AF722424

CONSENTING TO INTERNATIONAL LAW

The obligations stemming from international law are still predominantly considered, despite important normative and descriptive critiques, as being 'based' on (State) consent. To that extent, international law differs from domestic law where consent to the law has long been considered irrelevant to law-making, whether as a criterion of validity or as a ground of legitimacy. In addition to a renewed historical and philosophical interest in (State) consent to international law, including from a democratic theory perspective, the issue has also recently regained importance in practice. Various specialists of international law and the philosophy of international law have been invited to explore the different questions this raises in what is the first edited volume on consent to international law in the English language. The collection addresses three groups of issues: the notions and roles of consent in contemporary international law; its objects and types; and its subjects and institutions.

SAMANTHA BESSON holds the Chair of *International Law of Institutions* at the Collège de France, Paris, and is Professor of Public International Law and European Law at the University of Fribourg (Switzerland). She is an associate member of the Institute of International Law and Co-chair of the ILA Study Group on the International Law of Regional Organizations.

ASIL Studies in International Legal Theory

Series Editors

Mark Agrast, ASIL
Mortimer Sellers, University of Baltimore

Editorial Board

Samantha Besson, Collège de France & University of Fribourg
Allen Buchanan, Duke University
David Kennedy, Harvard University
Jan Klabbers, University of Helsinki
David Luban, Georgetown University
Larry May, Vanderbilt University
Mary Ellen O'Connell, University of Notre Dame
Helen Stacy, Stanford University
John Tasioulas, University of Oxford
Fernando Tesón, Florida State University

The purpose of the ASIL Studies in International Legal Theory series is to clarify and improve the theoretical foundations of international law. Too often the progressive development and implementation of international law has foundered on confusion about first principles. This series raises the level of public and scholarly discussion about the structure and purposes of the world legal order and how best to achieve global justice through law.

This series grows out of the International Legal Theory project of the American Society of International Law. The ASIL Studies in International Legal Theory series deepens this conversation by publishing scholarly monographs and edited volumes of essays considering subjects in international legal theory.

Books in the series

The Death Penalty's Denial of Fundamental Human Rights John Bessler

Theories of International Responsibility Law Edited by Samantha Besson

Human Dignity in International Law Ginevra Le Moli

Tipping Points in International Law: Commitment and Critique Edited by Jean d'Aspremont and John D. Haskell

Ethical Leadership in International Organizations: Concepts, Narratives, Judgment, and Assessment Edited by Maria Varaki and Guilherme Vasconcelos Vilaca

Whither the West?: Concepts on International Law in Europe and the United States Edited by Chiara Giorgetti and Guglielmo Verdirame

International Law as Behavior Edited by Harlan Grant Cohen and Timothy Meyer

Space and Fates of International Law: Between Leibniz and Hobbes Ekaterina Yahyaoui Krivenko

Why Punish Perpetrators of Mass Atrocities?: Purposes of Punishment in International Criminal Law Edited by Florian Jeßberger and Julia Geneuss

The Challenge of Inter-Legality Edited by Jan Klabbers and Gianluigi Palombella

The Nature of International Law Miodrag A. Jovanović

Reexamining Customary International Law Edited by Brian D. Lepard

Theoretical Boundaries of Armed Conflict and Human Rights Edited by Jens David Ohlin

Human Rights in Emergencies Edited by Evan J. Criddle

The Theory of Self-Determination Edited by Fernando R. Tesón

Negotiating State and Non-State Law: Global and Local Legal Pluralism Edited by Michael A. Helfand

Jus Post Bellum and Transitional Justice Edited by Larry May and Elizabeth Edenberg

Normative Pluralism and International Law: Exploring Global Governance Edited by Jan Klabbers and Touko Piipaerinen

The Future of International Law: Global Government Joel P. Trachtman

Morality, Jus Post Bellum, and International Law Edited by Larry May and Andrew T. Forcehimes

Global Justice and International Economic Law: Opportunities and Prospects Edited by Chios Carmody, Frank J. Garcia, and John Linarelli

Parochialism, Cosmopolitanism, and the Foundations of International Law Edited by M. N. S. Sellers

The Role of Ethics in International Law Edited by Donald Earl ChildressIII

The New Global Law Rafael Domingo

Customary International Law: A New Theory with Practical Applications Brian D. Lepard

International Criminal Law and Philosophy Edited by Larry May and Zachary Hoskins

Consenting to International Law

Edited by
SAMANTHA BESSON
Collège de France & University of Fribourg

With the assistance of
LOUIS HILL

CAMBRIDGE
UNIVERSITY PRESS

CAMBRIDGE
UNIVERSITY PRESS

Shaftesbury Road, Cambridge CB2 8EA, United Kingdom

One Liberty Plaza, 20th Floor, New York, NY 10006, USA

477 Williamstown Road, Port Melbourne, VIC 3207, Australia

314–321, 3rd Floor, Plot 3, Splendor Forum, Jasola District Centre, New Delhi – 110025, India

103 Penang Road, #05-06/07, Visioncrest Commercial, Singapore 238467

Cambridge University Press is part of Cambridge University Press & Assessment, a department of the University of Cambridge.

We share the University's mission to contribute to society through the pursuit of education, learning and research at the highest international levels of excellence.

www.cambridge.org
Information on this title: www.cambridge.org/9781009406451

DOI: 10.1017/9781009406444

© Cambridge University Press & Assessment 2024

This publication is in copyright. Subject to statutory exception and to the provisions of relevant collective licensing agreements, no reproduction of any part may take place without the written permission of Cambridge University Press & Assessment.

First published 2024

A catalogue record for this publication is available from the British Library.

Library of Congress Cataloging-in-Publication Data
NAMES: Besson, Samantha, 1973- editor.
TITLE: Consenting to international law / edited by Samantha Besson, Collège de France, Paris.
DESCRIPTION: Cambridge, United Kingdom ; New York, NY : Cambridge University Press, 2023. | SERIES: ASIL Studies in International Legal Theory | Includes index.
IDENTIFIERS: LCCN 2023029299 (print) | LCCN 2023029300 (ebook) | ISBN 9781009406451 (hardback) | ISBN 9781009406475 (paperback) | ISBN 9781009406444 (ebook)
SUBJECTS: LCSH: International law. | International and municipal law. | Consent (Law) | State, The. | Effectiveness and validity of law. | Legitimacy of governments. | Court of Justice of the European Union.
CLASSIFICATION: LCC KZ3410 .C6675 2023 (print) | LCC KZ3410 (ebook) | DDC 341–dc23/eng/20230710
LC record available at https://lccn.loc.gov/2023029299
LC ebook record available at https://lccn.loc.gov/2023029300

ISBN 978-1-009-40645-1 Hardback

Cambridge University Press & Assessment has no responsibility for the persistence or accuracy of URLs for external or third-party internet websites referred to in this publication and does not guarantee that any content on such websites is, or will remain, accurate or appropriate.

Contents

Contributors

Jean d'Aspremont is Professor of International Law at Sciences Po Law School, Paris, France, and at the University of Manchester, United Kingdom.

Samantha Besson is Professor at the Collège de France, Paris, where she holds the Chair of International Law of Institutions, and Professor of Public International Law and European Law at the University of Fribourg, Switzerland.

Laurence Boisson de Chazournes is Professor of International Law at the University of Geneva, Switzerland, and Director of the Geneva Centre for International Dispute Settlement (CIDS).

Fernando Lusa Bordin is Assistant Professor of International Law at the University of Cambridge, United Kingdom, John Thornely Fellow in Law at Sidney Sussex College, and Fellow of the Lauterpacht Centre for International Law.

Catherine Brölmann is Associate Professor of International Law and Research Fellow at the University of Amsterdam, Netherlands.

Jutta Brunnée is Dean, University Professor and James M. Tory Professor of Law at the University of Toronto, Canada.

Monique Chemillier-Gendreau is Emeritus Professor of Public Law and Political Science at the University of Paris Cité, France.

Louis Hill is former Research Assistant at the Chair International Law of Institutions, Collège de France, Paris.

Duncan B. Hollis is Laura H. Carnell Professor of Law at Temple Law School, Philadelphia, United States.

Eva Kassoti is Senior Researcher in International and European Law at the T.M.C Asser Institute, The Hague, Netherlands.

David Lefkowitz is Professor of Philosophy at the University of Richmond, Virginia, United States.

José Luis Martí is Associate Professor of Philosophy of Law at the University of Pompeu Fabra, Barcelona, Spain.

Georg Nolte is Judge of the International Court of Justice, The Hague, Netherlands, and Professor at the Humboldt University of Berlin, Germany.

Alain Pellet is Emeritus Professor of International Law at the University of Nanterre, France.

Yannick Radi is Professor of International Law at the Catholic University of Louvain, Belgium.

Christian J. Tams is Professor of International Law at the University of Paris, 1 Panthéon-Sorbonne, France.

Fuad Zarbiyev is Associate Professor of International Law at the Geneva Graduate Institute, Switzerland.

Preface

The obligations stemming from international treaties, but also from international legal sources in general – together with the jurisdiction of international courts and tribunals – are still predominantly considered, despite important normative as much as descriptive critiques, as being 'based' on (State) consent. To that extent, international law differs from domestic law, where consent to the law has long been considered peripheral or irrelevant to law-making, whether as a criterion of validity or as a ground of legitimacy.

This is, of course, an old chestnut in international legal theory, but one that still puzzles most theorists. In addition to a renewed historical and philosophical interest in (State) consent to international law, including from a democratic theory perspective, the question is still also highly relevant in practice. Thus, the notions of consent and agreement remain difficult to grasp in international treaty law, not to mention their controversial role in the formation of customary international law. Unexpectedly, given some of the original arguments to the contrary, the question of consent has also recently resurfaced, with other private law analogies, in debates pertaining to the normativity of international soft law and other forms of transnational regulation, raising issues as to what consent does and should amount to in those new normative practices. Moreover, after being, maybe too quickly, considered as outdated, the consensual jurisdiction of international courts and tribunals has also been given renewed attention lately. Finally, it has become increasingly common to refer to the 'will' of international organizations, including with respect to the law adopted by and within them, but also to the 'consent' of other private 'stakeholders' of international law-making.

Various specialists of both international law and the philosophy of international law were invited to explore those issues and many others in a conference that took place at the Collège de France in Paris on 23–24 June 2022. This volume gathers those contributions and a few additional chapters. It addresses (i) the notions and roles of consent in contemporary international law, but also (ii) its objects and types, and (iii) its subjects and institutions. The various chapters also shed light on the increasingly vexed topics of the normativity, authority and legitimacy of what we refer to as international 'law' today.

This volume could not have come into existence without the support of a great number of people and institutions. I would like to express my gratitude to Mr Louis Hill, former research assistant at the Collège de France, for his tremendous and unfailing assistance throughout the editorial process, and to Ms Nadia Signorell and Ms Shpresa Salihu, research assistants at the University of Fribourg, for proofreading the manuscript. Special thanks are also due to my administrative assistant at the Collège de France, Ms Sylvie Sportouch, who helped organize the June 2022 conference. I am also extremely grateful to Dr Sévrine Knuchel for translating one of the volume's contributions.

I would like to thank Ms Marianne Nield at Cambridge University Press for her support and kind forbearance during the process of putting this book together, and to Professor Tim Sellers for his willingness to include this volume in the ASIL International Legal Theory Series. I would also like to thank two anonymous reviewers for their feedback on the book proposal and for making me reflect further about the project. I hope they will be able to find traces of some of their constructive suggestions in the volume. Finally, I would like to express my gratitude to the Fondation du Collège de France for providing vital financial support for the June 2022 conference and for the English translation of one of the contributions.

Last but not least, special thanks are owed to all of the contributors and to the commentators, including Professor Pierre d'Argent and Professor Paolo Palchetti who decided not to publish with us, for making this ambitious project such a stimulating, formative and worthwhile experience, and for their lively and engaging discussions in a memorable conference in Paris.

Samantha Besson,
Paris, 2nd March, 2023

Consenting to International Law

An Introduction

SAMANTHA BESSON*

On 23–24 June 2022, a conference entitled *Consenting to International Law* was held at the Collège de France.[1] The painting illustrating the programme was *Divisio* from the *Allegory of Bad Government* by Ambrogio Lorenzetti. *Divisio*'s serene appearance is deceptive. With her saw, she is slowly, but surely dividing the city or civic body in two (as you can see from the 'Si' and 'No' on her robe). This representation of *Divisio* reminds us about how divided our world is and, by extension, the international community of States and peoples.

The representation also reminds us of the formidable, and much more painful, challenge we face every day when pressed to address issues of common concern, be it climate change, pandemics or peace. The challenge of adopting that kind of common law in circumstances of persistent disagreement is actually made even greater at the international level because of a central feature of international law-making: the requirement of State consent to international law. That requirement is the topic of the present volume.

The volume gathers the fifteen chapters presented at the conference or commissioned thereafter. It is the first edited volume dedicated entirely to consent to international law in the English language and the first one that brings international legal philosophers and international lawyers into a dialogue on the topic. This introduction sets the stage for the book's argument: first, it clarifies the relevance of the issue and the reasons that led to putting this collection of essays together; second, it introduces the main conceptual

* Many thanks to Louis Hill for his editorial assistance.

[1] Collège de France, 'Consenting to International Law' (23–24 June 2022). Available at: www.college-de-france.fr/fr/agenda/colloque/consenting-to-international-law, last accessed 7 December 2022.

and normative challenges addressed in the volume and explains what it hopes to achieve; third, it provides some information about how the book is structured; and, finally, it sketches out the content of its successive chapters and their articulation.

1 THE BACKGROUND TO THE VOLUME

'Private' law analogies were prevalent in the international law of the seventeenth and eighteenth centuries. They contributed in a central manner to the construction of what became known only much later as 'public' international law.[2]

One of those private law analogies was States' consent to international law or, more accurately, States' consent to 'be bound' by international law. According to the liberal and anthropomorphic approach to inter-State relations that was prevalent at that time, indeed, international treaties between States were commonly conceived of as contracts.[3] Drawing on that contractualist analogy, States were, and sometimes still are, depicted as free to consent to international treaties that would bind them, in the same way private persons are considered free to consent to a contract that would bind them following that exchange of consents. A further, albeit related, analogy between individual free will and State sovereignty actually explains how later on, and as epitomized by one of the dicta of the Permanent Court of International Justice in *The S.S. "Lotus"*,[4] State consent to international law became associated with a voluntarist approach to State sovereignty and, by extension, with a voluntarist brand of legal positivism.[5]

Today, those contractualist and voluntarist readings of international law are mostly considered as relics of a bygone era. Interestingly, however, the

[2] Sir Hersch Lauterpacht, *Private Law Sources and Analogies of International Law: With Special Reference to International Arbitration* (Clark, NJ: The Lawbook Exchange, 2013 (London: Longmans, Green and Co., 1927)).

[3] For a critique, see Chemillier-Gendreau, Chapter 13 in this volume; d'Aspremont, Chapter 5 in this volume.

[4] *The Case of the S.S. "Lotus" (France* v. *Turkey)* (Judgment) [1927] PCIJ Ser. A No. 10, p. 18.

[5] For a historical discussion, see Martti Koskenniemi, *From Apology to Utopia: The Structure of International Legal Argument* (Cambridge: Cambridge University Press, 2006), p. 310; Catherine Brölmann, *The Institutional Veil in Public International Law* (Oxford: Hart, 2007), p. 71; Richard Collins, 'Classical Legal Positivism in International Law Revisited', in Jörg Kammerhofer and Jean d'Aspremont (eds.), *International Legal Positivism in a Post-Modern World* (Cambridge: Cambridge University Press, 2014), pp. 23–49; Matthew Craven, 'The Ends of Consent', in Michael J. Bowman and Dino Kritsiotis (eds.), *Conceptual and Contextual Perspectives on the Modern Law of Treaties* (Cambridge: Cambridge University Press, 2018), pp. 103–135.

obligations stemming from international treaties, but also from international legal sources in general, together with the jurisdiction of international courts and tribunals, are still predominantly considered as being 'based'[6] on (State) consent.[7] This is the case in spite of the numerous normative[8] and descriptive[9] (especially quantitative) arguments for its demise in contemporary international law-making. To that extent, international law differs from domestic law, where consent has long been considered peripheral or irrelevant to the obligations arising from law-making – by contrast to its growing relevance in domestic private or criminal law where it has become more pervasive than ever, for example, to ground all sorts of obligations or, at least, liabilities arising from contracting or promising.[10] In domestic law and domestic legal theory, indeed, consent is not or, at least, no longer considered as a criterion of legal validity or as a ground or justification of the legitimate authority of law.[11]

6 On the polysemic term 'based' on consent, see Samantha Besson, 'State Consent and Disagreement in International Law-Making: Dissolving the Paradox' (2016) 29(2) *Leiden Journal of International Law* 289–316, at 290, footnote 5.

7 See, for example, *Legality of the Threat or Use of Nuclear Weapons* (Advisory Opinion) [1996] ICJ Rep. 226, paras. 18, 21; *Case concerning Military and Paramilitary Activities in and against Nicaragua (Nicaragua* v. *United States)* (Merits) [1986] ICJ Rep. 14, para. 135. See Jan Klabbers, 'Law-Making and Constitutionalism', in Jan Klabbers, Anne Peters and Geir Ulfstein (eds.), *The Constitutionalization of International Law* (Oxford: Oxford University Press, 2009), pp. 81–125, pp. 100, 114. See also the numerous textbooks that start by discussing consent, often critically, as a basis of international legal obligation, but that, independently from their conclusion in that first section, then invariably end up presenting and defending a consent-based account of international law-making: see, for example, James Crawford, *Brownlie's Principles of Public International Law*, 9th ed. (Oxford: Oxford University Press, 2019); Andrew Clapham, *Brierly's Law of Nations. An Introduction to the Role of International Law in International Relations*, 7th ed. (Oxford: Oxford University Press, 2012).

8 See, for example, Laurence R. Helfer, 'Nonconsensual International Law-Making' (2008) 1 *University of Illinois Law Review* 71–125; Andrew T. Guzman, 'Against Consent' (2012) 52(4) *Virginia Journal of International Law* 747–790; Gregory Shaffer, 'International Law and Global Public Goods in a Legal Pluralist World' (2012) 23(3) *European Journal of International Law* 669–693; Joost Pauwelyn, Ramses A. Wessel and Jan Wouters, 'When Structures Become Shackles: Stagnation and Dynamics in International Lawmaking' (2014) 25(3) *European Journal of International Law* 733–763.

9 See, for example and most recently, Joost Pauwelyn, 'Informal International Lawmaking: Framing the Concept and Research Questions', in Joost Pauwelyn, Ramses A. Wessel and Jan Wouters (eds.), *Informal International Lawmaking* (Oxford: Oxford University Press, 2012), pp. 13–34; Nico Krisch, 'The Decay of Consent: International Law in the Age of Global Public Goods' (2014) 108(1) *American Journal of International Law* 1–40.

10 For a critique, see Muriel Fabre-Magnan, *L'institution de la liberté* (Paris: Presses Universitaires de France, 2018), pp. 53–108.

11 See, for example, on consent and legal validity, Herbert L. A. Hart, *The Concept of Law*, 2nd ed. (Oxford: Oxford University Press, 1994), pp. 225–228; Liam Murphy, *What Makes Law: An Introduction to the Philosophy of Law* (New York: Cambridge University Press, 2014),

Of course, (State) consent to international law (short for consent to 'be bound by' international law in what follows) is an old chestnut in international legal theory. As just mentioned, its central role in international law has been heavily discussed and criticized, especially since the second half of the twentieth century.[12] Despite many of its original conceptual and normative flaws, consent is a chestnut that still puzzles or fascinates many international lawyers today, including the most critical ones.[13] It has actually become the

p. 179. See, on consent and legitimate authority: John A. Simmons, *Moral Principles and Political Obligations* (Princeton: Princeton University Press, 1979); Joseph Raz, *The Morality of Freedom* (Oxford: Oxford University Press, 1986), pp. 88–93; Joseph Raz, 'Government by Consent' (1987) 29 *Nomos* 76–95, at 85; Leslie Green, 'Law, Legitimacy, and Consent' (1989) 62(6) *Southern California Law Review* 795–825, at 814; Joseph Raz, *Ethics in the Public Domain: Essays in the Morality of Law and Politics*, 2nd ed. (Oxford: Oxford University Press, 1995), pp. 80–94; Joseph Raz, 'The Problem of Authority: Revisiting the Service Conception' (2006) 90(4) *Minnesota Law Review* 1003–1044, at 1028–1029, 1037–1040.

12 See, for example, James Leslie Brierly, 'The *Lotus* Case' (1928) 44 *Law Quarterly Review* 154–163; Gerald Fitzmaurice, 'Some Problems Regarding the Formal Sources of International Law', in Frederick M. van Asbeck (ed.), *Symbolae Verzijl* (Leiden: Martinus Nijhoff, 1958), pp. 153–176; Prosper Weil, 'Towards Relative Normativity in International Law' (1983) 77(3) *American Journal of International Law* 413–442; Bruno Simma, 'Consent: Strains in the Treaty System', in Ronald Saint John Macdonald and Douglas Millar Johnston (eds.), *The Structure and Process of International Law: Essays in Legal Philosophy Doctrine and Theory* (Leiden: Martinus Nijhoff, 1983), pp. 485–511, p. 503; Gaetano Arangio-Ruiz, 'Voluntarism versus Majority Rule', in Antonio Cassese and Joseph H. H. Weiler (eds.), *Change and Stability in International Law-Making* (Berlin: Walter de Gruyter, 1988), pp. 102–108; Alain Pellet, 'The Normative Dilemma: Will and Consent in International Law-Making' (1992) 12(1) *Australian Yearbook of International Law* 22–53; Thomas M. Franck, *The Power of Legitimacy among Nations* (Oxford: Oxford University Press, 1990); Daniel Bodansky and James Shand Watson, 'State Consent and the Sources of International Obligation' (1992) 86 *Proceedings of the Annual Meeting (American Society of International Law)* 108–111; Christian Tomuschat, 'Obligations Arising for States without or against Their Will' (Volume 241) *Collected Courses of the Hague Academy of International Law*, 1993, pp. 195–374; Shabtai Rosenne, *An International Law Miscellany* (Leiden: Martinus Nijhoff, 1993), pp. 357–377; Shabtai Rosenne, 'Consent and Related Words in the Codified Law of Treaties', in *Mélanges offerts à Charles Rousseau* (Paris: Pedone, 1974), pp. 229–248; Olufemi A. Elias and Ching Len Lim, *The Paradox of Consensualism in International Law* (Leiden: Brill, 1998); Philip Allott, 'The Concept of International Law' (1999) 10(1) *European Journal of International Law* 31–50; Ellen Hey, *Teaching International Law: State-Consent as Consent to a Process of Normative Development and Ensuing Problems* (The Hague: Kluwer Law International, 2003).

13 See, for example, Duncan B. Hollis, 'Why State Consent Still Matters: Non-State Actors, Treaties and the Changing Sources of International Law' (2005) 23(1) *Berkeley Journal of International Law* 137–174; Malgosia Fitzmaurice, 'Consent to Be Bound: Anything New under the Sun?' (2005) 74(3) *Nordic Journal of International Law* 483–508; Maurice Kamto, 'La volonté de l'État en droit international' (Volume 310) *Collected Courses of the Hague Academy of International Law*, 2004, pp. 19–428; Jutta Brunnée, 'Consent' (last updated January 2022), in Rüdiger Wolfrum (ed.), *Max Planck Encyclopedia of Public International Law* (Oxford: Oxford University Press, 2008). Available at: https://opil.ouplaw.com/display/10

object of renewed legal philosophical interest as of late, with a flurry of new publications on the topic and of attempts to provide justifications for the role of consent to international law in practice.[14] This is partly due to the rekindling of the philosophy of international law tradition in the last twenty years or so,[15] but also to the growing concerns about international law's democratic

.1093/law:epil/9780199231690/law-9780199231690-e1388, last accessed 13 December 2022; Timothy Meyer, 'From Contract to Legislation: The Logic of Modern International Lawmaking' (2014) 14(2) *Chicago Journal of International Law* 559–624; Besson, fn. 6; Eva Kassoti, 'Beyond State Consent? International Legal Scholarship and the Challenge of Informal International Law-Making' (2016) 63(2) *Netherlands International Law Review* 99–131; Werner G. Wouter, 'State Consent as Foundational Myth', in Catherine Brölmann and Yannick Radi (eds.), *Research Handbook on the Theory and Practice of International Lawmaking* (Cheltenham: Edward Elgar, 2016), pp. 13–31; Yota Negishi, 'Opinio Juris as (the Ultimate) International Secondary Rule of Recognition: Reconciling State Consent and Public Conscience' (2016) 7(4) *European Society of International Law (ESIL) 2016 Research Forum* 1–25. Available at: https://papers.ssrn.com/sol3/papers.cfm?abstract_id=2911989, last accessed 7 December 2022; Evangeline Reynolds, Amâncio Jorge Silva Nunes de Oliveira, Janina Onuki and Matthew S. Winters, 'Attitudes toward Consent-Based and Non-Consent-Based International Law in a Regional Power Context' (2018) 44(4) *International Interactions* 661–680; Stephen C. Neff, 'Consent', in Jean d'Aspremont and Sahib Singh (eds.), *Concepts for International Law: Contributions to Disciplinary Thought* (Cheltenham: Edward Elgar, 2019), pp. 127–140; Catherine Brölmann, 'Capturing the Juridical Will', in Sufyan Droubi and Jean d'Aspremont (eds.), *International Organizations, Non-State Actors, and the Formation of Customary International Law* (Manchester: Manchester University Press, 2020), pp. 42–61.

14 See, for example, Matthew Lister, 'The Legitimating Role of Consent in International Law' (2011) 11(2) *Chicago Journal of International Law* 663–691; Besson, fn. 6; Liam Murphy, 'Law beyond the State: Some Philosophical Questions' (2017) 28(1) *European Journal of International Law* 203–232; Samantha Besson, 'Law beyond the State: A Reply to Liam Murphy' (2017) 28(1) *European Journal of International Law* 233–240; Richard Collins, 'Consent, Obligation and the Legitimate Authority of International Law', in Patrick Capps and Henrik Palmer Olsen (eds.), *Legal Authority beyond the State* (Cambridge: Cambridge University Press, 2018), pp. 206–236; John Tasioulas and Guglielmo Verdirame, 'Philosophy of International Law', in Edward N. Zalta and Uri Nodelman (eds.), *The Stanford Encyclopedia of Philosophy* (Summer 2022 Edition). Available at: https://plato.stanford.edu/archives/sum2022/entries/international-law/, last accessed 7 December 2022.

15 See, for example, Samantha Besson, 'The Authority of International Law: Lifting the State Veil' (2009) 31(3) *The Sydney Law Review* 343–380; John Tasioulas, 'The Legitimacy of International Law', in Samantha Besson and John Tasioulas (eds.), *The Philosophy of International Law* (Oxford: Oxford University Press, 2010), pp. 97–116, p. 101; Samantha Besson, 'Theorizing the Sources of International Law', in Besson and Tasioulas, fn. 15, pp. 163–185; Timothy A. Endicott, 'Sovereignty: The Logic of Freedom and Power', in Besson and Tasioulas, fn. 15, pp. 245–259; Allen Buchanan and Robert O. Keohane, 'The Legitimacy of Global Governance Institutions' (2006) 20(4) *Ethics & International Affairs* 405–437; Brad R. Roth, *Sovereign Equality and Moral Disagreement: Premises of a Pluralist International Legal Order* (Oxford: Oxford University Press, 2011); Ronald Dworkin, 'A New Philosophy for International Law' (2013) 41(1) *Philosophy & Public Affairs* 2–30; Jörg Kammerhofer and Jean d'Aspremont, 'Introduction: The Future of International Legal Positivism', in Kammerhofer

legitimacy that has come with a special attention for self-determination and hence consent in international law-making.[16]

Importantly, those contemporary philosophical and doctrinal debates about consent to international law do not merely repeat earlier ones. Nor, by extension, do they repeat the latter's mistakes. They have (mostly) moved away from the original (and misguided) identifications between consensualism and contractualism or between consensualism and voluntarism.[17] They have also (mostly) realized how consent may not be considered as a criterion of international legal validity, a ground of the legitimacy of international law or a condition of State sovereignty.[18] Luckily, they have also (mostly) shifted away from the later (and often unhappy and Manichean) oppositions between 'objective' and 'subjective' international law, between 'communitarian' and 'individualistic' conceptions thereof, or between the 'public' and the 'private' in international law in which State consent was usually wrongly assimilated with and then reduced to the 'subjective', the 'individualistic' or 'self-interested' and the 'private' end of international law.[19] Of course, and as should be the case with an essentially contestable concept and especially with a legally constructed one such as consent,[20] new critiques may arise and be said to afflict contemporary versions of the notion and role of consent to international law.[21]

and d'Aspremont, fn. 5, pp. 1–20; Samantha Besson, 'Sovereign States and their International Institutional Order: Carrying Forward Dworkin's Work on the Political Legitimacy of International Law' (2020) 2(2) *Jus Cogens* 111–138; David Lefkowitz, *Philosophy and International Law: A Critical Introduction* (Cambridge: Cambridge University Press, 2020); Carmen E. Pavel, *Law beyond the State: Dynamic Coordination, State Consent and Binding International Law* (Oxford: Oxford University Press, 2021).

16 See, for example, Thomas Christiano, 'Democratic Legitimacy and International Institutions', in Besson and Tasioulas, fn. 15, pp. 119–137; Thomas Christiano, 'Climate Change and State Consent', in Jeremy Moss (ed.), *Climate Change and Justice* (Cambridge: Cambridge University Press, 2015), pp. 17–38; Thomas Christiano, 'Legitimacy and the International Trade Regime' (2015) 52(5) *San Diego Law Review* 981–1012; Besson, fn. 6, at 305–309; Samantha Besson and José Luis Martí, 'Legitimate Actors of International Law-Making: Towards a Theory of International Democratic Representation' (2018) 9(3) *Jurisprudence* 504–540; Craven, fn. 5.

17 Besson, fn. 6, at 298–305; Pellet, Chapter 1 in this volume.

18 See for an overview of those critiques: Besson, fn. 6, at 298–305; Lefkowitz, Chapter 2 in this volume.

19 On the consequences of some of those oppositions in international treaty law, see, for example, Vassilis Pergantis, *The Paradigm of State Consent in the Law of Treaties: Challenges and Perspectives* (Cheltenham: Edward Elgar, 2017).

20 On the role of disagreement in the law, see Samantha Besson, *The Morality of Conflict. Reasonable Disagreement and the Law* (Oxford: Hart, 2005).

21 See, for example, d'Aspremont, Chapter 5 in this volume. Most chapters in this volume are actually critical in one way or another and articulate various revision proposals to improve our theory and practice of consent in international law.

Besides or, rather, together with those re-ignited philosophical discussions of consent, the question has also regained in relevance in the recent practice of international law. This is the case in at least three respects: the sources of international law, international adjudication and the subjects of international law.

Thus, and starting with the sources of international law, the notions of consent and agreement have remained curiously informal and difficult to grasp in international treaty law, at all stages of treaty-making and treaty-interpreting. Recently, this has revived the discussion around the differences between treaties and other fast-developing forms of State commitments based on consent, such as inter-State 'contracts' or other international albeit non-legal 'agreements' like the increasingly common 'political commitments' of States.[22] Further, new consensual techniques are being experimented in multilateral treaty-making processes, especially in international environmental law,[23] and could be exported into law-making processes pertaining to other international public goods (such as health or peace) in the future. Turning to custom, one should also mention the vexed place of consent in the formation of customary international law, giving rise to new questions about the end of consent and the legality of so-called withdrawals from customary law.[24]

22 See, for example, Jan Klabbers, 'Not Re-Visiting the Concept of Treaty', in Alexander Orakhelashvili and Sarah Williams (eds.), *Forty Years of the Vienna Convention on the Law of Treaties* (London: British Institute of International and Comparative Law, 2010), pp. 29–40; Jan Klabbers, 'The Validity and Invalidity of Treaties', in Duncan B. Hollis (ed.), *The Oxford Guide to Treaties*, 2nd ed. (Oxford: Oxford University Press, 2020), pp. 545–567; Duncan B. Hollis, 'Defining Treaties', in Hollis, *The Oxford Guide to Treaties*, fn. 22, pp. 11–45; Timothy Meyer, 'Alternatives to Treaty-Making – Informal Agreements', in Hollis, *The Oxford Guide to Treaties*, fn. 22, pp. 59–81; Curtis A. Bradley, Jack L. Goldsmith and Oona A. Hathaway, 'The Rise of Nonbinding International Agreements: An Empirical, Comparative, and Normative Analysis' (in press, 2023) 90 *University of Chicago Law Review*; Hollis, Chapter 6 in this volume; Kassoti, Chapter 12 in this volume.

23 See, for example, Jutta Brunnée, 'COPing with Consent: Law-Making under Multilateral Environmental Agreements' (2002) 15(1) *Leiden Journal of International Law* 1–52; Jutta Brunnée, 'Reweaving the Fabric of International Law? Patterns of Consent in Environmental Framework Agreements', in Rüdiger Wolfrum and Volker Röben (eds.), *Developments of International Law in Treaty Making* (Berlin: Springer, 2005), pp. 101–126; Brunnée, Chapter 8 in this volume.

24 See, for example, Chin Leng Lim and Olufemi Elias, 'Withdrawing from Custom and the Paradox of Consensualism in International Law' (2010) 21(1) *Duke Journal of Comparative & International Law* 143–156; Curtis A. Bradley and Mitu G. Gulati, 'Withdrawing from International Custom' (2010) 120(2) *The Yale Law Journal* 202–275; Niels Petersen, 'Customary Law and Public Goods', in Curtis A. Bradley (ed.), *Custom's Future: International Law in a Changing World* (Cambridge: Cambridge University Press, 2016), pp. 253–274; Aymeric Hêche, 'L'élément subjectif dans la coutume internationale', in Samantha Besson, Yves Mausen and Pascal Pichonnaz (eds.), *Le consentement en droit* (Zurich: Schulthess, 2019), pp. 31–53.

Moreover, and unexpectedly given some of the original descriptions of soft and/or informal law *qua* 'non-consensual' law,[25] the question of consent has recently resurfaced, together with other private law analogies such as contracts, promises or pledges, in debates pertaining to the sources of the specific 'normativity' of international soft or informal law.[26] This development raises the question of what it is, if not consent, that makes that informal or soft law normative or even 'binding', albeit in a non-formal or non-legal way, and, by contrast, what this means for the specificity of consent to international law itself and especially, as will be argued in Section 2, for its institutional dimension. It also sheds a new light on the issue mentioned before of the distinction between binding treaties and so-called informal or non-binding agreements that are based on mutual consent like treaties, but allegedly do not bind like them or, at least, not legally. The development of such agreements calls for an inquiry into the normative or binding role of consent under contemporary international law and for a broader discussion about what makes international law 'law'.[27]

Turning to international adjudication, second, the consensual jurisdiction of international courts and tribunals has also attracted renewed attention lately. This has followed the assertive development of some international tribunals' case law pertaining to the interpretation of both their consent-based jurisdiction[28] and consent-based sources of international law.[29] In a mirroring exercise, certain States have reacted through withdrawals or, at least, qualifications of their jurisdictional clauses. After being maybe too quickly considered as outdated,[30] State consent to jurisdiction seems to have remained foundational and will be pivotal to the future of international adjudication.[31] In international responsibility law, consent works as an exception to another

[25] See, for example, Helfer, fn. 8; Guzman, fn. 8; Pauwelyn, fn. 9; Pauwelyn *et al.*, fn. 8; Krisch, fn. 9.

[26] See, for example, Melissa J. Durkee, 'The Pledging World Order' (2023) 48(1) *Yale Journal of International Law* 1–54.

[27] On some of these questions, see Kassoti, Chapter 12 in this volume; Radi, Chapter 15 in this volume.

[28] See Tams, Chapter 3 in this volume; Boisson de Chazournes, Chapter 10 in this volume.

[29] See Nolte, Chapter 9 in this volume.

[30] See, for example, Cesare P. R. Romano, 'The Shift from the Consensual to the Compulsory Paradigm in International Adjudication: Elements for a Theory of Consent' (2007) 39(4) *New York University Journal of International Law and Politics* 791–872.

[31] See, for example, Clément Marquet, *Le consentement étatique à la compétence des juridictions internationales* (Paris: Pedone, 2022); Rejla Radović, *Beyond Consent: Revisiting Jurisdiction in International Investment Treaty Arbitration* (Leiden: Brill, 2021); Tom Sparks, 'Reassessing State Consent to Jurisdiction: The Indispensable Third Party Principle before the ICJ' (2022) 91(2) *Nordic Journal of International Law* 216–252.

State's or international organization's responsibility. Lately, that exception has raised numerous questions in the context of the use of force and regarding the identity of the consenting subject and the limits to State consent.[32]

Finally, the right to consent to international law seems to have been extended to other subjects and institutions than States in the international institutional order. Thus, it is now common to refer to the 'consent' of international organizations (hereafter IOs), including with respect to the law adopted by them[33] or, at least, by States within them,[34] even if the legal regime and normative implications of that consent still differ from those of State consent and require reverting to those organizations' Member States' consent. One should also mention the increasing inclusion of private persons, such as non-governmental organizations (hereafter NGOs), in international law-making processes, sometimes vesting them with similar rights to consent to international obligations. For instance, they are considered as 'participants' alone or alongside consenting States, in so-called multi-stakeholders agreements, and their participation rights often emulate the modalities of State consent.[35]

2 THE AIMS OF THE VOLUME

Although the topic has been addressed quite regularly in the form of articles and chapters,[36] there have been, surprisingly for such a central topic, few monographs on consent to international law in general and no edited volume, if one excludes major commentaries and textbooks on the international law of treaties.[37]

32 See, for example, Federica Paddeu, 'Military Assistance on Request and General Reasons against Force: Consent as a Justification for the Use of Force' (2020) 7(2) *Journal on the Use of Force and International Law* 227–269; Aurélie Galetto, 'Des formes du consentement étatique et de ses limites: Analyse au regard de l'excès de mandat par des forces armées étrangères', in Besson *et al.*, fn. 24, pp. 256–278.

33 See, for example, Brölmann, fn. 13; Brölmann, Chapter 4 in this volume; Bordin, Chapter 11 in this volume; Kassoti, Chapter 12 in this volume.

34 See, for example, Brölmann, Chapter 4 in this volume; Besson and Martí, Chapter 14 in this volume.

35 See, for example, Hollis, fn. 13; Melissa Loja, *International Agreements between Non-State Actors as Source of International Law* (London: Hart, 2022); Kassoti, Chapter 12 in this volume.

36 See, for example, the references in fn. 7–9, 12–14.

37 See, for example, Jan Klabbers, *The Concept of Treaty in International Law* (The Hague: Kluwer Law International, 1996); Mark E. Villiger, *Commentary on the 1969 Vienna Convention on the Law of Treaties* (Leiden: Brill, 2009); Orakhelashvili and Williams, fn. 22; Olivier Corten and Pierre Klein (eds.), *The Vienna Convention on the Law of Treaties:*

Moreover, the existing monographs on consent to international law are not general in scope. There have been quite a few monographs published recently on the topic, but they pertain to specific sources or regimes of international law, and especially either to international treaty law or to the jurisdiction of international courts and tribunals.[38] Regarding consent itself, they do not usually expand beyond the odd definitional pages, and certainly do not address the many issues pertaining to the notions, roles, objects, types, subjects and institutions of consent to international law. There have been at least two exceptions, of course. However, the two general monographs are already twenty years old and are either focused on sources for one or relatively succinct for the other.[39]

For all the reasons identified earlier, and especially its current philosophical and practical relevance, it is important to re-examine the issue of consent to international law in depth and in the contemporary circumstances of international law. The best way to do so in a rich and nuanced way is to give a voice to many authors at the same time on the matter, and this is the purpose of the present volume.

The volume has at least two aims: a first, conceptual aim, and a second one, more normative and critical. Both aims are intertwined in any legal argument, of course, and this is confirmed in almost all the chapters of the volume.

The primary, conceptual aim of this collection of essays is to address and reflect over three groups of issues one may identify in the current scholarship about the consent to international law and in its practice: the notions and roles of consent; the objects and types of consent; and the subjects and institutions of consent. Note that those issues are not exclusive, either mutually or in themselves. Moreover, they should not be read to detract from the legal nature of consent itself: consent is best constructed as a legal right or power, on the one hand, and the consenting subject or institution is instituted legally as such

A Commentary (Oxford: Oxford University Press, 2011); Anthony Aust, *Modern Treaty Law and Practice*, 2nd ed. (Cambridge: Cambridge University Press, 2013); Robert Kolb, *The Law of Treaties: An Introduction* (Cheltenham: Edward Elgar, 2016); Brölmann and Radi, fn. 13; Bowman and Kritsiotis, fn. 5; Oliver Dörr and Kirsten Schmalenbach (eds.), *Vienna Convention on the Law of Treaties: A Commentary*, 2nd ed. (Berlin: Springer, 2018); Hollis, *The Oxford Guide to Treaties*, fn. 22.

38 See, for example, Pergantis, fn. 19; Katharina Berner, *Subsequent Agreements and Subsequent Practice in Domestic Courts* (Berlin: Springer, 2017); Irina Bugua, *Modification of Treaties by Subsequent Practice* (Oxford: Oxford University Press, 2018); Alexis Marie, *Le silence de l'État comme manifestation de sa volonté* (Paris: Pedone, 2018); Marquet, fn. 31; Radović, fn. 31.

39 See Elias and Lim, fn. 12; Hey, fn. 12.

before or while it is given that right or power to consent to international law, on the other hand.

First of all, the notions and roles of consent in contemporary international law need to be clarified.

To start with the *notions* of consent to international law, one may approach consent as a descriptive or as a normative concept.[40] It suffices here to review the range of terms used to refer to it: a practice or a state, on the one hand, and a right, a power, an axiom or a principle of international law, on the other hand. More specifically, indeed, consent may be understood both as an intentional state and/or an expression thereof and as the normative right or power to alter one's own normative position and, by extension, another's in most cases, for instance, by incurring obligations or liabilities. Finally, consent may be approached not only as a process – as it is the case in this volume as *per* its title – but also as its outcome, and hence, by extension or not, as form, but also as content.[41]

Turning to the *roles* of consent in contemporary international law, they are mostly normative. Consent has, rightly or wrongly, been related, even if it cannot be reduced to them as explained in Section 1, and in various and very distinct ways, to the validity of international law and/or to its legitimacy.[42] It has also been said to be an expression of sovereignty or, depending on the subject, of autonomy[43] and self-government.[44] This is how it came to be related to other distinctive notions such as 'will',[45] 'intention',[46] 'agreement',[47] 'consensus', 'convention', 'contract', 'commitment', 'acceptance',[48] 'self-government', 'participation' or 'veto',[49] all notions whose exact relationship to consent, however, remains a topic of controversy in contemporary international law and scholarship.[50] The same may be said of the related limits to consent to international law: if consent is justified by reference to autonomy[51] or

40 See Lefkowitz, Chapter 2 in this volume.

41 See Zarbiyev, Chapter 7 in this volume; Brölmann, Chapter 4 in this volume.

42 See Lefkowitz, Chapter 2 in this volume; Besson and Martí, Chapter 14 in this volume; Chemillier-Gendreau, Chapter 13 in this volume.

43 See Radi, Chapter 15 in this volume.

44 See Besson and Martí, Chapter 14 in this volume.

45 See Pellet, Chapter 1 in this volume.

46 See Zarbiyev, Chapter 7 in this volume.

47 See Hollis, Chapter 6 in this volume.

48 See Besson, fn. 6, at 295.

49 On consent, 'veto' and 'participation', see Besson and Martí, Chapter 14 in this volume.

50 See d'Aspremont, Chapter 5 in this volume.

51 See Radi, Chapter 15 in this volume.

self-determination,[52] the original legal institution of the latter also implies inherent legal limits thereto.[53] This is the case, for instance, of the egalitarian limits to consent, but also of all those other features that are constitutive of that autonomy legally and considered as inherent limits to consent in international law, as exemplified by imperative rights and duties under international human rights law.[54]

Second, the objects and types of consent to international law also need to be clarified.

Starting with the *objects* of consent, indeed, consent pertains to 'obligations' or 'liabilities' arising from different sources of international law, such as treaties or custom, and arguably unilateral acts.[55] It also pertains to such obligations or liabilities arising from adjudication, thereby giving rise to a controversy about the differences between consent to obligation and consent to jurisdiction (i.e. a third-party's power to adjudicate) over those obligations[56] and about the importance of who controls both kinds of consent and their objects.[57] As explained in Section 1, the normative or binding dimension of the object of consent when it is consent to international 'law' calls for a distinction from other 'norms' as in inter-State 'contracts' or 'political commitments', and from other forms of promises or pledges one usually classifies as informal or soft law in international law.[58]

Turning to the *types* of consent in contemporary international law, consent is usually understood through binary oppositions:[59] it may be considered individual or institutional, individual or collective,[60] unilateral or mutual, tacit or explicit, single or continuous, unique or fragmented,[61] domestic or international,[62] and original or subsequent.[63] One also opposes consent as a

52 See Besson and Martí, Chapter 14 in this volume.

53 See Fabre-Magnan, fn. 10.

54 See Besson and Martí, Chapter 14 in this volume.

55 See Lefkowitz, Chapter 2 in this volume.

56 See Tams, Chapter 3 in this volume; Nolte, Chapter 9 in this volume; Boisson de Chazournes, Chapter 10 in this volume.

57 See Tams, Chapter 3 in this volume; Kassoti, Chapter 12 in this volume.

58 See Hollis, Chapter 6 in this volume; Brunnée, Chapter 8 in this volume; Kassoti, Chapter 12 in this volume.

59 For a critique of those binary oppositions, see d'Aspremont, Chapter 5 in this volume.

60 See Brunnée, Chapter 8 in this volume; Pellet, Chapter 1 in this volume; Radi, Chapter 15 in this volume.

61 See Brunnée, Chapter 8 in this volume.

62 See Brunnée, Chapter 8 in this volume.

63 See Nolte, Chapter 9 in this volume.

threshold to substantive consent, for interpretation purposes for instance,[64] or consent to rule to consent to regime.[65]

Third, and finally, the subjects and institutions of consent to international law are also in need of clarification.

The *subjects* of consent may be individual persons or, more commonly, groups of persons such as peoples – whether they have been instituted into States or other public institutions or into civil society organizations, such as NGOs and transnational corporations. Their *institutions* may also consent to international law. The latter's power or right to do so for their peoples under international law and hence to represent them actually contributes to instituting them as such.[66] Those institutions encompass States, of course, but also IOs,[67] cities or regions.

This distinction between the subjects and institutions of consent to international law is not always sufficiently clear in contemporary discussions, and deserves to be addressed more clearly in the future. Of course, it comes with complexities, and especially important limitations to the analogy between individual and institutional consent, vexed questions of (especially, but not only democratic) representation of the subjects,[68] and difficult issues of attribution of the consent of individual agents, or further institutions, to their institutions.[69] Further difficulties arise also when the subjects and/or institutions consenting to one another are not of the same kind, as with informal 'arrangements' or 'agreements' between States and non-State actors or between IOs such as the European Union (hereafter EU) and non-State actors.[70] More generally, the institutionalized context of contemporary international law-making affects the nature and role of consent.[71]

From the perspective of those primary, conceptual goals, the proposed study of the legal regime of consent in international law may be described as a study in general international law. It proceeds from the identification and comparison of general or generalizable features of consent across various special regimes of international law and across different international institutions.

64 See Zarbiyev, Chapter 7 in this volume; Nolte, Chapter 9 in this volume.

65 See Tams, Chapter 3 in this volume; Zarbiyev, Chapter 7 in this volume, by reference to Neff, fn. 13.

66 See Besson and Martí, Chapter 14 in this volume; Kassoti, Chapter 12 in this volume; d'Aspremont, Chapter 5 in this volume.

67 See Bordin, Chapter 11 in this volume.

68 See Besson and Martí, Chapter 14 in this volume.

69 See Besson, fn. 6, at 295–296; Brölmann, Chapter 4 in this volume; Bordin, Chapter 11 in this volume.

70 See Kassoti, Chapter 12 in this volume; Hollis, Chapter 6 in this volume.

71 See Brölmann, Chapter 4 in this volume; Brunnée, Chapter 8 in this volume; Radi, Chapter 15 in this volume.

The recent debates about the notions and roles of consent, about its objects and types, and about its subjects and institutions may indeed be observed in all regimes of international law, but especially in international environmental law,[72] international human rights law[73] and international humanitarian law.[74] The various specialists of international law and the philosophy of international law invited to contribute to this volume have been asked to explore those issues in the regimes mentioned, but also in many others.

The volume also has a secondary, more normative and critical aim. The exploration of the notions, roles, objects, types, subjects and institutions of consent to international law should indeed also shed light on the increasingly vexed questions of the origins of the normativity and authority of international law *qua* 'law' by contrast to the many other types of consensual 'norms' that increasingly apply within contemporary international relations. Tying the question of consent to international law more closely to its subjects and institutions could also contribute to clarifying the issue of the legitimacy of international law as the law of public institutions by contrast to mere 'actors' of international law.

Indeed, even if the time of anthropomorphism and of the related private law analogies is long past in international law, and even if legal positivism is no longer wedded to voluntarism, consensualism has undoubtedly retained some of its private law flavour. If unattended (and this volume's second aim is precisely to attend to this), the current consolidation of the normative role

[72] See, for example, Malgosia Fitzmaurice, 'Expression of Consent to Be Bound by a Treaty as Developed in Certain Environmental Treaties', in Jan Klabbers and René Lefeber (eds.), *Essays on the Law of Treaties: A Collection of Essays in Honour of Bert Vierdag* (Leiden: Martinus Nijhoff, 1998), pp. 59–80; Brunnée, 'COPing with Consent', fn. 23; Brunnée, 'Reweaving the Fabric of International Law?', fn. 23.

[73] See, for example, Curtis A. Bradley and Jack L. Goldsmith, 'Treaties, Human Rights, and Conditional Consent' (2000) 149(2) *University of Pennsylvania Law Review* 399–468; Matthew Craven, 'Legal Differentiation and the Concept of the Human Rights Treaty in International Law' (2000) 11(3) *European Journal of International Law* 489–519; Ryan Goodman, 'Human Rights Treaties, Invalid Reservations and State Consent' (2002) 96(3) *American Journal of International Law* 531–560; Jan Klabbers, 'On Human Rights Treaties, Contractual Conceptions and Reservations', in Ineta Ziemele (eds.), *Reservations to Human Rights Treaties and the Vienna Convention Regime: Conflict, Harmony and Reconciliation* (Leiden: Martinus Nijhoff, 2004), pp. 149–182; Lea Brilmayer, 'From "Contract" to "Pledge": The Structure of International Human Rights Agreements' (2006) 77(1) *British Yearbook of International Law* 163–202; Samantha Besson, 'Human Rights Waivers and the Right to Do Wrong under the ECHR', in *Mélanges for Dean Spielmann* (Nijmegen: Wolf Legal Publishers, 2015), pp. 23–35.

[74] See, for example, Eliav Lieblich, 'Why Can't We Agree on When Governments Can Consent to External Intervention? A Theoretical Inquiry' (2020) 7(1) *Journal on the Use of Force and International Law* 5–25; Paddeu, fn. 32.

of consent outside the formal sources of international law may contribute to the ongoing process of privatization of public international law.[75] How, indeed, could a legal order that began by treating public institutions by analogy with private persons now resist their privatization and, conversely, the treatment of those private persons by analogy with public institutions and their publicization?[76]

It is, for instance, in a private law guise that consent features in recent discussions pertaining to the normativity of international soft and/or informal law.[77] States are simply assimilated to other 'actors', public or private, when they consent to those soft and/or informal norms, and vice versa.[78] This assimilation of States to private individuals reduces States to their governments. In so doing, it dispenses State consent from representing that State's people's consent, and hence from any requirements of attribution and from additional domestic law requirements of parliamentary or popular approval. The equal role recognized to State consent and that of other 'non-State actors' in those contexts contributes to undermining the specificity of the consent of States *qua* public and sovereign institutions representing their peoples in international law-making. In turn, those new normative practices also exclude States' consent from the scope of protection of the international legal framework that usually applies and actually vests that consent with the normative power to bind under international law in the first place, and especially under international treaty law. This leaves weaker States unprotected from stronger ones, or (States)peoples unprotected from powerful private 'stakeholders'. The erosion of the right not to consent to soft law of certain States, weaker than others, actually epitomizes the problem.[79]

The privatization of consent does not stop with States, however. One may observe a similar 'personification' of IOs in the debates pertaining to their autonomous 'will' or 'consent' in international treaty-making or customary

75 Samantha Besson, *The Public-Private Relation and International Law* (Leiden: Brill, in press, 2024); Anne Peters, 'Privatisation under and of Public International Law', Hersch Lauterpacht Memorial Lectures 2017 (7–10 March 2017). Available at: www.mpil.de/files/pdf5/0_Handout_Lauterpacht_07032.pdf, last accessed 7 December 2022; Frédéric Mégret, 'Are There "Inherently Sovereign Functions" in International Law?' (2021) 115(3) *American Journal of International Law* 452–492.

76 For a full argument, see Besson, fn. 75.

77 This applies to 'agreements' between States and non-State actors (see, e.g., Kassoti, Chapter 12 in this volume), as much as to 'agreements' between non-State actors themselves (see, e.g., Loja, fn. 35).

78 For a general critique, see Samantha Besson, *Reconstructing the International Institutional Order* (Paris: OpenEdition Books/Éditions du Collège de France, 2021).

79 See, for example, Lorenz Langer, 'Implications of Soft Law Regimes for Small States: The Experience of Switzerland and Liechtenstein' (2020) 30(2) *Swiss Review of International and European Law* 235–264.

practice.[80] The focus on IOs' legal personality in that debate and the legal analogies between States and IOs have actually kept international lawyers from addressing the far more pressing institutional questions of the multiple and continuous representation of the same peoples by IOs and their Member States.[81] In turn, the prevalence of the functionalist understanding of IOs and their law-making powers and its contribution to the latter's privatization may be a cause of additional concern in this respect.[82] It could, indeed, lead to understand consent by IOs, but also by extension by States in IOs, as any other type of individual consent, and not as that of a public institution representing (States)peoples.

What one may coin the 'private return of consent' in international law implies that the alleged rise of 'non-consensual' international law,[83] far from signalling the demise of consent, may actually only have marked the demise of States' consent (and arguably other public institutions') *qua* public institutions' consent in international law-making. Keeping consent in place while displacing States (and those other public institutions), the inadequately called 'non-consensual' international law has in fact contributed to the ongoing process of recontractualization of international law-making and to its privatization,[84] at the price of its publicness and of the international rule of law.[85]

This process has actually been facilitated by the parallel albeit dubious reduction, in international law scholarship, of State consent to a subjective, individualistic, self-interested and private posture, as mentioned before. This reduction has led to the promotion, instead, of an objective, collective, communitarian and public conception of international law, a conception that has been, however, severed from State consent rather than constructed around it.[86] In turn, this has left those new processes of 'regulation' of alleged

[80] See Brölmann, fn. 13; Brölmann, Chapter 4 in this volume; Bordin, Chapter 11 in this volume; Kassoti, Chapter 12 in this volume.

[81] See Samantha Besson, 'Book Review: Fernando Lusa Bordin: The Analogy between States and International Organizations' (2020) 31(2) *The European Journal of International Law* 771–776; Besson, 'Sovereign States and Their International Institutional Order', fn. 15.

[82] On the privatization of IOs through functionalism and on the privatization of Member States by those IOs by extension, see Samantha Besson, 'The International Public: A Farewell to Functions in International Law' (2021) 115 *American Journal of International Law Unbound* 307–311.

[83] See, for example, Helfer, fn. 8; Guzman, fn. 8; Shaffer, fn. 8; Pauwelyn, fn. 9; Pauwelyn *et al.*, fn. 8; Krisch, fn. 9.

[84] See, for example, Peters, fn. 75; Mégret, fn. 75; Besson, fn. 75; Durkee, fn. 26.

[85] See Besson, fn. 75. For a more general critique of the institutional blind spot of contemporary international law, see Besson, fn. 78.

[86] For a critique, see Samantha Besson, 'Community Interests in International Law: Whose Interests Are They and How Should We Best Identify Them?', in Eyal Benvenisti and Georg

international public goods entirely in the hands of 'private actors', of insufficiently institutionalized and uncontrolled 'trustees', of unchecked 'judges' or, even worse, of a handful of powerful States using the now largely inegalitarian and privatized institutional structures of IOs[87] or soft law mechanisms to rule over weaker ones.

Of course, as we all know from the ticking clock of climate change and the many other public goods such as health, peace or science, in urgent need of protection by international law, international law-making is often paralyzed by disagreements among States and hence by the withholding of a few States' consent. This may explain why so many today are ready to dispense with State consent despite the lack of opposability of new norms, both internationally in terms of the formal sources of international law and domestically in terms of respect of the requirements of foreign relations law.

One may, however, beg to differ with the argument many draw from this observation against the role of State consent in international treaty-making or in IOs. It is true that giving States a veto or, at least, refusal rights in international law-making has become part of the problem. However, abandoning State consent altogether is too high a price to pay and the consent of (States) peoples has to be part of any legitimate solution to those challenges. One should protect all self-determining (States) peoples' right to equal consent, albeit as a right that is duly revised so as to become more egalitarian, inclusive and participative.[88] This is the only way to strengthen international law as the kind of public, hard and representative law one may not only deem more effective, but also democratically legitimate.

Breaking away from the pragmatic resignation that often prevails among international law scholars on the question of State consent,[89] it is time therefore for international lawyers to turn to the reform of international institutions and procedures so as to enforce a new, and especially more democratic, conception of State consent that enables States, and arguably other public institutions,[90] to represent all peoples and their public interests

Nolte (eds.), *Community Interests across International Law*, online ed. (Oxford: Oxford University Press, 2018), pp. 50–69.

87 See Samantha Besson, 'Democratic Representation within International Organizations: From International Good Governance to International Good Government' (2022) 19 *International Organizations Law Review* 489–527; Besson and Martí, Chapter 14 in this volume.

88 See Besson and Martí, Chapter 14 in this volume; Chemillier-Gendreau, Chapter 13 in this volume.

89 See Besson, fn. 6, at 315.

90 See Besson and Martí, 'Legitimate Actors of International Law-Making', fn. 16.

effectively in international law-making.[91] Such an account of democratic State consent would not only fit and justify the contemporary practice of the formal sources of international law, where consent retains a central albeit changing role. With its revised understanding, justification and limits, such an account may also contribute to bringing States and their peoples back to these sources in the future, and away from informal and soft law-making processes. This would not only enhance the accountability of international law to all peoples, but also benefit domestic democracy by protecting it from populism and from the sirens of other forms of withdrawal and exit.

3 THE STRUCTURE OF THE VOLUME

To reflect the three dimensions of the process of consenting to international law, identified in Section 2, this volume is divided into three parts. Part I pertains to the notions and roles of consent to international law, Part II to its objects and types, and Part III to its subjects and institutions. Those three parts correspond to the three dimensions of consent that are discussed the most, as explained before, in current debates in international law.

Each of those three parts comprises five chapters written by international lawyers and philosophers of international law (some authors qualify and consider themselves as both). This mixed authorship avoids a common but fake opposition between the theory and practice of international law, and makes the exchanges more fluid between the two groups of authors. This edited volume is indeed the first one to open a dialogue, and hopefully a fruitful one, between international lawyers and legal philosophers on the topic of consent to international law. The issues raised by consent to international law are notably difficult, indeed. They pertain to the nature, validity and legitimate authority of international law, and to its interpretation, as well as to the sovereignty of States and their sovereign equality, international legal personality and international institutional representation. Such issues are not usually addressed together and in all their philosophical complexity by existing international law accounts of consent. Those issues cannot, however, be solved in an informed way by legal philosophers alone either. The latter often tend to overgeneralize and fail to grasp the sheer complexity of the practice of international law-making, whether it pertains to sources of international law, to international adjudication or to IOs.

[91] See Besson, fn. 6, at 305–312.

Coming back to the tripartite structure of the volume, there may be overlaps between some of those parts' topics and the respective chapters therein, as it is often the case when addressing complex international law issues. It is difficult, indeed, to classify any given argument about consent to international law as pertaining only to its nature or role and not to its objects and types, and vice versa. This is why some of the chapters in Part I pertain to consent to treaties and jurisdiction, two topics that are also addressed in Part II. By contrast to the latter, however, the former focus on the nature of consent and its role therein.[92] In the same vein, the subjects of consent affect the role it may have in international law, and especially its contribution to the legality and the legitimacy of international law, and vice versa. That is why some of the chapters in Part I pertain to IOs and, more generally, the institutionalized context of international law-making, albeit from the perspective of the nature of consent,[93] and not only from that of its subjects and institutions as in the chapters in Part III. This is also why, conversely, some chapters in Part III draw conclusions from the increasingly private subjects of consent to international law for the role of consent as a criterion for the legality of international law in the first place.[94] Importantly, however, those overlaps have been identified, and have been addressed in the relevant chapters.

Of course, the idea has not been to ask contributors in the later parts to endorse what was said in earlier ones (as a matter of fact, most contributors disagree on many of the issues discussed in the other chapters), but to ask them to refer to those arguments provided their own argument required them to do so and to explain how they agreed or disagreed with what was said earlier in the volume. Chapter 15 that closes the volume actually reverts to some of those shared objects of contention and to the open controversies between contributors. It also identifies the remaining open questions and a few directions for future research.

As it is the case in any edited volume, and especially on a topic like consent to international law, there are many issues that were identified as the project went along and could not be covered. They will have to be addressed in future research. Many of those issues are mentioned at the end of the respective chapters. Among them, however, two need to be singled out here.

First of all, even if Part III addresses people as the ultimate subjects of their States and other international institutions' consent to international law,[95] the

92 See Tams, Chapter 3 in this volume; by contrast to Boisson de Chazournes, Chapter 10 in this volume.

93 See Brölmann, Chapter 4 in this volume; by contrast to Bordin, Chapter 11 in this volume.

94 See Kassoti, Chapter 12 in this volume; by contrast to Hollis, Chapter 6 in this volume.

95 See especially Besson and Martí, Chapter 14 in this volume; Chemillier-Gendreau, Chapter 13 in this volume.

notion and role of individuals' direct consent to obligations or liabilities under international law would need to be addressed more specifically and for itself. This is the case in international human rights law in particular, but individual consent is a fast developing practice in almost all regimes of international law that have individuals as direct subjects. Second, the domestic or internal law dimension of States' or IOs' consent would also need to be discussed in more detail, especially through the lenses of comparative foreign relations law. This does not only matter for democratic legitimacy purposes when linking our institutions' international consent to the peoples they represent, as discussed in Part III,[96] but also, more generally, to identify new ways of protecting the autonomy of consenting subjects in international law, for instance, through further limits on State or other public institutions' consent.[97]

4 THE CONTENTS OF THE VOLUME

As mentioned before, this volume is divided in three parts: Part I pertains to the notions and roles of consent in international law; Part II to its objects and types; and Part III to its subjects and institutions.

Part I is composed of five chapters and pertains to the notions and roles of consent in international law. Those chapters address different aspects of the question. Whereas Chapter 1 delineates consent from other related concepts and Chapter 2 addresses in what sense consent may contribute to the legitimacy of international law, Chapter 3 pertains to how control over consent has become the new focus of the practice of international dispute resolution and Chapter 4 addresses the way in which the institutionalization of international law has affected both the concept of consent and its relevance. Chapter 5 takes stock of the debate and assesses its theoretical underpinnings critically.

In Chapter 1, 'Consenting Is Not Willing', Alain Pellet argues that 'will' and 'consent' are different. According to him, no State's will is entirely free. However, this does not preclude its consent from being valid. State consent displays different shades of will: while unilateral acts are the epitome of 'willing consent', the degree of willingness required when accepting a treaty is weaker, until it almost disappears in the case of custom, or general principles of law. The author argues that *opinio juris* and consent are also different notions: you may feel legally bound even if consent is very remote. However, whatever role 'will' plays in the formation of rules, once the rules exist, States

96 Besson and Martí, Chapter 14 in this volume; Chemillier-Gendreau, Chapter 13 in this volume.

97 Radi, Chapter 15 in this volume.

are, according to Alain Pellet, bound and their will is trapped. The author makes the argument that if neither will nor consent explains the basis of a State's obligation when it is no longer willing to implement it, they nonetheless have a stabilizing and legitimizing role. He argues that consent makes the acceptability of the obligation stronger, by comforting its legitimacy, which also makes its implementation more effective.

In Chapter 2, 'State Consent and the Legitimacy of International Law', David Lefkowitz argues that while State consent does contribute to international law's legitimacy, it does not do so by providing a justification for it. States are not bound to obey international law because they have chosen to submit to its authority. Rather, international law provides them with a reason for action, and indeed they have a moral duty to obey it, if and only if they will do better at realizing justice if they act as the law directs them to act than if they act on their own judgment. As a means for crafting international law, State consent is, according to the author, valuable insofar as it yields international legal norms that satisfy this condition. He argues, that in a few cases, it may also constitute an intrinsically valuable expression of trust in the international political community or an international institution that exercises political authority.

In Chapter 3, 'Controlling Consent: Insights from Binding Dispute Settlement', Christian Tams assesses the role of consent in processes of binding dispute resolution before international courts and tribunals. He seeks to demonstrate that – notwithstanding its general relevance across wide fields of international law – 'consent' has a particular role in binding dispute resolution. According to him, this particular role derives from the special nature of binding dispute resolution processes. These processes are intrusive and characterized by their uncertain outcome: the implications of State consent to the dispute resolution process crucially depend on decisions of an independent entity, namely an international court or tribunal. Because this is so, States insist on the need for consent, as a precondition of any binding dispute resolution process. What is more, consent is typically formal, explicit and directly expressed, reflecting continued State control over binding dispute resolution. At the same time, once consent has been given, control shifts to the competent international court or tribunal. As far as the scope of consent is concerned, the decisions of this court or tribunal are binding on the State concerned. States renounce control over the scope of consent and have to accept the court's or tribunal's decision, as well as its application and interpretation of the applicable law in particular disputes. Moreover, by virtue of their decision-making authority, many international courts and tribunals have managed to assert at least a persuasive influence over proper construction of the legal rules at stake, extending beyond the cases immediately pending before them. The chapter traces these peculiarities and – by reference to two pen pictures – examines how the tension between State and courts' authority plays out in particular disputes.

In Chapter 4, 'International Organizations and the Disaggregation of Consent', Catherine Brölmann examines how 'consent', traditionally taken as a foundational element in international law, fares in the context of IOs. The central argument is that IOs, both as actors consenting to international law and as institutional spaces for other actors doing so, have changed the operation or even the nature of consent in international law as they have made the components of the act of consent disaggregate. Catherine Brölmann argues that the IO's expression of consent has become detached from the psychological or 'intentional' state that is presumed to be underlying in the legal subject. Where the organization appears as an institutional space for the consent of others, the object of consent in many instances is detached especially in substance from the normative effect created for the consent-giver.

In Chapter 5, 'Consenting to International Law in Five Moves', Jean d'Aspremont seeks to unpack five of the main discursive moves witnessed in the literature and case law pertaining to the question of consent to international law. He argues that these five specific discursive moves are performed by almost anyone engaging with the question of consent to international law, be such engagement on the more orthodox side or on the more critical side of the argumentative spectrum. The author claims that these five discursive moves correspond to the reproduction of a very modernist understanding of authority, the constitution of the very subject that is consenting, the anonymization of the author of consent, the reversal of the temporality of the legal discourse on consent and the adoption of very binary patterns of thought. This chapter shows that discursive moves made by international lawyers around the idea of consent bears heavily upon the type of political legitimacy, the type of geography, the type of responsibility, the type of temporality and the type of hermeneutics that international law is serving.

Part II is dedicated to the objects and types of consent in international law. It is comprised of five chapters. Those chapters address different aspects of the question, by focusing, for the first three chapters, Chapters 6 to 8, on consent in international treaty law-making and treaty interpretation and, for the next two chapters, Chapters 9 and 10, on consent to international adjudication or within international adjudication.

In Chapter 6, 'Do International Agreements Have a Consent Problem?', Duncan B. Hollis explores how consent functions as commitment, content and constitution for international agreements. He argues that consent constructs all forms of international commitment, not just those governed by international law (treaties), but those governed by national law (contracts), and those not governed by law at all (political commitments). According to him, consent elucidates an agreement's contents – what the agreement 'is' in terms of scope and substance. Consent can also function as a constitution – delimiting not only 'primary' rules encapsulated by an agreement's existence and contents, but 'secondary rules' determining who can make agreements, how they must do so, and ways to recognize, adjust and end them. The author further argues that, for all these functions, consent remains an under-examined and undifferentiated concept. Today, almost any of consent's functions can be established by almost any formal or informal means. This leaves ample room for inconsistent understandings, unaligned expectations, and disputes about the existence of treaties or other forms of international agreements, their contents, and their relevant constitutive rules. Alongside existing proposals (presumptions/defaults and content-based criteria), this chapter proposes that international law should pursue more – and different – formalities for consent. Having different forms of consent follow its different functions may, according to the author, improve the efficacy of consent and with it the efficacy of international agreements overall.

In Chapter 7, 'Consenting to Treaty Commitments: Endorsing Rules or Endorsing a Regime of Discursive Commitments?', Fuad Zarbiyev examines the place of consent in treaty interpretation at the time of the marginalization of the role of the intention of the parties. Whether the characterization of international law as a legal system grounded in State consent has ever been empirically true is, as he argues, open to discussion. For him, the law of treaties, however, is commonly seen as 'a bastion of consensualism'. This sense of confidence has, however, never sat easily with treaty interpretation. The author claims that, despite the lip service sometimes paid to the fiction of the common intention of the parties, the official doctrine of treaty interpretation rests on the primacy of the terms of the treaty.

In Chapter 8, 'State Consent in the Evolving Climate Regime: Individual and Collective Aspects', Jutta Brunnée examines the interplay between the individual and collective dimensions of treaty-based law-making and standard-setting processes in the United Nations climate regime, which boasts a broad spectrum of approaches to regime development. They range from formal consent to its component treaties or amendments to these treaties and standard-setting by plenary bodies to recourse to non-binding commitments. The reason why the author attempts to elucidate the interplay between the individual and collective dimensions of treaty-based law-making is that multilateral treaties have been the main anchors for international environmental law-making. In this context, State consent not only has individual effects, but also feeds into a collective process. The chapter begins by exploring the United Nations Framework Convention on Climate Change and the Kyoto Protocol. It then turns to the Paris Agreement and the shift to what has been described as a 'bottom-up' approach. The perhaps most striking feature of this approach is its reliance on non-binding, 'nationally determined contributions' (hereafter NDCs) that each party must 'prepare, communicate and maintain'. The author argues that, from the vantage point of State consent, the most significant consequence of the Paris Agreement's NDC approach is a shift away from the anchoring of consent to climate action in treaty-based processes, and hence from the linkages that adoption and entry into force requirements establish between multiple parties' individual expressions of consent.

In Chapter 9, 'Consent and Sources: The European Court of Human Rights and the International Law Commission', Georg Nolte's starts by observing that discussions about the foundations and the limits of the powers of international courts, including those of the European Court of Human Rights (hereafter ECtHR), turn around the aims of achieving legal certainty, ensuring legitimacy and justice, and avoiding conflicting obligations that may emanate from different regimes of international law. The chapter reflects on these aims from the perspective of consent as the common basis of the main sources of international law, listed in Article 38 of the Statute of the International Court of Justice. Proceeding from the case law of the ECtHR, the chapter explores how the recent work of the International Law Commission conceives the role of consent in respect of the main sources of international law, and whether the jurisprudence of the ECtHR remains within the framework of general international law so enunciated.

In Chapter 10, 'Variations around the Notion of Consent in Investment Arbitration', Laurence Boisson de Chazournes seeks to illustrate the multiplicity of thoughts and varied techniques deployed in interpreting consent in investment arbitration. The jurisdiction and right to adjudicate of international courts and tribunals is based on the consent and agreement of the subjects, that is, litigants. Given the clear terms in which international courts and tribunals have formulated and upheld the principle of consent, it could be expected that this principle would not evoke confusion or extensive discussion. However, this chapter shows that the steady rise of varied international disputes has generated significant debate about the interpretation and application of the principle of consent. International courts and tribunals are being increasingly criticized by States for their jurisdictional overreach. The underlying problem, as the author sees it, may well be whether the contours of consent to arbitration are clear. Investment arbitration tribunals while dealing with the question of State consent have shown sharp divisions on the notion of consent. The varied approaches taken by arbitral tribunals to State consent highlights the indeterminacy of the contours of consent. The chapter finds support for its argument in a case study of the issue of State consent in the context of the interpretation of Most-Favoured Nation clauses.

Part III pertains to the subjects and institutions of consent in international law. It comprises five chapters. Those chapters address different sides of the issue, by focusing, for the first two chapters, Chapters 11 and 12, on consent by IOs and by so-called non-State actors' and, for the third and fourth chapters, Chapters 13 and 14, on the democratic legitimacy of State consent to international law within or outside IOs and hence on (States) peoples as the primary subjects of that consent. The fifth and final chapter of Part III, Chapter 15, concludes the volume by reverting to some of the conceptual questions it opened with and especially the issue of the autonomy of the consenting subject and the limits that autonomy places on consent to international law.

In Chapter 11, 'The Consent of International Organizations in the Making of General and Conventional Rules of International Law', Fernando Lusa Bordin attempts to answer the following question: in an international legal system of which States are no longer the only subjects, what is the role that the consent of IOs plays in the creation of rights and obligations that apply on the international plane? The chapter reflects on the legal agency that IOs enjoy, *qua* subjects of international law, in the process of formation of general international law and in the acquisition of treaty rights and obligations. In so doing, it advances two claims. The first is that even though IO practice can and should be taken into account in the identification of customary rules, it is not a necessary element in the process of formation of those rules. As a result, the applicability of custom to IOs is not premised upon their participation in the customary process. The second claim of the chapter is that, under current law, IOs can only be bound by treaty rules to which they have consented, which may give rise to problematic gaps between the treaty obligations of IOs and the treaty obligations of their members. In pursuing those claims, the chapter offers some reflections on the systemic and normative implications of the formal involvement of IOs in the making of rules of general and conventional international law.

In Chapter 12, 'Consent and Informal Law-Making: The View From the Court of Justice of the European Union', Eva Kassoti explores how the Court of Justice of the European Union (hereafter CJEU) has dealt with issues of consent as a trigger of commitment in the context of treaty-making by focusing on its practice pertaining to informal arrangements concluded between the EU and third parties aimed at replacing international agreements. The main arguments advanced in the chapter are: (a) that the Court has largely followed mainstream international legal thinking by identifying consent as the 'objective' common intention of its authors to be legally bound – as this is manifested on the basis of an instrument's actual terms and the circumstances attending its making; and (b) that the Court has acknowledged the constitutive function of consent when it comes to treaty-making with non-State actors. The chapter also illustrates an important blind spot in the current debate on consent. The examination of the CJEU's case law shows that political factors may have a bearing on the ascertainment of the consent to be legally bound. This, in turn, entails, the author argues, that attempts at theorizing how international law can remain sociologically clever and keep pace with current developments on the ground should be cognizant of the danger of over-relying on judicial practice.

In Chapter 13, 'Consent as a Guarantee of the Democratic Legitimacy of International Law', Monique Chemillier-Gendreau makes the case for a new understanding of the role of consent in international law. She begins by noting that the question of consent should be as central to international law as it is in other fields of law because legal norms give rise to power relations and impose constraints upon those to whom they apply, and those in power want these constraints to be accepted. Yet, the question of consent was, as the chapter claims, never raised in the classical era when State sovereignty made it possible for States to adopt international norms without their subjects' consent. With the Enlightenment, however, the people's consent through representation became the foundation of domestic law. Yet, most of the time, representation is, according to the author, formal and serves to justify the law as if it were produced by the general will. Because international law reflects the fickle concurrence of States' wills, the world community's law does not rely on popular consent. The world community is confronted with difficult challenges, and it needs, more than ever, norms that can meet this moment. For the author, the international system, as it is currently conceived around the central notion of sovereignty, is unable to effectively address such challenges. Institutional innovations will be crucial to confronting such challenges, but they have yet to be imagined.

In Chapter 14, 'From Equal State Consent to Equal Public Participation in International Organizations: Institutionalizing Multiple International Representation', Samantha Besson and José Luis Martí begin by observing that most obligations of international law are still regarded as 'based' on State consent even if, strictly speaking, consent can neither be a condition of that law's validity nor amount to a moral reason to comply with it. There are, the authors argue, good reasons for this, especially from a democratic legitimacy perspective. Still, the principle of State consent, even in its qualified version of 'democratic State' consent, suffers from important shortcomings that call for correctives or, at least, for complements in terms of international democratic representation. The chapter focuses on State consent in IOs. It starts by accounting for the democratic value of State consent in IOs before addressing some of its democratic deficits. It then articulates several institutional proposals to correct or, at least, complement the role of equal State consent in the institution, the operation and the control of IOs. While being aware of the high complexity and diversity of IOs, the authors develop a non-ideal normative argument for the latter's political re-institution to enhance their democratic legitimacy, drawing on the case of the World Health Organization (WHO). That re-institution has to start, the chapter argues, with the replacement of the principle of equal State consent by that of equal public participation in IOs: this does not only avoid reducing State consent in IOs to State veto or refusal rights, but it also extends the personal scope of those participatory rights to other non-State public institutions. The chapter's proposal should be read as one dimension of the institutionalization of a system of multiple representation of the world's peoples *qua* multiple instituted publics.

In Chapter 15, 'Autonomy in International Law: About the Legal and Societal Limits to the Exercise of Consent', Yannick Radi attempts to unravel the close conceptual and practical connection between consent and autonomy. The chapter argues that consent is the vehicle of autonomy, vehicle through which States give themselves their own rules, both primary rules and secondary rules. Because the exercise of autonomy in the international society faces contextual limits, linked to the self (*auto*) and to the law (*nomos*), it is claimed, that consent appears not only to be characterized by power, but also by limitations. This holds true for consent in international law-making as much as for consent in international dispute settlement. The chapter focuses on both categories, discussing the theory of sources and institutional law-making with respect to the former and jurisdictional matters and applicable law with respect to the latter. It concludes – prospectively – with some thoughts on the future of autonomy and consent in international legal theory and practice.

PART I
Notions and Roles of Consent

1

Consenting Is Not Willing

ALAIN PELLET*

Legal theories are not – at least, not only – innocuous intellectual games. They have concrete consequences and may become political challenges.

It seems in order nowadays to apologize for being 'mainstream'. In some respects, I am 'critical', but not on the general approach to international law. I remain convinced that the biggest theoretical problem – and the one of greatest practical importance – is that of the foundation of public international law: what makes it 'law', that is, what makes it a system of norms of behaviour that the addressees consider as legal?[1] And I also maintain two important beliefs, which explain the developments that follow:

- The only theories that have a real explanatory value with respect to the legal character of rules (or norms – I maintain that there is no material difference between them) are voluntarism (to which I do not adhere) or sociological objectivism (to which I do adhere, but not in its Scellian and moralizing version, rather in a so-called Marxian – and maybe outmoded – perspective).
- I also persist in thinking that the venerable notion of 'sources of law' retains an irreplaceable explanatory virtue.[2] Indeed, law is not a mere form, but it needs form and, in this respect, the concept of sources of international law continues to be useful and enlightening despite its despisers. What is a source of law (I speak of formal sources)? Nothing

* With thanks to Tessa Barsac for her helpful assistance in the preparation of this chapter.

1 I will confine myself to inter-State law, but I consider of course that States are not the only 'subjects' of public international law.

2 No need to expand on these two postulates: they form the substratum of my *Cours général de droit international public*: see Alain Pellet, 'Le droit international à la lumière de la pratique: L'introuvable théorie de la réalité' (Volume 414) *Collected Courses of the Hague Academy of International Law*, 2021, pp. 28–547.

> but a method to evaluate the acceptability of a rule within a given circle. It is the test through which you can determine whether a political project or wish has penetrated into the legal sphere or, in the words of Jacques Dehaussy, '*tout processus juridique créateur de normes générales destinées à régir des rapports internationaux*'.[3]

I intend to illustrate these purely doctrinal postulates and show their explanatory efficacy by revisiting and updating an old paper that appeared in the *Australian Yearbook of International Law* in 1992 under the title 'The Normative Dilemma: Will and Consent in International Law-Making'.[4] It has, of course, aged a little, but, on the whole, I still adhere to the essence of what I said more than thirty years ago. I think that the fundamental 'message' still holds true: neither will nor consent are explanatory factors of international law even if both are taken into account by international law – but in somewhat different ways.

In my last century's article, I had made much of the distinction between 'consent' and 'will'. I still value the distinction between both notions – and maintain that it was (and is) appropriate to differentiate between 'will' and 'consent'. Hence the title of this chapter: 'Consenting Is Not Willing'. But, upon reflection, I think I was a bit confused about the respective desirable use of the two words.

In reality, what I have (now) in mind is that 'will' is an affirmative attitude: 'I *want* this', 'this is my *will*' – and I would add: 'this is what I *really* want'; it has a psychological and subjective component. 'Consent' is different; indeed, it belongs to the same 'family' of expressions in that it too conveys a sense of assent or acceptance; but it implies (or may imply) something more 'passive' and includes resignation, discouragement or even dismay and, notwithstanding these aspects, it will produce legal effects – upon legally rather well-defined conditions.

A consent can be valid even if it expresses a reluctant will. And it is primarily in that sense that will does not equate with consent. The shade in meaning of

[3] Jacques Dehaussy, 'Sources du droit international' (1958) 1(10) *Jurisclasseur de Droit international*: 'any legal process creating general norms intending to govern international relations' (my translation). Unfortunately, in his last – and stimulating – book, the eminent writer changed this excellent definition and restricted it to the individual or collective *decisions* whose effect is '*de créer une norme* ayant valeur obligatoire *dans un système de droit*' ('*to create a norm* with binding force *in a system of law*') (my translation) (emphasis added): see Jacques Dehaussy, *Propos sur les sources du droit international* (Paris: Pedone, 2017), p. 23. I strongly disagree with this restriction: see, for example, the text from fn. 55–58.

[4] Alain Pellet, 'The Normative Dilemma: Will and Consent in International Law-Making' (1992) 12(1) *Australian Yearbook of International Law* 22–53.

both words might not be as clear in English as it is in French. 'Consent' in the sense used in this paper can be an equivalent to what other writers have in mind when they use the word 'consensus'.[5] The point here is that States may not 'want' a particular rule of international law, but, even if their will is not free, they can consent to that rule, not because they *want* it, but because they have no real choice.

Yet, the distinction is rarely made. Thus, in her article in the *Leiden Journal* (2016), Samantha Besson notes: 'A cursory survey of the use of the term "consent" in international law reveals that consent is used to refer both to the "free will" of States and to their "acceptance" of international law.'[6] This is true indeed and this is precisely what the 1969 Vienna Convention on the Law of Treaties[7] (hereafter VCLT) does: the word 'consent' is used there sixty-two times but, in reality, it is 'discredited' or 'conditioned' in more than half of its occurrences – that is, every time the Convention provides for the conditions of a 'valid' consent. However, leaving aside the VCLT, the reverse is nearly as common and 'will' (or in French '*volonté*') is used instead of consent.[8]

This is regrettable and I would urge both international courts and tribunals as well as colleagues not to conflate both notions. As the International Court of Justice (hereafter ICJ) rightly noted in the *Genocide (Croatia* v. *Serbia)* case, 'there is a distinction between the legal nature of ratification of, or accession to, a treaty, on the one hand, and on the other hand, the process by which a State becomes bound by a treaty as a successor State or remains bound as a continuing State'. In the first case, there 'is a simple act of will on the part of the State manifesting an intent' to become a party.

> In the case of succession or continuation on the other hand, the act of will of the State relates to an already existing set of circumstances, and amounts to a recognition by that State of certain legal consequences flowing from those

5 See Anthony D'Amato, *The Concept of Custom in International Law* (Ithaca: Cornell University Press, 1971); Jutta Brunnée, 'Consent' (last updated January 2022), in Rüdiger Wolfrum (ed.), *Max Planck Encyclopedia of Public International Law* (Oxford: Oxford University Press, 2008). Available at: https://opil.ouplaw.com/display/10.1093/law:epil/9780199231690/law-9780199231690-e1388, last accessed 13 December 2022.

6 Samantha Besson, 'State Consent and Disagreement in International Law-Making: Dissolving the Paradox' (2016) 29(2) *Leiden Journal of International Law* 289–316, at 295.

7 The Vienna Convention on the Law of Treaties, 1155 UNTS 331 (adopted 23 May 1969, entered into force 27 January 1980).

8 See, for example, *Legality of the Threat or Use of Nuclear Weapons* (Advisory Opinion) [1996] ICJ Rep. 226, Separate Opinion of Judge Guillaume, p. 291, para. 10; Brunnée, fn. 5: 'States can easily come to be bound by customary law without their explicit consent. In fact, they may even incur obligations against their *will*' (emphasis added). Interestingly, the *Max Planck Encyclopedia*, in which this paper is published, does not include an entry 'Will'.

> circumstances, so that any document issued by the State concerned, being essentially confirmatory, may be subject to less rigid requirements of form.[9]

Strictly speaking (and even though the Court mentions an 'act of will' in both cases), 'consent' would more properly mark a less clearly affirmed will.

Even though consent itself is not a univocal concept – or maybe more exactly, the manifestations of consent in the international legal sphere are quite diverse – the difference between both notions is more effectively represented on a scale than by determining a threshold. It is rather easy (even if probably over-simplistic) to construct a scale showing the various degrees of will and consent implied by the various ascertained sources of international law, their varying respective intensity and their unequal legitimizing and stabilizing effects.

Unilateral acts of the State are probably the epitome of 'willing consent', at least when they aim at imposing obligations on their own author; and this is also true for reservations to treaties (and objections to them) made in accordance with Articles 19–23 of the VCLT.[10]

It is well established that States can bind themselves by unilateral expressions of will.[11] This is compatible with the voluntarist approach. But when such declarations have been made, 'the unilateral undertaking resulting from these statements cannot be interpreted as having been made in implicit reliance of an arbitrary power of reconsideration'.[12] *Acta sunt servanda* in the same way as *pacta sunt servanda*.

[9] *Application of the Convention on the Prevention and Punishment of the Crime of Genocide (Croatia* v. *Serbia)* (Preliminary Objections) [2008] ICJ Rep. 412, p. 450, para. 109.

[10] On the very complex issues made by the law applicable to reservations with regard to the respect due to the will of the reserving State and the will of the other parties to the treaty, see International Law Commission (hereafter ILC), 'Guide to Practice on Reservations to Treaties', *Yearbook of the International Law Commission* (2011) Vol. II, Part Two, UN Doc. A/66/10, pp. 26–38; see also the challenging views expressed by Vassilis Pergantis, *The Paradigm of State Consent in the Law of Treaties: Challenges and Perspectives* (Cheltenham: Edward Elgar, 2017), pp. 234–323.

[11] *Nuclear Tests Case (Australia* v. *France)* (Judgment) [1974] ICJ Rep. 253, p. 270; *Case concerning Armed Activities on the Territory of the Congo (New Application: 2002) (Democratic Republic of the Congo* v. *Rwanda)* (Jurisdiction and Admissibility) (Judgment) [2006] ICJ Rep. 6, pp. 27–28; *Obligation to Negotiate Access to the Pacific Ocean (Bolivia* v. *Chile)* (Judgment) (Merits) [2018] ICJ Rep. 507, p. 554.

[12] *Nuclear Tests (Australia* v. *France)*, fn. 11, p. 270; *The Enrica Lexie Incident (Italy* v. *India)*, PCA, Provisional Measures (29 April 2016), 177 ILR 651, paras. 128–131. On unilateral acts and their termination, see, for example, Alfred P. Rubin, 'The International Legal Effects of Unilateral Declarations' (1977) 71(1) *American Journal of International Law* 1–30; Jean-Didier Sicault, 'Du caractère obligatoire des engagements unilatéraux en droit international public' (1979) 83(3) *Revue générale de droit international public* 633–688, at 650–656.

However, the degree of willingness required when accepting a treaty is weaker. As noted by Philip Allott: 'Negotiation is a process for finding a third thing which neither party wants but both parties can accept.'[13] Indeed, being bound by a treaty is a voluntary, supposedly free, decision – to the point that the VCLT is replete with provisions supposed to ensure that the consent of the State is effective and 'free'; and I have in mind not only Articles 46–53 on the 'Invalidity of treaties', but also Articles 7 and 8 on full powers, 11 *et sequitur* on the means of expressing consent to be bound or Article 40 on amendments to treaties. With these provisions, the VCLT postulates that, when a State follows the usual procedure and concludes a treaty without error or fraud, corruption or coercion in the sense of the VCLT, its will is free.

But this, in fact, is pure hypocrisy. It is not enough to will; it is also necessary *to be able to will*. And it is quite clear that in the international society, if States are equal, some are 'more equal', sometimes much more equal, than others. It is obvious that the 'will' of small and weak States is 'less free' than that of wealthy powerful ones; but this certainly does not prevent them from validly expressing their 'consent' to be bound by treaties or to participate *volens nolens* to the formation of customary rules. This is all in the name of the principle of sovereignty – which, nevertheless, must be recognized as having other virtues.[14]

This is not the place to enter into a lengthy discussion on the effects of coercion on the validity of international law norms or obligations, which, even limited to treaty law, the painstaking compromise embodied in Article 52 of the VCLT and the joint Declaration included in the Final Act of the Conference, are far from solving. This results in a marked reluctance of international courts and tribunals to recognize the invalidity of a treaty on grounds of coercion or to interpret it widely. Thus, in its 1973 judgments in the *Fisheries Jurisdiction* case, the ICJ refused to admit that the mere inequality of power between the United Kingdom and the Federal German Republic, on the one hand, and Iceland, on the other hand, could, in itself, void the relevant fisheries agreements.[15] To give a more recent example: in

[13] Philip Allott, 'The Concept of International Law' (1999) 10(1) *European Journal of International Law* 31–50, at 43.

[14] See Pellet, fn. 1, p. 490, paras. 852–857; Alain Pellet, 'Le droit international à l'aube du XXIème siècle (La société internationale contemporaine: Permanences et tendances nouvelles)', in Alain Pellet, *Le droit international entre souveraineté et communauté* (Paris: Pedone, 2014), pp. 19–112, pp. 48–55.

[15] *Fisheries Jurisdiction Case (United Kingdom* v. *Iceland)* (Judgment) [1973] ICJ Rep. 3, p. 14, para. 24; *Fisheries Jurisdiction Case* (*Federal Republic of Germany* v. *Iceland*) (Judgment) [1973] ICJ Rep. 49, p. 58, para. 24. For another example of the Court's reluctance when

the Advisory Opinion on the *Chagos*, the ICJ observed that, given the circumstances in which the Mauritian representatives had given their 'consent' to the territorial detachment of the archipelago on the eve of independence, this 'was not based on the free and genuine expression of the will of the people concerned'. However, the Court was careful not to characterize these circumstances (independence in exchange for detachment) as coercion within the meaning of the law of treaties, preferring the ground of violation of the colony's right to territorial integrity.[16]

That said, there can be no doubt that consent is not incompatible with at least a certain amount of coercion.[17] It must be admitted that coercion *lato sensu* is a component of international society as of any society; but this does not impede States in validly consenting to rules of, and obligations under, international law.

In reality, no State's will is entirely free. Great powers have different kinds of constraints to those of small countries, notably because they are, in fact, more deeply involved in international relations and therefore would usually care more for reputation, influence, soft power or interdependence. They too must compromise and consent to rules that do not necessarily correspond to their best interest at the time of conclusion of the treaty. Communality is indeed for all States an important incentive for consenting to legal rules – being of course accepted that 'depending on whether you are powerful or powerless' ('*selon que vous serez puissant ou misérable*'),[18] it will be easier to get out of the legal chains thus accepted. It remains that, as Tom Franck wrote, 'membership confers a desirable status which is manifested when the members have internalized socially functional and status-rooted privileges and duties'.[19]

Whatever the conditions for a valid consent, when they express their 'consent' in conformity with these rules, States buy a 'one-way ticket'.

coercion is invoked: *Case concerning Territorial and Maritime Dispute (Nicaragua v. Colombia)* (Judgment) (Preliminary Objections) [2007] ICJ Rep. 832, p. 859, para. 79; see also the strong formulas in *Aminoil* v. *Kuwait*, Arbitral Tribunal, Award (24 March 1982) 21 ILM 976.

16 Judgment, *Legal Consequences of the Separation of the Chagos Archipelago from Mauritius in 1965* (Advisory Opinion) [2019] ICJ Rep. 95, p. 137, para. 172. In that case, the Court addressed the consent of the people; but this does not matter for my purpose, which is to approach the limits of consent in a context of coercion.

17 Monique Chemillier-Gendreau, 'Le droit international entre volontarisme et contrainte', in *Mélanges offerts à Hubert Thierry: L'évolution du droit international* (Paris: Pedone, 1998), pp. 93–105.

18 Jean de La Fontaine, 'Les animaux malades de la peste', in Jean de La Fontaine, *Les Fables de la Fontaine* (Paris: Aubert, 1842), pp. 7–9, p. 9.

19 Thomas M. Franck, 'Legitimacy in the International System' (1988) 82(4) *American Journal of International Law* 705–759.

Take a case like *The S.S. "Wimbledon"*.[20] By its consent, whether it corresponded to its real will or not,[21] Germany entered into the Treaty of Versailles. Obviously, when the events that gave rise to the dispute occurred, Germany had changed its will and was no longer willing to apply that part of the Treaty concerning the Kiel canal – and for quite respectable reasons. Nevertheless, the Court rightly answered: *Pacta sunt servanda*.[22] But the formula is very ambiguous and this sacrosanct slogan of voluntarism as used here means in reality the very contrary of voluntarism: 'whatever its will, a State must abide by the law it entered into'.

This same idea of a 'will trap' is conveyed by the recent judgment on the preliminary objections in *Guyana* v. *Venezuela*. Commenting on the wording of the Agreement by which the Parties had 'conferred on the Secretary-General the authority to choose among the means of dispute settlement provided for in Article 33 of the Charter "until the controversy has been resolved"', the Court observed that the Parties had thus 'conferred on the Secretary-General the authority to choose the most appropriate means for a definitive resolution of the controversy'.[23] Then, noting that the decision taken accordingly by the Secretary-General 'would not be effective … if it were subject to the further consent of the Parties for its implementation' and 'would be contrary to the object and purpose of the Agreement', the Court concluded 'that the consent of the Parties to the jurisdiction of the Court is established in the circumstances of this case'. In other words, in spite of its strong struggle against the ICJ's jurisdiction,[24] the procedural conditions being fulfilled, Venezuela could not go back on the will clearly expressed in the Agreement concluded fifty-four years earlier. Professor Christian Tams will further explain that while State consent remains an indispensable condition for binding dispute settlement, States lose control over what they have

20 *Case of the S.S. "Wimbledon" (Great Britain* v. *Germany)* [1923] PCIJ Rep. Ser. A No. 1.

21 But the Court did not question that Germany had expressed a free consent, and the Treaty of Versailles was not subjected to the principle of the prohibition of the use of force in international relations: see ibid., pp. 25, 30.

22 Ibid., pp. 29–30. However, the Court does not expressly refer to the Latin formula.

23 *Arbitral Award of 3 October 1899 (Guyana* v. *Venezuela)* (Judgment) [2020] ICJ Rep. 455, p. 478, paras. 83, 84.

24 Venezuela did not only object to the Court's jurisdiction, it systematically refused to participate in the proceedings until 28 November 2019 when it sent a 'Memorandum' objecting to the admissibility of the Guyanese Application; it also made a lot of declarations and a press communiqué vociferously stating that the Court lacked jurisdiction and that it would not comply with any judgment on the merits, including after the Court's judgment asserting jurisdiction: see ibid.

consented to once the process is under way – it is then an independent third party that will determine, affirm and interpret the scope of consent.[25]

It would therefore seem that consent is only an explanation for one part of the process: the access to the treaty. It does not explain the basis of a State's obligation when that State is no longer willing to implement a treaty – in this respect, I join Samantha Besson who rightly drew attention to the importance of 'disagreement'.[26]

This does not mean, of course, that treaties are established *ne varietur*. It is necessary to be aware that treaty law changes and lives as does any part of any legal system, either through an informal evolution (mainly thanks to interpretation), or formally through amendments. As also stressed by Allott: 'A treaty is not the end of a process, but the beginning of another process.'[27] But it is suggested that there is no symmetry between the two processes: what has been done willingly cannot be changed or terminated by merely expressing a new unilateral will.

Indeed, except in a very few conceivable cases (e.g. in the field of human rights or of the environment), at least two States must express their consent to be bound. However, when it enters into an agreement, a State acts unilaterally: ratification, accession, acceptance, signature, etc., are unilateral acts – even though means of expressing consent to be bound show an increased flexibility in the conclusion of treaties. But, as underlined by Jutta Brunnée, the treaty-making process can progress, and the treaty take effect, only when a collectivity of States so agrees.[28] Similarly, when they want to amend or terminate the treaty, the Parties must act together: 'all States' must express the same will (except, of course, if the treaty itself prescribes otherwise); if not, the recalcitrant State will be responsible for its violation of the treaty. This is the clear result of Articles 54 and 56–60 of the VCLT. And the rules in this regard demonstrate an increase of formal rigidity, notably with the pressure of the treaty bodies that are jealously guarding the integrity of the treaty and of its membership.[29] It can be maintained that will is not absent from this process. But it is not State will, not even majority will, but communal consensus, in a very strict sense – the consent (be it implicit) of each and every party, not of one or a few or even many of them; this very much looks like unanimity. And this confirms Vassilis Pergantis' remark in his excellent

[25] Tams, Chapter 3 in this volume.
[26] Besson, fn. 6, at 292: 'consent, when it is required in international law-making, does not amount to strict agreement only, but rather to an agreement to disagree further'.
[27] Allott, fn. 13, at 43.
[28] Brunnée, Chapter 8 in this volume.
[29] On this approach, see Pergantis, fn. 10, pp. 154–188.

book on *The Paradigm of State Consent in the Law of Treaties*: 'States can exist only within a collaborative framework (legal order), which means we are forced ... to "construct" their will on the basis of communitarian ideals.'[30]

However, it can happen that some liberties are taken with apparently strict rules embodied in the VCLT. Thus, the famous Smithsonian Institute Agreement, which was instrumental in changing the Bretton Woods monetary system in 1971, was a purely informal agreement that certainly does not meet the requirements of Article XXVIII of the International Monetary Fund (hereafter IMF) Statutes.[31] In the same vein, the short-lived Protocol 14 bis to the European Convention on Human Rights of 27 May 2009,[32] simplifying the procedure for examining applications to the European Court of Human Rights (hereafter ECtHR), entered into force following its acceptance by only three States, whereas the Convention and Protocol 14, which it replaced pending its entry into force, required unanimity.[33] In these cases, the initial *pactum* was not respected, it was modified: the communal consent achieved what isolated State wills could not have done.

It is also true that the law of treaties offers an apparent safety net to States in the form of the famous doctrine of fundamental change of circumstances, to which Article 62 of the VCLT is dedicated.[34] According to this principle, a

30 Ibid., p. 3.

31 'Communiqué from the Group of Ten (Washington, 18 December 1971)' (1971) 1 *Bulletin of the European Communities* 19–21; see also the 'habilitation clause', adopted by the General Agreement on Tariffs and Trade (hereafter GATT) at the end of the Tokyo Round in 1979, which undoubtedly should have been voted for unanimously but, instead, was adopted by consensus: see GATT, 64 UNTC 187 (adopted 30 October 1947, entered into force 1 January 1948); Olivier Long, 'La place du droit et ses limites dans le système commercial multilateral du GATT' (Volume 192) *Collected Courses of the Hague Academy of International Law*, 1983, pp. 13–142, p. 76.

32 Protocol No. 14 bis to the Convention for the Protection of Human Rights and Fundamental Freedoms, Amending the Control System of the Convention, *Council of Europe Treaty Series*, No. 204 (adopted 27 May 2009, entered into force 1 October 2009).

33 Jean-François Flauss, 'Le protocole n°14 bis de la Convention européenne des droits de l'homme' (2009) 3 *Revue Générale de Droit International Public* 621–634; Linos-Alexandre Sicilianos, 'Le protocole 14 bis à la convention européenne des droits de l'homme: un instrument (heureusement) éphémère' (2009) 55 *Annuaire français de droit international* 729–742; Annelise Quast Mertsch, 'The Reform Measures of ECHR Protocol No. 14 and the Provisional Application of Treaties', in Malgosia Fitzmaurice and Panos Merkouris (eds.), *The Interpretation and Application of the European Convention of Human Rights* (Leiden: Martinus Nijhoff, 2012), pp. 33–71.

34 See, for example, Philippe Cahier, 'Le changement fondamental de circonstances et la Convention de Vienne de 1969 sur le droit des traités', in *Le droit international à l'heure de sa codification: études en l'honneur de Roberto Ago*, Vol. 1 (Milan: Giuffrè, 1987), pp. 167–186; Aymeric Hêche, 'Les conditions d'application de la *clausula rebus sic stantibus*' (2014) 1 *Revue Belge de Droit International* 322–354; Thomas Giegerich, 'Article 62', in Oliver Dörr and

treaty can be terminated provided circumstances have changed in a radical way and this change affects the very scope of the treaty. This well-established rule of law[35] puzzles voluntarists as it is not easy to be reconciled with the idea of will. Voluntarists have tried, by claiming that any treaty embodies an implicit clause providing for its termination in case of fundamental changes of circumstances: *clausula rebus sic stantibus*. This problem cannot be discussed here in any detail, but it is clear that the *clausula* is a purely fictitious explanation: 'Such clauses, if ever employed, are not now generally employed.'[36] In fact, it is certainly more convincing to root this principle – which does exist in all systems of law – in the necessities of social life: the function of legal rules is to meet social needs; when social needs change legal rules lose legitimacy and lose their binding force.

Thus, it appears that treaties or unilateral commitments, praised as they may be in voluntarist doctrine, flow effectively from the consent of States; but when they enter into force, they negate the notion of sovereign will. Once a State, by an apparent act of its free will has entered into a treaty or a unilateral commitment, the trap closes; its will is captive and can be freed only through processes in which the will of an individual State has little or nothing to do.[37]

Moreover, it is not clear that, in the prevailing conditions of modern international life, a formal expression of consent is always necessary. The rules embodied in the so-called 'codification treaties' which, more often than not, are 'progressive development treaties' can, nevertheless, be or become binding upon all States, even if not in force.[38] At any rate these general treaties certainly provide 'general indications' of what the law is.[39] And it can be recalled that in *Continental Shelf (Tunisia/Libyan Arab Jamahiriya)*, the Court considered that it 'would have had *proprio motu* to take account of

Kirsten Schmalenbach (eds.), *Vienna Convention on the Law of Treaties: A Commentary*, 2nd ed. (Berlin: Springer, 2018), pp. 1143–1181; or Julian Kulaga, 'A Renaissance of the Doctrine of *Rebus Sic Stantibus*?' (2020) 69(2) *International & Comparative Law Quarterly* 477–497.

35 *Fisheries Jurisdiction Case (United Kingdom* v. *Iceland)*, fn. 15, p. 18; *Fisheries Jurisdiction Case* (*Federal Republic of Germany* v. *Iceland*), fn. 15, p. 63, para. 36.

36 Clive Parry, 'The Law of Treaties', in Max Sørensen (ed.), *Manual of Public International Law* (London: Macmillan, 1968), pp. 175–245, p. 234.

37 See, for example, Pergantis, fn. 10, p. 157.

38 Thus, the VCLT was referred to by the ICJ before its entry into force in 1980: see *Legal Consequences for States of the Continued Presence of South Africa in Namibia (South West Africa) notwithstanding Security Council Resolution 276* (Advisory Opinion) [1971] ICJ Rep. 16, p. 47; *Fisheries Jurisdiction Case (United Kingdom* v. *Iceland)*, fn. 15, p. 18, para. 24.

39 *Interpretation of the Agreement of 25 March 1951 between the WHO and Egypt* (Advisory Opinion) [1980] ICJ Rep. 73, p. 94, para. 46.

the progress made by the [Third United Nations Conference on the Law of the Sea] even if the parties had not alluded to it in their Special Agreement'.[40]

In any case, whatever the role of State will in treaty-making – where consent is, nevertheless, predominant – it is clear that its influence is even less regarding other means of formation of legal rules.

Thus, concerning customary obligations, Prosper Weil himself, the most rigorous advocate of voluntarism in the last century, has defined them as 'the Achilles heel of consensualist outlook'.[41] This is indeed confirmed by a very quick look at the classical theory based on the well-known two 'elements' of custom, as enunciated by Article 38 of the ICJ Statute.

First, as far as the so-called 'material element' is concerned, that is, the 'general practice', States' behaviour converging towards such a practice can be said, in a way, to be 'voluntary'. But State wills are aimed here at doing something, not at elaborating a rule of law. If a national court renders makes a decision on State immunity, its judgment will be part of the general practice; that, however, was not the aim of the court's decision: its only concern was to decide on the precise dispute it had to solve. Therefore, concerning our inquiry, the only question is whether the requirement of an *opinio juris* – the 'psychological element' – is a confirmation of voluntarist theories. The answer must be in the negative for several reasons which I only mention:

– Both elements are not on the same footing. The practice is 'constitutive'; except in the special case of the '*coutume sauvage*'[42] which

[40] *Case concerning the Continental Shelf (Tunisia/Libyan Arab Jamahiriya)* (Judgment) [1982] ICJ Rep. 18, p. 38, para. 24.

[41] Prosper Weil, 'Towards Relative Normativity in International Law?' (1983) 77(3) *American Journal of International Law* 413–442, at 433; Georges Abi-Saab, 'La coutume dans tous ses états ou le dilemme du développement du droit international général dans un monde éclaté', in *Le droit international à l'heure de sa codification: Études en l'honneur de Roberto Ago*, fn. 34, pp. 53–65; Maarten Bos, 'The Identification of Custom in International Law' (1982) 25 *German Yearbook of International Law* 9–83; Jean Combacau, 'Ouverture: De la régularité à la règle' (1986) 3 *Droits* 3–10; Serge Sur, 'La coutume internationale: Sa vie, son œuvre' (1986) 3 *Droits* 111–124; Brigitte Stern, 'La coutume au cœur du droit international: Quelques réflexions', in *Le droit international: Unité and diversité: Mélanges offerts à Paul Reuter* (Paris: Pedone, 1981), pp. 479–499; Ielbo Marcus Lobo de Souza, 'The Role of State Consent in the Customary Process' (1995) 44(3) *The International & Comparative Law Quarterly* 521–539; Maurice Kamto, 'La volonté de l'État en droit international' (Volume 310) *Collected Courses of the Hague Academy of International Law*, 2004, pp. 13–428, pp. 262–312; Aymeric Hêche, 'L'élément subjectif dans la coutume internationale', in Samantha Besson, Yves Maussen, Pascal Pichonnaz (eds.), *Le consentement en droit* (Zürich: Schulthess, 2019), pp. 31–53.

[42] See René-Jean Dupuy, 'Coutume sage et coutume sauvage', in *La communauté internationale: Mélanges offerts à Charles Rousseau* (Paris: Pedone, 1974), pp. 75–87; René-Jean Dupuy, 'Droit déclaratoire et droit programmatoire: De la coutume sauvage à la "soft law"', in Société

relates more to the law-making by the General Assembly; *opinio juris* can only appear after the event. States cannot 'feel that they are conforming to what amounts to a legal obligation', in the words of the ICJ in the *North Sea Continental Shelf cases*,[43] if this legal obligation does not already exist.

- The wording used by the Court is revealing: a 'feeling' that an obligation exists is a very different thing from a will and certainly corresponds more to the ideas of consent or consensus than to those of will or agreement; thus the International Law Commission (hereafter ILC) noted in its commentaries of its Draft conclusions on identification of customary international that '[t]he Latin term *opinio juris* has been retained in the draft conclusions and commentaries alongside "acceptance as law" because of its prevalence in legal discourse ... and also because it may capture better the particular nature of the subjective element of customary international law as referring to legal conviction and not to formal consent'.[44]
- Above all, this 'feeling', or even 'acceptance' in the wording of Article 38 of the Statute of the ICJ, is, by no means achieved by the expression of will of individual States, but by a general, communal acceptance of some more or less openly expressed conviction by States or by international bodies. In its 1984 Judgment, the Chamber of the ICJ constituted in *Gulf of Maine* contented itself with an examination of 'the legal conviction ... of all States' ('*de l'ensemble des États*').[45] As late President Jimenez de Arechaga has underlined, the Court 'has not required strict proof of the specific acceptance of the defendant State, thus rejecting the voluntarist conception of custom'.[46] Moreover and very significantly, new States find, in their birth crib, the whole body of customary rules existing at the time together with their sovereignty. Customary obligations as lying on a tacit agreement is a totally misleading fable.

française pour le droit international, *L'élaboration du droit international public: Colloque de Toulouse* (Paris: Pedone, 1975), pp. 132–148.

43 *North Sea Continental Shelf Cases (Federal Republic of Germany/Denmark; Federal Republic of Germany/Netherlands)* (Judgment) [1969] ICJ Rep. 3, p. 44, para. 77.

44 ILC, 'Draft Conclusions on Identification of Customary International Law, with Commentaries', in ILC, 'Report on the work of the seventieth session' (2018), UN Doc. A/73/10, pp. 122–156, p. 123, fn. 665.

45 *Case concerning Delimitation of the Maritime Boundary in the Gulf of Maine Area (Canada/United States of America* (Judgment) [1984] ICJ Rep. 246, p. 299, para. 111.

46 Eduardo Jimenez de Arechaga, 'Custom', in Antonio Cassese and Joseph H. Weiler (eds.), *Change and Stability in International Law-Making* (Berlin: De Gruyter, 1988), pp. 1–4, p. 3.

It is, of course, impossible to ignore the 'persistent objector' doctrine. But it must be observed that it is, at best, a 'contracting out' doctrine and that it is largely unrealistic: in most cases, States do not care; practice develops without them being aware of the process. When they 'awake', that is, when the time of *opinio juris* has arrived, it is too late – the evil is done and the rule does exist.[47] Of course, nothing impedes a State from expressly accepting a customary rule, but no theoretical conclusion can be inferred from this: 'Acceptance of a rule contributes to its effectiveness',[48] but is not a prerequisite for its existence.

And, it must be stressed that what has been said about treaties is *a fortiori* true for custom. Whatever role their will plays in the formation of customary rules, once these rules exist, States are bound – and even more strongly than by treaty rules. The reason for this is that it is virtually impossible for a State or a group of States to repudiate an existing custom by which they are bound.

From this very quick overview of custom, it can at least be concluded that State will contributes very little to its formation, while some form of soft consent can be presumed.

This conclusion is even more obvious regarding general principles of law. They are such a problem for voluntarist authors that most of them deliberately ignore these principles and deny them the quality of an autonomous source of law.[49]

This position is quite easy to understand. If, arguably, custom could be equated with a tacit agreement – *quod non* – such a conjuring trick is clearly impossible as regards general principles of law. If Article 38(1)(c) of the World Court's Statute has an autonomous meaning, those principles represent the degree zero in State consent: they are deduced from domestic laws whose rules have been elaborated without any intent as to their role as the source of obligations in international law. Of course, it is plain that State will has nothing to do with such rules: from a voluntarist point of view, this is a condemnation to death! Most certainly, these principles do exist in domestic

47 For an illustration see, for example, *Military and Paramilitary Activities in and against Nicaragua (Nicaragua* v. *United States of America)* (Judgment) (Merits) [1986] ICJ Rep. 14, p. 107, para. 204.

48 Cassese and Weiler, fn. 46, p. 16.

49 See Alain Pellet, *Recherches sur les principes généraux de droit en droit international*, thèse Paris II, 1974. Available at: www.alainpellet.eu/ouvrages, last accessed 18 November 2022, pp. 334–338; for an update see, for example, Jean d'Aspremont, 'What Was Not Meant to Be: General Principles of Law as a Source of International Law', in Riccardo Pisillo Mazzeschi and Pasquale De Sena (eds.), *Global Justice, Human Rights and the Modernization of International Law* (Berlin: Springer, 2018), pp. 163–184. For more moderate views, see Samantha Besson, 'General Principles in International Law: Whose Principles?', in Samantha Besson and Pascal Pichonnaz (eds.), *Principles in European Law* (Zürich: Schulthess, 2011), pp. 19–64.

legal orders; but in no way have they been created in order to apply at the international level and, in fact, there are cases when they do not apply. This has nothing to do with State will: it depends entirely on the question of whether or not the international society can be compared with national society – and it can only be with great caution.[50]

And yet, according to both the dominant doctrine and the international case law, all these sources are 'equal'. Well, equal 'in dignity' maybe; but, concretely, things are different: the intensity of recourse to one or the other of the sources I have mentioned is quite proportional to the 'consent load' in each source. No doubt the preference given to written law is in part dictated by practical convenience: it is easier to refer to treaties, declarations or resolutions than to customs or general principles. However, this is not the only reason: the intensity of consent and, consequently, of legitimacy – which is a main factor for the acceptability of the rule – impregnating the respective obligations also plays a role in this preference. Now, it would be erroneous to draw a 'voluntarist' conclusion from this: customary obligations are not less binding legally speaking than treaty obligations.[51] Simply handling customary norms is more difficult and their acceptability is lower.

But there is more: *jus cogens*. Perhaps can it be interpreted 'as some form of older natural law thinking'; at any rate, it is clearly 'an updated denial of [voluntarist] positivism'.[52]

Contrary to a voluntarist recurring criticism, the definition given by Article 53 of the VCLT of a 'peremptory norm' is less blurry than that of an 'international custom' by Article 38 of the ICJ Statute, under which it is unclear whose 'general practice' must be taken into account and by whom it must be 'accepted as law'. For its part, a peremptory norm must be 'accepted and recognized *by the international community of States as a whole*'; this clearly means that acceptance and recognition are not given by individual States but by their 'community', which surely goes beyond a simple majority but just as surely does not require unanimity.[53] This acceptance relates to the

[50] See Pellet, fn. 49, pp. 294–318.

[51] See *Military and Paramilitary Activities in and against Nicaragua (Nicaragua* v. *United States of America)*, fn. 47, pp. 94–95, para. 177.

[52] Maarten Bos, 'Will and Order in the Nation-State System: Observations on Positivism and International Law', in Ronald St. J. Macdonald and Douglas M. Johnston (eds.), *The Structure and Process of International Law*, 2nd ed. (Leiden: Martinus Nijhoff, 1986), pp. 51–78, p. 51; Dan Dubois, 'The Authority of Peremptory Norms in International Law: State Consent or Natural Law?' (2009) 78 *Nordic Journal of International Law* 133–175.

[53] See, for example, ILC, 'Text of the draft conclusions on peremptory norms of general international law (*jus cogens*) and commentaries thereto', in ILC, 'Report on the Work of the Seventy-first Session', pp. 147–208, p. 170, para. 6; *Smith* v. *Socialist People's Libyan Arab*

particular quality of the norm, its imperative nature, which results in a strengthened, but not necessarily unanimous, *opinio juris* and means that no derogation is allowed. Indeed, peremptory norms of general international law are the only rules that are truly binding in the sense that they cannot be derogated from, even by the common will of the transgressors.

Now, the role of *opinio juris* is not confined to custom (whether 'normal' or peremptory): it is an indispensable test applying to all legal obligations. I would go even further: it is *the* very criterion of law that differentiates it from ethics or religion, even more so from political sciences or economic so-called laws. You could call it 'conventialism' but I must say I do not favour the expression that reduces to a single set of sources that have in common that they give rise to binding rules only if they are based on some form of 'consent', but the manifestations of this consent are so diverse and its 'intensity' so variable that the word seems to me to be rather reductive.

Moreover, I do not totally accept Dame Rosalyn Higgins' assertion that 'what one identifies as international law will be closely dependent upon what one believes is the basis of legal obligation'[54] since I suspect that, under the eminent author's pen, 'legal obligation' means 'binding commitment'. Personally, I cannot accept that law be reduced to this. It is wider than that – legal norms exist when the addressees have a feeling that a conduct, whether binding or desirable, is expected from them – that they must *or should* do something.[55] But I fully agree that they are 'closely dependant upon what one believes is the basis of legal obligation'. And this has a name: *opinio juris*.

Opinio juris and consent are different notions. In many cases, you may feel legally bound even if consent is very remote: willy-nilly you accept that through the legal system, obligations can be imposed upon you. Now, it goes without saying that the effectiveness of the obligation will be enhanced if the addressee has consented to it: by consenting to the obligation, it becomes subjectively legitimate, and legitimacy clearly is a guarantee of increased effectiveness.

Why do you comply? For a lot of reasons that you can find outside the law: this is the totally convincing 'no-law hypothesis' ('*hypothèse du non-droit*') once proposed by Dean Carbonnier.[56] As very aptly explained by the late Tom Franck:

Jamahiriya, 101 F.3d 239 (2nd Cir. 1996), p. 242; Dubois, fn. 52, p. 135; João Ernesto Christófolo, *Solving Antinomies between Peremptory Norms in Public International Law* (Zürich: Schulthess, 2016), p. 125.

54 Rosalyn Higgins, 'The Identity of International Law', in Bin Cheng (ed.), *International Law: Teaching and Practice* (London: Stevens, 1982), pp. 27–45, p. 32.

55 See fn. 58 and accompanying text.

56 Jean Carbonnier, 'L'hypothèse du non-droit' (1963) *Archives de philosophie du droit* 55–74.

> [C]oercion is not law's whole story. Persons also comply with law because they think it right to do so. Why do they think it right? One reason is that they believe the law to be legitimate. This belief in a law's legitimacy has to do with properties of the legal text: how it was enacted, its clarity, pedigree, and how it fits into the overall framework and skein of the legal system.[57]

The question of State consent and legitimacy is carefully developed by David Lefkowitz[58] so I will not discuss it at length and I apologize for making apparently exciting ideas totally banal and a bit pedestrian, but I think that this simply means that legitimacy stems from the belief that an obligation exists because the interested persons are convinced that it has a 'legal basis' – let us say, if I dare to be even more banal and pedestrian, because they can recognize its *source*. It does not mean that the addressees are happy with it, that they approve it, but they know they must comply whether they like it or not. Law is law; *dura lex sed lex*.... However, whatever positivist voluntarists may say, this does not mean that they are in favour of the obligation in question – simply, 'objectively' they are prepared to comply with it. They have no real will to do so but they comply.

There is no doubt that consent can play a crucial role in creating or reinforcing this feeling and consequently in making the acceptability of the obligation stronger by comforting its legitimacy, and its implementation more effective. Indeed, the correlation is far from absolute between consent and effectiveness but there is no doubt that it helps. Let me just illustrate this with a few examples:

– Acceptation of the ICJ's jurisdiction (or, for that matter, any international court or tribunal) clearly gives rise to fewer difficulties when it is given in a Special Agreement or – but to a lesser extent – in the compromissory clause of a treaty, than when it is given rather abstractly in an optional declaration under Article 36, paragraph 2, of the Statute which is a nest for preliminary objections.[59] And you may think also of China's virulent opposition to the *South China Sea* Arbitration.[60]

[57] Thomas M. Franck, 'Fairness in the International Legal and Institutional System (General Course on Public International Law)' (Volume 240) *Collected Courses of the Hague Academy of International Law*, 1993, pp. 9–498, p. 41.

[58] Lefkowitz, Chapter 2 in this volume.

[59] Since 1947, preliminary objections have been raised in fifty cases introduced by a unilateral application (out of 183).

[60] *The South China Sea Arbitration (The Republic of Philippines* v. *The People's Republic of China)*, PCA, Award on Jurisdiction and Admissibility (29 October 2015) 55 ILM 805, Award (12 July 2016); Chinese Society of International Law, 'The South China Sea Arbitration Awards: A Critical Study' (2018) 17(2) *Chinese Journal of International Law* 207–748.

Indeed, as Rüdiger Wolfrum noted, 'international law proceeds from the assumption that the establishment of continuous obligations is possible by a single original consent'[61] and, in this case, you have a compromissory clause in the United Nations Convention on the Law of the Sea[62] (hereafter UNCLOS), and you could allege that China gave its consent when ratifying. But such a remote one – just at the time of ratification and, most probably, with the feeling that its declaration under Article 288 was a sufficient precaution.

– And, another example among others, showing the stabilizing role of consent: the evolution of the law of the sea. No need to elaborate but just have in mind the major stages in the extension of maritime spaces: three nautical miles; slight marginal unilateral differences; massive claims (in particular, the Truman declarations) almost instantaneously endorsed by a great majority of States; two successive waves of treaty law that have permitted to stabilize the situation including among States that have not ratified UNCLOS. Moreover, the role of consent as a stabilizing factor is also crystal clear when one thinks about maritime delimitation: equidistance/special circumstances; virulent objections (the negative, destabilizing, side of consent) in the name of equity; destruction of the rule; patient reconstruction with the passive acceptance (consent) of the community of States; stabilization. And the same goes with space law: the need for legal rules has called for immediate consent at least to general principles – so stringently that some have spoken of instant custom;[63] then, again stabilization through a wide series of resolutions followed by treaties. Hardening of consent – progressive stabilization.

Consent has another virtue: it can be given to non-binding norms. In such a case, it expresses an intent, it fixes a target, without creating strict obligations to act for the addressees. Contemporary international law is replete with such instruments – foremost among them the recommendations of the collective bodies of international organizations, which lack the capacity to impose obligations or prohibitions on their addressees, but which nevertheless seek to influence the conduct of those addressees and do not necessarily fail to do so any

61 Rüdiger Wolfrum, 'Legitimacy of International Law from a Legal Perspective: Some Introductory Considerations', in Rüdiger Wolfrum and Volker Röben (eds.), *Legitimacy in International Law* (Berlin: Springer, 2008), pp. 1–24.

62 United Nations Convention on the Law of the Sea, 1833 UNTS 397 (adopted 12 October 1982, entered into force 16 November 1994).

63 Bin Cheng, 'United Nations Resolutions on Outer Space: "Instant" International Customary Law?' (1965) 5 *Indian Journal of International Law* 23–48.

more than treaties. As Sir Hersch Lauterpacht magnificently explained in the separate opinion he attached to the ICJ Advisory Opinion of 7 June 1955 in one of the many cases concerning South-West Africa, this does not mean

> that a recommendation is of no legal effect whatsoever. A Resolution recommending to an Administering State a specific course of action creates some legal obligation which, however rudimentary, elastic and imperfect, is nevertheless a legal obligation and constitutes a measure of supervision. The State in question, while not bound to accept the recommendation, is bound to give it due consideration in good faith. If . . . it decides to disregard it, it is bound to explain the reasons for its decision.[64]

In these cases, collective consent is at the origin of flexible (soft) norms intended to guide the conduct of the members of the Organization, without imposing binding obligations. And, while it has sometimes been argued that a recommendation is binding on a State that, by its vote, has contributed to its adoption, based on the principle of good faith, good faith is not violated merely because a State does not implement a recommendation it has voted for. Similarly, as the ICJ rightly stressed in its Judgment of 1 October 2018, a State's 'participation in the consensus for adopting some resolutions . . . does not imply that [it] has accepted to be bound under international law by the content of these resolutions'.[65]

Nevertheless, like the ratification of a treaty or a unilateral commitment, a vote in the United Nations General Assembly or the Security Council or any other organ of an international organization expresses the consent of the State that casts it. It may reflect the deep-seated will of the State or it may be coerced within the limits imposed by the prohibition on the use of force in international relations: in all cases it is consent, not necessarily a commitment. Thus, consent irrigates 'the great shades of nuance that permeate international law'[66] and contributes to the 'infinite variety' of international law.[67] But, definitely consenting is not willing.

64 *Voting Procedure on Questions relating to Reports and Petitions concerning the Territory of South-West Africa* (Advisory Opinion) [1955] ICJ Rep. 67, Separate Opinion of Judge Lauterpacht, pp. 90–123, p. 120.

65 *Obligation to Negotiate Access to the Pacific Ocean (Bolivia* v. *Chile)* (Judgment) (Merits) [2018] ICJ Rep. 507, p. 562, para. 171.

66 *Accordance with International Law of the Unilateral Declaration of Independence in Respect of Kosovo* (Advisory Opinion) [2010] ICJ Rep. 403, Declaration of Judge Simma, pp. 478–481, p. 481, para. 9.

67 Richard R. Baxter, 'International Law in "Her Infinite Variety"' (1980) 29(4) *The International & Comparative Law Quarterly* 549–566.

2

State Consent and the Legitimacy of International Law

DAVID LEFKOWITZ*

2.1 INTRODUCTION

Like all law, international law is a practice of reason-giving, one in which agents invoke legal norms to justify their conduct. Practitioners of international law generally proceed on the assumption that those norms do, in fact, justify the conduct they sanction. Theorists, in contrast, tend to take a more critical stance towards the practice of international law, including the assumption that the law succeeds in providing a justification for its subjects' conduct. Why treat the claim that international law prohibits Φ-ing as in itself a reason not to Φ?[1] Or using the terminology I will employ in this chapter, what makes an international legal norm prohibiting Φ-ing legitimate? In the modern era, the consent of States to be bound by international law has played an increasingly prominent role in addressing these questions, with some theorists going so far as to maintain that only State consent can explain why international law binds; that is, why it provides States (and their subjects) with reasons for action. Though not uncontested, the belief in the centrality of State consent to international law's legitimacy remains widespread today.

In this chapter, I argue that while State consent does contribute to international law's legitimacy, it does not do so by providing a justification for it. States are not bound to obey international law because they have chosen to submit to its authority. Rather, international law provides them with a reason for

* For their comments on earlier iterations of this chapter, I wish to thank Terry McConnell, Oisin Suttle, Samantha Besson, Jose Luis Martí, and the participants in the 'Consenting to International Law' conference at the Collège de France.

1 One response is that to participate in the practice of international law just is to treat a norm that prohibits Φ-ing as a reason not to Φ. But, arguably, that offers a descriptive-explanatory response to what is a normative question, namely what reason is there to participate in the practice of treating a norm prohibiting Φ-ing as a reason not to Φ.

action, and indeed they have a moral duty to obey it, if and only if they will do better at realizing justice if they act as the law directs them to act than if they act on their own judgment. As a means for crafting international law, State consent is valuable insofar as it yields international legal norms that satisfy this condition.

My defence of these claims begins in Section 2.2 with a characterization of the concepts of consent and legitimacy (or legitimate authority), and the justifications for according agents the normative powers to which those concepts refer. In Section 2.3, I argue that the consent of the governed cannot justify a claim to political authority, and so the duty of the governed to obey its directives. The role consent can play in building and expressing trust in a practical authority, including a political one, is the subject of Section 2.4. Though trust can provide a basis for a duty to obey the law, it does so only if the law is already legitimate, and so already law an agent ought to obey. In Section 2.5, which comprises the second half of this chapter, I draw on arguments developed in the first three sections to examine the myriad ways in which State consent contributes, or could contribute, to the legitimate exercise of international legal authority.

2.2 CONCEPTUAL AND NORMATIVE BACKGROUND

2.2.1 *The Concept and Justification of Consent*

The term 'consent' picks out two related but distinct concepts, a narrower normative one and a broader descriptive one. The narrower concept refers to an agent's exercise of a normative power to alter another agent's normative position (e.g. to grant that agent permission to perform an act that she would otherwise have no right to perform). Agents occupy normative positions in virtue of their standing in various relationships to other agents, relationships that are constituted by norms that accord them various rights, duties, powers and immunities. Those norms may be moral, social or legal, though as we shall see, the latter provide moral reasons for action only if they are legitimate.

Following Joseph Raz, I maintain that consent is given by any act or omission undertaken in the belief that:

- It will change the normative situation of another;
- It will do so because it is undertaken with such a belief;
- It will be understood by its observers to be of this character.[2]

[2] Joseph Raz, *The Morality of Freedom* (Oxford: Oxford University Press/Clarendon Press, 1986), p. 81.

Normally, an agent's behaviour constitutes a successful instance of consent if and only if these beliefs are correct. The third condition that characterizes the performance of consent follows from the rationale for according an agent a normative power to alter another's normative position, namely that doing so serves to enhance that agent's control over some aspect of her life, or over the life of another agent. One can exercise that control only if other agents acknowledge that one's act or omission counts as an instance of consent, and act accordingly.

But what justifies according an agent control over some aspect of her life, or that of another agent? First, agents may often be best placed to determine whether and when a change in another agent's normative position will advance their own well-being, or that of another. Such a change may be instrumentally valuable, namely if it conduces to the attainment of a good distinct from the normative relationship, as in the case of an ordinary market transaction. Or it may be intrinsically valuable, if it (also) serves to constitute a relationship that is good in itself. Second, the exercise of control over one's life may be intrinsically valuable apart from whatever contribution it makes to the realization of other elements of a good or flourishing life. If so, then there may be grounds for according agents a normative power to alter another's normative position even in cases where their exercise of that power detracts from their own or another's attainment of other goods. Or, to the contrary, it may be that the intrinsic value of self-determination is conditional on the value of what is chosen; choice is good in itself, but only if what is chosen is good, either in itself or as a means to something that is good in itself. I return to this point later in the chapter, when I consider respect for political self-determination as a reason to hold that States, or at least sufficiently democratic States, should for the most part only be subject to exercises of international authority to which they consent.

The broader descriptive notion of consent refers to the fact of agreement, typically to terms that purport to structure interactions between the parties to it. Oftentimes, such agreements accurately reflect the exercise of a normative power to alter another's normative position by one or more of the parties to it. But not always; the agreement may concern the performance of an act the parties have no right to perform, or it may be reached under conditions at odds with the underlying rationale for according agents a normative power to alter another's normative position. Thus, we may say that a person who responds to the threat 'your money or your life!' by handing over her money consents to the transfer of her property, in the sense that she agrees to it, but also maintain that her consent is not genuine, meaning not a successful exercise of her normative power to alter another's normative position (in this case, by granting another a property right in her money).

2.2.2 *The Concept and Justification of Legitimacy (or Legitimate Authority)*

Now consider the concept of legitimacy, understood here as a property of law. Law is legitimate, I contend, if and only if it constitutes a justifiable exercise of practical authority by one agent over another, that is, if it consists of directives issued by an agent with a moral right to rule to an agent with a correlative duty to obey that agent's directives. A attempts to exercise practical authority over B with respect to some domain of conduct if and only if A maintains that B ought to defer to A's judgment regarding what B should do. When A does so, she maintains that her directives provide B with content-independent and exclusionary reasons for action. So, if A claims authority over B and she directs B not to Φ, then she maintains that B has a reason not to Φ simply because A instructed him not do so, a reason that makes no reference to the content of A's direction to B (i.e. what Φ-ing is). Moreover, she maintains that B ought to treat A's instruction not to Φ as a reason to exclude from his deliberation some or all of the reasons that bear on whether he ought to Φ. From B's perspective, to treat A's directive as a content-independent and exclusionary reason just is to defer to A's judgment, or in other words, to recognize her as having practical authority over him.[3]

As in the case of consent, we require a normative theory of legitimate authority, one that explains why we are justified in according A the moral power to impose on B a duty to defer to A's judgment regarding what B ought to do. Following Raz again, I maintain that A's claim to practical authority over B is justifiable when the following two conditions are met:

- The Normal Justification Condition (hereafter NJC): the subject would better conform to reasons that apply to him anyway (i.e. to reasons other than the directives of the authority) if he intends to be guided by the authority's directives than if he does not.
- The Independence Condition (hereafter IC): the matters regarding which the first condition is met are such that with respect to them it is better to conform to reason than to decide for oneself, unaided by authority.[4]

[3] For further elaboration and defence, see Raz, fn. 2, pp. 38–69; David Lefkowitz, *Philosophy and International Law: A Critical Introduction* (Cambridge: Cambridge University Press, 2020), pp. 99–107.

[4] Joseph Raz, 'Problem of Authority: Revisiting the Service Conception' (2006) 90 *Minnesota Law Review* 1003–1044, at 1014.

A's claim to authority over B is justified, then, if B is more likely to act as he has most reason to act by deferring to A's judgment regarding what he should do, than by acting on his own judgment, except in cases where it is more important that B decide what to do for himself than that he decides correctly. Raz labels this the service conception of legitimate authority.

Three brief expository remarks are in order, since they bear on the contribution that State consent can make to international law's legitimacy. First, the NJC entails that law's legitimacy may be piecemeal, its claim to practical authority justifiable on some matters, or with respect to some agents, but not others. Second, the service conception provides an account of the rationality of deferring to authority; a description of the conditions under which practical authority enables us to better conform or respond to any of the reasons for action that apply to us. Questions of legitimate authority, however, only concern a subset of the reasons that apply to us, namely moral ones. Only in those cases where an agent is more likely to act as she is morally required to act by deferring to another's practical authority does she have a moral duty to do so.

Finally, the same understanding of rationality, as responsiveness to reasons, that justifies deference to authority also provides two reasons not to do so. One is instrumental; in some cases, an agent is likely to do better in the long run at acting on right reason if she develops her own prudential or moral judgment than if she relies on the judgment of another. For example, the fact that parents will not always be available to instruct their children on what to do provides a weighty reason for them to develop their children's ability to make good judgments. Like any skill, however, judgment can only be developed with practice, and that requires giving children the opportunity to act on their own judgment even though they will sometimes err when doing so. The other reason why agents should not defer to another's judgment is non-instrumental: certain valuable experiences, accomplishments and relationships can only be realized if an agent chooses them for herself. This is true of intimate relationships, for example, which are partly constituted by individuals' choosing to make themselves exceptionally vulnerable to one another. The fact that there are certain reasons for action that agents cannot better conform to by acting on another's judgment places an inherent limit on the scope of justifiable practical authority.

2.3 PRINCIPLED ARGUMENTS AGAINST CONSENT AS A JUSTIFICATION FOR LEGITIMATE AUTHORITY

The service conception of legitimate authority undergirds the first of three principled objections to grounding international law's legitimacy in State consent.[5] Recall that the justification for according agents a normative power to alter their normative position is that doing so serves to enhance their ability to advance or honour something valuable. Deference to another's authority does so if and only if the NJC and IC are satisfied. Thus, if A claims authority over B, and A satisfies the NJC and IC vis-à-vis B with respect to the conduct at issue, then B already has a duty to defer to A's judgment regarding the performance of that conduct. From the standpoint of justifying A's right to rule and B's correlative duty to obey, B's consent to A's rule is superfluous.

Suppose A does not yet claim authority over B. Will not B's consent to A's rule change B's normative position? If so, does that not prove that consent can and often does justify one agent's claim to authority over another? These questions reflect a common confusion. B may agree to A's rule (e.g. to accept the jurisdiction of the International Court of Justice (hereafter ICJ) in a particular dispute), and it is true that absent that agreement A would not claim a right to rule B. Nevertheless, the question that concerns us is why, having agreed to A's rule, B now has a moral duty to defer to A's judgment regarding what to do, rather than ignoring it, or treating A's directive as merely advisory? To say that agreements must be kept (*pacta sunt servanda*) is simply to restate the problem. Why must B keep its agreement to obey A? The answer, I maintain, is that B has a duty to do so if and only if B is more likely to conform to right reason by deferring to A's judgment than if B acts on its own judgment, and it is more important that B get it right than that B act on its own judgment. Of course, B might still have compelling reasons to act as A directs even if A lacks a legitimate claim to authority over B. Doing so may be prudent, or the best available means for avoiding or mitigating injustice. Nevertheless, if A does not satisfy the criteria set out in the service conception of authority, B has no moral duty to do what A directs because A so directs, regardless of whether B has consented to rule by A.

In Section 2.2.2, I noted that consent may be justifiable in part because it constitutes an intrinsically valuable exercise of autonomy or self-determination. Might the intrinsic value of self-determination justify a duty

[5] Much of the criticism of State consent as a basis for international law's legitimacy targets the existing practice of soliciting and giving consent on the grounds that it is not free, or informed, or both. That an act must satisfy these conditions in order to qualify as an exercise of the normative power to alter another's normative position follows from the rationale for according agents that power. These objections are moot if *in principle* State consent cannot provide a basis for international law's legitimacy. They remain relevant to the success of purported exercises of consent to alter another agent's normative position that do not involve granting the latter authority, however. Examples include one State granting another a right to military overflights, or to tariff-free trade.

to obey an authority to whom an agent has consented even in cases that do not satisfy the NJC and IC? Raz maintains that it cannot justify an individual's consent to rule by the government (State) that claims her as a subject because 'governments typically claim authority to govern any and all aspects of their subjects' lives', and so may act in ways that directly or indirectly deprive their subjects of their autonomy.[6] Just as a proper regard for the value of liberty is incompatible with selling oneself into slavery, so too a proper regard for the value of autonomy is incompatible with consenting to the rule of an agent who claims comprehensive authority to determine what one ought to do. Nicole Roughan suggests that this argument does not apply to international legal authorities because (the political community constituted by) international law does not advance a claim to comprehensive authority.[7] This response may confuse empirical facts regarding how the international community currently exercises its authority with a conceptual claim regarding the authority law (or a political community) necessarily claims over its subjects, namely that of having the final say on any moral question, including the conditions for its own legitimacy and whether it satisfies them in any particular case. If so, then even assuming that the exercise of political self-determination by (the community constituted by) a State is intrinsically valuable, that State's consent to the rule of international law cannot justify its duty to obey it.

Two further considerations warrant a sceptical response to the argument that, in virtue of its constituting an intrinsically valuable exercise of autonomy, an agent's consent to rule by another justifies a duty to obey the other's directives. First, as I noted previously, it may be that the exercise of autonomy is valuable only when it is exercised well, that is, when an agent chooses to do something that is valuable, or warranted by an undefeated reason. If so, then consent to another's authority is valuable only if an agent has an undefeated reason to do so, and that will be the case only when the other agent satisfies the NJC and IC. Second, consent to another's authority over some aspect of one's life is not so much an exercise of self-government as it is an abdication of it. The fact that one chooses to grant another control over that aspect of one's life does not change the fact that, from that point forward, it is the other agent and not you who decides what you should do in that domain. That need not be a bad thing; we should not make a fetish of autonomy, but instead recognize that in some cases it is more important that we get it right than

6 Joseph Raz, 'Government by Consent' (1987) 29 *Nomos* 76–95, at 85.

7 Nicole Roughan, 'Mind the Gaps: Authority and Legality in International Law' (2016) 27(2) *European Journal of International Law* 329–351, at 334–340.

that we decide for ourselves. Nowhere is that claim more compelling than with respect to the just treatment of others.

On the basis of the foregoing arguments, I conclude that the consent of the governed cannot justify a political community's or its agents' claim to legitimate authority over them.

2.4 CONSENT, TRUST AND RESPECT FOR LAW

Thus far, we have considered consent as an act whereby an agent alters his normative position vis-à-vis another agent. But Raz observes that consent can also serve as a means for expressing trust or loyalty.[8] Consent is most likely to carry this expressive meaning when it constitutes a change in an agent's normative relationship to another that the consenting agent views as leaving him or her exceptionally vulnerable to the other agent(s).[9] Indeed, it is the fact that consent will have this consequence that makes it a suitable vehicle for expressing one's trust in another agent. As expressions of trust, acts of consent serve to constitute valuable relationships, such as those between lovers, or among friends. This constitutive role in creating, sustaining and deepening intrinsically valuable relationships makes trust-expressing acts of consent intrinsically valuable.

Raz maintains that under certain conditions agents can express their trust in, and loyalty to, the political community with which they identify by consenting to the rule of its government. As an example, consider the practice of requiring individuals who wish to become members of a political community to take an oath of allegiance to it. As we have seen, a promise to obey the law creates a moral obligation to do so only if the NJC and IC are satisfied, and where that is the case agents have a duty to obey the law regardless of whether they have promised or consented to do so. Nevertheless, the ritual of pledging allegiance to the political community offers individuals an opportunity to publicly express their trust in, and loyalty to, the other members of that community, as well as the institutions through which the community governs itself. Like all expression of trust, however, a pledge of allegiance to a political community has value only where it serves to constitute a valuable relationship. Therefore, a promise to obey the law counts as an intrinsically

[8] Raz, fn. 2, pp. 90–94; Raz, fn. 6, at 90–93.

[9] 'Exceptionally' indicates a deviation from the normal or standard degree of physical or emotional vulnerability that characterizes relationships between agents in a given society.

valuable expression of trust in, and loyalty to, a political community only if its government's rule is generally legitimate.[10]

A constitutive element of trust in government is an attitude Raz labels respect for law. As he describes it, respect for law 'takes the form (among others) of trusting these institutions, taking it on trust that they have the authority to do what they do, not questioning their conduct too closely to see whether they exceed their authority'.[11] Where respect for law is warranted, it may involve 'a certain slackening of vigilance regarding the two conditions of legitimacy [the NJC and IC]' so that 'while the conditions themselves are unaffected, people would be justified in maintaining that the government has authority on evidence that would not be sufficient to reach such conclusions but for the trust they have in the government'.[12] Note that consent is not a necessary condition for respect for law; one may have trust in one's government, and so an attitude of respect for law, even if one has never consented to its rule (e.g. one has never pledged allegiance to it). Nor does Raz maintain that one has a moral duty to cultivate trust in, or loyalty to, one's government, and so an attitude of respect for law, even if one's government is worthy of those attitudes. Nevertheless, identification or a sense of community with others with whom one cooperates to realize justice can certainly contribute to a flourishing life, and insofar as the performance of an act of consent contributes to the creation or strengthening of that bond, agents have a compelling reason to do so.[13]

Reflection on the role that consent plays in other contexts highlights the contribution that seeking consent, and restricting one's interactions with another to those forms of treatment to which they have consented, can make to sustaining and deepening trust. For example, a number of bioethicists argue that the requirement of informed consent to treatment in both medical practice and research is partly justified by the need to sustain (or restore) people's trust in both their particular medical providers and the field of medicine as a whole.[14] In the latter case, the rationale appears entirely instrumental; medical professionals' ability to advance human well-being will be severely curtailed if potential or actual patients or test-subjects do not trust them. In some cases of

[10] Raz, fn. 6, at 92.

[11] Raz, fn. 4, at 1028.

[12] Ibid., at 1028–1029.

[13] For various qualifications to this claim, see Leslie Green, 'Law, Legitimacy, and Consent' (1989) 62(6) *Southern California Law* 795–825.

[14] See, for example, Onora O'Neill, *Autonomy and Trust in Bioethics* (Cambridge: Cambridge University Press, 2002); Jennifer Jackson, 'Promise-Keeping and the Doctor-Patient Relationship', in Raanan Gillon (ed.), *Principles of Health Care Ethics*, 1st ed. (Chichester: John Wiley & Sons), pp. 489–497.

interactions between patients and medical providers, the soliciting and offering of consent may also be a constitutive element of a genuinely fiduciary relationship. Such a relationship is one in which (a) the provider is motivated by the trust the patient places in her, and not simply conformity to professional ideals (which may be restated or specified in the law) or fear of the (legal) consequences of violating that trust, and (b) the patient treats that motivation on the part of the provider as a reason to trust her. Typically, genuinely fiduciary relationships develop over time through repeated interactions, and when they do, patients tend to adopt an attitude of respect for professional judgment that is analogous to the attitude of respect for law a person manifests if she trusts her government. The increasingly bureaucratic and industrial nature of medicine in many parts of the world raises significant obstacles to the development of genuinely fiduciary relationships between patient and provider. If trust figures at all in this environment, it does so in the form of patients' trust 'in the institution', a belief in the practitioner having been formed by professional training and a professional culture so that the patient is warranted in taking it on faith that the practitioner will treat her with a proper regard for her rights and interests.

In sum, giving, seeking and honouring consent can all serve as vehicles for expressing and building trust, including in political authorities. To trust a political authority is, in part, to presume that it satisfies the conditions for legitimate authority, and so to take oneself to have a duty to obey it. Trust in political authorities is justifiable, however, only if it is merited, and only political authorities that generally meet the conditions set out in the service conception of legitimate authority do so. Thus, trust-expressing and trust-building acts of consent provide a supplemental justification for obeying the law, a reason to do so in addition to, and conditional on, the law constituting an exercise of legitimate authority.

2.5 STATE CONSENT'S CONTRIBUTIONS TO INTERNATIONAL LAW'S LEGITIMACY

The arguments set out in Section 2.3 entail that international law's legitimacy is not a product of States' exercise of a moral power to subject themselves to another agent's rule, but is instead a function of the extent to which specific exercises of international authority satisfy the NJC and IC. And indeed, there are a number of ways in which international law can help those over whom it claims jurisdiction improve their conformity to right reason.[15] It can correct

[15] I focus here solely on what *makes* an exercise of international legal authority legitimate, and set aside questions regarding what counts as evidence, or *reason to believe*, that an exercise of

for ignorance or mistaken beliefs that lead even well-intentioned agents to act unjustly. Multilateral treaties, for instance, are likely to reflect more information than any single party to them would be able to acquire on its own, and the process of crafting a treaty to which all parties can agree can serve as a useful corrective to biases that undergird mistaken beliefs. International law can also protect its subjects against volitional defects. For example, State officials may come under great pressure from more powerful States, representatives of multinational corporations or domestic interest groups to engage in conduct that promotes those actors' perceived interests but that is contrary to right reason. International law provides a mechanism for resisting such pressure, by enabling officials to claim that their hands are tied.[16]

Perhaps most importantly, international law can enhance its subjects' conformity to right reason by facilitating coordination on common standards of right conduct.[17] In some cases, it may do so by rendering more determinate a shared but vague standard, where the parties are rightly indifferent between any of a number of possible ways in which the abstract standard may be made more concrete. Far more common, however, are disputes over what the standard of right conduct is. Examples include disagreements regarding the moral principles that govern the use of force, international migration, trade, financial transactions and the use of and control over the oceans or the Earth's atmosphere. In all of these cases international actors are generally likely to do better at approximating justice by conforming to common standards set out in international law than by acting on their own judgment. In some instances, such as addressing climate change, this may be because justice can only be achieved via the cooperation of (nearly) all States. In others, the attempt by a State or international organization to act on its own understanding of what justice requires, even when it is accurate, may well result in an overall increase in international (and perhaps domestic) injustice. That is partly because one State's genuinely just war or trade policy may appear to another to be an act of aggression or beggar-thy-neighbour protectionism. But in addition, State officials acting in bad faith may offer the example of another State's just but illegal

international legal authority is legitimate. For discussion of the latter issue, see Lefkowitz, fn. 3, pp. 107–111.

16 John Tasioulas, 'The Legitimacy of International Law', in Samantha Besson and John Tasioulas (eds.), *The Philosophy of International Law* (Oxford: Oxford University Press, 2010), pp. 97–116, p. 101.

17 Samantha Besson, 'The Authority of International Law: Lifting the State Veil' (2009) 31(3) *Sydney Law Review* 343–380, at 352–357; Tasioulas, fn. 16, p. 102; Allen Buchanan and Robert Keohane, 'The Legitimacy of Global Governance Institutions' (2006) 20(4) *Ethics and International Affairs* 405–437, at 407–408.

conduct as cover for their own unjust conduct. Both of these observations provide reasons to conclude that injustices are likely to follow when States and other international legal subjects deviate from the common standards of right conduct set out in international law. Indeed, Samantha Besson speaks for many political and legal theorists when she writes that 'in conditions of pervasive and persistent reasonable disagreement about justice, the creation of a legal order as a means of general co-ordination over matters of justice is actually in itself a requirement of justice'.[18]

Given this understanding of what makes international law legitimate, we can now consider the role that State consent plays, or should play, in generating justifiable claims to international authority. All else equal, a legal order should be designed so that, as much as possible, it claims authority if and only if it is justified in doing so.[19] The international legal order includes two mechanisms for issuing authoritative directives. One is the practice of customary international law, while the other is the practice of using treaties to create institutions imbued with legislative (rule-making) or adjudicative (rule-applying) authority, or both. Thus, the question regarding the contribution that State consent makes to international law's legitimacy takes two specific forms. Given the morally mandatory aim of optimizing international law's legitimacy, what considerations (if any) justify the persistent objector rule, according to which a norm of customary international law is binding on a State only if that State does not persistently object to being so bound when the norm is first emerging or 'crystalizing'? And what considerations, if any, justify the norm that States are usually subject to authoritative institutions only if they agree ('consent') to be ruled by those institutions, as well as the exceptions to that norm?

The service conception of legitimate authority provides a framework we can use to answer these questions. Broadly, State consent contributes to international law's legitimacy if, but only if, it makes it more likely that international legal actors' exercise of authority satisfies the NJC and the IC. State consent can do so by enhancing the ability of international legal authorities to improve international legal subjects' conformity to right reason. Or it can do so by serving as an acknowledgement of the limits of legitimate claims to authority, that is, as a means for recognizing cases where it is more important that international legal subjects act on their own judgment than that they act

[18] Besson, fn. 17, at 353.

[19] Thus, we should infer who should rule, and what procedures they should follow in doing so, from the service conception's account of what it is to rule well. For a contrasting approach to theorizing political legitimacy, see Besson and Martí, Chapter 14 in this volume.

as they have most reason to act. In what follows, I explore each of these potential contributions in greater detail.

2.5.1 *State Consent and De Facto Legitimacy*

The ability of any legal order to contribute to the production of social order in the way law purports to contribute depends primarily on the treatment of its norms as legitimate, that is, on the law normally being treated as a sufficient justification for action. Where law is so treated, it enjoys de facto legitimacy. In a vertically organized or hierarchical legal order, one characterized by a considerable degree of specialization in legislation, adjudication and enforcement, the law can contribute to the production of social order as long as most officials treat it as legitimate, even if many ordinary subjects do not. The latter may simply view legal norms as a means for predicting how legal officials will respond to various types of conduct.[20] But in a largely horizontal legal order like the international one, it is the members of the community constituted by law that must view it as legitimate. That is because responsibility for determining whether an agent is complying with the law, as well as for enforcing it in the case of violations, lies with the members themselves, acting either collectively or via the collective authorization of individual States.

The importance of creating, sustaining and strengthening international law's de facto legitimacy provides a weighty consideration in favour of treating international legal actors as subject only to those norms to which they agree to be subject, or at least those to which they do not persistently object. To do otherwise – that is, to subject States to norms against their will to be so bound – risks not only their disregard for the norms in question, or where prudence favours it, their resentful and possibly incomplete compliance. It also risks a loss of trust in other members of the community that can erode the de facto legitimacy of other international legal norms, and indeed, faith in the very conception of the international legal order as an attempt to contribute to the realization of justice through the enactment, application and enforcement of legitimate law. And where trust in other members of the community and faith in that conception of international law is already lacking, subjecting States to norms against their will may well reinforce existing cynicism and scepticism. These reactions may lead in turn to conduct that is both unjust and further weakens international law's ability to help its subjects conform to right reason.

[20] Herbert L. A. Hart, *The Concept of Law*, 3rd ed. (Oxford: Oxford University Press/Clarendon Press, 2012), p. 117. Of course, law is likely to make a greater contribution to social order if both legal officials and ordinary subjects view it as legitimate.

Consequently, even if a legal norm would satisfy the NJC and IC were it treated as legitimate by the international legal subjects to whom it is addressed, the fact that some of them will not do so, and may well respond in ways that significantly weaken international law's legitimacy, militates against adopting, issuing or finding that norm.[21] To illustrate this point, John Tasioulas observes that were international law to deny borrowing privileges to States that systematically and persistently flouted certain basic human rights against discrimination on the grounds of sex, the upshot might be a backlash against international law leading to all sorts of undesirable geopolitical consequences.[22] Thus, due regard for international law's de facto legitimacy places a pragmatic constraint on the directives an international authority should issue, namely that they apply only to those States that agree ('consent') to their application, or in the case of a norm of customary international law, only to States who do not persistently object to its application. The constraint is pragmatic because it is a concession to a failing on the part of some international legal subjects, namely their refusal to acknowledge certain legal norms as legitimate even though they satisfy the NJC and IC. It contrasts with the principled limits on legitimate authority discussed earlier, which follow from the nature of reasons and rationality (i.e. the capacity to respond or conform to reasons).

2.5.2 *State Consent and the Satisfaction of the Normal Justification Condition*

Earlier in this section, I noted several ways in which international law can satisfy the NJC, and so enable States and other international legal subjects to better conform to the reasons that apply to them. These include facilitating coordination on common standards of right conduct, correcting for mistaken beliefs that reflect bias or ignorance, and buttressing the commitment to conform to norms in the face of a temptation to defect from them. State consent, in the sense synonymous with agreement on terms, plays a critical role in producing legal norms with these features. For example, States' consent to a third party's authority to resolve disputes regarding (non)conformity to an international legal norm can enhance that norm's capacity to facilitate coordination on a common standard of right conduct. The need to secure consent to an exercise of international authority often provides States

[21] The same conclusion holds for interpretations of an existing legal norm.

[22] John Tasioulas, 'Human Rights, Legitimacy, and International Law' (2013) 58(1) *The American Journal of Jurisprudence* 1–25, at 21.

with an incentive to work together to craft norms acceptable to all, a process of negotiation that can generate both more information and better understanding among the parties. And the act of agreeing to ('consenting to') obey the directives issued by an international authority can 'stiffen the spine' of an international legal actor in much the same way that promising to tell the truth can strengthen a witness's commitment to fulfilling her duty to do so.

Some theorists maintain that the consent of (sufficiently) democratic States to the rule of international law is especially or even uniquely valuable. For example, Thomas Christiano argues that in circumstances characterized by the moral necessity of coordination on common standards of right conduct and disagreement as to what those standards should be, justice requires that people organize their lives together on the basis of rules that publicly treat them as equals.[23] This entails that law, including international law, must be made democratically.[24] To defend these claims, Christiano introduces three concepts: fundamental interests, the facts of judgment and the fundamental interests in judgment. An agent's fundamental interests are those that figure centrally in a person's well-being. Justice, Christiano maintains, requires the equal advancement of fundamental interests. The facts of judgment include (a) diversity in people's cultural surroundings; (b) cognitive biases in the interpretation of their own and others' interests (including what counts as their advancement) and the importance of their own interests in comparison to that of others; and (c) fallibility in both moral and non-moral judgment. The facts of judgment explain why disagreement as to what justice truly requires will be rife, even amongst those committed to the equal advancement of interests. Finally, the fundamental interests in judgment consist of the interest in correcting for others' cognitive biases, the interest in being at home in the world, and the interest in being treated as a person with equal moral standing. Each of these interests provides a moral basis for a claim against others that one's judgment regarding matters of justice be given equal weight in the collective task of determining how the shared aspects of social life ought to be arranged.

Against a background constituted by diversity, cognitive bias and fallibility, and the pervasive disagreement to which they give rise, agents will have compelling reason to believe that their fundamental interests in judgment, and so their other fundamental interests, are not being unjustifiably set back only if political power is exercised within institutions that publicly realize

[23] Thomas Christiano, *The Constitution of Equality: Democratic Authority and Its Limits* (Oxford: Oxford University Press, 2008), pp. 75–130, pp. 231–259.

[24] Democracy refers here not only to voting and a majoritarian decision procedure but also formal and informal practices of public deliberation and contestation.

equality. Democratic decision-making satisfies this criterion, since it 'enables us all to see that we are being treated as equals despite disagreements [regarding the true demands of justice] as long as we take into account the facts of judgment and the interests that accompany them'.[25] Interestingly, Christiano argues against the creation of a global parliament that creates international law via a majoritarian decision-making process. Instead, he defends a fair democratic association as the optimal institutional structure for exercising international legal authority in a manner that publicly treats all people as equals. In such an association, law is the product of agreement ('consent') by sufficiently democratic States to terms reached via a fair process of negotiation.[26]

On Christiano's account, democratic State consent yields legitimate law in part because of its instrumental value in correcting for cognitive biases and ignorance. Importantly, the consent of democratic States to an exercise of international authority can serve this end even if some of the other States that consent to it are not democratic. Still, we should not exaggerate this contribution. Democratic States are likely to be insufficiently responsive to the perspectives of individuals in other States, since those individuals have no formal say on what policies the State pursues, and limited opportunities for participating in its public deliberation. Moreover, the absence of fair bargaining conditions may distort the terms to which democratic States are willing to agree. These observations point to a possible caveat to the claim that, with a few exceptions, no democratic State should be subject to an exercise of international authority without its consent (i.e. without its agreement to be subject to that authority).[27] If other democratic States have agreed ('consented') to submit to an exercise of international legal authority, and there are compelling reasons to conclude that a particular democratic State's decision not to consent to that authority owes to the aforementioned shortcomings in its deliberations, then extending the authority's jurisdiction to that State may well be warranted even in the absence of its consent. Or, at least, this is so insofar as the rationale for treating democratic State consent as a necessary condition for legitimate authority is the instrumental one under discussion here.[28]

25 Christiano, fn. 23, p. 76.

26 Thomas Christiano, 'Democratic Legitimacy and International Institutions', in Besson and Tasioulas, fn. 16, pp. 119–137, pp. 129–136; Thomas Christiano, 'Legitimacy and the International Trade Regime' (2015) 52(5) *San Diego Law Review* 981–1012.

27 Samantha Besson, 'State Consent and Disagreement in International Law: Dissolving the Paradox' (2016) 29(2) *Leiden Journal of International Law* 289–316, at 306.

28 Again, a concern for international law's de facto legitimacy may offer a pragmatic justification for not asserting a claim to authority over a State, even if that exercise of authority would be legitimate.

I doubt that obedience to law in any international political–legal order short of a fair democratic association can honour all people's fundamental interests in being at home in an egalitarian world, or in being treated as a person with equal moral standing. Neither obedience to the authority of a political community composed partly of non-democratic States nor to institutions that owe their existence and claim to authority in part to the consent of non-democratic States, can carry that meaning. Yet it is not clear that either of these fundamental interests provide an independent basis for (international) law's legitimacy. Like the exercise of autonomy or self-determination, the value of feeling at home in the political society one inhabits, rather than alienated from it, may well be conditional on how well that society's institutions do at advancing justice.[29] If so, then even if identification with one's political society is an element of human well-being, it is only a secondary and dependent reason for creating and obeying legal authorities that enable one to better fulfil one's duty to treat others justly. As for the interest in being treated as a person with equal moral standing, given that Christiano characterizes it as one of our fundamental interests *in judgment*, it seems plausible to describe it as grounding an equal right to have one's moral judgment taken into account when determining the form that morally necessary collective action ought to take. We have already considered an instrumental justification for such a right, namely that its exercise serves to correct for cognitive biases. But why think the exercise of judgment, or at least of moral judgment, is valuable even if it fails to track the truth?[30] If it is not, then the fact that democratic government accords equal moral standing to all of the governed is also a secondary and dependent basis for the legitimacy of democratically enacted law. The primary justification for deferring to democratically enacted law is that one will better respond to the reasons for action provided by others fundamental interests, or what is the same, one will do better at treating others justly.

[29] Christiano acknowledges this point when he maintains that the fundamental interest is in being at home in an *egalitarian* world.

[30] One common answer is that we owe others respect for their exercise of moral judgment, so long as it is reasonable: see, for example, David Lefkowitz, 'A Contractualist Defense of Democratic Authority' (2005) 18(3) *Ratio Juris* 346–364; Besson, fn. 17; Jeremy Waldron, *Law and Disagreement* (Oxford: Oxford University Press, 1999). I am less confident than I once was in this response, and persuaded that instrumental considerations suffice to justify democratic rule.

2.5.3 *State Consent and Principled Limits on Legitimate Authority: The Instrumental Argument for Cultivating Moral Judgment*

The successful exercise of moral judgment depends on the integration of information and understanding. The former consists of data, both contemporary (e.g. the maternal mortality rate), and historical (e.g. changes in maternal mortality rates over time). The latter consists in theoretical constructions of data, either causal-explanatory or normative. In attempting to design legal institutions that optimize our ability to act on the basis of correct moral judgments, we must pay careful attention to the capacity of different actors to gather information, and to comprehend it. We should also recognize that the exercise of moral judgment is a skill, and so must be developed through practice. Finally, we should take as our aim maximizing conformity to right reason over time (or across all times), and not simply at one point in time, such as the present. Taken together, these considerations point to a limitation on the ability of one agent to exercise legitimate authority over another, namely where the latter will do better on the whole or in the long run at acting on right reason if they cultivate their own moral judgment rather than relying on that of another.

Plausibly, justice is most likely to be realized through the development of a multi-level institutional structure that includes local, sub-State regional, national, supra-State regional and global legal institutions. That is because some permutation of such an institutional structure will generate the best possible integration of information and understanding that human beings can achieve.[31] If so, one implication is that States ought not to agree to ('consent to') the rule of the international community or specific international institutions, if doing so will result in less overall conformity to right reason. Moreover, because long-run improvements in conformity to right reason will often depend on the honing of State officials' and citizens' facility at making moral judgments, they will need to retain some degree of freedom to make and act on their judgments even when, in the immediate or near term, they would do better at acting as they should, were they to defer to the rule of an international authority.

As will likely be clear, the instrumental argument for cultivating moral judgment can be used to justify several features of the existing international legal order. These include the development or adoption of abstractly formulated human rights norms that leave States a good deal of latitude when it

[31] I set aside here breakdowns between judgment and action, as occurs when executive agents fail to exhibit sufficient fidelity to the ideal of government in accordance with the rule of law.

comes to their application in domestic legislation or courts, as well as some international courts' adherence to the margin of appreciation doctrine when adjudicating human rights disputes. However, the instrumental argument for acknowledging or preserving States' freedom to act on their own moral judgment is conditional on the fact that doing so produces greater conformity to right reason in the long run. That conclusion is most plausible in the case of States that effectively secure the conditions for the development of better moral judgment, which includes respect for human rights, robust democratic politics, fidelity to the rule of law and a commitment to reasoned inquiry. It may still be persuasive in States that fall short to a considerable degree on one or more of these metrics, insofar as there remains some reasonable prospect of its leaders and citizens improving their moral judgment, including recognition of those changes they need to make to refine it still further. Where this is not the case, the instrumental argument for cultivating moral judgment provides no justification for treating a State's subjection to international authority as conditional on its agreement, even if other considerations, such as the need to preserve international law's de facto legitimacy, do so.

2.5.4 *State Consent and Principled Limits on Authority: The Intrinsic Value of (Political) Autonomy*

As I noted earlier in this chapter, all human beings have a fundamental interest in autonomy, the exercise of some degree of control over the shape or course of their lives. That is partly because individuals are often more likely to judge correctly what will best serve their other interests, fundamental or not, than is any other agent. But it also owes to autonomy's intrinsic value; self-government is good in itself, and not simply in virtue of its consequences. Where individuals' exercise of control over the shape of their lives includes a say in how they are governed – for example, in the crafting, application and/or enforcement of a community's law – then the community's political self-determination is also intrinsically valuable. Of course, it is impossible for a community to realize the value of political self-determination if, on every issue of government, it defers to another agent's judgment. Thus, the intrinsic value of political self-determination appears to provide a justification for a State's refusal to agree to ('consent to') rule by an international authority. Though hardly uncontroversial, I contend that the foregoing (and highly condensed) argument becomes much more problematic if we add the following claim: the intrinsic value of political self-determination precludes or defeats an international agent's claim to legitimate authority even in those cases where a State will do better at realizing justice if it defers to that international agent than if it acts on its own judgment.

While acknowledging the complexity of the issue, Tasioulas concludes that 'it is plausible that, when it comes to at least some human rights matters, the idea of a "margin of appreciation" or "subsidiarity" can be defended in part in terms of the importance of communal self-determination, even if the cost of recognizing this discretion is an inferior outcome with respect to conformity with human rights morality on the point at issue'.[32] Besson also invokes respect for autonomy to justify the conclusion that so long as a State is democratic it should enjoy a good deal of freedom to act on its own judgment of what justice requires, rather than that of an international authority.[33] Yet when what is at issue is one agent's just treatment of another, it is hard to see why the intrinsic value of acting on one's own judgment should ever outweigh getting the right answer. Indeed, while acting on one's own moral judgment may be intrinsically valuable, I submit that the realization of that value is conditional on one judging correctly what morality requires. When (or if) we experience a sense of accomplishment in acting on our own moral judgment, or take pride in having done so, we do so in the belief that we have judged well. Where this condition is not met, we do not feel pride or a sense of accomplishment, even if we have a compelling excuse for why we judged erroneously. These responses are evidence that we take the value of having chosen to perform a certain act to be conditional on our having an undefeated reason to perform that act – something that is not normally true of unjust conduct.

It may be that certain demands of justice are characterized by a degree of ineliminable vagueness or indeterminacy. While some specifications of the demand are inferior to others, there are two or more where either no compelling reason to believe that one is superior to the other will be forthcoming (ineliminable vagueness), or there is no fact of the matter as to which is superior to the other (indeterminacy). This may be true of many human rights. While some conduct clearly violates the right to be free from cruel or degrading punishment, or the right to engage in peaceful assembly consistent with due regard for national security and public order, some conduct is likely to fall into a 'gray area' in which disagreement is not only reasonable but also rationally irresolvable. It is also possible that certain values are incommensurable, meaning that there is no common measure that can be used to compare or rank those values, and thereby provide a rational basis for making trade-offs

[32] Tasioulas, fn. 22, at 21.

[33] Besson, fn. 27, at 305–308.

between them. This may be true of the right to freedom of religion and the right to freedom from discrimination on the basis of sex or gender. Each of these considerations – ineliminable vagueness, indeterminacy and incommensurability – can justify making a State's subjection to the jurisdiction of an international authority conditional on that State's agreement ('consent'). Where these properties characterize the demands of justice, either States will not better conform to right reason if they defer to the international authority than if they act on their own judgment, or they might, but it is impossible to determine whether this is so. In such cases, States have no duty to submit to an international authority, and given the intrinsic value of political self-determination, they may prefer to act on their own judgment.

2.5.5 *State Consent and Respect for Law*

To reiterate a point I made in Section 2.4, trust in another agent is partly constituted by a distinctive sort of respect for them, namely a less careful policing of their conduct to determine whether they are conforming to standards of right conduct than one would carry out in the absence of that trust. Thus, trust in one's government involves a strong presumption that it satisfies the conditions for legitimate authority, and so a belief that one ought to defer to its authority by obeying the law. Though not a necessary condition for the cultivation of trust in a practical authority, a practice of limiting claims to authority to those who consent to be subject to them, and only on those matters to which they consent, can serve to foster it. The agent whose consent is sought may take the request for it as a demonstration of the other agent's appropriate regard for his or her rights and interests, while the agent whose request for consent is granted may take that fact as evidence that the consenting agent views him or her as morally upstanding.

Besson suggests in passing that State consent to international legal authority may be valuable because it generates respect for law.[34] Presumably the idea is that by consenting to the rule of an international authority, States express their trust in it (e.g. in the international community), and in doing so contribute to the constitution of a relationship characterized by respect for that authority's directives (e.g. norms of customary international law). Yet State consent can serve as a means for expressing trust in an international authority only if it is publicly understood as doing so, and it is far from clear that the participants in the international legal order share such an understanding. Moreover, even if

[34] Besson, fn. 17, at 371; Besson, fn. 27, at 300.

State consent is available to serve as a means for expressing trust, it seems likely that many State officials do not intend to use it for that purpose when they agree ('consent') to an international institution's exercise of authority over them, or do not persistently object to an emerging norm of customary international law.

Still, it may be worth investigating whether certain instances of State consent do constitute trust-expressing or trust-building acts. Consider, for example, North Atlantic Treaty Organization (hereafter NATO) Member States' consent to a unified command for planning and executing military operations: the Supreme Allied Commander Europe (hereafter SACEUR). Admittedly, SACEUR does answer to the North Atlantic Council, which consists of permanent representatives from each of the Member States. Nevertheless, the willingness of the other twenty-nine (and counting) States to have an American officer serve as SACEUR, and so exercise the authority to order their military personnel to risk their lives, may serve in part to express their trust in the United States' commitment to the collective defence of NATO's Member States.

In some cases, States' consent to the jurisdiction of the ICJ may serve in part to express their trust in that institution, and its ability to satisfy the criteria for legitimate authority. In submitting their dispute to the ICJ, and so agreeing to abide by its judgment, States may act in the belief that the judges' professional training and culture warrant taking it on faith that they will act with a proper regard for the parties' rights and interests. Moreover, consent to the ICJ's jurisdiction may also express States' trust in one another, and in particular, in the commitment of officials in the other State to the ideal of government in accordance with the rule of law. Note that in making the case that State consent expresses trust, and so constitutes a trust-building act, there is no need to maintain that trust alone explains why States consent to an international authority. States may also count on international authorities' and other international actors' prudential interests motivating them to act with proper regard for the States' rights and interests. But then the same is often true for individuals; attaching legal penalties or punishment to violations of patients' fundamental interests can provide medical practitioners with a prudential incentive to respect them, and so provide patients with assurance that they will do so, without crowding out trust as a motivation for both parties' actions.

2.6 CONCLUSION

As a slogan, the consent of the governed has its virtues. For example, it expresses the belief that legitimate rule requires accountability to the ruled, and perhaps also that the purpose of government is to serve the needs of the governed. It also misleads, however, in that it suggests that the justification for a political community's right to rule its members owes to their exercise of a moral power conferring that right upon the community or its agents. Hopefully, a clearer understanding of how consent contributes to legitimate government, and how it does not, can aid us in improving the legitimacy of the practice of government constituted by international law.

3

Controlling Consent

Insights from Binding Dispute Settlement

CHRISTIAN J. TAMS*

3.1 INTRODUCTION

Consider the following hypotheticals, inspired by real disputes about the scope of State consent in processes of binding dispute resolution:

- Example 1: In the early 2010s, an investor comes across the text of an old-generation multilateral investment treaty, the 1981 Organization of Islamic Cooperation (hereafter OIC) Investment Agreement, which it invokes in its investment dispute against a foreign host State. The OIC Agreement contains a clause mentioning the possibility of binding dispute settlements but does not clearly and unequivocally state that such disputes can unilaterally be submitted to investment arbitration. In an award rendered in 2014, the tribunal determines that the clause does contain a standing offer to arbitrate, made by each and every party to the multilateral treaty. It reaches that conclusion by reading the clause against the background of hundreds of more recent clauses that do indeed contain the host State's unequivocal consent to arbitration. The decision is considered by commentators to have 'opened up a huge new world of possible investment claims'. A few years later, many investors explore this 'new world', by filing claims against State parties to the new treaties. States voice surprise that in 1981, they had in fact made a standing offer to arbitrate.
- Example 2: In an inter-State dispute involving questions of military force, the respondent relies on self-defence as a justification for its actions recognized under customary international law. The International Court of Justice (hereafter ICJ) rejects this justification, finding that the respondent could not invoke self-defence. In support of

* I am grateful to Dr Federica Paddeu (Cambridge University) for her comments on earlier versions of this contribution.

that finding, it holds that self-defence under customary international law could only be used against an 'armed attack', and that only the 'most grave forms' of forcible conduct would so qualify.

The two hypotheticals point towards the questions that I would like to explore in this chapter: What is the role of consent in the framework of binding dispute resolution, and who controls the meaning of such consent? I aim to explore this question in two main steps: by highlighting the basic tension affecting consent in proceedings before international courts and tribunals (hereafter ICaTs) (Section 3.2); and by illustrating how this tension plays out in two current debates (Section 3.3). Both steps are an attempt to initiate discussions about the role of consent in a particular setting – binding dispute resolution in arbitral and judicial proceedings before ICaTs – that is dear to international lawyers and, symbolically as well as practically, relevant to international law's claim to be rule-oriented.

This attempt is informed by a traditional perspective on international arbitration and adjudication, and proceeds from a straightforward hypothesis. The traditional perspective leads me to approach arbitral and judicial proceedings primarily as dispute settlement procedures. This is unlikely to be a controversial approach: ICaTs were set up to resolve disputes; arbitration and adjudication continue to be classified as means of dispute settlement; and the role of consent in this regard is clearly marked out. Of course, ICaTs perform other functions: in José E. Alvarez' terminology, we can think of these as 'fact finding', 'law-making' and 'governance' functions.[1] These other functions implicate consent differently; I indicate how by looking at the 'law-making' role of ICaTs (even though I will describe it in different terms). But my discussion remains focused on dispute settlement as the original function of ICaTs.

This discussion proceeds from a straightforward hypothesis: the role of consent in binding dispute resolution is peculiar, and not the same as in other settings, such as State responsibility, the law of obligations, the sources of international law and international institutional law.[2] It is peculiar in at least two ways. First, consent to dispute settlement is only the starting-point. It marks the acceptance, by a State, of a particular process in which an ICaT is to play a central role. Adapting distinctions introduced by Stephen

[1] José E. Alvarez, 'What Are International Judges for? The Main Functions of International Adjudication', in Cesare P. R. Romano, Karen J. Alter and Yuvan Shany (eds.), *The Oxford Handbook of International Adjudication* (Oxford: Oxford University Press, 2014), pp. 158–178, p. 159.

[2] Comp. Brunnée, Chapter 8 in this volume; Bordin, Chapter 11 in this volume; Kassoti, Chapter 12 in this volume; Nolte, Chapter 9 in this volume.

Neff, one might view consent to binding dispute settlement as an instance of 'regime consent' (as opposed to 'outcome consent' or 'rule consent').[3] Second, unlike in other fields, consent remains the central pillar of the system of binding dispute settlement. It is much maligned, but elevated to the level of a governing principle, that of *consensualism*.

Section 3.2 discusses consensualism, but recognizes that it is but the beginning of a process, 'the outcome of which' (to adapt Ellen Hey's phrase) 'is undetermined at the time at which that consent is given'.[4] But one thing is clear: 'regime consent' to the settling of a dispute implies a duty to accept the (yet undetermined) outcome of the process. As will be shown in the following, this relatively basic fact is key to understanding control over consent, which shifts in the course of the process of dispute settlement. Section 3.2 spells out this shift in a general manner. Section 3.3 illustrates how, in particular dispute settlement regimes, States and ICaTs vie for control and influence over binding dispute settlement. Section 3.4 offers brief concluding observations.

3.2 THE BASIC TENSION: INDISPENSABLE STATE CONSENT, FIRMLY CONTROLLED BY COURTS

The role of consent in arbitral and judicial proceedings reflects the nature of these two forms of binding dispute settlement. Arbitration and adjudication are not the same, but share essential characteristics. Both are optional and highly formalized ways of resolving controversies over questions of law or fact, which result in a binding decision by an independent institution (an international court or international tribunal). They are available only in exceptional circumstances, namely if States have accepted them. This acceptance implies a significant transfer of authority, as an ICaT scrutinizes State conduct, assesses it against the benchmarks of the applicable law, and pronounces on it, with binding force.

These considerations point to the basic tension of State consent in binding dispute settlement, which remains indispensable (Section 3.2.1) and yet, once given, is firmly controlled by ICaTs (Section 3.2.2). Both aspects make consent to binding dispute settlement peculiar: State consent to binding dispute settlement is more important than in other settings, and yet States renounce control more fully than elsewhere. The subsequent sections work through these two central features.

3 Stephen C. Neff, 'Consent', in Jean d'Aspremont and Sahib Singh (eds.), *Concepts for International Law: Contributions to Disciplinary Thought* (Cheltenham: Edward Elgar, 2019), pp. 127–140, p. 128.

4 Ellen Hey, *Teaching International Law: State-Consent as Consent to a Process of Normative Development and Ensuing Problems* (The Hague: Kluwer Law International, 2013), p. 13.

3.2.1 *The Heartland of Voluntarism: No Binding Dispute Settlement without Prior State Consent*

The first aspect is straightforward: State consent 'retains a sweeping hold'[5] on binding dispute settlement. Only State consent enables ICaTs to exercise jurisdiction, that is, to perform their primary role. What is more, consent typically is formal, direct and contained in a written document, making it easy to 'find'. This distinguishes binding dispute settlement from other areas where consent operates in less formalized and direct ways.[6]

Formally and directly expressed consent is required for the simple reason that international law, reflected in Article 2(3) of the United Nations (hereafter UN) Charter, merely requires States to settle their disputes peacefully, but beyond good faith negotiations,[7] does not prescribe a particular method of such settlement. State consent is required to limit the discretion of States and to move from the free choice of means[8] to binding dispute settlement.[9]

In the standard accounts of arbitration and adjudication, this basic fact is referred to as the 'fundamental principle of consent'.[10] All ICaTs acknowledge this principle and recognize the consensual basis of their jurisdiction – from the ICJ's statement that 'jurisdiction is based on the consent of the parties and is confined to the extent accepted by them',[11] via investment tribunals affirming that 'states are subject to binding third party dispute settlement procedures only

5 Jutta Brunnée, 'Consent' (last updated January 2022), in Rüdiger Wolfrum (ed.), *Max Planck Encyclopedia of Public International Law* (Oxford: Oxford University Press, 2008). Available at: https://opil.ouplaw.com/display/10.1093/law:epil/9780199231690/law-9780199231690-e1388, last accessed 13 December 2022, para. 4.

6 Ibid. Jutta Brunnée mentions law-making, but the point equally applies to international claims and their settlement, State responsibility, etc.

7 These have been described as 'an intrinsic element of the principle of [peaceful] dispute settlement': see Anne Peters, 'International Dispute Settlement: A Network of Cooperational Duties' (2003) 14(1) *European Journal of International Law* 1–34, at 11; ICJ, *North Sea Continental Shelf Cases (Federal Republic of Germany/Denmark; Federal Republic of Germany/Netherlands)* (Judgment) [1969] ICJ Rep. 3, p. 44, para. 77.

8 See UNGA Res. 2625 (24 October 1970), Principle 5, para. 4: 'International disputes shall be settled on the basis of the sovereign equality of States and in accordance with the principle of free choice of means'.

9 See *Status of Eastern Carelia* (Advisory Opinion) [1923] PCIJ Ser. B No. 5, p. 27: 'no state can, without its consent, be compelled to submit its disputes with other States either to mediation or to arbitration, or to any other kind of pacific settlement'.

10 *Case concerning Application of the International Convention on the Elimination of All Forms of Racial Discrimination* (Judgment) [2011] ICJ Rep. 70, para. 131. Reports 2011, 64, para. 131.

11 *Case concerning Armed Activities on the Territory of the Congo (New Application: 2002) (Democratic Republic of the Congo* v. *Rwanda)* (Jurisdiction and Admissibility) (Judgment) [2006] ICJ Rep. 6, para. 88.

if they so consent to it',[12] to the acknowledgement by a British–French arbitral tribunal that it 'derive[d] its competence from the consent of both the Parties to the present arbitration',[13] and finally the European Court of Human Rights' (hereafter ECtHR) recognition that it would have to declare 'incompatible ratione personae' complaints directed against entities that were not 'a Contracting Party to the [European] Convention'.[14]

The ways and means by which States manifest their acceptance of the 'fundamental principle of consent' no doubt vary, reflecting different designs of international courts and tribunals.[15] Specialized institutions like the ECtHR or the World Trade Organization (hereafter WTO) dispute settlement organs typically operate on the basis of generalized 'one-step consent',[16] manifested in a State's decision to join a treaty regime with mandatory arbitration or adjudication. Other courts and tribunals offer greater flexibility, notably because they (like the ICJ, or International Centre for Settlement of Investment Disputes (hereafter ICSID) tribunals) require 'two-step' or 'dual' consent, first to a particular framework establishing the institution and then activating it for a particular dispute or class of disputes.[17]

Cutting across these structural variations, consent can be granted in a circumscribed manner, perhaps even *post hoc* after a particular dispute has arisen and only in relation to it – but the majority of instances (as illustrated by Example 1) today involve general consent given *ante hoc*, covering particular categories of future disputes.[18] This is the model followed by courts operating

[12] *ConocoPhillips* v. *Bolivarian Republic of Venezuela*, ICSID, Decision on Jurisdiction and the Merits (3 September 2013) Case No. ARB/07/30, para. 254.

[13] *Delimitation of the Continental Shelf between the United Kingdom of Great Britain and Northern Ireland, and the French Republic (UK, France)* [1977], 18 RIAA 3, at 24.

[14] *Behrami and Behrami* v. *France, Saramati* v. *France, Germany and Norway* (No. 71412/01 and 78166/01) (2007) 45 EHRR SE10, GC, paras. 152, 144.

[15] Shabtai Rosenne, 'International Court of Justice (ICJ)' (last updated June 2006), in Wolfrum, fn. 5, para. 8: '[t]he law is, in principle, indifferent to how the consent is manifested'.

[16] Chittharanjan F. Amerasinghe, *Jurisdiction of International Tribunals* (The Hague: Kluwer Law International, 2002), p. 77.

[17] Ibid., pp. 82–89; Yuval Shany, 'No Longer a Weak Department of Power? Reflections on the Emergence of a New International Judiciary' (2009) 20(1) *European Journal of International Law* 73–91, at 79–80. Exceptionally, international tribunals are established on the basis of powers granted to (organs of) international organizations, in which case State consent is derivative or indirect. The International Criminal Tribunal for the former Yugoslavia (hereafter ICTY) and International Criminal Tribunal for Rwanda (hereafter ICTR) are obvious examples: see Amerasinghe, fn. 16, p. 89. In the *Tadic Case*, the ICTY assessed the propriety of its establishment, which some commentators had questioned: see *Prosecutor* v. *Dusko Tadic* (Appeals Chamber Decision on the Defense Motion for Interlocutory Appeal on Jurisdiction) [1995] ICTY, Case IT-94-1, para. 18; Bernhard Graefrath, 'Jugoslawientribunal: Präzedenzfall trotz fragwürdiger Rechtsgrundlage' (1993) 10 *Neue Justiz* 433–480.

[18] For more on this, see Rosenne, fn. 15, paras. 8–9.

on the basis of one-step consent, which can exercise jurisdiction over all States parties to the regime-creating treaty (United Nations Convention on the Law of the Sea[19] (hereafter UNCLOS), European Convention on Human Rights[20] (hereafter ECHR), WTO, etc.), but also accounts for the bulk of inter-State or investment cases brought on the basis of generally worded compromissory clauses containing offers to litigate[21] or, in the case of the ICJ, matching optional clause declarations.[22]

While the paths to jurisdiction are diverse, the basic principle remains: 'jurisdiction is always a limited one, existing only in so far as States have accepted it'.[23] And owing to the formalized nature of binding dispute settlement, such acceptance is almost inevitably expressed very visibly. Unlike in other settings, in which consent is discussed, consent to jurisdiction is nearly always in writing: only in rare instances can it be inferred from conduct or based on oral declarations.[24] For the rest, unlike in other areas, assessing consent is a matter of interpreting written statements, emanating from States' highest authorities capable of representing the State internationally. This does not mean that the validity of consent is never at issue: a number of decisions have turned on the status of the jurisdiction-conferring instrument, or on whether a party has succeeded to an earlier instrument.[25] But these instances pale in comparison with the major issues raised by the validity of consent in other fields – notably in the *jus ad bellum*[26] or in debates about the

[19] United Nations Convention on the Law of the Sea (hereafter UNCLOS), 1833 UNTS 397 (adopted 12 October 1982, entered into force 16 November 1994).

[20] Convention for the Protection of Human Rights and Fundamental Freedoms (hereafter ECHR), 213 UNTS 221 (adopted 4 November 1950, entered into force 3 September 1953).

[21] See, for example, Convention on the Settlement of Investment Disputes between States and Nationals of Other States (hereafter ICSID Convention) 575 UNTS 159 (adopted 18 March 1965, entered into force 14 October 1966), Art. 25(1); Art. 36(1) of the ICJ Statute.

[22] Art. 36(2) of the ICJ Statute.

[23] *Case concerning the Factory at Chorzów* (Jurisdiction) [1927] PCIJ Ser. A No. 9, p. 32.

[24] *Forum prorogatum* in particular continues to interest commentators; but this interest probably exceeds the real-life relevance of the concept. For helpful comments, see Sienho Yee, 'Forum Prorogatum to the International Court of Justice' (2003) 16(4) *Leiden Journal of International Law* 701–713.

[25] For examples from the ICJ's jurisprudence, see *Case concerning Maritime Delimitation and Territorial Questions between Qatar and Bahrain* (Judgment) [1994] ICJ Rep. 112, pp. 120–121; *Case concerning Application of the Convention on the Prevention and Punishment of the Crime of Genocide (Croatia* v. *Serbia)* (Judgment) [2008] ICJ Rep. 412, pp. 449–455.

[26] For detailed discussions, see, for example, Max Byrne, 'Consent and the Use of Force: an Examination of "Intervention by Invitation" as a Basis for US Drone Strikes in Pakistan, Somalia and Yemen' (2016) 3(1) *Journal on the Use of Force and International Law* 97–125.

formation of custom,[27] where the status of the allegedly consenting actor is central. All this confirms Jutta Brunnée's assessment that consent retains a 'sweeping hold'[28] on binding dispute settlement. This is the first of the basic parameters shaping the role of consent.

3.2.2 *Courts in Control: State Consent during Processes of Binding Dispute Settlement*

The above account of consent as a condition to the exercise of jurisdiction may seem trite. It looks at the role of consent at the beginning of a potentially lengthy process. An expression of consent opens the door to processes of binding dispute settlement,[29] but (as Example 1 illustrates) it may take decades before anyone actually walks through that door. When the door is used, ICaTs work with State consent, previously expressed. Reflecting the variable scope of consent, this can happen in processes of 'routinized litigation on a set of clearly defined issues arising'[30] under one treaty (such as the Inter-American Convention on Human Rights (hereafter IACHR), or the Energy Charter Treaty)[31]. It can also remain an altogether exceptional, 'episodic' occurrence relating to a wide array of legal issues (e.g. in proceedings before the ICJ).[32] But whether 'episodic' or 'routinized', the use of consent marks a shift of control. Once (ostensibly and plausibly) granted, State consent is to be given effect, and interpreted, by ICaTs. ICaTs determine what States have consented to and spell out the implications of this consent in particular disputes. In simple terms, States lose control over what they have consented to, and *in extremis*, over whether they have consented to binding dispute settlement at all. This loss of control is not explicit; it is the necessary

27 See, for example, the International Law Commission's (hereafter ILC) work on the identification of customary international law, notably Draft Conclusions 4–7 (and commentaries): see ILC, 'Draft Conclusions on Identification of Customary International Law, with Commentaries', in ILC, 'Report on the Work of the Seventieth Session' (2018), UN Doc. A/73/10, pp. 122–156, pp. 130–135.

28 Brunnée, fn. 5, para. 4.

29 Clément Marquet speaks of State consent as an entry point ('point d'accès') to dispute resolution: see Clément Marquet, *Le consentement étatique à la compétence des juridictions internationales* (Paris: Pedone, 2022), p. 131; for a non-metaphorical take see Nico Krisch, 'The Decay of Consent: International Law in an Age of Global Public Goods' (2014) 108(1) *American Journal of International Law* 1–40, at 7, footnote 38 ('consent … *at one remove*') (emphasis added).

30 See Benedict Kingsbury, 'International Courts: Uneven Judicialisation in Global Order', in James Crawford and Martti Koskenniemi (eds.), *The Cambridge Companion to International Law* (Cambridge: Cambridge University Press, 2012), pp. 203–227, p. 210.

31 The Energy Charter Treaty, 2080 UNTS 95 (adopted 17 December 1994, entered into force 16 April 1998).

32 Kingsbury, fn. 30.

implication of two prerogatives enjoyed by each and every international court or tribunal: its 'jurisdiction to determine its own jurisdiction';[33] and its power to resolve authoritatively disputes submitted to it. The subsequent sections assess how these two powers – referred to by shorthand terms as '*la compétence de la compétence*' and 'authority of decision' – affect the role of State consent, first by looking at control over jurisdiction, and then at the implication of decisions on the understanding of the law.

3.2.2.1 *Compétence de la compétence*

The first principle – *la compétence de la compétence* (or, in more convoluted German, *Kompetenz-Kompetenz*) – is the flip side to State consent to jurisdiction.[34] Many statutory instruments enshrine it, for example, stating that '[i]n the event of dispute as to whether the Court has jurisdiction, the Court shall decide',[35] or in the more focused language of the ICSID Convention, that '[a]ny objection by a party to the dispute that that dispute is not within the jurisdiction of the Centre, or for other reasons is not within the competence of the Tribunal, shall be considered by the Tribunal'.[36] In their jurisprudence, ICaTs have typically 'c[o]me down heavily and forcefully in favour of the view that [they] had a general unlimited jurisdiction to decide on their own jurisdiction'.[37] Hersch Lauterpacht's view that this power was 'the most fundamental principle of international – and national – jurisprudence' is instructive.[38] Described as 'inherent', the principle does not depend on any express recognition in a court's or tribunal's constitutional documents: according to the WTO Appellate Body, 'the right to determine whether [panels] have jurisdiction in a given case' counts among the 'powers that are inherent in their adjudicative function',[39] while the International

33 ICTY, fn. 17.

34 Brown considers it as 'perhaps the best known example of an inherent power': see Chester Brown, *A Common Law of International Adjudication* (Oxford: Oxford University Press, 2007), p. 63; see further Marquet, fn. 29, p. 203.

35 Art. 32(2) ECHR; and similarly Art. 36(6) ICJ Statute; Art. 288(4) UNCLOS.

36 Art. 41 ICSID Convention.

37 Amerasinghe, fn. 16, p. 136.

38 *Case of Certain Norwegian Loans (France* v. *Norway)* (Judgment) [1957] ICJ Rep. 9, p. 44; and further *Nottebohm Case (Liechtenstein* v. *Guatemala)* (Judgment) [1953] ICJ Rep. 111, p. 119. 'As regards ICSID, suffice it to mention that the decision of the annulment committee in *Klöckner* v. *Cameroon* which considered it 'neither contestable nor contested that the arbitrators have "the power to determine their own jurisdiction" ("la competence de la competence")': see *Klöckner* v. *Cameroon*, ICSID, Award (21 October 1983) Case No. ARB/81/2, para. 17.

39 *Mexico – Taxes Measures on Soft Drinks*, WTO, Report of the Appellate Body (6 March 2006) WT/DS308/AB/R, para. 45.

Criminal Tribunal for the former Yugoslavia (hereafter ICTY) referred to it as 'a necessary component of the judicial function'.[40]

How do the two sides of the coin – State consent and *Kompetenz-Kompetenz* – relate to each other? Alexander Orakhelashvili provides a starting point: 'While jurisdictional instruments are created by [State] consent, the precise ambit of the jurisdictional conferral depends on the interpretation of these instruments.'[41] But this is perhaps too matter-of-factly. In the world of binding dispute settlement, increasingly shaped by claims filed unilaterally, 'the precise ambit of the jurisdictional conferral' is often in doubt, especially as generalized consent (as opposed to *post hoc* consent) has become the norm.[42] As Orakhelashvili rightly notes, in determining the precise ambit of a jurisdictional conferral, ICaTs engage in an interpretative exercise, almost always seeking to make sense of written jurisdictional clauses. In this, they are guided by international law's principles of interpretation, but the vagueness of these principles, the recognition of maxims pointing in different directions (e.g. textual vs purposive) and the absence of clear directives as to the relative weight of each maxim in an individual case, means that they enjoy a significant measure of discretion.[43] As long as the protocols of interpretation are followed, there is limited room for a meaningful scrutiny of the outcome of a court's exercise of its *compétence de la compétence*. Adapting Jutta Brunnée's phrase, one might say that it grants ICaTs a 'sweeping hold'[44] over the construction of consent, which (outside rare exceptions) they typically exercise at one single level of decision-making,[45] and without subsequent scrutiny.[46]

40 *Prosecutor* v. *Dusko Tadic*, fn. 33.

41 Alexander Orakhelashvili, 'Consensual Principle' (last updated April 2020), in Wolfrum, fn. 5, para. 9.

42 See Section 3.2.1.

43 In its work on the law of treaties, the ILC recognized that 'recourse to many of these principles [of interpretation] is discretionary rather than obligatory', suggesting famously that 'the interpretation of documents is to some extent an art, not an exact science': see ILC, 'Documents of the Second Part of the Seventeenth Session and of the Eighteenth Session', *Yearbook of the International Law Commission* (1966) Vol. II, UN Doc. A/CN.4/SER.A/1966/Add.1, p. 218.

44 Brunnée, fn. 5, para. 4.

45 The key exceptions are the two-tiered systems established in the WTO Dispute Settlement Understanding (hereafter DSU) and the ECHR, as well as the limited annulment control exercised by annulment committees under Art. 52 of the ICSID Convention. But these systems of control merely clarify how ICaTs exercise their *Kompetenz-Kompetenz*; they do not affect the shift of control from States to ICaTs.

46 The main exception is the subsequent control of domestic courts over the recognition and enforcement of investment awards rendered outside the ICSID Convention; this will often involve some control over the tribunals' approach to jurisdiction.

Example 1, as given above, illustrates that disputes about the proper meaning of a jurisdictional title can have significant implications: in the real-life scenario on which Example 1 is based, tribunals, sitting decades after the conclusion of a multilateral treaty, made what has been termed 'a fabulous discovery',[47] finding that in 1981, in the wake of fervent arguments for a new international economic order emphasizing State control over foreign investment, dozens of Islamic States had made a standing offer inviting foreign investors to litigate investment disputes against them before international arbitral tribunals.[48] As the dozens or so claims submitted since the 'fabulous discovery' suggest, construing the 'precise ambit' of a jurisdictional clause, tribunals have indeed, as was predicted, 'open[ed] a new perspective to arbitration and to investment in the Islamic world'.[49] They have done so in decisions that are binding on the States that can only be challenged under very narrow grounds.[50]

The real OIC treaty disputes that inspired Example 1 are illustrative of a long list of cases that highlight the potentially significant implications of decisions construing the 'precise ambit of a jurisdictional conferral'. In fact, it might be interesting to write the history of international adjudication by reference to controversial jurisdictional holdings that construed State consent in unexpected ways – and may have surprised the State whose consent was at stake. While any list is subjective, the ICJ's *Nicaragua* Judgment would likely occupy an important place, as it did shake '[t]he Court's authority and the system of [jurisdiction under] the optional clause',[51] basing jurisdiction under Article 36(5) of the ICJ Statute on a transferred 'declaration never made'[52] and creatively bypassing a standard reservation made by the respondent.[53] Beyond *Nicaragua*, a 'best of' list of controversial and unexpected jurisdictional holdings might include decisions by human rights bodies of the *Temeltasch/*

47 Walid Ben Hamida, 'A Fabulous Discovery: The Arbitration Offer under the Organization of Islamic Cooperation Agreement Related to Investment' (2013) 30(6) *Journal of International Arbitration* 637–663.

48 In the interest of transparency, I should disclose that I have acted as counsel in two of the (many) cases on which the hypothetical Example 1 draws.

49 Ben Hamida, fn. 47.

50 Namely in annulment proceedings for awards rendered under the ICSID Convention (see Art. 52) and in domestic proceedings concerning recognition and enforcement for other, non-ICSID awards.

51 James Crawford, 'Military and Paramilitary Activities in and against Nicaragua Case (Nicaragua v United States of America)' (last updated 2019), in Wolfrum, fn. 5, para. 41.

52 Ibid., para. 9.

53 *Case concerning Military and Paramilitary Activities in and against Nicaragua (Nicaragua v. United States of America)* (Judgment) [1984] ICJ Rep. 392. For succinct and critical comment, written from a distance of twenty-five years, see Crawford, fn. 51, paras. 6–18.

Belilos type (asserting an institutional competence to declare reservations impermissible and yet severable, thus preserving State consent *minus* the reservation)[54] or the series of awards by ICSID tribunals progressively pushing the boundaries of 'investments' and 'foreign investors' protected under Bilateral Investment Treaties (hereafter BITs), and thus covered by the standing offer of host States to accept 'arbitration without privity'.[55]

But drawing up such lists would only go so far. ICaTs may simply have been correct in asserting jurisdiction, even where this surprised States or observers. And more importantly, having consented to binding dispute settlement, States have accepted the possibility of jurisdictional surprises and at least within the confines of the particular dispute settlement process, have *ex ante* acquiesced in an ICaT's construction of the applicable jurisdictional instrument: as much as they may disagree with the instrument's interpretation – as long as the protocols of interpretation were followed, this is a case of *curia locuta, causa finita*: in Shotaro Hamamoto words 'from a strictly legal point of view, such an argument [criticizing jurisdictional holdings that bring "surprises"] is without merit since "[i]n the event of a dispute as to whether the Court has jurisdiction, the matter shall be settled by the decision of the Court"'.[56] As Hamamoto goes on to note, the renunciation of control is almost absolute, as the principle of '*compétence de la compétence*, combined with the lack of instance of review – except with respect to investment arbitration – makes it practically impossible for any frustrated disputing party to see the decision in question rendered null and void'.[57] All this reinforces the basic point: by exercising their power to identify 'the precise ambit of the jurisdictional conferral', ICaTs gain a 'sweeping hold' over the scope of consent. The *Kompetenz-Kompetenz* principle effects this shift.

3.2.2.2 Authority of the Decision

While the power to determine the scope of their jurisdiction is the most obvious prerogative of ICaTs, their influence on the scope of State consent

54 *Belilos* v. *Switzerland* (No. 10328/83) (1988) 10 EHRR 466; *Temeltasch* v. *Switzerland* (No. 9116/80) (1983) 5 EHRR 417.

55 Jan Paulsson, 'Arbitration without Privity' (1995) 10(2) *ICSID Review* 232–257, at 232. The (real or perceived) jurisdictional creep of investment tribunals is surveyed by Chen Huiping: see Chen Huiping, 'The Expansion of Jurisdiction by ICSID Tribunals: Approaches, Reasons and Damages' (2011) 12(5) *The Journal of World Investment and Trade* 671–687, at 671.

56 Shotaro Hamamoto, 'Legitimacy of International Adjudication' (last updated October 2020), in Hélène Ruiz Fabri (ed.), *Max Planck Encyclopedia of International Procedural Law* (Oxford: Oxford University Press, 2020). Available at: https://opil.ouplaw.com/display/10.1093/law-mpeipro/e3159.013.3159/law-mpeipro-e3159, last accessed 13 December 2022, para. 12.

57 Ibid.

goes further. By resolving disputes submitted to them through authoritative decisions, ICaTs also impact States' rights and duties under those rules of international law that are at stake in the case at hand. ICaTs can thereby shape the meaning of international rules on whose interpretation the dispute submitted to them turns – and in respect to which States consented to jurisdiction. This influence on the interpretation of rules is exercised during dispute settlement processes, and in that sense might be termed as a 'side effect' – at least as long as it is recognized that in certain fields of international dispute settlement, this side effect has real implications for the understanding of legal rules.

Unlike with respect to *Kompetenz-Kompetenz*, the link between the authority of a decision and the principle of State consent is more difficult to conceptualize: rather than of 'sweeping holds', this is the terrain of shared control over the construction of legal rules. Through the authority of their decisions, ICaTs gain some control, but much depends on the characteristics of the different dispute settlement regimes. Reflecting as much, the subsequent considerations remain somewhat general and tentative.[58]

The premise: These considerations proceed from the undisputed premise that ICaTs, as part of their judicial function, resolve disputes submitted to them by rendering final decisions that impose upon parties binding obligations. This general principle is clearly enshrined in the constitutional documents of almost all ICaTs,[59] which recognize (as noted in the 1899 Hague Convention) that '[r]ecourse to arbitration implies an engagement to submit in good faith to the award'.[60] Unsurprisingly, 'submission in good faith' implies a duty to comply with the decision's construction of the international legal rights and obligations that are at stake. In Example 2 mentioned at the outset, this would comprise the duty of the respondent to accept the ICJ's interpretation of self-defence as a justification only available in response to 'armed attacks', and the Court's further clarification that a use of force only qualifies as an 'armed attack' if it reaches the threshold of a 'most grave' use of

58 The considerations set out in the following aims to outline general features of ICaT authority over the construction of legal rules; Section 3.3. goes beyond this general discussion by looking in more detail at attempts to strengthen the degree of influence of certain ICaTs.

59 See, for example, Arts. 59, 60 ICJ Statute, read in conjunction with Art. 94(1) of the UN Charter; Art. 46(1) ECHR; Art. 53(1) ICSID Convention; Art. 296 UNCLOS; Art. 68(1) IACHR. The WTO DSU is the exception that proves the rule (Art. 19.1 DSU).

60 See Art. 37(2), 54 of the Convention for the Pacific Settlement of International Disputes, UKTS 6 (adopted 18 October 1907, entered into force 26 January 1910) UKTS 6 (1907), 1 Bevans 577, 2 AJIL Supp. 43 (1908).

force.[61] By the same token, respondent States in human rights or investment cases are required to accept the ICaT's construction of (to give just two examples) a treaty clause requiring respect for an individual's right to life or the fair and equitable treatment of investors. In each of these instances, the construction adopted by an ICaT may well conflict with the State's understanding of what it had consented to. But by agreeing to participate in the dispute settlement process, the State has conferred upon the international court or tribunal the competence to construe the scope of the legal rule, and to determine the meaning of its initial consent to the rule. Just as with respect to jurisdictional instruments, this may be described as a renunciation of control over the scope of the rights and obligations at stake in the proceedings.

At the same time, this renunciation, when looked at from the perspective of the constituent documents of ICaTs, only goes so far. The constituent documents typically limit the binding effect of decisions rendered by ICaTs in two respects: first, carefully guarding against any law-making inclinations, the constitutive documents of ICaTs regularly rein in the effect of decisions, which 'have no binding force except between the parties and in respect of that particular dispute'.[62] Second, as far as the parties and the dispute are concerned, the duty to comply primarily relates to the outcome of the decision, that is, its operative part,[63] possibly extended to cover the reasoning where it was 'necessarily entailed' in the *dispositif*, but not 'peripheral or subsidiary matters, or *obiter dicta*'.[64] These two factors could be said to 'defuse' the tension with State consent: where a State (as in Example 2) is concerned that an ICaT had overstretched the meaning of a provision, it can take comfort in the fact that this construction is only binding upon it within the framework of a particular dispute settlement process. Beyond that – in relations with other States, or in future disputes, in future debates about the scope of self-defence – nothing in the constituent documents would require respondent States to accept an ICaT's construction of the underlying legal rule. The firm (perhaps even 'sweeping') hold of ICaTs over the construction of rules of international law is limited to the case at hand.

61 See Section 3.1.

62 See, for example, Art. 296(2) UNCLOS; and further: Art. 59 ICJ Statute.

63 *Case concerning Application of the Convention on the Prevention and Punishment of the Crime of Genocide (Bosnia and Herzegovina* v. *Serbia and Montenegro)* (Judgment) [2007] ICJ Rep. 43, para. 123: 'The operative part of a judgment of the Court possesses the force of *res judicata*'; *Polish Postal Service in Danzig* (Advisory Opinion) [1925] PCIJ Ser. B No. 11, pp. 29–30.

64 *Bosnian Genocide*, fn. 63, para. 126; *Request for Interpretation of the Judgment of 11 June 1998 in the Case concerning the Land and Maritime Boundary between Cameroon and Nigeria (Cameroon* v. *Nigeria), Preliminary Objections* (Judgment) [1999] ICJ Rep. 31, para. 10.

This, of course, is but the formal part of the assessment, which looks at the legally binding effects of decisions.[65] While the constituent documents limit this binding force, they do not tell the whole story. The real tension with State consent arises not from the limited *binding* effects of decisions, but from the impact of decisions on the development of international law: to the extent that ICaTs, as a side effect of their decisions, shape the understanding of rules of international law, they limit the discretion of States in advancing their own understanding of the rule in a more subtle way. This impact is not a matter of binding constructions: as their constituent documents make clear, ICaTs are not able to 'make' international law single-handedly, let alone through binding precedent; and many of them have recognized as much.[66] Rather, it is a matter of contributing to the development of international law 'in the practice of its interpretation'.[67]

In the orthodox discussion, this contribution has typically been said to be *persuasive*, and decisions have been portrayed as 'persuasive precedents'.[68] The exact influence of these 'persuasive precedents' on the proper understanding of international law is not easy to assess, and much depends on the design of a dispute settlement regime. As regards the ICJ and the Permanent Court of International Justice (hereafter PCIJ), whose impact has been studied in most detail, the influence is broad and diffuse, reflecting the diversity of international legal issues litigated before the 'World court', with a focus on

65 The following is a highly condensed summary of points developed in earlier writings: see, for example, Christian J. Tams, 'The ICJ as a "Law-Formative Agency": Summary and Synthesis', in Christian J. Tams and James Sloan (eds.), *The Development of International Law by the International Court of Justice* (Oxford: Oxford University Press, 2013), pp. 377–396; Christian J. Tams, 'The World Court's Role in the International Law-Making Process', in Jost Delbrück, Ursula Heinz, Kerstin Odendahl, Nele Matz-Lück and Andreas von Arnauld (eds.), *Aus Kiel in die Welt: Kiel's Contribution to International Law* (Berlin: Duncker & Humblot, 2013), pp. 139–164; Christian J. Tams and Alexandre Belle, '*Erga Omnes* Effects of Judicial Decisions' (last updated September 2021), in Ruiz Fabri, fn. 56.

66 *Pars pro toto*, in the *Nuclear Weapons* opinion, it was said to be '*clear* that the Court cannot legislate.... Rather its task is to engage in its normal judicial function of ascertaining the existence or otherwise of legal principles and rules': *Legality of the Threat or Use of Nuclear Weapons* (Advisory Opinion) [1996] ICJ Rep. 226, para. 18 (emphasis added).

67 Armin Von Bogdandy and Ingo Venzke, 'The Spell of Precedents: Lawmaking by International Courts and Tribunals', in Romano *et al.*, fn. 1, pp. 503–522, p. 505. Conversely, the fact that ICaTs cannot 'make law' single-handedly does not stop them from influencing the understanding of the law through their decisions: from the perspective of legal development, '[t]he formal nature of a judicial finding does not matter': Daniel Terris, Cesare P. R. Romano and Leigh Swigart, *The International Judge: An Introduction to the Men and Women Who Decide the World's Cases* (Oxford: Oxford University Press, 2007), p. 121.

68 See, for example, Mohammad Shahabuddeen, *Precedent in the World Court* (Cambridge: Cambridge University Press, 1996), p. xiv.

questions of State responsibility and boundary delimitations, and occasional forays into international law's specialized branches.[69] As regards the specialized regimes of binding dispute settlement, the contribution of ICaTs is far more concentrated (typically on the treaty, or set of treaties, within their jurisdiction) and often more marked, simply because routine litigation permits courts to develop a *jurisprudence constante* on the 'home turf' of 'their' treaty.

As will be shown subsequently,[70] these factors shape how, in the context of particular dispute settlement regimes, ICaTs can exercise interpretative influence through their decisions. But it is central to acknowledge that this influence is a matter of degree. ICaTs contribute to the development of international law by advancing normative propositions about the proper understanding of international law (e.g. through the proper interpretation of a treaty provision, or the existence of a rule of customary international law). In a system lacking centralized law-interpreters, such normative propositions are unlikely to be dismissed out of hand: international lawyers need (in the words of Sir Franklin Berman) 'beacons, guides and orientation points, all the more so because of the non-structured, non-hierarchical nature of [international law's] rules',[71] which may explain why many pronouncements are often accorded 'a truly astonishing deference'.[72] But this deference is not automatic. ICaTs do not have 'the last word in the adaptation, formulation and ... elaboration ... of the rules of international law'.[73] Nothing stops their audiences from rejecting the proposed understanding, and there are well-known instances of States 'bypassing' the interpretation favoured by an ICaT, among them the subsequent 'correction' of the PCIJ's holding in *The S.S. "Lotus"* on port State jurisdiction over collisions on the high seas.[74]

To illustrate such competing considerations, it may be useful to briefly trace the 'fate' of the decision that inspired Example 2 set out in the Introduction to

[69] For details see the contributions to Tams and Sloan, fn. 65.

[70] See Section 3.3.1.

[71] Sir Franklin Berman, 'The International Court of Justice as an "Agent" of Legal Development?', in Tams and Sloan, fn. 65, pp. 7–21, p. 21.

[72] Daniel Patrick O'Connell, *International Law*, Vol. 1, 2nd ed. (London: Stevens and Sons, 1970), p. 32.

[73] Alain Pellet and Daniel Müller, 'Article 38', in Andreas Zimmermann and Christian J. Tams (eds.), *The Statute of the International Court of Justice: A Commentary*, 3rd ed. (Oxford: Oxford University Press, 2019), pp. 819–962, para. 336.

[74] Art. 1 of the International Convention relating to the Arrest of Seagoing Ships (hereafter 1952 Brussels Convention) 439 UNTS 193 (adopted 10 May 1952, entered into force 24 February 1956); and further Vaughan Lowe and Antonios Tzanakopoulos, 'The Development of the Law of the Sea by the International Court of Justice', in Tams and Sloan, fn. 65, pp. 177–196, p. 184.

this chapter, namely the ICJ's *Nicaragua* Judgment of 1986. Looking at a decade of discussions on the matter, it seems clear that the ICJ's construction of the 'armed attack' requirement – requiring, as a threshold condition, an attack to involve a qualified (grave) breach of the ban against force – has come to shape the international legal discourse: while not binding beyond the remit of the particular case, it has radiated, as States arguing in favour of a narrow conception of self-defence (or concerned about 'normative drift'[75] in the law on self-defence) have claimed that their understanding was supported by the World Court's jurisprudence.[76] Thirty-five years of engaged struggle over the proper construction of self-defence confirm that the ICJ's decision has made it more difficult for competing constructions of self-defence (e.g. those not viewing 'armed attacks' as a 'most grave forms' of force)[77] to be accepted. On the other hand, the ICJ's decision has not 'frozen' the law, and even those cautioning against 'normative drift' tend to accept that international practice and opinion may not always neatly fit with the World Court's earlier pronouncement – whose impact needs to be assessed, cannot simply be taken for granted.[78] By the same token, arbitral and judicial pronouncements in other fields have, for example, made it more difficult to cling to a narrow construction of the notion 'investment' under Article 25 of the ICSID Convention or to a peacetime view of human rights that considers them not to apply during armed conflict. On these and dozens of other questions of legal constructions, arbitral and judicial pronouncements provide guidance that favours particular constructions and limits the plausibility of others. But they do so as part of a broader process of legal development, in which the voice of ICaTs, while distinctive, is not a solo voice.

75 The term is Daniel Bethlehem's: see Daniel Bethlehem, 'International Law and the Use of Force: The Law as It Is and as It Should Be' (written evidence to the Select Committee on Foreign Affairs: Minutes of Evidence, 8 June 2004). Available at: https://publications.parliament.uk/pa/cm200304/cmselect/cmfaff/441/4060808.htm, last accessed 1 December 2022, para. 21.

76 For a representative spectrum of views see the contributions in Mary Ellen O'Connell, Christian J. Tams and Dire Tladi, *Self-Defense against Non-State Actors* (Cambridge: Cambridge University Press, 2019).

77 On the particular question of self-defence and the threshold of armed attack, see James A. Green, *The International Court of Justice and Self-Defense in International Law* (Oxford: Hart, 2009), pp. 31–33.

78 To illustrate, in Olivier Corten's work, which restates the traditional account of self-defence comprehensively, the jurisprudence of the ICJ is one factor among many: see Olivier Corten, *The Law against War: The Prohibition on the Use of Force in Contemporary International Law* (Oxford: Hart, 2012), p. 194.

3.2.3 *Interim Conclusions*

The preceding sections highlight the basic tension affecting the role of consent in binding dispute settlement. They illustrate the importance of looking at dispute settlement as a process – conditioned by State consent, but, once under way, dominated by the power of ICaTs to render binding decisions. This power explains why consent is taken so seriously. At the same time, it implies a 'takeover' of control over the meaning of State consent to jurisdiction and means that, through their decisions, ICaTs influence the proper rules of international law. In that sense, the discussion emphasizes Ellen Hey's observation that, when agreeing to submit to the jurisdiction of ICaTs, States accept to join a 'process of normative development, the outcome of which is undetermined at the time at which ... consent is given'.[79] Surprises need to be priced in. Conversely, it is precisely because ICaTs play, during the dispute settlement process, such an influential role, that States jealously control consent to jurisdiction, insisting that jurisdiction is never general, and must be formally conferred.

3.3 NAVIGATING THE TENSION: TWO PEN PICTURES

The preceding discussion might suggest a relatively linear understanding of the basic tension, in which initial State control over consent is over time replaced by subsequent ICaT control over its construction. That would be misleading, though. In reality, the tension is constantly navigated: States continually consider whether to grant jurisdiction to ICaTs, for example, by negotiating jurisdiction-conferring instruments, by pondering whether to join treaty regimes envisaging recourse to arbitration or adjudication, by reflecting on the scope of reservations, or by (in the field of investment law) providing for consent in their national legislation. ICaTs in turn constantly apply and interpret jurisdictional clauses and, through their decisions, construe rules of international law with binding force for litigants, and with persuasive force for others. Observers have sought to translate the broad trends of this constant adaptation exercise in catchy phrases. 'Judicialisation' and 'juridification' seemed to capture the seemingly inevitable rise of binding dispute settlement, as from the 1990s larger numbers of States conferred upon ICaTs more significant jurisdictional mandates, to the point where some commentators sensed 'a shift from the consensual to the compulsory paradigm'.[80] Twenty

79 Hey, fn. 4.

80 Cesare P. Romano, 'The Shift from the Consensual to the Compulsory Paradigm in International Adjudication: Elements for a Theory of Consent' (2007) 39(4) *New York University Journal of International Law* 791–872.

years later, such assessments appear naive and short-sighted, terms such as 'backlash' and 'pushback' have come to reflect marked dissatisfaction with ICaTs and as some of the more prominent among them have been paralyzed: the pendulum seems to swing back.

Sections 3.3.1 and 3.3.2 illustrate the dynamics of consent at a more concrete level: they offer two pen pictures that sketch out how States and ICaTs work from within the parameters set out in Section 3.2, and adapt them. The pen pictures take us back to the fault lines identified above, that is, the uncertain scope of ICaTs' contribution to legal development and the tension between State consent and the *compétence de la compétence* of ICaTs.

3.3.1 *Normative Acquis and* Res Interpreta *versus Reassertions of State Control: The Struggle over Interpretative Authority*

The first pen picture depicts current debates about the influence of ICaTs on the development of international law. As noted above, beyond the basic parameters – no law-making power, but at least some de facto influence – the degree of this influence is uncertain. As has also been noted, whether ICaTs have more or less influence primarily depends on the context of the particular jurisdictional regime. As part of this context, the number and density of decisions is the key variable: where a court such as the ICJ, or *ad hoc* arbitral tribunals, due to 'the occasional and adventitious nature of [its] caseload … is unlikely to be given the opportunity to revisit successively particular areas of substantive international law',[81] its influence on the development of international law is likely to remain limited, and to the extent it exists, be exercised in tandem with other interpretative processes.[82] The picture is different for specialized ICaTs that render greater number of decisions and can regularly 'revisit', and finesse, the interpretation of international legal rules argued before them. In relation to regional human rights treaties, the WTO covered agreements and the more diffuse body of standards recognized in international investment agreements, this has enhanced ICaTs' control over legal development. Unsurprisingly, it is here that the struggle over interpretative authority plays out most visibly. While the moves in that struggle reflect the design features of the different regimes, they follow a

[81] Berman, fn. 71, p. 20.

[82] As regards the ICJ, the partnership with the ILC is particularly significant, often resulting in forms of 'normative ping-pong': see Christian J. Tams, 'Meta-Custom and the Court: A Study in Judicial Law-Making' (2015) 14(1) *Law and Practice of International Courts and Tribunals* 51–79, at 74.

general pattern, with ICaTs seeking to consolidate their influence and States warning against activist judicial law-making.

3.3.1.1 Normative Acquis and *Res Interpretata*

Most ICaTs have moved cautiously, aware of concerns about (perceptions of) judicial activism. But certain moves can be detected. In the field of investment law, tribunals have sought to consolidate their influence by seeking to ensure consistency across arbitral proceedings, which in a system lacking central governance structures is anything but easy. Reflecting this, the debate has primarily been *between* arbitral tribunals, some of which have asserted a duty of tribunals to 'stay in line'. A much-quoted statement from the *Saipem* award was the high water mark of this approach – but even this statement leaves room for deviation, and it does not look at the application of the law outside arbitral settings: According to the tribunal, it had

> subject to compelling contrary grounds, ... a duty to adopt solutions established in a series of consistent cases ... [and], subject to the specifics of a given treaty and of the circumstances of the actual case, ... a duty to seek to contribute to the harmonious development of investment law.[83]

Other bodies have been less cautious. The language used by WTO dispute settlement institutions is more assertive. The central take is the oft-quoted assertion that adopted Panel and AB reports 'are an important part of the GATT acquis' and 'should be taken into account where they are relevant to any dispute'.[84] While typically followed by the caveat that reports 'are not binding',[85] this reflects how much authority to interpret the law is being centralized. Over time, the Appellate Body has become slightly more robust in its language, for example, noting that reports are a contribution to 'security and predictability', 'impl[ying] that, absent cogent reasons, an adjudicatory body will resolve the same legal question in the same way in a subsequent case'.[86] While primarily directed at panels, there is – unlike with respect to investment law – an attempt to interpret the law generally, and not just for

[83] *Saipem SpA* v. *The People's Republic of Bangladesh*, Decision on Jurisdiction and Recommendation on Provisional Measures (21 March 2007) ICSID Case No. ARB/05/07, 48 ILM 996, para. 67.

[84] *Japan – Alcoholic Beverages II*, WTO, Report of the Appellate Body (4 October 1996) WTDS8/AB/R, p. 14; *US – Shrimp* (22 October 2001) WT/DS58/AB/RW, paras. 107–109.

[85] *Japan – Alcoholic Beverages II*, fn. 84.

[86] *US – Stainless Steel (Mexico)*, WTO, Report of the Appellate Body (30 April 2008) WT/DS344/AB/R, paras. 158, 159–162 (relying on Art. 3.2 DSU).

future dispute settlement proceedings: as part of the 'acquis', interpretations set out in adopted reports 'create legitimate expectations among WTO Members', who 'take into account the legal interpretation … developed in adopted panel and Appellate Body reports'.[87]

It is in the context of *regional human rights treaties* that international courts have gone furthest in asserting a general authority to interpret the law. Recent debates in the ECHR context illustrate the state of play.[88] Here the focus is now firmly on the ECtHR's attempt to control the interpretation of human rights law *generally*, notably insofar as they are invoked in domestic courts.[89] These attempts – drawing on the Court's recognized role as a guardian of the Convention[90] – have a long history: already in *Ireland v UK*, the ECtHR felt that its judgments 'serve not only to decide those cases brought before the Court but, more generally, to elucidate, safeguard, *and develop* the rules instituted by the Convention, thereby contributing to the observance by the States of the engagements undertaken by them as Contracting Parties'.[91] In later judgments, the Court stated that its mission was 'to determine issues on public-policy grounds in the common interest, thereby raising the general standards of protection of human rights and extending human rights jurisprudence throughout the community of the Convention States'.[92] The implications of this understanding for State authorities are set out clearly in, for example, *Opuz* v. *Turkey*:

> [T]he Court will consider whether the national authorities have sufficiently taken into account the principles flowing from its judgments on similar issues, even when they concern other States.[93]

87 *Japan – Alcoholic Beverages II*, fn. 84; *US – Stainless Steel (Mexico)*, fn. 86.

88 The debate is not limited to the ECtHR though: in the IACHR context, similar issues arise in debates about the possibility of the IACtHR's exercise of 'conventionality control': see, for example, *Almonacid Arellano* v. *Chile* (Preliminary Objections, Merits, Reparations and Costs) (26 September 2006) IACHR, para. 124; Jorge Contesse, 'The Final Word? Constitutional Dialogue and the Inter-American Court of Human Rights' (2017) 15(2) *International Journal of Constitutional Law* 414–435.

89 For much more on the issues sketched out in the following, see Samantha Besson, 'The *Erga Omnes* Effect of Judgments of the European Court of Human Rights: What's in a Name?', in Samantha Besson (ed.), *La Cour européenne des droits de l'homme après le Protocole 14* (Zürich: Schulthess, 2011), pp. 125–175; Oddný Mjöll Arnardóttir, 'Res Interpretata, *Erga Omnes* Effect and the Role of the Margin of Appreciation in Giving Domestic Effect to the Judgments of the European Court of Human Rights' (2017) 28(3) *European Journal of International Law* 819–843.

90 See notably Arts. 19, 32 ECHR.

91 *Ireland* v. *United Kingdom* (No. 5310/71) (1979–1980) 2 EHRR 25, para. 154 (emphasis added); and further *Karner* v. *Austria* (No. 40016/98) (2004) 38 EHRR 24, para. 26.

92 *Rantsev* v. *Cyprus and Russia* (No. 25965/04) (2010) 51 EHHR 1, para. 197.

93 *Opuz* v. *Turkey* (No. 33401/02) (2010) 50 EHRR 28, para. 163.

As is clear from this statement, the ECtHR's claim to control the interpretation of the Convention is now made forcefully, to the point where the traditional parameters come under strain.[94] Where States are required, as part of their duty to comply with regional human rights law, to respect the 'principles of ECtHR jurisprudence', the limiting effect of Article 46(1) is easily bypassed: commentators have recognized as much, opting to speak of the '*erga omnes* effects' of ECtHR decisions, and noting the emergence of 'the principle of *res interpretata*' in the Court's jurisprudence.[95]

3.3.1.2 Reassertion of State Control

These attempts to consolidate the interpretative authority of courts have not gone unchallenged. In all three regimes, States have voiced concern about 'activist' ICaTs. At least occasionally, States have sought to translate these concerns into strategies for reasserting control over the interpretative process. Three different strategies can be distinguished.

Rejecting the claims of ICaTs is the obvious approach. In the WTO, well before moving on to a more forthright attack, the United States (hereafter US) had expressed concern about the Appellate Body's claim to be clarifying law with effect for all WTO members. For example, in a statement made in 2003, the US described the idea of *erga omnes* effects of Reports 'to be squarely at odds with the fundamentally bilateral nature of the WTO and the General Agreement on Tariffs and Trade ("GATT") dispute settlement'.[96] In the ECHR context, similar concerns made their way into the *Report of the Steering Committee for Human Rights*, which (rejecting claims to recognize the ECtHR's interpretative authority, made, for example, in the *Interlaken Declaration*) explicitly 'oppose[d] the proposal that there should be a Convention-based legal obligation upon States Parties to abide by final judgments of the Court in cases to which they are not parties'.[97]

[94] Arnardóttir, fn. 89, at 820: 'contrary to the *prima facie* appearance of a more lenient and deferential Court, the emerging approach in fact signals the Court's ambition for more direct influence and a deeper penetration of its jurisprudence into the legal systems of the contracting states'.

[95] See fn. 89.

[96] Statement cited in Laurence R. Helfer, 'The Effectiveness of International Adjudicators', in Romano *et al.*, fn. 1, pp. 464–482, p. 471.

[97] Council of Europe, Steering Committee for Human Rights, 'CDDH Report on the Longer-Term Future of the System of the European Convention on Human Rights, 11 December 2015', CDDH(2015)R84. Available at: https://rm.coe.int/cddh-2015-r84-addendum-i-en-/16806585d8, last accessed 2 December 2022.

Second, beyond these defensive moves, the most common strategy is for States to make an effort to limit the room for judicial activism. In the WTO context, Member States sought to do this prophylactically, by circumscribing the mandate of WTO panels and the Appellate Body in the final clause of Article 3(2) of the Dispute Settlement Understanding (hereafter DSU): 'Recommendations and rulings of the DSB cannot add to or diminish the rights and obligations provided in the covered agreement.' The more obvious strategy has been for Member States to move towards greater specificity in the wording of substantive provisions that are to be interpreted by ICaTs. Investment law, traditionally characterized by terse and vague treaty language, provides the most instructive examples in point. Among these, the move from 'laconically drafted' Fair and Equitable Treatment (hereafter FET) clauses in traditional BITs to the 'precise drafting with enumerated examples' in more recent treaties[98] stands out: from nine words ('Each Party shall accord investors fair and equitable treatment'), the FET clause of the EU-Canada Comprehensive Economic and Trade Agreement (hereafter CETA) has exploded in size, comprising seven paragraphs and 360 words. Whether this helps, is another matter: the actual interpretation in proceedings remains the task of the tribunal, after all. But the intention is clear: the parties to the treaty have aimed for a 'guided and constrained'[99] formulation, which of course is meant to 'guide and constrain' tribunals.[100]

In certain cases, States parties have opted for a more 'robust' response and expressly asserted a power to interpret the meaning of provisions subject to judicial or arbitral jurisdiction.[101] This power, to be sure, exists under the general principles of interpretation reflected in Article 31(3)(a) and (b) of the Vienna Convention on the Law of Treaties.[102] However, these provisions

98 Flavien Jadeau and Fabien Gelinas, 'CETA's Definition of the Fair and Equitable Treatment Standard: Toward a Guided and Constrained Interpretation' (2016) 13(1) *Transnational Dispute Management*. Available at: https://papers.ssrn.com/sol3/papers.cfm?abstract_id=2931503, last accessed 2 December 2022.

99 Ibid.

100 Eleni Methymaki and Antonios Tzanakopoulos, 'Masters of Puppets? Reassertion of Control through Joint Investment Treaty Interpretation', in Andreas Kulick (ed.), *Reassertion of Control over the Investment Treaty Regime* (Cambridge: Cambridge University Press, 2017), pp. 155–181, p. 157: 'the struggle of States parties to reassert control over their IIAs was prompted by the fact that arbitral tribunals ... at times (many times) approached their interpretative function very liberally with respect to both jurisdiction and the substantive standards of protection'.

101 Ibid.

102 Vienna Convention on the Law of Treaties, 1155 UNTS 331 (adopted 23 May 1969, entered into force 27 January 1980).

make its exercise very difficult.[103] Such exercise has become a more realistic prospect under treaties that set up committees and vests them with interpretative authority. Again, investment law provides the most instructive examples. Many of the more recent treaties[104] set up treaty bodies that can authoritatively determine the meaning of treaty clauses. The 'mother' of these treaty bodies, the Free Trade Commission (hereafter FTC) of the North American Free Trade Agreement (hereafter NAFTA), did so on a number of occasions, including in relation to the FET standard.[105] And while its statements, lacking specificity, left some wriggle room to tribunals, these duly acknowledged the FTC's authority: '[W]e have the Parties themselves – all the Parties – speaking to the Tribunal. No more authentic and authoritative source of instruction on what the Parties intended to convey in a particular provision of NAFTA is possible.'[106]

The various moves surveyed in the preceding sections reflect how much the struggle over interpretative authority has become 'regime specific'. In navigating the basic tension outlined above, ICaTs and States define their respective spheres of influence within each particular dispute settlement regime. As a result, the degrees of influence enjoyed by ICaTs varies significantly. In the field of investment arbitration, States are most active in seeking to reassert control; while in the WTO, some of them have opted for more ruthless tactics of court-curbing. Their strategies can be seen as attempts to limit the power of ICaTs to define the meaning of WTO rules and investment protection standards. This involves occasional shots across the bow, but at least in investment law, also includes the creation of State-driven centres of interpretative authority. By contrast, the ECtHR's assertion of interpretative authority has met with much less resistance. Of the different systems looked at here,

[103] ILC, 'Subsequent Agreements and Subsequent Practice in Relation to the Interpretation of Treaties', in ILC, 'Report on the Work of Its Seventieth Session', UN Doc. No. A/73/10 (2018), pp. 11–116, Draft Conclusion 4, pp. 27–37.

[104] Office of the United States Trade Representative, '2012 U.S Model Bilateral Investment Treaty'. Available at: https://ustr.gov/sites/default/files/BIT%20text%20for%20ACIEP%20Meeting.pdf, last accessed 2 December 2022, Art. 30; Indian Government, 'Model Text for the Indian Bilateral Investment Treaty' (2015). Available at: www.mygov.in/sites/default/files/master_image/Model%20Text%20for%20the%20Indian%20Bilateral%20Investment%20Treaty.pdf, last accessed 2 December 2022, Art. 14.9(iv); Electronic Database of Investment Treaties, 'Canada Model BIT' (2004). Available at: https://edit.wti.org/document/show/d15e4f5d-0310-4db4-a1ed-85e5d19f8ee1, last accessed 2 December 2022.

[105] NAFTA Free Trade Commission, 'North American Free Trade Agreement: Notes of Interpretation of Certain Chapter 11 Provisions' (2001). Available at: www.sice.oas.org/tpd/nafta/commission/ch11understanding_e.asp, last accessed 2 December 2011, Art. 1130.

[106] *ADF Group, Inc.* v. *United States*, ICSID, Award (9 January 2003) Case No. ARB(AF)/00/1, para. 177.

it is the ECHR that has gone furthest in the direction of 'court control': the response to the *Interlaken* process suggests that Member States are unwilling to formally accept the *res interpretata* doctrine; but in the practice of everyday dispute settlement, 'the ECHR is what the Strasbourg Judges say it is'.

3.3.2 *Concerns about Mandate Creep and How to Respond*

The second pen picture sketches out a different debate: rather than a struggle for degrees of influence, it depicts a more direct confrontation between ICaTs and States. This confrontation – the struggle over jurisdiction – proceeds from a clear-cut allocation of power: as noted above, when determining the scope of their jurisdiction, the principle of *compétence de la compétence* puts ICaTs firmly 'in control'. As has also been noted,[107] in exercising this competence, ICaTs have quite regularly upheld their jurisdiction over the objections of States who felt their consent did not in fact go that far. Recent judicial and arbitral experience illustrates the potential for conflicts as ICaTs have frequently been accused of 'mandate creep' – and yet it suggests that the power of ICaTs to determine the scope of their jurisdiction is not seriously in doubt. Instead, the very real concerns felt by a number of States over problems of (real or alleged) mandate creep are channelled in two different ways: many States have become a lot more vigilant before consenting to the exercise of jurisdiction, while in a significant number of cases, States have withdrawn from existing systems of binding dispute settlement. The subsequent sections sketch out these trends in turn.

The first point to note is that, notwithstanding high-profile confrontations, the *compétence de la compétence* of ICaTs is not seriously contested. No doubt, many States have voiced serious concerns about what they perceive as unduly expansive construction of jurisdictional titles. This, to be sure, is not new, but the tone of the debate has become shrill: The *South China Sea* award is but the most dramatic instance on a list of controversial jurisdictional holdings, which also includes investment awards (including those rendered on the basis of the OIC Agreement, referred to in Example 1 at the outset), and the *Campbell* decision of the Southern African Development Community (hereafter SADC) tribunal. In their responses to these decisions, States have voiced serious concern and accused ICaTs of overstepping the limits of consent, at times criticizing (as the Chinese Foreign Minister put it in response to the *South China Sea* award) the 'Arbitral Tribunal's ...

[107] See Section 3.2.2.1.

self-expansion of power', which had led it to act 'ultra vires', which meant the award 'has no legal effect'.[108] At times, as part of their critique, States asserted that the principle of *Kompetenz-Kompetenz* was to be exercised within the limits of accepted principles of treaty interpretation: in the Chinese government's terms, 'the tribunal itself is not given the absolute right to determine whether it has the jurisdiction or not'.[109] But even the most critically minded States soon seem to realize that (to quote Hamamoto again) 'from a strictly legal point of view, such an argument is without merit', as the ICaTs' decision is protected as an exercise of its *compétence de la compétence*.

While struggling to attack concrete controversial jurisdictional decisions from within the systems of dispute settlement, States have frequently sought to respond at a more general level, by redefining the scope of consent. Their reactions are informed by the States' own view of the proper understanding of their consent, but they are designed to produce effects beyond the scope of the individual dispute in which the controversial decision was rendered. Withdrawing from jurisdiction is the most obvious response – without effect on disputes already pending, but (depending on the notice period) removing the possibility of future proceedings. Withdrawing is permitted under virtually all jurisdiction-conferring instruments: a State opting to withdraw certainly sends a signal – and at the same time, it makes use of a right expressly granted to it. Significantly, States use this right rather frequently. The precise 'drivers'[110] are not always easy to discern; often it may be dissatisfaction with a controversial jurisdictional holding *and* with the outcome of the decision on the merits. But at least for certain withdrawals, there seems to be a clear link with a court's or tribunal's prior, controversial construction of a jurisdictional title. The reaction, by the US, to controversial jurisdictional rulings by the ICJ illustrates the 'power of withdrawal' in response to perceived jurisdictional overreach:

- Following *Nicaragua*, the US left the ICJ's optional clause system and never returned: it did so, stating that the Court Judgment on jurisdiction and admissibility 'represents an overreaching of the Court's limits'.[111]

[108] Remarks by Chinese Foreign Minister Wang Yi on the Award of the So-called Arbitral Tribunal in the South China Sea Arbitration. Available at: www.mfa.gov.cn/ce/ceus//eng/zt/abc123/t1380241.htm, last accessed 2 December 2022.

[109] Ibid. This echoed points made by the US following the ICJ's *Nicaragua* judgment: see Security Council, 'Verbatim Record of the 2716th Meeting' (1986), UN Doc. S/PV.2718, p. 46; *Nicaragua* v. *United States of America*, fn. 53.

[110] Joost Pauwelyn and Rebecca J. Hamilton, 'Exit from International Tribunals' (2018) 9(4) *Journal of International Dispute Settlement* 679–690.

[111] United States, 'Statement concerning US Withdrawal from the Proceedings Initiated by Nicaragua in the International Court of Justice' (1985) 24 ILM 246. The link with the earlier

- Perhaps exhausted by a series of Iranian lawsuits based on the 1955 Treaty of Amity,[112] including claims that tested the scope of the Court's jurisdiction, the US expressed its desire to terminate the Treaty in 2018.[113]
- Having (largely unsuccessfully) defended a number of cases under the 1963 Vienna Convention on Consular Relations,[114] the US in 2005 withdrew from the Optional Protocol establishing the ICJ's jurisdiction.[115]

Similar responses can be observed in the field of investment arbitration, where withdrawal from jurisdiction-conferring International Investment Agreements (hereafter IIAs) has become a significant factor. While the concerns are manifold, often merging substantive and jurisdictional objections to the approach of investment tribunals, the EU Member States' concerted action to terminate intra-EU BITs is a clear example of a withdrawal driven by controversial jurisdictional decisions, which ignored the demands of EU integration rules: notwithstanding *Achmea*,[116] investment arbitration for the past five years have continued to uphold their jurisdiction under intra-EU BIT,[117] to the point where the majority of EU Member States now have

Nicaragua decision upholding jurisdiction is clearly drawn by William Michael Reisman, 'Has the International Court Exceeded Its Jurisdiction?' (1986) 80(1) *American Journal of International Law* 128–134.

112 Treaty of Amity, Economic Relations, and Consular Rights, 284 UNTS 93 (adopted 15 August 1955, entered into force 16 June 1957).

113 The US National Security Advisor at the time explained the withdrawal in 'jurisdictional terms', noting (with respect to the ICJ's provisional measures order in the *Alleged Violations of the 1955 Treaty of Amity, Economic Relations, and Consular Rights Case* (Provisional measures order) [2018] ICJ Rep. 623) that 'we are disappointed that the ICJ failed to recognize that it has no jurisdiction to issue any order with respect to sanctions the United States imposes to protect its own essential security under the treaty': see American Rhetoric, 'John Bolton Remarks on the Withdrawal from the Optional Protocol on Dispute Resolution to the Vienna Convention on Diplomatic Relations' (6 August 2019). Available at: www.americanrhetoric.com/speeches/johnboltonviennaoptionalprotcolsuswithdrawl.htm, last accessed 2 December 2022.

114 Vienna Convention on Consular Relations, 596 UNTC 261 (adopted 24 April 1963, entered into force 19 March 1967).

115 Charles Lane, 'US Quits Pact Used in Capital Cases', *Washington Post* (10 March 2005). Available at: https://archive.globalpolicy.org/empire/un/2005/0310deathpenalty.htm, last accessed 2 December 2022.

116 CJEU, *Slovak Republic* v. *Achmea BV*, Case C-284/16, EU:C:2018:158; CJEU, *Republic of Moldova* v. *Komstroy LLC*, Case C-741/19, EU:C:2021:655.

117 See, for example, *RREEF Infrastructure (G.P.) Limited, RREEF Pan-European Infrastructure Two Lux S.à.r.l* v. *Kingdom of Spain*, ICSID, Decision on Jurisdiction (6 June 2016) Case No. ARB/13/30, paras. 74–75; and many references in Julian Scheu and Petyo Nikolov, 'Jurisdiction of Tribunals to Settle Intra-EU Investment Treaty Disputes' (2021) 36(1) *ICSID Review* 171–188, at 171–172, footnote 6.

pledged to phase out and terminate intra-EU BITs through express treaty action.[118] As with the United States conduct referred to above, such withdrawal cannot take away jurisdiction in pending cases; but it limits State exposure prospectively.

More briefly, one can at least plausibly speculate that controversial jurisdictional rulings have affected States' attitudes towards the granting of consent to jurisdiction, and prompted them to leave ICaTs a more limited interpretative leeway. That at least seems to be suggested by State practice under the optional clause of Article 36(2) of the ICJ Statute. As has been observed elsewhere, the incremental rise in the number of optional clause declarations has been accompanied by a preference for longer declarations, which include broader and more comprehensive reservations.[119] Of the twenty-five declarations submitted since the year 2000, only three are without reservation.[120] In formulating reservations, States such as the United Kingdom, Japan or India have added significant new reservations on top of existing ones,[121] in Japan's case, in what has been termed a 'pre-emptive strike' against potential future cases about sensitive questions of whaling.[122] By the same token, for common reservations concerning military matters or prior disputes, the trend is towards comprehensive exclusions, reflecting careful planning on how undesirable cases can be avoided.[123]

Stepping back from the details, these impressionistic comments point to a link between (a) the general acceptance of the *compétence de la compétence* principle and (b) the relatively regular practice of States modifying their jurisdictional consent in response to negative surprises. Unlike with respect to the struggle for interpretative authority surveyed in Section 3.3.1, the fault lines are clear: ICaTs have a 'sweeping hold' over the meaning of jurisdictional titles – States that feel they have to respond against real or perceived mandate creep cannot respond 'from within'. Absent non-compliance,

[118] Agreement for the Termination of Bilateral Investment Treaties between the Member States of the European Union, OJ 2020 No. L169/1 (signed 5 May 2020, entered into forced 29 August 2020).

[119] For details, see Christian Tomuschat, 'Article 36', in Zimmermann and Tams, fn. 73, pp. 712–798, paras. 70–72.

[120] ICJ, 'Declarations Recognizing the Jurisdiction of the Court as Compulsory'. Available at: www.icj-cij.org/en/declarations, last accessed 2 December 2022. The list includes 'unreserved' declarations submitted by Dominica, Timor-Leste and Djibouti.

[121] For details: see ibid.

[122] Michael A. Becker, 'Japan's New Optional Clause Declaration at the ICJ: A Pre-Emptive Strike?' (2015) *EJIL: Talk!* Available at: www.ejiltalk.org/japans-new-optional-clause-declaration-at-the-icj-a-pre-emptive-strike/, last accessed 2 December 2022.

[123] *Pars pro toto*, see the declarations submitted by Germany and Nigeria: ICJ, fn. 120.

withdrawing from jurisdiction, and the more careful phrasing of jurisdictional conferrals, are the main tools at their disposal. The power of courts to determine the scope of their jurisdiction is unassailable, but only its prudent exercise ensures continued State consent to binding dispute settlement.

3.4 CONCLUSION

This piece proceeded from a straightforward hypothesis: that the role of State consent in dispute settlement is peculiar and differs from the roles of consent in others fields. The preceding considerations have focused on bringing out the roles of consent in dispute settlement – so to facilitate comparison with consent in other settings. It seems to me that any such comparison needs to reflect four central takeaways.

First, State consent to dispute settlement is consent to a regime, or better still: to a process. This process has an uncertain outcome and it regularly involves decisions that determine, affirm and interpret the scope of consent.

Second, these decisions are beyond the control of States: they are taken by an independent entity (an ICaT) that has the authority to make binding decisions (in fact is set up to make them) and that is only superficially constrained by agreed principles of interpretation.

Third, in making decisions determining the scope of State consent, ICaTs exercise a clearly established authority, granted to them in constituent documents or derived from their universally recognized inherent powers. While their decisions can rarely be challenged within a particular dispute resolution proceeding, their wider impact on future disputes between future litigants remains uncertain and varies from one dispute settlement regime to another.

Fourth, while (and perhaps because) States' control over consent during processes of dispute settlement is qualified, State consent remains an indispensable condition for the exercise of jurisdiction. State consent to jurisdiction is nearly always formal, express and direct; reflecting a high degree of State control over access to binding dispute settlement.

4

International Organizations and the Disaggregation of Consent

CATHERINE BRÖLMANN

4.1 INTRODUCTION

This chapter examines how 'consent', traditionally taken as a foundational element in international law, fares in the institutionalized environment of contemporary international legal life. The central argument is that international organizations (hereafter IOs), both as actors consenting to international law and as institutional spaces[1] for other actors, have changed the operation or even the nature of consent in international law, as they have made the components of the act of consent come apart.

The notion of consent appears in more than a few ways. This is to say that the elements of definition (acceptance of a norm of international law),[2] and also the explanatory angle may vary. It is thus helpful to mention also some perspectives not taken in this chapter. Many studies proceed from consent as a prerequisite imbedded in some way in international law. This prerequisite may then be addressed with an analytical approach (e.g. identifying a trend of 'nonconsensualism' at work in public international law as a whole)[3] or a normative approach (e.g. '[consent] creates a cumbersome status quo bias').[4] In the latter category is also the proposition to understand (equal State) consent not as a right to repudiate a norm, but as a right to (equal State)

[1] 'Institutionalized' and 'institutional' in this chapter refer to the institutional character and structure of IOs in particular.

[2] This chapter's working definition is loosely adopted from Samantha Besson, 'State Consent and Disagreement in International Law-Making: Dissolving the Paradox' (2016) 29(2) *Leiden Journal of International Law* 289–316, at 295.

[3] Nico Krisch, 'The Decay of Consent: International Law in an Age of Global Public Goods' (2014) 108(1) *American Journal of International Law* 1–40.

[4] Andrew T. Guzman, 'The Consent Problem in International Law' (2011) *UC Berkeley Working Paper Series* 1–63. Available at: https://escholarship.org/content/qt04x8x174/qt04x8x174.pdf?t=lnrx4u, last accessed 11 January 2023, at 2.

participation in the formation of the norm.[5] Either way, important questions, for instance, regarding legitimacy, are raised.[6] This chapter, however, is not primarily concerned with the role of consent for the general sphere or – depending on the lens – system of international law.

Rather, the starting point of this chapter is consent as an act of the subject. When the notion is further unpacked, it shows at least four facets, which tend to be alternately emphasized in legal discourse but rarely articulated as such. These are consent as an intentional state; consent as an agreed (symbolic) expression of that intentional state; the object of consent; and the manifestation thereof as a concrete legal-normative situation binding the subject. In the archetypal image of consent, most likely because of its connection with situations involving the natural person, these facets are closely or even inextricably linked. The intentional state and the agreed symbol(s) for its expression are taken together – summarized here as 'giving consent' – while the object of consent is close to the normative outcome. This is the picture in which one person expresses consent to another and vice versa, in order to create mutual rights and obligations, on the precise substance of which clear agreement exists; as when X buys a good from Y. While all consent can be said to amount to acceptance of a rule as law, this scenario emphasizes the 'unanimous (intersubjective) acceptance for the same reasons'.[7] It may be summarized as 'consent as agreement'. There is also a picture in which X accepts a given rule as law without the intersubjective dimension, and this may be denoted by the general term of 'consent as acceptance'.[8] Both dynamics play a role in international law.

The argument made in this chapter is that in the context of IOs these different facets of consent have disaggregated. When the organization itself gives consent, the symbolic expression has come to be separated from the underlying intentional state. Where the organization appears as an institutional space for the consent of others, the object of consent can be far removed in time and especially in substance from the *Rechtsmoment* at which the consent bears normative effect for the consent-giver. In these instances the object of consent may not overlap with the eventual normative effect.

5 Besson, fn. 2.

6 Thomas Christiano, 'The Legitimacy of International Institutions', in Andrei Marmor, *The Routledge Companion to Philosophy of Law* (New York: Routledge, 2014), pp. 380–393; Besson, fn. 2.

7 Besson, fn. 2, at 295.

8 I use these expressions without engaging with the (convincing) argument about how consent is not an 'agreement' in the substantive sense, made by Samantha Besson: see ibid.

Why is this relevant? After all, it is abstract and formal-doctrinal language, which over the years has lost considerable persuasive power. Indeed, it has been pointed out how in recent decades social change is often brought about not by adjusting the law, but by moving outside the sphere of formal international law altogether.[9] Unsurprisingly, 'informal law' (a notion that leaves us to explore whether it amounts to 'international law' or not)[10] and 'soft law' (a notion that predominantly is taken to refer to non-law) have been studied extensively in recent years. It is one reason for which this chapter chooses to focus precisely on consent as a formal-legal tool and, while 'consent' can be used to refer to a commitment to 'law' in the full variety of normative shades, to start squarely within the formal-legal realm with a concomitantly formal and binary notion of consent.

Disaggregation of consent in all cases can, arguably, be traced to the same origin – the mechanistic view of organizations as legal subjects ultimately in the service of States, mentioned in Section 4.2. It is not equally apparent in all cases however. The distinction and possibly separation between the intentional state and its expression is an elusive phenomenon and arguably under-theorized. In contrast, the separation between the object of consent, on the one hand, and the normative outcome for the consent-giver, on the other hand, is well documented – albeit as part of a different narrative. A prime example of such separation are the cases of delegated powers and ensuing possibilities for majority decision-making, often within a formal institutional structure.

In order to advance the claim of disaggregation, this chapter aims to capture particular features of the act of consent in the context of organizations. The disaggregation of consent performed by IOs themselves (Section 4.2) is determined largely *a contrario*, on the basis of what is not said, against the background of the way in which the 'juridical will' of organizations in general has been construed. The act of consent of States within the institutional space of organizations (Section 4.3) is addressed through a more straightforwardly descriptive approach. The chapter concludes with some remarks on the implications of the disaggregation of consent (Section 4.4).

4.2 CONSENT AS INTENTIONAL STATE AND AS EXPRESSION

Giving consent thus has two dimensions: one is the psychological condition or mental state, for which this chapter uses the term 'intentional state' because of

9 Krisch, fn. 3, at 2: 'international law is often sidelined'.

10 Joost Pauwelyn, 'Informal International Lawmaking: Framing the Concept and Research Questions', in Joost Pauwelyn, Ramses A. Wessel and Jan Wouters (eds.), *Informal International Lawmaking* (Oxford: Oxford University Press, 2012), pp. 13–34.

its association with directedness.[11] It is a particular manifestation of the 'juridical will'[12] – the construct that serves to operationalize the legal agency of actors that are allowed participation in a legal system and thus become legal subjects or persons. The other is the conduct symbolizing or signifying that intentional state. Seen through a semiotic lens, to give consent comprises the *signifié* (the realm of content) and the *signifiant* (its expression). This duality is borne out by the classic reference in the Vienna Conventions on the Law of Treaties (hereafter VCLT) to 'expression of consent to be bound'.[13] The concept underscores that both facets of giving 'consent' (leaving aside the distinction between law and obligation) are present in international law. They are generally not separated, and an emphasis on one of them, depending on the context, is only implicit.

In one account '[b]y the end of the eighteenth century', for treaties, 'emphasis was placed upon the meeting of minds, or upon the expression of a "mutual will" through reciprocal consent to the terms of the agreement'.[14] Meanwhile the ability to perform consent, as a manifestation of will, had come to be firmly located in the State.[15] By the nineteenth century, the State's unique corporate and fictional nature had largely disappeared from view,[16] facilitating the incorporation of domestic law analogies in international law and the idea of the State as a 'natural person' amounting to a *personne morale*.

The anthropomorphic view of the State was to some extent dismantled by interbellum scholarship,[17] with States rediscovered as corporate entities alongside other international actors.[18] In truth, however, international law doctrine

[11] John R. Searle, 'What Is an Intentional State?' (1979) 88(349) *Mind* 74–92.

[12] Taken as a construct, in contrast to the notion of 'will' as a specific psychological state in, for example, the analysis of Alain Pellet, 'The Normative Dilemma: Will and Consent in International Law-Making' (1992) 12(1) *Australian Yearbook of International Law* 22–54; Pellet, Chapter 1 in this volume.

[13] Arts. 11–17 of the Vienna Convention on the Law of Treaties (VCLT), 1155 UNTS 331 (adopted 23 May 1969, entered into force 27 January 1980).

[14] Matthew Craven, 'The Ends of Consent', in Michael J. Bowman and Dino Kritsiotis (eds.), *Conceptual and Contextual Perspectives on the Modern Law of Treaties* (Cambridge: Cambridge University Press, 2018), pp. 103–135, p. 113.

[15] See different forms of consent identified by de Vattel: see Emer de Vattel, *Le droit des gens, ou Principes de la loi naturelle appliqués à la conduite et aux affaires des nations et des souverains*, Vol. 1, translated by Charles G. Fenwich (Washington, DC: Carnegie institution of Washington, 1916), p. 9.

[16] Martti Koskenniemi, 'The Wonderful Artificiality of States' (1994) 88 *Proceedings of the Annual Meeting of the American Society of International Law* 22–29.

[17] Such as by Kelsen, Brierly and Nekam: see Catherine Brölmann, *The Institutional Veil in Public International Law: International Organisations and the Law of Treaties* (Oxford: Hart, 2007), pp. 70–71.

[18] Besson, fn. 2, at 295.

and practice have always remained at ease with the attribution of legally relevant 'states of mind' to States. It has been pointed out how in the course of the twentieth century the ability to *think* became linked to the doctrine of 'fundamental' rights of States.[19] References to psychological agency and the attribution of will, such as consent, to legal actors are, as in domestic (private) law, common in international law. Witness classic references such as '[t]he signed text is … the … expression of the common will of the parties'.[20] As before, '[o]rthodox international law proceeds from the assumption that States have a legal conscience, [even if] it has no workable or operational way to explain how this is supposed to work',[21] and it operates 'as if governments, let alone States, had determinable states of mind'.[22]

This is decidedly different when it comes to IOs, as was brought to light by the codification process of the law of treaties once its scope was to be expanded to include IOs.[23] It is important to note that this is not about the actual possibility of corporate entities such as organizations forming a 'will'. Political theory and political philosophy have shown how group agents are distinct from the sum of their component parts because of a particular decision-making structure,[24] and how by the ability to formulate a separate, collective will, they would become susceptible to bearing responsibility.[25] Philosophy of language can explain how (groups of) human individuals may 'impose intentionality on governments or international organisations', and how *opinio juris* as part of the formation of custom may amount to

[19] Jean d'Aspremont, 'The Doctrine of Fundamental Rights of States and Anthropomorphic Thinking in International Law' (2015) 4(3) *Cambridge Journal of International and Comparative Law* 501–520, at 515.

[20] International Law Commission (hereafter ILC), 'Third Report on the Law of Treaties, by Sir Humphrey Waldock, Special Rapporteur', *Yearbook of the International Law Commission* (1964) Vol. II, UN Doc. A/CN.4/167 and Add. 1–3, pp. 5–66, p. 56 (my translation); ILC, 'Reports of the International Law Commission on the Second Part of Its Seventeenth Session and on Its Eighteenth Session', *Yearbook of the International Law Commission* (1966) Vol. II, UN Doc. A/6306/Rev.1, pp. 169–364, p. 220 (my translation).

[21] Anthony Carty, 'Doctrine versus State Practice', in Bardo Fassbender and Anne Peters (eds.), *The Oxford Handbook of the History of International Law* (Oxford: Oxford University Press, 2012), pp. 972–996, p. 976.

[22] Philip Allott, 'The Concept of International Law' (1999) 10(1) *European Journal of International Law* 31–50, at 39.

[23] Brölmann, fn. 17.

[24] Philip Pettit, 'Collective Persons and Powers' (2002) 8(4) *Legal Theory* 443–470; Fleur Johns (ed.), *International Legal Personality* (Farnham: Ashgate, 2010), pp. xi–xxix, footnote 87.

[25] From the angle of the international relations scholarship: see, for example, Toni Erskine, 'Assigning Responsibilities to Institutional Moral Agents: The Case of States and "Quasi-States"', in Toni Erskine (ed.), *Can Institutions Have Responsibilities? Collective Moral Agency and International Relations* (London: Palgrave Macmillan, 2003), pp. 19, 20.

an 'institutional object', brought about by speech acts that express beliefs and intentions.[26]

Thus considered, the attribution of an intentional state to one composite actor (e.g. an IO) should not require more effort than the attribution to another composite actor (e.g. a State). However, legal doctrine seems unconnected to such philosophical and psychological considerations. As has been pointed out, 'the collective and institutional structure of states has not been discussed by international law scholars'.[27] From an immanent perspective we find that a legal actor's capability to have an intentional state depends foremost on the legal framework, and on the legal imaginary within which the actor is situated. The traditional hesitation to attribute full-fledged agency to IOs and the ensuing mechanistic image of organizations as international actors would naturally affect the subjective, psychological dimension of the organization's legal consent. This appears to be confirmed in doctrine and practice, but it leaves only subtle traces.

Now, the intentional state of a consent-giver may be disregarded when agreed symbolic conduct exists for the expression of such juridical will. We find this in the law of treaties, as in 'signature' for 'consent',[28] or the 'passing of twelve months' for 'acceptance'.[29] In these cases, a presumption of consent as an intentional state can exist without the need for its ascertainment.

On the other hand, where an agreed symbolic expression is lacking, the intentional state (the 'juridical will') as such must be established, which is a more intricate process. This process can, however, be fluid and flexible when an actor's capacity in this regard is uncontested, as in the case of States. The powerful image of States as legal actors capable of a psychological condition, summarized as 'will', is reflected, for example, in the weight traditionally given to the State's 'intention' to consent to a juridical agreement, or conversely to a

[26] Sufyan Droubi, '*Opinio Juris*: Between Mental States and Institutional Objects', in Sufyan Droubi and Jean d'Aspremont (eds.), *International Organisations, Non-State Actors, and the Formation of Customary International Law* (Manchester: Manchester University Press, 2020), pp. 62–101, p. 79.

[27] Specifically in relation to the tenability of 'any analogy between state and individual consent' and to the view of 'states as unitary subjects of international law', which 'reduces states to individuals in a domestic setting': see Besson, fn. 2, at 295. Somewhat different from the corporate dimension, see the collective dimension of the responsibility of both States and organizations treated in Samantha Besson (ed.), *Theories of International Responsibility Law* (Cambridge: Cambridge University Press, 2022); see, more specifically, Paolo Palchetti, 'Responsibility of Members of an International Organization: Collective and/or Individual?', in Besson, *Theories of International Responsibility Law*, ibid., pp. 143–164.

[28] Art. 12 VCLT.

[29] Art. 20(5) VCLT.

non-legal arrangement.[30] In contrast, the restricted agency of IOs[31] is reflected, for instance, in the fact that so far no cases appear to exist in which the subjective intentional state of an IO has prevailed.

This again turns on the particular conceptualization of organizations in which they have been accommodated as legal persons but not wilful legal persons or *personnes morales*.[32] The codification process of the 1986 Vienna Convention on the Law of Treaties between States and International Organizations or between International Organizations (hereafter the 1986 Convention), from 1971 to 1986, gives evidence of that. From the text, the commentaries and the *travaux* in general emerges, next to a States' concern about the possibility of independent action on the part of organizations, primarily a mechanistic view of IOs as legal actors.[33] To be sure, according to the regime of the 1986 Convention, IOs could engage in treaty-making, especially if they can produce an agreed sign of a legal will expressed to this effect, such as the formal 'expression of consent to be bound by a treaty'. At the same time, IOs as such are not ascribed the moral and political 'considerations', and 'intentions' that go with the legal *persona* projected upon States. Thus, the 1986 Convention envisages the possibility of error or fraud in the conclusion of a treaty on the part of an organization, but in order to ascertain that this is the case, the claimant must resort to the internal institutional order of the IO, or – in other words – to the Member States.[34] The Convention provides that States 'acquiesce in the validity of the treaty', while organizations must be seen to have 'renounced the right to invoke that ground [of invalidity]' based on the passing

30 A novel focus on external conduct rather than the intentional state of the disputing parties is found in *Case concerning Maritime Delimitation and Territorial Questions between Qatar and Bahrain (Qatar* v. *Bahrain)* [1994] ICJ Rep. 112. A classic reliance on the state's intention is found in *Iron Rhine Arbitration (Belgium/Netherlands)*, PCA, Award (24 May 2005) 140 ILR 130, para. 142; *Dispute concerning Delimitation of the Maritime Boundary in the Bay of Bengal* (*Bangladesh/Myanmar*), Judgment of 14 March 2012, ITLOS Reports 2012, p. 4.

31 Catherine Brölmann, 'Capturing the Juridical Will of International Organisations', in Droubi and d'Aspremont, fn. 26, pp. 42–61.

32 On 'moral personality' in the civil law tradition see, for example, Frederic W. Maitland, 'Moral Personality and Legal Personality' (1905) 6(2) *Journal of the Society of Comparative Legislation* 192–200; Évelyne Pisier-Kouchner, 'La notion de personne morale dans l'oeuvre de Léon Duguit' (1974) 11/12(2) *Quaderni fiorentini per la storia del pensiero giuridico moderno* 667–684.

33 This proposition is elaborated in Brölmann, fn. 17.

34 Arts. 48, 49 of the Vienna Convention on the Law of Treaties between States and International Organizations or between International Organizations (hereafter 1986 Convention), UN Doc. A/Conf.129/15 (adopted 21 March 1986); ILC, 'Report of the International Law Commission on the Work of Its Thirty-Fourth Session', *Yearbook of the International Law Commission* (1982) Vol. II, Part Two, UN Doc. A/37/10, p. 53, para. 2 (regarding Art. 48(2)).

of a certain stretch of time.[35] In a general sense, the position of IOs is clear from the fact that 'the [International Law] Commission thought it worthwhile to point out that, in the present state of international law, it is States that are called upon to establish or recognize peremptory norms'.[36] The reluctance to ascribe juridical will, or an intentional state, to IOs is also reflected in the long-time idea of the impossibility of an IO's wrongdoing: ('[i]s it really conceivable that . . . organisations may . . . employ, the threat or use of force . . .?'),[37] while in relation to an early version of the Draft Articles on State Responsibility the International Law Commission (hereafter ILC) had stated that 'it must not be forgotten that, by their very nature, international organizations normally behave in such a manner as not to commit internationally wrongful acts'.[38] Clearly the adoption of the 2011 ILC Draft articles on the responsibility of international organizations[39] has confirmed an extent of IOs' coming of age,[40] in the sense of their being capable of wrongful conduct; however, this has not altogether changed the underlying mechanistic view of the legal subjectivity of organizations.

Also illustrative is the doctrinal discourse of *opinio juris*, which in some accounts of sources theory is the embodiment of consent, and in some other accounts too, at least in part, as practice and *opinio juris* cannot be separated to begin with.[41] The ascertainment of *opinio juris*, in the absence of agreed symbolic behaviour, focuses on the intentional state of legal actors. The search for a subjective psychological condition can be gleaned from the range of expressions used by the International Court of Justice (hereafter ICJ) to render the notion of *opinio juris*, which include 'feeling', 'belief', 'deliberate intention', 'awareness', 'conviction', 'general feeling' and 'actual consciousness'.[42]

35 Arts. 45(1)(b), 45(2)(b) of the 1986 Convention.

36 ILC, fn. 34, p. 56, para. 3 (regarding Art. 53).

37 Ibid., p. 55, para. 2.

38 ILC, 'Report of the International Law Commission on the Work of Its Twenty-Seventh Session', *Yearbook of the International Law Commission* (1975) Vol. II, Part One, UN Doc. A/10010/Rev.1, p. 87, para. 3 (emphasis added); both the article and the commentary were adopted in an unaltered version in 1996.

39 ILC, 'Draft Articles on the Responsibility of International Organizations', *Yearbook of the International Law Commission* (2011) Vol. II, Part Two, UN Doc. A/66/10, pp. 40–105, paras. 87–88.

40 On this point and the 'coming of age' frame see Brölmann, fn. 31, p. 59.

41 Besson, fn. 2, at 295: 'contexts, like customary international law-making . . . in which consent occurs not by expressing or stating, but by doing'. Proceeding from the view that both practice and *opinio juris* are a form of practice; John Tasioulas, 'Custom, *Jus Cogens*, and Human Rights', in Curtis A. Bradley, *Custom's Future: International Law in a Changing World* (Cambridge: Cambridge University Press, 2016), pp. 95–116, pp. 103–105.

42 Collected in the context of the ILC project on the identification of custom; see ILC, 'Second Report on the Identification of Customary International Law, by Sir Michael Wood, Special

Given the aforementioned mechanistic image of the IO as a legal subject, the fact that *opinio juris* is not communicated by an agreed expression coupled with the ensuing reliance on an underlying intentional state, would affect the position of organizations. This is confirmed by the modest role in the process of international custom formation accorded to IOs by the ILC in its 2018 Conclusions on identification of customary international law (hereafter 'the ILC Conclusions'),[43] with one reference to the practice of organizations[44] and no reference to their *opinio juris*.[45]

The minor role of IOs in the process of international custom formation[46] is consistent with the general reticence on the part of international lawyers and policy-makers in regard of organizations, and with the limits in international law's imagery when it comes to IOs as full-fledged legal subjects. These are factors that may explain how, for the establishment of customary international law, both the element of *opinio juris* and the element of (distinctly willed) practice can pose a challenge when these must be ascertained in an IO.

The language of consent, whether one takes it as alluding to 'self-limitation' or rather to 'authority assertion', has a strong connotation of legal agency. It 'invites us to think about the State, in organic terms, as a morally autonomous agent capable of pursuing "the dictates of its own will"'.[47] This goes to underline the relevance of studying consent in relation to IOs, precisely because it also points to the challenge of incorporating organizations in international law; the construction of organizations' legal agency is closely connected to the role that organizations are *allowed* to play in international life, perhaps more than to any particular formal institutional features. As has

Rapporteur', *Yearbook of the International Law Commission* (2014) Vol. II, Part One, UN Doc. A/CN.4/672, pp. 163–203, para. 67.

43 ILC, 'Draft Conclusions on Identification of Customary International Law, with Commentaries', in *Yearbook of the International Law Commission* (2018) Vol. II, Part Two, UN Doc. A/73/10, pp. 119–200.

44 Ibid., p. 119, Conclusion 4(2): 'In certain cases, the practice of international organizations also contributes to the formation, or expression, of rules of customary international law.' For commentaries, see ibid., p. 130, paras. 5–6; Bordin, Chapter 11 in this volume.

45 Implicitly in the commentary to Conclusion 4(2): see ILC, fn. 43, p. 130, paras. 5–6.

46 While organizations have a modest role in the text of the ILC Conclusions, it is true that the commentary to Conclusion 10 (2) states that it 'applies *mutatis mutandis* to forms of evidence of acceptance as law (*opinio juris*) of international organizations': see ibid., p. 141, para. 7. As emerges from the cited materials in the footnotes of the Third Report of the Special Rapporteur, this might be called groundbreaking in respect of previous times: see ILC, 'Third Report on Identification of Customary International Law, by Sir Michael Wood, Special Rapporteur', *Yearbook of the International Law Commission* (2015) Vol. II, Part One, UN Doc. A/CN.4/673, pp. 93–134, paras. 68–797; at the same time, in absolute terms the role of organizations is certainly modest when compared to that of States.

47 Craven, fn. 14, p. 112.

been argued elsewhere, this may be related to the historical development of international law doctrine; to limitations to our legal imagination; or to philosophical considerations such as that the IO is not a 'natural' political community, and less suited for protecting all people's interests; or to legal considerations such as that an IO is ultimately too transparent as a legal structure, with the Member States all too present; or to political considerations such as a wish not to share power.[48]

4.3 THE OBJECT OF CONSENT AND ITS MANIFESTATION

Not only are IOs actors who give consent, they also exist as an institutional space for other actors, especially States, consenting to international law.[49] An 'institutional space' in this chapter is epitomized by the framework of a formal intergovernmental organization, but the vertical dynamic, captured early on by the notion of 'centralization' that Hans Kelsen used in relation to the United Nations (hereafter UN),[50] is present also in less formal intergovernmental arrangements, such as treaty regimes with a 'constitutional character', for instance, featuring a compliance mechanism or a mechanism for subsequent decisions by treaty parties. Here as well the focus is on the formal rule-making framework, while a variety of 'soft law' made by and in organizations[51] is left out of account.

Where the organization acts as an institutional space, the disaggregation of consent does not so much concern the intentional state of consent and its expression, but rather points to a distance between the object of consent (in treaty-making comprising *consensus ad idem*, as part of mutual consent), on the one hand, and its effect as a 'processual trigger providing for the imposition of certain obligations',[52] on the other hand. These facets, traditionally closely linked, can become separated in an institutional context – with the distance between them specifically relating to substance, rather than to time.

[48] Brölmann, fn. 31, pp. 59–60.

[49] Important actors such as individuals and non-governmental organizations (NGOs) are left out of account here because of the formal framework.

[50] Hans Kelsen, *The Law of the United Nations: A Critical Analysis of Its Fundamental Problems* (London: Stevens and Sons, 1950), p. 329. He saw centralization as a precondition for the differentiation between the 'duties, rights and competences' of the organization and those of the Member States.

[51] See the findings of José E. Alvarez who takes an effect-based approach rather than a pedigree-based approach: see José E. Alvarez, *International Organisations as Law-Makers* (Oxford: Oxford University Press, 2005).

[52] With regard to treaties specifically, see Craven, fn. 14.

Of course, organizations are known also for providing the infrastructure for acts of consent where such a distance does not exist. This is the case of the law-making treaties concluded under the auspices of the UN,[53] or the Conventions prepared and 'sponsored' by the International Labour Organization (hereafter ILO).[54] Frequently then, the institutional structure facilitates stages in the process leading up to the act of formal consent, which as such is largely outside, or parallel to, the institutional framework of the organization. Still, it is noteworthy that also in the early stages of the treaty-making process leading up to final consent, in the institutional space results may be obtained that are unfeasible in a completely open, contractual space. Thus, when the Conference on Disarmament did not succeed in reaching consensus on the adoption of the text of the Comprehensive Nuclear Test-Ban Treaty, the text was famously submitted by Australia to the UN General Assembly[55] and could be adopted with support even exceeding the required two-thirds majority.[56]

The mixing of contractual and institutional elements in States' treaty-making in the context of IOs is a long-time phenomenon, with the ILO still as a striking example among contemporary IOs, some eighty years after France repudiated the ILO constitution for the organization's encroachment upon State sovereignty through the convention-making technique.[57] The object of consent, however, in these instances, remains close to the normative effect.

In contrast, it is with the various forms of organizations' legal acts that a separation between the object of consent and its manifestation or 'outcome' is at issue. In the context of decision-making by organizations, we see the enactment of decisions and standards that are typically based on a constitutive treaty and which doctrinally appear as a produced part of the law of treaties canon; at the same time the conceptual boundaries of the 'treaty' become

[53] Many of the multilateral treaties deposited with the Secretary-General: see United Nations, 'Multilateral Treaties Deposited with the Secretary-General'. Available at: https://treaties.un.org/Pages/ParticipationStatus.aspx?clang=_en, last accessed 12 January 2023.

[54] Art. 19 of the Constitution of the ILO (Part XIII of the Treaty of Versailles (adopted 28 June 2013, entered into force 10 January 1935)).

[55] UN Doc. A/50/L.78 (6 September 1996).

[56] Art. 18(2) Charter of the United Nations and Statute of the International Court of Justice (adopted 24 June 1945, entered into force 24 October 1945); United Nations General Assembly, 'Adoption of the Agenda and Organization of Work: Comprehensive Test-Ban Treaty: Letter dated 22 August 1996 from the Permanent Representative of Australia to the United Nations addressed to the Secretary-General', 26 August 1996, UN Doc. A/50/1027.

[57] Charles Rousseau, *Droit international public* (Paris: Recueil Sirey, 1953), p. 39; Catherine Brölmann, 'ILO Convention Practice Mixed Methods in Norm-Setting for Social Justice', in George Politakis, Tomi Kohiyama and Thomas Lieby (eds.), *ILO100: Law for Social Justice* (Geneva: International Labour Office, 2019), pp. 137–149.

apparent. The phenomenon is most stark in cases of majority rule-making, which as yet seem to be concentrated in IOs with a predominantly technical field of operation.[58] In an IO with near-universal membership, this can in certain areas move written legal rules from a context of freedom of treaty to one of institutional obligation. But outside an institutional context, 'there is no evidence that . . . members of the international community endorse *legislative* techniques based on majority law-making'.[59]

For instance, in the International Civil Aviation Organization (hereafter ICAO), 'standards' are adopted or amended by the Council by a two-thirds majority, which become effective unless the majority of the members register an objection within three months.[60] In the ICAO, where the opting-out system originates, the element of centralization is particularly apparent, as the Council is not a plenary organ. Comparable procedures for the enactment of 'regulatory acts' exist, for instance, in the World Health Organization (hereafter WHO) (where, however, the law-making function resides in the plenary organ)[61] and in several other Specialized Agencies.[62] In the category of – less formal-institutional – Multilateral Environmental Arrangements, the procedure laid down in the 1987 Montreal Protocol on Substances that Deplete the Ozone Layer for the enactment of 'adjustments' to the original standards with regard to controlled substances, goes further than the ICAO regime on 'standards' in that such adjustments – failing consensus adopted by a two-thirds majority – are explicitly said to be binding on all parties to the Protocol.[63] It is arguable that instances such as these, in which the object of consent is detached from its manifestation (in effect because the object was

[58] Leaving aside the general difficulty of making a distinction between political and technical organizations, or between organizations that mainly act as a forum for inter-State negotiation, on the one hand, and organizations that act primarily as a machinery for technical rule-making activities, on the other hand: see, for example, Anne Peters and Simone Peter, 'International Organizations: Between Technocracy and Democracy', in Fassbender and Peters, fn. 21, pp. 170–197.

[59] A – still tenable – statement by Gennady Danilenko: see Gennady Danilenko, *Law-Making in the International Community*, 3rd ed. (Leiden: Martinus Nijhoff, 1993). He refers to comments of States participating in the third United Nations Conference on the Law of the Sea (1973–1982): see ibid., pp. 67–68 (emphasis added).

[60] Arts. 37, 54 (l) and (m) of the Convention on International Civil Aviation (Chicago Convention), 15 UNTS 295 (adopted 7 December 1944, entered into force 4 April 1947).

[61] Arts. 21, 22 of the Constitution of the WHO, 14 UNTS 185 (adopted 22 July 1946, entered into force 7 April 1948).

[62] Jan Klabbers, *An Introduction to International Organizations Law* (Cambridge: Cambridge University Press, 2022), pp. 164–165.

[63] Arts. 2(9), 11 (b) of the Montreal Protocol on Substances that Deplete the Ozone Layer, 1522 UNTS 3 (adopted 16 September 1987, entered into force 1 January 1989).

not clearly defined to begin with), are only possible in a, to some degree, centralized, 'constitutionalized' environment – whether this environment be a formal institutional space, as in an organization, or a specific field of law such as environmental law or human rights law, with self-reflective mechanisms (e.g. the 'living instrument' doctrine in treaty interpretation).

The disaggregation of consent within an institutional space is relatively well documented, for one because the decision-making powers of IOs have been an element in debates, for instance, concerning the legitimacy of IOs,[64] the publicness of public international law[65] or the protection, and production, of global public goods.[66]

There has been considerable debate as to whether the aforementioned regulatory acts of IOs and regimes should be considered as 'treaty practice', that is, whether they are to be considered as 'treaty obligations' for the organization's Member States deriving from the constituent treaty, or on the contrary as 'legislative acts' issued by an organization simply binding its Member States. One important factor in the classification of these standard-setting acts is the legal image of IOs: as relatively open 'treaty regimes' that maintain a clear connection with their constituent treaties, or as independent 'legal orders' with a relatively closed structure.

The doctrinal stance of grounding IOs' decisions in the consent to the constitutive treaty, in accordance with a somewhat old-fashioned 'treaty analogy', points to the first choice. It was the approach of the ICJ, when it treated the conflict between the 1971 Montreal Convention and SC Resolution 748 – originating in the UN Charter – as a traditional case of conflicting treaties.[67] It was also the perspective of the Court of First Instance of the European Communities in the 2005 *Kadi Case*,[68] before the Grand Chamber of the

64 See, for example, Jochen von Bernstorff, 'Procedures of Decision-Making and the Role of Law in International Organizations', in Armin von Bogdandy, Rüdiger Wolfrum, Jochen von Bernstoff, Philipp Dann and Matthias Goldmann (eds.), *The Exercise of Public Authority by International Institutions: Advancing International Institutional Law* (Berlin: Springer, 2010), pp. 777–806.

65 See, for example, an early enquiry, including into the place of the UN, in Bruno Simma, 'From Bilateralism to Community Interest in International Law' (Volume 250) *Collected Courses of the Hague Academy of International Law*, 1994, pp. 217–384.

66 Krisch, fn. 3.

67 *Case concerning Questions of Interpretation and Application of the 1971 Montreal Convention Arising from the Aerial Incident at Lockerbie (Libyan Arab Jamahiriya* v. *United States of America)* (Provisional Measures) [1992] ICJ Rep. 114, p. 126.

68 Court of First Instance, *Yassin Abdullah Kadi* v. *Council of the European Union and Commission of the European Communities* (*Kadi I CFI*) (Case T-315/01) EU:T:2005:332 [2005] ECR II-3649, 21 September 2005.

European Court of Justice (hereafter ECJ) in 2008[69] resorted to an unprecedented 'constitutional' approach.

At some point in the life of an organization, the latter perspective may come to prevail for reasons of practical and doctrinal necessity, as such perhaps part of a broader dynamic of 'sectoral constitutionalization',[70] and the organization itself may adopt a 'legislative' discourse. An example is the European Union legal order, where obligations stemming from 'community legislation' (Article 288 of the Treaty of the Functioning of the European Union) are clearly set apart from obligations stemming from treaty practice of the Member States, the 'primary' European Union law.

This aside, the opposition between the categories of 'treaty law' and 'international legislation' does not alter the fact that decisions by IOs, also where these in some accounts transcend the category 'treaty norms', are generally seen as grounded in the consent on the part of the States involved. Here the consent element is subsumed in the institutional space, engendering the construct of *consent ex ante*. The notion of consent as such then tends to 'acceptance', as mentioned in Section 4.1. Relatedly and at a more concrete, doctrinal level the delegation theory prevails over the treaty analogy theory.[71]

In short, this is not an argument about 'non-consensualism'.[72] Rather, the foregoing indicates how consent is remarkably resilient in international law.[73] That the classic image of consent appears stretched, is precisely because of the disaggregation of its components.

4.4 CONCLUSION

The global environment of today is marked by institutionalization, which in the context of this chapter refers first of all to IOs. Organizations can be seen both to give consent to international law and to act as institutional spaces for

69 CJEU, *Yassin Abdullah Kadi and Al Barakaat International Foundation* v. *Council of the European Union and Commission of the European Communities* (*Kadi I*) (Joined Cases C-402/05 P and C-415/05 P) EU:C:2008:461 [2008] ECR I-6351, 3 September 2008, GC.

70 Anne Peters, 'Constitutionalisation', in Jean d'Aspremont and Sahib Singh (eds.), *Concepts for International Law: Contributions to Disciplinary Thought* (Cheltenham: Edward Elgar, 2019), pp. 141–153, pp. 144–146.

71 Klabbers, fn. 62, pp. 161–163; Pieter Jan Kuijper, 'Delegation and International Organizations' (Volume 426) *Collected Courses of the Hague Academy of International Law*, 2022, pp. 9–239.

72 In a different vein, and on how majority decision-making in organizations (without a right to opt out) is compatible with the principle of 'equal state consent' once consent is taken in the sense of 'participation', see Besson and Martí, Chapter 14 in this volume.

73 Krisch, fn. 3, at 39; Besson, fn. 2.

the consent of others, notably States. The central argument of this chapter is that IOs have brought about a disaggregation of consent. This can be gleaned from the separation of the presumed intentional state and the expression thereof – two components that traditionally are taken together. It can also be observed in the distance brought between the object of consent, on the one hand, and its manifestation in an actual legal relation or obligation, on the other hand.

IOs are often presented as the essential non-State actors' success story, because, in the course of a century, they seemingly have come to act as legal actors on a par with States. But the legal agency of organizations has more to it. A look at the development of organizations as international legal actors since their entry on the international stage, including the facet of 'legal will' – as a shorthand for various intentional states, in addition makes clear that this development is closely connected to the role that organizations have been allowed to play in international law.

In the act of giving consent, both the psychological condition or 'intentional state' to commit to a particular obligation, arrangement or relation, and the expression thereof are traditionally presumed present in international law. Given the general reservations vis-à-vis full-fledged legal agency of organizations in the way of States, the underlying psychological dimension of consent has been inevitably underserved. It then logically follows that where IOs are involved, more reliance exists on the external, symbolic expression of consent.

Because of its disaggregation, the consent given by IOs constitutes a break with the traditional and persisting picture of a legal act by an anthropomorphic subject.[74] This can in turn be said to underline the 'mechanization' of the organization as a legal subject. In the long run, it might counterbalance threshold notions of 'natural' and 'original' legal persons, and may contribute to the opening up of international law in terms of legal personality and facilitate the inclusion of other actors. Or in a more general spirit, the disaggregation of consent brought about by organizations contributes to the awareness regarding the institutional nature of all consenting subjects in international law, including States.[75] The declining relevance of the intentional state fits a long-reported general trend of deformalization and objectivization in international law, which pertains first of all to States.

[74] See fn. 17, 18 and accompanying text.

[75] See Samantha Besson, *Reconstructing the International Institutional Order* (Paris: OpenEdition Books/Editions du Collège de France, 2021). Available at: https://books.openedition.org/cdf/12335, last accessed 12 January 2023.

An example is the 'objectivization of intention' that was key to the landmark ICJ *Qatar* v. *Bahrain*.[76]

When States in an institutional space perform their act of consent, disaggregation occurs when the object of consent and the outcome become detached, notably when the object has not been clearly defined so as to leave room for further normative choices. This is the case of (majority) decision-making of organizations that at the doctrinal level tends to be explained on the basis of a theory of delegation.[77] A particular concern in this regard is that where flexibility increases, predictability and formality decrease. This is helpful for addressing problems, but not necessarily for levelling an uneven playing field among powerful and less powerful States. This argument runs along similar lines as the one on the (dis)advantages of informality in law-making, which have been mentioned frequently, and the continuous effort to strike a balance.[78] One author has pointed out that the structures created by 'non-consensualist' initiatives (which here refers to majority decision-making), 'in formal or informal guise', reduce the number of decision-makers, and they do so 'typically not in an egalitarian fashion but in a way that entails a loss of control for all but the most powerful players'.[79]

It is noteworthy that the term 'non-consensualism' is used frequently to refer to majority decision-making. Indeed, the flexibility of such mechanisms is considerable, up to a point that for some observers it would amount to 'non-consensual' law-making. This chapter is not as such focused on 'non-consensualism' as a general trend, but the question as to the scope of (the concept of) consent is a fair one. There may be a boundary to that scope (or to 'consensualism') – after which a legal relation or obligation would, in form and time, be so remote from an act of consent, that it would lapse into an instance of non-consensualism. How to locate that boundary, however, remains unclear. Such because of the inherent subjectivity, the link with certain doctrinal pre-assumptions (regarding, e.g., State sovereignty, or delegation of powers), and the concept of consent that is adopted (e.g. consent as 'acceptance' might tolerate more of a separation of components than consent as 'agreement'). Either way, it seems that in doctrine and in discursive practice, consent persists as a foundation for the creation of formal legal rules stemming from organizations' acts, irrespective of whether these acts are conceptualized

[76] *Qatar* v. *Bahrain*, fn. 30, para. 27.

[77] See fn. 71 and accompanying text. These references to 'delegation theory' as traditionally referred to in international law, especially in relation to a separate legal order, leave aside possible issues of unanimity of consent: Besson and Martí, Chapter 14 in this volume.

[78] Pauwelyn, fn. 10.

[79] Krisch, fn. 3, at 31.

as treaty law or as legislation. This is confirmed by the fact that 'the pressure for change has mostly been absorbed not through new binding international rules and formal institutions, but through alternative means of regulation'. To this, the author adds that it is 'ones in which consensual elements are weak and hierarchies are often pronounced'.[80]

The different conceptualizations of consent – emphasizing agreement and acceptance, respectively, as proposed at the outset of this chapter – may tie in with the private and public law procedural characteristics that international law combines. At first blush, it would seem that when consent is given in an institutional context, disaggregation of the object of consent and its manifestation occur in a 'public law dynamic', such as with decisions and 'acts', accompanied by an understanding of consent as 'acceptance'. On the other hand, less disaggregation appears to occur when consent is given through a legal act with a contractual flavour in a 'private law dynamic', such as treaty-making in the institutional space of the organization. The understanding of consent then tends towards that of 'agreement'.

Finally, from the chapter it appears that the act of consent in international law responds to all things institutional. What common meaning can be found in the two very different institutional scenarios – the IO giving consent and the IO acting as an institutional space for the consent of others? Perhaps the most prominent aspect is a break – sadly and wisely – with the anthropomorphic picture in law that of old has had a strong hold, also in international law: 'consent [as] an expression of the individual's desires and commitments'.[81]

80 Krisch, fn. 3, at 34.

81 George P. Fletcher, *Basic Concepts of Legal Thought* (Oxford: Oxford University Press, 1996), p. 118.

5

Consenting to International Law in Five Moves

JEAN D'ASPREMONT

5.1 INTRODUCTION

Consenting to international law is the object of a very prolific literature and case law. What consenting to international law possibly means, entails, requires, prescribes, performs, hides and orders seems to indefinitely call for new studies and scholarly discussions.[1] At the risk of indulging in oversimplification, this chapter contends that the abundant literature and case law pertaining to consent to international law can be reduced to five key discursive moves.[2] These five moves are performed, as is claimed here, by almost anyone engaging with the question of consent to international law, be such engagement on the more orthodox side or the more critical side of the argumentative spectrum. Indeed, whether they hold that consent has always been the foundation of international law and inevitably remains so,[3] whether they hold

[1] Duncan B. Hollis, 'Why State Consent Still Matters: Non-State Actors, Treaties, and the Changing Sources of International Law' (2005) 23(1) *Berkeley Journal of International Law* 137–174, at 173: 'maligned as the doctrine may be, international law needs more scholarship, not less, on the doctrine of consent as a basis of obligation in international law, looking at who is consenting, on whose behalf, and to whom such consent is being given'; Stephen C. Neff, 'Consent', in Jean d'Aspremont and Sahib Singh (eds.), *Concepts for International Law: Contributions to Disciplinary Thought* (Cheltenham: Edward Elgar, 2019), pp. 127–140, p. 138: 'If there is universal agreement on the importance of consent in international law, there is all too little agreement on anything else about it. It may be considered a sad comment on the intellectual state of international law that there can be, even now, so much uncertainty on so vital a subject. Putting the matter in the best light, one might say instead that the diversity of views on the subject is a sign of healthy debate within international legal circles.'

[2] On the notion of discourse, see generally Hayden White, *Tropics of Discourse: Essays in Cultural Criticism* (Baltimore: Johns Hopkins University Press, 1978), pp. 4–5.

[3] Andrew T. Guzman, 'Against Consent' (2012) 52(4) *Virginia Journal of International Law* 747–790; Nico Krisch, 'The Decay of Consent: International Law in an Age of Global Public Goods' (2014) 108(1) *American Journal of International Law* 1–40; Jutta Brunnée, 'Consent'

that consent has been a criterion of validity and inevitably remains so,[4] whether they hold that consent is receding either as a foundation or as a validity criterion,[5] whether they claim that consent has never played the ultimate role in terms of legal validity,[6] whether they attempt to refine the role of consent,[7] whether they claim that consent plays no role in relation to a whole range of international legal rules,[8] whether they seek to promote what they construe as non-consensual law-making processes,[9] whether they claim

(last updated January 2022), in Rüdiger Wolfrum (ed.), *Max Planck Encyclopedia of Public International Law* (Oxford: Oxford University Press, 2008). Available at: https://opil.ouplaw.com/display/10.1093/law:epil/9780199231690/law-9780199231690-e1388, last accessed 13 December 2022, paras. 16–17.

4 Theodore Christakis, 'Human Rights from a Neo-Voluntarist Perspective', in Jörg Kammerhofer and Jean d'Aspremont (eds.), *International Legal Positivism in a Post-Modern World* (Cambridge: Cambridge University Press, 2014), pp. 421–450, p. 423; Eva Kassoti, 'Beyond State Consent? International Legal Scholarship and the Challenge of Informal International Law-Making' (2016) 63(2) *Netherlands International Law Review* 99–131.

5 Krisch, fn. 3. On the decline of State consent in WTO Law, see Joost Pauwelyn, 'Sources of International Trade Law: Mantras and Controversies at the World Trade Organization', in Samantha Besson and Jean d'Aspremont (eds.), *The Oxford Handbook on the Sources of International Law* (Oxford: Oxford University Press, 2017), pp. 1027–1046, p. 1039.

6 Herbert L. A. Hart, *The Concept of Law*, 2nd ed. (Oxford: Oxford University Press, 1994), p. 225; Alain Pellet, 'The Normative Dilemma: Will and Consent in International Law-Making' (1992) 12(1) *Australian Year Book of International Law* 22–53, at 22; Jean d'Aspremont, *Formalism and the Sources of International Law: A Theory of the Ascertainment of Legal Rules* (Oxford: Oxford University Press, 2011), pp. 21–24; Thomas M. Franck, *The Power of Legitimacy among Nations* (Oxford: Oxford University Press, 1990), p. 187; Jean d'Aspremont, 'Herbert Hart in Today's International Legal Scholarship', in Kammerhofer and d'Aspremont, fn. 4, pp. 114–150, p. 145. On Hart's rejection of consent as a foundation and a criterion of validity, see Dennis Patterson, 'Transnational Governance Regimes', in Kammerhofer and d'Aspremont, fn. 4, pp. 401–420, p. 411; Richard Collins, 'Sources and the Legitimate Authority of International Law: A Challenge to the "Standard View"', in Besson and d'Aspremont, fn. 5, pp. 703–723, p. 713.

7 Olusoji Elias and Chin L. Lim, *The Paradox of Consensualism in International Law* (Leiden: Brill, 1998).

8 Christian Tomuschat, 'Obligations Arising for States Without or Against Their Will' (Volume 241) *Collected Courses of the Hague Academy of International Law*, 1993, pp. 195–374; Anne Peters, 'Global Constitutionalism Revisited' (2005) 11 *International Legal Theory* 39–69; Bruno Simma, 'From Bilateralism to Community Interest in International Law' (Volume 250) *Collected Courses of the Hague Academy of International Law*, 1993, pp. 217–384; Pellet, fn. 6, at 23; Bruno Simma and Andreas L. Paulus, 'The Responsibility of Individuals for Human Rights Abuses in Internal Conflicts: A Positivist View' (1999) 93(2) *American Journal of International Law* 302–316, at 304.

9 Laurence R. Helfer, 'Nonconsensual International Lawmaking' (2008) 1 *University of Illinois Law Review* 71–125; Guzman, fn. 3; Joel P. Trachtman, *The Future of International Law: Global Government* (Cambridge: Cambridge University Press, 2013).

that consent both as a foundation or as a criterion of validity is a myth or conceptually impossible,[10] whether they contend that consent as a foundation and/or a criterion of validity is an actuality that is detrimental to international law and that should be unmade,[11] whether they claim that consent follows the variations of the forms of international law-making processes,[12] whether they

[10] Hersch Lauterpacht, *The Function of Law in the International Community* (Oxford: Oxford University Press, 1933), pp. 420–421; Andrew Clapham, *Brierly's Law of Nations: An Introduction to the Role of International Law in International Relations*, 7th ed (Oxford: Oxford University Press, 2012), pp. 50–51; Gerald Fitzmaurice, 'The Foundations of the Authority of International Law and the Problem of Enforcement' (1956) 19(1) *Modern Law Review* 1–13; Gerald Fitzmaurice, 'The General Principles of International Law Considered from the Standpoint of the Rule of Law' (Volume 92) *Collected Courses of the Hague Academy of International Law*, 1957, pp. 1–227, p. 45; Iain Scobbie, 'Legal Theory as a Source of International Law: Institutional Facts and the Identification of International Law', in Besson and d'Aspremont, fn. 5, pp. 493–512, pp. 502–508; Wouter G. Werner, 'State Consent as Foundational Myth', in Catherine Brölmann and Yannick Radi (eds.), *Research Handbook on the Theory and Practice of International Lawmaking* (Cheltenham: Edward Elgar, 2016), pp. 13–31; Samantha Besson, 'Sources of International Human Rights: How General Is General International Law?', in Besson and d'Aspremont, fn. 5, pp. 837–870, pp. 845–846.

[11] Peters, fn. 8; Guzman, fn. 3; Jan Klabbers, 'International Legal Positivism and Constitutionalism', in Kammerhofer and d'Aspremont, fn. 4, pp. 264–290, pp. 286–287; Jonathan I. Charney, 'Universal International Law' (1993) 87(4) *American Journal of International Law* 529–551; Ingo Venzke, 'Post-modern Perspectives on Orthodox Positivism', in Kammerhofer and d'Aspremont, fn. 4, pp. 182–212, p. 187. For a rejection of international law being identified through the past material or historical conditions of its production and a claim to make law derived from characteristics that belong to the norms themselves, see Roberto Ago, 'Positive Law and International Law' (1957) 51(4) *American Journal of International Law* 691–733.

[12] Krisch, fn. 3; Guzman, fn. 3, at 789–790; Anthony Carty, 'Conservative and Progressive Visions in French International Legal Doctrine' (2005) 16(3) *European Journal of International Law* 525–537; David Kennedy, 'The Sources of International Law' (1987) 2(1) *American University Journal of International Law and Policy* 1–96, at 20; David Kennedy, 'When Renewal Repeats: Thinking Against the Box' (1999–2000) 32 *New York University Journal of International Law and Politics* 335–500, at 355, 366. On the need to distinguish consent and formalism, see also d'Aspremont, *Formalism and the Sources*, fn. 6, pp. 21–24; Samantha Besson, 'Theorizing the Sources of International Law', in Samantha Besson and John Tasioulas (eds.), *The Philosophy of International Law* (Oxford: Oxford University Press, 2010), pp. 163–186, p. 166; Elias and Lim, fn. 7, p. 193; Olivier Corten, *Méthodologie du droit international public* (Brussels: Éditions de l'Université de Bruxelles, 2009), pp. 53–54, 58; Alain Pellet, 'Lotus que de sottises on profère en ton nom! Remarques sur le concept de souveraineté dans la jurisprudence de la Cour mondiale', in Edwige Belliard (ed.), *L'état souverain dans le monde d'aujourd'hui: Mélanges en l'honneur de Jean-Pierre Puissochet* (Paris: Pedone, 2008), pp. 215–230.

espouse[13] or reject[14] a custom-formation role for consent,[15] whether they deem inescapable the role of consent in treaty,[16] whether they lament the poor descriptive virtues of consent when it comes to international law-making

[13] Dionisio Anzilotti, *Scritti di diritto internazionale pubblico* (Padua: CEDAM, 1956–1957), p. 38; Heinrich Triepel, *Völkerrecht und Landesrecht* (Aalen: Scientia Verlag, 1899), p. 95; Grigory I. Tunkin, *Theory of International Law*, translated by William E. Butler (Cambridge, MA: Harvard University Press, 1974), p. 124; Charles Chaumont, 'Cours général de droit international public' (Volume 129) *Collected Courses of the Hague Academy of International Law*, 1970, pp. 333–546, p. 440. For an illustration of the occasional resilience of the association between custom and consent in international legal thought, see Hugh Thirlway, *The Sources of International Law*, 2nd ed. (Oxford: Oxford University Press, 2019), p. 16; John Tasioulas, 'Custom, *Jus Cogens*, and Human Rights', in Curtis A. Bradley (ed.), *Custom's Future: International Law in a Changing World* (Cambridge: Cambridge University Press, 2016), pp. 95–116; Niels Petersen, 'The Role of Consent and Uncertainty in the Formation of Customary International Law', in Brian D. Lepard (ed.), *Reexamining Customary International Law* (Cambridge: Cambridge University Press, 2017), pp. 111–130; Werner, fn. 10, p. 13; Klabbers, fn. 11, p. 284; Upendra Baxi, 'Sources in the Anti-Formalist Tradition: "That Monster Custom, Who Doth All Sense Doth Eat"', in Besson and d'Aspremont, fn. 5, pp. 225–244, p. 232; José Luis Martí, 'Sources and the Legitimate Authority of International Law: Democratic Legitimacy and the Sources of International Law', in Besson and d'Aspremont, fn. 5, pp. 724–748, p. 739.

[14] Akbar Rasulov, 'The Doctrine of Sources in the Discourse of the Permanent Court of International Justice', in Christian Tams and Malgosia Fitzmaurice (eds.), *Legacies of the Permanent Court of International Justice* (Leiden: Martinus Nijhoff, 2013), pp. 271–318, p. 276; Hersch Lauterpacht, 'Decisions of Municipal Courts as a Source of International Law' (1929) 10 *British Yearbook of International Law* 65–95, at 83; Clapham, fn. 10, p. 50; Josef L. Kunz, 'The Nature of Customary International Law' (1953) 47(4) *American Journal of International Law* 662–669, at 664; Maurice Mendelson, 'The Subjective Element in Customary International Law' (1995) 66(1) *British Yearbook of International Law* 177–208, at 185; Guzman, fn. 3, at 775–776; Pellet, fn. 6, at 36–37; Krisch, fn. 3, at 2–3; James Patrick Kelly, 'The Twilight of Customary International Law' (2000) 40(2) *Virginia Journal of International Law* 449–543, at 473; Maiko Meguro, 'Customary International Law and Non-State Actors: Between Anthropomorphism and Artificial Unity' (17 November 2017) *Amsterdam School Research Paper Series, No.* 2018-29. Available at: https://papers.ssrn.com/sol3/papers.cfm?abstract_id=3071305, last accessed 4 October 2022; Iain Scobbie and Sufyan Droubi (eds.), *Non-State Actors and the Formation of Customary International Law* (Manchester: Manchester University Press, 2018).

[15] For a discussion on the relationship between consent and custom, see generally Anthony Carty, *The Decay of International Law? A Reappraisal of the Limits of Legal Imagination in International Affairs* (Manchester: Manchester University Press, 2019), pp. 61–65; Fernando Lusa Bordin, 'A Glass Half Full? The Character, Functions and Value of the Two-Element Approach to Identifying Customary International Law' (2019) 21(3–4) *International Community Law Review* 283–306, at 291–293; Brunnée, fn. 3, paras. 16–17; Neff, fn. 1, pp. 131–134.

[16] On the function of consent in treaty law, see Thirlway, fn. 13, p. 17; Brunnée, fn. 3, paras. 5–14; Shabtai Rosenne, 'Consent and Related Words in the Codified Law of Treaties', in *Mélanges offerts à Charles Rousseau* (Paris: Pedone, 1974), pp. 229–248; Matthew Craven, 'The Ends of Consent', in Michael J. Bowman and Dino Kritsiotis (eds.), *Conceptual and Contextual Perspectives on the Modern Law of Treaties* (Cambridge: Cambridge University

processes,[17] whether they foreground the serious shortcomings of consent as a source of legitimacy of international law,[18] most scholars and judges make the discursive moves depicted in this chapter. The five discursive moves that are discussed in turn in the following sections can be summarized as corresponding to the reproduction of a very modernist understanding of authority (Section 5.2), the constitution of the very subject that is consenting (Section 5.3), the anonymization of the author of consent (Section 5.4), the reversal of the temporality of the legal discourse on consent (Section 5.5) and the adoption of very binary patterns of thought (Section 5.6).

Before outlining these five discursive moves made by almost all those who engage with consent to international law, an important preliminary remark about the aim of this chapter is warranted. Reducing international lawyers' discussions of consent to a handful of discursive moves seeks to show neither that such moves are ridiculous nor that they are conceptually compelling. In fact, this chapter has no other ambition than to shed light on what international lawyers do when they mobilize the inscriptions that compose the international legal discourse in their discussion of the question of consent to international law. And yet, the account offered here remains premised on the idea that the discursive moves made by international lawyers around the idea of consent bear heavily upon the type of political legitimacy, the type of geography, the type of responsibility, the type of temporality and the type of hermeneutics that international law is serving.

5.2 'PASTICHING' MODERN AUTHORITY

The literature and case law discussing the idea of consent to international law can be read as a crude iteration of the modern model of authority, that is one whereby legitimate and valid authority ought to be grounded in the consent of those subjected to it.[19] From this modernist perspective, consenting to international law boils down not only to securing the consent of those subjected to

Press, 2018), pp. 103–135; Klabbers, fn. 11, p. 284; Werner, fn. 10; see Hollis, Chapter 6 in this volume.

[17] Werner, fn. 10, p. 28; Krisch, fn. 3, at 1–40.

[18] Besson and Martí, Chapter 14 in this volume. On the idea that consent cannot be a ground for international law's legitimate authority, see Samantha Besson, 'State Consent and Disagreement in International Law-Making: Dissolving the Paradox' (2016) 29(2) *Leiden Journal of International law* 289–316; Matthias Goldmann, 'Sources in the Meta-Theory of International Law: Exploring the Hermeneutics, Authority, and Publicness of International Law', in Besson and d'Aspremont, fn. 5, pp. 447–468, p. 465; Martí, fn. 13, pp. 739–744.

[19] In the same vein, see Martti Koskenniemi, 'The Politics of International Law' (1990) 1 *European Journal of International Law* 4–32, at 4–6; Martti Koskenniemi, *From Apology to*

its rules but also to projecting a contractual image of international law. Indeed, by virtue of the idea of consent, international law comes to mirror the social contract so dear to modern political theorists. In that sense, the modern necessity to consent to international law and the contractual approach to international law[20] mutually support one another in projecting an image of a non-coerced[21] but produced[22] international law.

The modern model of authority that informs engagements with consent to international law is certainly very tangible in debates on the history of international law where the 1648 Peace of Westphalia[23] narrative has come to serve no other role than embedding international law in the modern story of the social contract.[24] This modern concept of authority can similarly be witnessed in the scholarly findings about the serious shortcomings of consent

Utopia: The Structure of International Legal Argument (Cambridge: Cambridge University Press, 2006), pp. 21–22; Craven, fn. 16; Neff, fn. 1, pp. 128–129; Collins, fn. 6, pp. 712–714.

20 On the rise of the contractual approach to international law (with an emphasis on the work of Francisco Suarez), see the considerations of Stephen C. Neff, *Justice among Nations: A History of International Law* (Cambridge, MA: Harvard University Press, 2014), pp. 153–158.

21 In the same vein, see Werner, fn. 10, p. 15; Craven, fn. 16, pp. 103–135.

22 On the centrality of the idea of production in modern thought, see Michel de Certeau, *L'écriture de l'histoire* (Paris: Gallimard, 1975), pp. 27–28.

23 For Andreas Osiander, the birth of the story of Westphalia can be located in the work of Nys: see Andreas Osiander, 'Sovereignty, International Relations, and the Westphalian Myth' (2001) 55(2) *International Organization* 251–287. For José-Manuel Barreto, the origin of this periodization goes back as early as 1845 with Henry Wheaton: see José-Manuel Barreto, 'Cerberus: Rethinking Grotius and the Westphalian System', in Martti Koskenniemi, Walter Rech and Manuel Jimenez Fonseca (eds.), *International Law and Empire* (Oxford: Oxford University Press, 2017), pp. 149–176, pp. 159–160. For the claim that the myth of Westphalia was created by Leo Gross in the middle of the twentieth century, see Luis Eslava, Michael Fakhri and Vasuki Nesiah, *Bandung, Global History, and International Law: Critical Pasts and Pending Futures* (Cambridge: Cambridge University Press, 2017), p. 15; Leo Gross, 'The Peace of Westphalia, 1648–1948' (1948) 42(1) *American Journal of International Law* 20–41; see also the remarks of Jennifer Pitts, 'Empire and Legal Universalism in the Eighteenth Century' (2012) 117(1) *American Historical Review* 92–121. On the arbitrariness of the choice for 1648, see Matthew Craven, 'Introduction: International Law and Its Histories', in Matthew Craven, Malgosia Fitzmaurice and Maria Vogiatzi (eds.), *Time, History and International Law* (Leiden: Martinus Nijhoff, 2007), pp. 1–25, p. 8; Bardo Fassbender, 'Peace of Westphalia (1648)' (last updated February 2011), in Rüdiger Wolfrum (ed.), *Max Planck Encyclopedia of Public International Law* (Oxford: Oxford University Press, 2008). Available at: https://opil.ouplaw.com/display/10.1093/law:epil/9780199231690/law-9780199231690-e739?prd=MPIL, last accessed 13 December 2022, paras. 7, 18–19.

24 It is important to note that Westphalia is not only a pastiche of modern authority. It is also a historical marker meant to locate the birth of international law in Europe and make the history of international law a part of the history of Western civilization. On the idea that 1648 makes the history of international law so European and Northern and pushes to the margins of the experience of African, Asian or South American societies, see Craven, 'Introduction', fn. 23.

as a source of legitimacy of international law and the need for correctives.[25] The care for ensuring a non-coerced consent in the law of treaties can also be construed as a continuation of this modern blueprint of submission to authority. The same quest for a modern grounding of authority pervades debates on the consent to jurisdiction of international courts and tribunals.[26]

It must be acknowledged that the modernism of international lawyers' engagements with consent is not only that which pertains to the modern blueprint of authority. The literature and the case law on consent can also be read as a modern pastiche, for they replicate one of the modern techniques of insertion into the real.[27] In fact, providing a consenting subject to a text, a constitution, a statute, a treaty, is a way to anchor it into the real.[28] From this perspective, international law is even more real – and less a literary construction – once the consent of those subjected to it has been secured and evidenced. In that sense, requiring that international law be consented to is yet another way in which international lawyers[29] have tapped into the modern primacy enjoyed by discourses about the real.[30] The discourse on

[25] Besson and Martí, Chapter 14 in this volume. On the idea that consent cannot be a ground for international law's legitimate authority, see Besson, fn. 18.

[26] On the question of consent to jurisdiction, see Boisson de Chazournes, Chapter 10 in this volume; Tams, Chapter 3 in this volume; Clément Marquet, *Le consentement étatique à la compétence des juridictions internationales* (Paris: Pedone, 2022); United Nations General Assembly (hereafter UNGA), 'Declaration on Principles of International Law concerning Friendly Relations and Co-operation among States in accordance with the Charter of the United Nations' (24 October 1970), A/RES/25/2625, s. 1, Principle 2, para. 5: 'International disputes shall be settled on the basis of the Sovereign equality of States and in accordance with the principle of free choice of means.' There is also an abundant case law on the question of consent to jurisdiction. Among others, see *Status of Eastern Carelia* (Advisory Opinion) [1923] PCIJ Ser. B No. 5, p. 27; *East Timor (Portugal* v. *Australia)* [1995] ICJ Rep. 90, para. 34; *Interpretation of Peace Treaties with Bulgaria, Hungary and Romania* (Advisory opinion) [1950] ICJ Rep. 65, p. 71; *Chevron Corporation and Texaco Petroleum Company* v. *The Republic of Ecuador (II)*, PCA, Third Interim Award on Jurisdiction and Admissibility (27 February 2012) Case No. 2009-23, para. 4.61.

[27] Compare with the argument of Alain Pellet, for whom consent is a nineteenth-century construction meant to give a scientific explanation to international law: see Pellet, fn. 6, at 23.

[28] Michel Foucault, *L'ordre du discours* (Paris: Gallimard, 1971), pp. 29–30.

[29] On the primacy of the real in international law, see generally the remarks of Jean d'Aspremont, 'The Rage against Scienticism in International Law' (2022) 33(2) *European Journal of International Law* 679–694; Jean d'Aspremont, 'A Worldly Law in a Legal World', in Andrea Bianchi and Moshe Hirsch (eds.), *International Law's Invisible Frames* (Oxford: Oxford University Press, 2021), pp. 110–123.

[30] On the modern primacy of discourses about the real over other discourses, see generally Hayden White, *The Content of the Form: Narrative Discourse and Historical Representation* (Baltimore: John Hopkins University Press, 1987), p. 57; Michel Foucault, *Les mots et les choses* (Paris: Gallimard, 1966), p. 89. Foucault later claimed that determining exactly when discourses about the real became the carrier of a truth is irrelevant: see Michel Foucault, *La*

consent to international law, as it is found in the literature and case law, can thus be read as a many-sided pastiche of modern thought.

5.3 CONSTITUTING THE CONSENTING SUBJECT

This second discursive move pertains to the constitution of the very subject consenting to international law, its regimes or its rules. Indeed, each time consent is required, ascertained, evidenced or contested, a consenting subject is constituted. This is no accident. Because it seeks to reproduce a very modern model of submission to authority, whereby those subjected to authority must consent to that authority,[31] the literature and case law on consent to international law cannot avoid defining the consenting subject, that is, the subject that will be subjected to the authority that is consented to. Just like modern political theorists had to define and give a content to the beings consenting to the modern government instituted,[32] the literature and case law discussing consent must define whom consent must be secured from. In that respect, it is noteworthy – and certainly not benign – that the literature and case law on consent to international law has always elevated States and international organizations (hereafter IOs) into the consenting subjects rather than, say, the individuals populating the planet, the beings whose exploitation is legitimized by international law or the companies benefiting from international legal rules.[33] The literature and case law on consent thus projects an image of the world to which international law applies as a world of States and IOs.[34] This is nothing new, but yet very determinative of what type of world is

naissance de la biopolitique: Cours au Collège de France (1978–1979) (Paris: Gallimard, Seuil, 2004), p. 38; Bruno Latour, *Nous n'avons jamais été modernes: Essai d'anthropologie symétrique* (Paris: La Découverte, Syros, 1997), p. 24; Jürgen Habermas, *The Philosophical Discourse of Modernity: Twelve Lectures*, translated by Frederick G. Lawrence (Cambridge: Polity Press, 1987), p. 19.

31 See Section 5.2.

32 On the famous 1755 challenge of Thomas Hobbes' humanity by Jean-Jacques Rousseau, see Jean-Jacques Rousseau, *Discours sur l'origine et les fondements de l'inégalité parmi les hommes* (Paris: Flammarion, 2008).

33 See, for example, *The Case of the S.S. "Lotus" (France* v. *Turkey)* (Judgment) [1927] PCIJ Ser. A No. 10, p. 18: 'International law governs relations between independent States. The rules of law binding upon States therefore emanate from their own free will as expressed in conventions or by usages generally accepted as expressing principles of law and established in order to regulate the relations between those co-existing independent communities or with a view to the achievement of common aims.'

34 On the idea of the discourse on consent as empowering States and international organizations, see Craven, fn. 16.

constituted by international law.[35] In that sense, the whole discussion on consenting to international law is very conducive to a specific spatial definition of the world and a very specific geography.[36]

The literature and case law on consent is not only constitutive of the world of States and IOs to which international law applies, but also of those very States and IOs that ought to consent to international law.[37] In other words, the literature and case law on consent comes with a very particular and often uniform[38] understanding of what a State or an IO is. In that regard, one cannot help being struck by the deep irony that permeates the literature and case law on consent. Indeed, while excluding individuals from its spatial representation of the world and providing States and IOs with the privilege of consenting to international law, the literature and case law on consent come to define those States – and, to a lesser extent, IOs[39] – anthropomorphically, that is, as endowed with a human intellect enabling them to consent.[40] Said differently, the current discourse on consent to international law invites us to think of States – and possibly IOs – in organic terms as individually autonomous agents capable of promoting, individually or collectively, their views or interests.[41] It is even fair to say that the literature and case law on consent to international law is where the modern anthropomorphism of the international legal discourse is at its peak.[42] The modern individual, albeit preliminary excluded by the discourse on consent, is

35 See generally d'Aspremont, 'A Worldly Law', fn. 29.

36 On the idea that consent projects a territorial division of the world in unitary sovereign States, see Werner, fn. 10, p. 15.

37 Compare with the constitution of the human subject through the rise of human sciences, see Michel Foucault, *Dits et écrits, I (1954–1975)* (Paris: Gallimard, 2001), p. 691. The constitution of the subject by the frameworks through which it is discussed has been construed as a move typical of structuralism: see Étienne Balibar, *Passions du concept: Épistémologie, théologique et politique: Écrits II* (Paris: La Découverte, 2020), p. 257; on the idea that international legal thought is very structuralist, see Jean d'Aspremont, *After Meaning: The Sovereignty of Forms in International Law* (Cheltenham: Edward Elgar, 2021), pp. 5, 9; Jean d'Aspremont, 'Two Attitudes towards Textuality in International Law: The Battle for Dualism' (2022) 42(4) *Oxford Journal of Legal Studies* 963–984.

38 On the idea that consent carries the assumption of the consenting subject as a unitary actor, see Werner, fn. 10, pp. 15, 27; Simma and Paulus, fn. 8, at 305.

39 This is the argument of Catherine Brölmann for whom international law appears reluctant to attribute an intentional state to IOs: see Brölmann, Chapter 4 in this volume.

40 Compare with Jan Klabbers, *The Concept of Treaty in International Law* (Leiden: Martinus Nijhoff, 1996), p. 65: 'Not only is intent difficult to identify but it also imbues those who conclude agreements with a psychological state they may never really have had.'

41 Craven, fn. 16.

42 In the same vein, see Brölmann, Chapter 4 in this volume.

rehabilitated and comes to inhabit those States and IOs that ought to consent to international law,[43] be it at the price of acrobatic conceptual contortions.[44]

5.4 DE-AUTHORING CONSENT

The performative effect of the literature and case law on consent that has been described in Section 5.3 goes beyond that of the constitution of a State-centric human-minded consenting subject. For instance, it is also constitutive of the space where consent can be expressed, as well as the modes of expressing consent.[45] It would be of no avail to dwell upon these other constitutive effects of the discourse on consent here. What matters is, rather, to show that the constitution of the consenting subject is, in the literature and case law on consent, followed by an obliteration of that consenting subject. This is yet another discursive move that informs most of the literature and case law on consent. Indeed, as soon as it has been constituted by virtue of the discursive move examined in Section 5.3, the consenting subject is immediately forgotten. Being plunged into forgetfulness, the consenting subject is nowhere to be found and consent is left authorless. Such a discursive move can be described as a move of de-authoring the consent to international law. Said differently, once constituted, and once put at the centre of the world, according to the second discursive move, described in Section 5.3, the constituting subject is pulled out of that world, leaving the process of subjection to international law objectified and uncontested.[46] In other words, by virtue of such a de-authoring move, the consenting subject becomes a central absentee in the name of

43 On anthropomorphic thinking about the State, see generally Jean d'Aspremont, 'The Doctrine of Fundamental Rights of States and Anthropomorphic Thinking in International Law' (2015) 4(3) *Cambridge Journal of International and Comparative Law* 501–520; see anthropomorphic thinking at work in the expression of opinio juris, see Jean d'Aspremont, 'The Practicians', in Jean d'Aspremont, *The Discourse on Customary International Law* (Oxford: Oxford University Press, 2021), pp. 59–87.

44 International lawyers have often realized that their constructions of the consenting subject does not work all the way and calls for some *ad hoc* adjustments: see Bordin, Chapter 11 in this volume; Hollis, fn. 1, at 172; for an overview of such scholarly contortions, see Jean d'Aspremont, 'Introduction: Non-State Actors in International Law: Oscillating between Concepts and Dynamics', in Jean d'Aspremont (ed.), *Participants in the International Legal System: Multiple Perspectives on Non-State Actors in International Law* (Abingdon: Routledge, 2011), pp. 1–21.

45 Craven, fn. 16.

46 Compare with the death of the human in human sciences as a result of human sciences never discovering human nature, see Foucault, fn. 37, p. 691; Foucault, *Les mots et les choses*, fn. 30, p. 398.

whom international law can be perpetually deployed, mobilized, interpreted and re-interpreted.[47]

It must be acknowledged that de-authoring is a move that has been extensively theorized in critical literary theory. Whilst it is widely recognized that the author is a useful category that allows one to give unity and coherence to the text, to provide it with an origin, and even to explain (and accept) the contradictions perceived in the text,[48] critical literary theory has long shown that any literary work always carries with it the death of its author. Indeed, once a literary work has been produced and released, it is argued in literary theory that the individual having authored the work is condemned to be nothing more than the author of that literary work.[49] This entails that the author of the text is bound to always be an extension of that very text[50] and can thus not be the origin of such text any longer.[51]

The way in which consent to international law is thought and discoursed in the literature and the case law is no different. In fact, the consenting subject, just like the author from the perspective of critical literary theory, cannot survive the inscription it is supposed to have engendered. Once the inscription consented to has become an inscription for the sake of the international legal

[47] On this discursive technique, see Foucault, *Les mots et les choses*, fn. 30, pp. 19–31; Balibar, fn. 37, p. 257.

[48] Foucault, fn. 28, p. 28; Foucault, fn. 37, p. 850.

[49] Roland Barthes, 'La mort de l'auteur', in Roland Barthes, *Le bruissement de la langue: Essais critiques IV* (Paris: Seuil, 1984), pp. 61–68, p. 63; Foucault, fn. 37, pp. 688, 821, 829. Jonathan Culler speaks of the text being 'orphaned': see Jonathan Culler, *Structuralist Poetics*, 2nd ed. (New York: Routledge Classics, 2002), p. 155.

[50] On Derrida's famous claim that there is nothing outside the text see Jacques Derrida, *De la grammatologie* (Paris: Éditions de Minuit, 1967), pp. 225–226; see also the remarks of Geoffrey Bennington, *Jacques Derrida* (Paris: Seuil, 1991), p. 83; Peter Salmon, *An Event Perhaps: A Biography of Jacques Derrida* (London: Verso, 2020), p. 143. With an emphasis on legal studies, see the remarks of Pierre Legrand, 'Foreign Law: Understanding Understanding' (2011) 6(2) *Journal of Comparative Law* 67–177, at 80; Foucault, fn. 37, p. 829.

[51] On the idea that the origin of texts always ensues the texts themselves and thus cannot be the origin of that form anymore, see generally Jacques Derrida, *Marges de la philosophie* (Paris: Éditions de Minuit, 1972), pp. 12–17; Jacques Derrida, *L'écriture et la difference*, 1st ed. (Paris: Seuil, 1967), p. 410; Derrida, fn. 50, p. 87. On this aspect of Derrida, see the remarks of Bennington, fn. 50, p. 4; Salmon, fn. 50, pp. 50–51. In rejecting the common claim of an origin of the sign as being outside the sign, Derrida transposed his criticism of Husserl's phenomenology as resting on a pre-conceptual originary moment to his critique of structuralism: see Jacques Derrida, *Marges de la philosophie*, fn. 51, pp. 185–207; Jacques Derrida, *Le problème de la genèse dans la philosophie de Husserl* (Paris: Presses Universitaires de France, 2010); Jacques Derrida, *La voix et le phénomène: Introduction au problème du signe dans la phénoménologie de Husserl* (Paris: Presses Universitaires de France, 2016). In the same vein and in relation to the international legal discourse, see d'Aspremont, *After Meaning*, fn. 37.

discourse, the consenting subjects are condemned to vanish behind that inscription and be nothing more than an extension of that inscription. Nowhere is such retreat of the consenting subject more tangible than in the law of treaties. This is what I have called elsewhere the '"magic descendance" of the treaty'.[52] Indeed, once the parties to a treaty have consented to the treaty, they can only be the parties to the treaty of which they are an extension. As an extension of the treaty, the parties are thus dematerialized, dehumanized and, more generally, put out of time and out of space. It is true that every now and then, the name of the consenting parties must be invoked. For instance, those invoking the treaty will feel the need to refer to the consenting parties when the nature of the treaty as a treaty must be vindicated. Likewise, the consenting parties must also be invoked when content must be given to the text of the treaty.[53] Yet, on such occasions, the consenting parties are not retrieved, traced or resuscitated, but they are simply invoked without those invoking them in any need of even re-creating or re-inventing the consenting parties. In other words, the consenting parties have already vanished the moment they are mobilized or referred to and do not need to be called back.[54]

This discursive move whereby, after constituting the consenting subject, the treaty obliterates them, is not innocent. Indeed, as a result of this disappearance of the consenting parties, the treaty is shrouded in an anonymity of sorts that those invoking the treaty can conveniently take advantage of. Since the consenting parties are absorbed into the treaty, of which they are condemned to be only an extension, the treaty-making process is actually anonymized. By virtue of such anonymity, the treaty – and all that is claimed under its name – enjoys a life of its own out of time and out of space. As a result of this anonymity and life outside space and time, the treaty brings about non-responsibility: no one is made responsible for the treaty and what is claimed under its name. In other words, the treaty allows the consenting parties to evade responsibility for both the good and the suffering caused in the name of

52 Jean d'Aspremont, 'Current Theorizations about the Treaty in International Law', in Duncan B. Hollis (ed.), *The Oxford Guide to Treaties*, 2nd ed. (Oxford: Oxford University Press, 2020), pp. 46–58, 55.

53 See, however, Zarbiyev, Chapter 7 in this volume.

54 One could object that the consenting parties are, to some extent, reconstructed or resuscitated for law-ascertainment and content-determination purposes. But even if this were the case, that would mean that such consented authors had been obliterated or forgotten in a way that requires the subsequent reconstruction. Reconstruction or resuscitation of the consenting parties necessitates an earlier forgetfulness or a disappearance. On this idea, see generally Foucault, fn. 37, p. 836.

the treaty. Thanks to this perpetual absence of the consenting parties, those invoking the treaty can conveniently present themselves as the naïve followers walking the trail blazed by the absent consenting parties.

This third discursive move found in the literature and case law about consent calls for a final observation of a more epistemological nature. This move whereby the consenting subject that had just been constituted is obliterated can simultaneously be construed as the expression of the modern primacy of scienticism.[55] Indeed, if international law deserves the riveted status of a scientific discipline,[56] it ought to have no identified author, for disciplines, contrary to doctrines, are not meant to have authors.[57] In other words, if international law is meant to be received as a lofty and scientific discourse, it ought to be stripped of its representation as the crude production of self-interested and vile States (or Statespersons). The consenting subjects that were necessary to uphold the validity and legitimacy of the submission to international law's authority conveniently vanish to ensure that international law – and all that can be invoked under its name – earns its recognition as a scientific discourse.

5.5 DE-ARTICULATING TEMPORALITY

This fourth discursive move pertains to the temporality at work in the discourse on consent. Scholars and judges engaging with the question of consent to international law commonly presuppose that consent pre-exists the international legal order, the jurisdiction, the treaty, the rule (etc.), which it gives rise to, validates or legitimates. In other words, consent is always approached

55 See generally d'Aspremont, 'The Rage', fn. 29.

56 For some classical exposition of international law as a science, see Lassa Oppenheim, 'The Science of International Law: Its Task and Method' (1908) 2(2) *American Journal of International Law* 313–356; Robert Ago, 'Science juridique et droit international' (Volume 90) *Collected Courses of the Hague Academy of International Law*, 1956, pp. 851–958; Frede Castberg, 'La méthodologie du droit international public' (Volume 43) *Collected Courses of the Hague Academy of International Law*, 1934, pp. 313–383; Alexander Somek, 'Legal Science as a Source of Law: A Late Reply by Puchta to Kantorowicz' (2013) *University of Iowa Legal Studies Research Paper Series, No.* 13-7. Available at: https://papers.ssrn.com/sol3/papers.cfm?abstract_id=2175235, last accessed 5 October 2022. On the consolidation of this self-representation, see the remarks of Anne Orford, 'Scientific Reason and the Discipline of International Law' (2014) 25(2) *European Journal of International Law* 369–385.

57 Régis Debray, *Le scribe: Genèse du politique* (Paris: Grasset, Fasquelle, 1980), pp. 161–162. In the Middle Ages, before the advent of modernity, scientific texts had to be attributed to an author whose reputation or status would confer truth status to them. On the distinction between the role of authorship in scientific discourses and in non-scientific discourses, see Foucault, fn. 28, p. 29; Foucault, fn. 37, pp. 827–828; Barthes, fn. 49, pp. 61–63.

in the literature and the case law as the origin of what is being consented to. The time of consent is thus a time that begins with the production of consent and ends with the object created by consent. As intuitive as such temporality may appear, it is argued here that, in approaching time this way, scholars and judges actually disarticulate the temporality that accompanies the very idea of consent. Notwithstanding the fact that consent is always construed in the literature and the case law as pre-existing its object, it is submitted here that consent is bound to be apprehended, discussed or contested *after the coming into being of its object*. In other words, consent cannot be the origin of its object, for it always is secondary to it. Be it the consent to the legal order as a whole, to a regime, to a treaty or to a rule, consent can only be the consent to that legal order, regime, treaty or rule. So, contrary to the common presupposition that consent precedes its object, the object of consent always comes to pre-exist the consent that generates, validates or legitimizes it. Said differently, the time of international law, of its rules, of its regimes always comes to precede the time of the consent that engenders them.[58] As a result, the time of consent is thus a time that stretches from the object of consent to an *a posteriori* consent and not the opposite. This is why international lawyers, by always construing consent as being the origin of what is being consented to, come to distort the temporality of consent.

That international lawyers engaging with consent put forward a disarticulated temporarily is nothing sensational. After all, the temporality brought about by the international legal discourse is always contingent on that discourse.[59] In other words, there is nothing like a natural temporality that would be inherent in the international legal discourse. The distorted temporality that accompanies the literature and case law on consent is similarly unspectacular, for it remains the expression of a very modern temporality, that is, a temporality that is serial, linear and one-directional.[60] In that sense, the discourse on

58 One could even say that all forms always begin before they begin. In other words, the origin of forms always ensues the forms themselves and thus cannot be the origin of that form anymore: see Jacques Derrida, *Positions* (Paris: Éditions de Minuit, 1972), p. 23; Jacques Derrida, *Spectres de Marx*, 1st ed. (Paris: Galilée, 1993), pp. 255–256; Barthes, fn. 49, p. 41.

59 On the idea of time as a social creation, see François Ost, *Le Temps du Droit* (Paris: Odile Jacob, 1999), pp. 21–22, pp. 176–179. On the idea that law creates the space–time continuum of its application, see Bruno Latour, *La fabrique du droit: Une ethnographie du Conseil d'État*, 2nd ed. (Paris: La Découverte, 2004), p. 299.

60 On the seriality, linearity and one-directionality of the temporality of modern thought, see Paul Ricoeur, *La mémoire, l'histoire, l'oubli* (Paris: Seuil, 2000), pp. 386–401; Peter Sloterdijk, *Après nous le déluge*, 1st ed., translated by Olivier Mannoni (Paris: Éditions Payot & Rivages, 2016), p. 63; Latour, fn. 30, p. 99; de Certeau, fn. 22, p. 15; Henri Bergson, *La pensée et le mouvant* (Paris: Flammarion, 2014), p. 205; Foucault, *Les mots et les choses*, fn. 30, p. 14;

consent in the literature and case law is no rupture from the modern temporality that commonly informs the international legal discourse.[61] And yet, the disarticulation of the temporality of consent that is witnessed in the literature and the case law on consent constitutes a very noteworthy discursive move because it comes to redefine the present into the past and the past into the present. Indeed, the finding or interpretation of consent can only be a present event, one that is provoked or demanded for by a past and already existing legal order, regime, treaty or rule. As was said in this section, the object of consent can only pre-exist the consent that allegedly generates, validates or legitimizes it. The literature and case law on consent thus offer a wonderful example of redefinition of the past into the present and of the present into the past.[62]

5.6 DUALIZING THE DISCOURSE

The discourse on consent is the place of some very intense deferral of meaning between a wide variety of forms. Indeed, in the discourse on consent, whether found in the literature or the case law, meaning is passed between many different words, idioms, aphorisms and texts.[63] It suffices to mention how common it is to associate consent with voluntarism,[64] legal positivism,[65]

Habermas, fn. 30, p. 5; François Hartog, *Régime d'historicité: Présentisme et expérience du* temps (Seuil, 2003).

61 For an example of a rupture from the modern temporality of international law, see Jean d'Aspremont, 'Time Travel in the Law of International Responsibility', in Samantha Besson (ed.), *Theories of International Responsibility Law* (Cambridge: Cambridge University Press, 2022), pp. 252–278.

62 Such a move is not unheard of. For a similar redefinition of the past into the present and the present into the past in the doctrine of customary international law, see d'Aspremont, *The Discourse on Customary International Law*, fn. 43, pp. 48–58; Jean d'Aspremont, 'The Custom-Making Moment in Customary International Law', in Panos Merkouris, Jörg Kammerhofer and Nina Arajärvi (eds.), *The Theory, Practice, and Interpretation of Customary International Law* (Cambridge: Cambridge University Press, 2022), pp. 29–39.

63 On the idea that consent itself is an empty signifier that defers meaning to many other forms, see d'Aspremont, fn. 52; Werner, fn. 10, pp. 19–20; Tams, Chapter 3 in this volume.

64 Christakis, fn. 4, pp. 423–424; Brunnée, fn. 3, para. 1; Simma and Paulus, fn. 8, at 303; Tams, Chapter 3 in this volume. For some criticisms of this association, see d'Aspremont, *Formalism and the Sources*, fn. 6; Jean d'Aspremont and Jörg Kammerhofer, 'Introduction: The Future of International Legal Positivism', in Kammerhofer and d'Aspremont, fn. 4.

65 See, for example, Thirlway, fn. 13, p. 14; Brunnée, fn. 3, para. 1; Hollis, fn. 1, at 140; Patrick Capps, 'International Legal Positivism and Modern Natural Law', in Kammerhofer and d'Aspremont, fn. 4, pp. 213–240, p. 219. For an attempt to debunk the association between consent and legal positivism, see Besson, fn. 18; Besson, fn. 12, at 166; Richard Collins, 'Classical Legal Positivism in International Law Revisited', in Kammerhofer and d'Aspremont, fn. 4, pp. 23–49; Besson, fn. 10, p. 845; d'Aspremont, 'Herbert Hart', fn. 6, p. 145; Duncan

formalism,[66] the sources of international law,[67] Article 38 of the Statute of the International Court of Justice,[68] sovereign equality,[69] hard law,[70] or *pacta sunt servanda*.[71]

Such intense deferral of meaning is certainly not an oddity, for it is the very condition of forms as forms.[72] More striking, however, is the very dualism that dominates the way in which scholars and judges solicit meaning from the many forms of the discourse on consent. In fact, it is not only that meaning is passed between a wide variety of forms. It is also that, in the discourse on consent to international law, the deferral of meaning is guided by very binary patterns.[73] For instance, it is common for those engaging with the question of

B. Hollis, 'Sources in Interpretation Theories: An Interdependent Relationship', in Besson and d'Aspremont, fn. 5, pp. 422–446, pp. 435–436.

66 Krisch, fn. 3; Guzman, fn. 3, at 789–790; Carty, fn. 12; Kennedy, 'The Sources of International Law', fn. 12, at 20; Kennedy, 'When Renewal Repeats', fn. 12, pp. 355, 366. For some criticisms of the association of consent with formalism, see d'Aspremont, *Formalism and the Sources*, fn. 6, pp. 21–24; Besson, fn. 12, p. 193; Corten, fn. 12, at 53–54 and 58; Pellet, fn. 12.

67 Lassa Oppenheim, *International Law: A Treatise*, Vol. 1, 1st ed. (London: Longmans, Green and Company, 1905), pp. 21–24; Tomuschat, fn. 8, p. 216; Christian Tomuschat, 'General Course on Public International Law' (Volume 281) *Collected Courses of the Hague Academy of International Law*, 1999, pp. 9–438, p. 24; Karl Zemanek, 'The Legal Foundations of the International System' (Volume 266) *Collected Courses of the Hague Academy of International Law*, 1997, pp. 9–335, p. 144. For some criticisms of the association of consent with the sources of international law, see Godefridus J. H. Van Hoof, *Rethinking the Sources of International Law* (The Hague: Kluwer Law International, 1983), p. 289; Gerald Fitzmaurice, 'Some Problems Regarding the Formal Sources of International Law', in Frederik M. van Asbeck (ed.), *Symbolae Verzijl* (Leiden: Martinus Nijhoff, 1958), pp. 153–176, p. 164; Mehrdad Payandeh, 'The Concept of International Law in the Jurisprudence of HLA Hart' (2010) 21(4) *European Journal of International Law* 967–995, at 970–971; Hollis, fn. 65, pp. 435–436.

68 Hollis, fn. 1, at 142–143.

69 Werner, fn. 10, pp. 15, 21–26. For an attempt to debunk the association between consent and State sovereignty, see Besson, fn. 18.

70 On the idea that soft law mechanisms are alien to consent, see Guzman, fn. 3, at 789–790. For a rebuttal of that argument, see Hollis, Chapter 6 in this volume; Pellet, fn. 6, at 27.

71 On consent as the evidentiary vehicle by which *pacta sunt servanda* assigns treaties their binding force, see Hollis, Chapter 6 in this volume. For some criticisms of the association of consent with *pacta sunt servanda*, see Pellet, fn. 6, at 33.

72 This is an argument that I have developed elsewhere: see d'Aspremont, *After Meaning*, fn. 37; d'Aspremont, 'Two Attitudes', fn. 37. In the same vein, see Peter Goodrich, 'Europe in America: Grammatology, Legal Studies, and the Politics of Transmission' (2001) 101(8) *Columbia Law Review* 2033–2084, at 2059; Fuad Zarbiyev, *Le Discours interprétatif en droit international* (Brussels: Bruylant, 2015), pp. 37–45; see more generally, Derrida, *Positions*, fn. 58, p. 54.

73 The dominance of binary patterns of thought in the discourse on consent is not exclusive of the occasional resort to sophisticated three-pronged distinctions. On the distinction between outcome-consent, rule-consent and regime-consent see, for example, Neff, fn. 1; on the

consent to international law to organize the discourse around a distinction between will and consent,[74] between consent as law-ascertaining form and consent as substance to be interpreted,[75] between consent as discursive construction and consent as an empirical reality[76] or between normative and descriptive understandings of consent.[77] The findings of contradictions in the discourse on consent similarly manifest a dualist type of thinking.[78] Surely, such a binary mode of thinking is no surprise at all. After all, like many of the other discursive moves discussed here, the dualism at stake here is primarily inherited from the philosophical tradition associated with the Enlightenment[79] and which still dominates the English-speaking international legal discourse.[80]

As this short overview of the main discursive moves that inform the literature and case law pertaining to the question of consenting to international law comes to an end, a final remark is in order. Whatever their reason for engaging with consent to international law, those mobilizing, contesting or reforming the discourse on consent all espouse, in a way or another, the discursive moves that have been depicted here. As was said in the Introduction of this chapter, none of those moves can be reduced to benign social facts. It has been one of

distinction between consent as commitment, consent as a content, consent as constitution, see Hollis, Chapter 6 in this volume; on the distinction between consent as an intentional state, consent as symbolic expression of the intentional state, and consent as the activation of a particular obligation, see Brölmann, Chapter 4 in this volume.

74 Matthew Craven argues that will is suggestive of power to create law whilst consent evokes the passive idea of acceptance of concession: see Craven, fn. 16. Alain Pellet argues that consent can accommodate a certain amount of coercion and that States can consent to a rule even the rule does not correspond to their will, that is to what they want: see Pellet, fn. 6, at 41.

75 Tams, Chapter 3 in this volume; Brölmann, Chapter 4 in this volume. This also corresponds to the distinction made by Fuad Zarbiyev between threshold consensualism and substantive consensualism: see Zarbiyev, Chapter 7 in this volume. Such distinction also informs the case law: see, for example, *Request for Interpretation of the Judgment of 15 June 1962 in the Case concerning the Temple of Preah Vihear (Cambodia* v. *Thailand)* (Judgment) [2013], ICJ Rep. 281, p. 30, para. 75.

76 Zarbiyev, Chapter 7 in this volume.

77 Lefkowitz, Chapter 2 in this volume.

78 Werner, fn. 10, p. 30. Alain Pellet argues that *Pacta sunt servanda* means the contrary to voluntarism: whatever its will, the State is bound and must abide by the law: see Pellet, fn. 6, at 33.

79 On the idea that modernity generalized modes of thinking articulated around identity and differences, see Timothy Mitchell, *Questions of Modernity* (Minneapolis: University of Minnesota Press, 2000), p. 17; de Certeau, fn. 22, p. 59; Foucault, *Les mots et les choses*, fn. 30, p. 68.

80 See generally d'Aspremont, 'Two Attitudes', fn. 37; d'Aspremont, 'A Worldly Law', fn. 29; d'Aspremont, *After Meaning*, fn. 37.

the ambitions of this chapter to stress that such discursive moves cannot be perpetuated without at least some degree of awareness for what they do to the world. Hence, it will be up to all those scholars and judges continuing to mobilize, contest or reform the discourse on consent to appreciate the consequences of their discursive moves. For now, one is left to admire the splendid sophistications and intricacies of the discourse on consent to international law.

PART II

Objects and Types of Consent

6

Do International Agreements Have a Consent Problem?

DUNCAN B. HOLLIS

6.1 INTRODUCTION

The last decade has witnessed rising attention to non-consensual law-making in international law.[1] When it comes to the law of treaties, however, the role of consent appears unbowed.[2] Consent may not itself be the basis for the treaty obligation – that honour goes to *pacta sunt servanda*.[3] But, consent very much

[1] For some, non-consensual law-making promises more effective global governance, see, for example, Andrew T. Guzman, 'Against Consent' (2012) 52(4) *Virginia Journal of International Law* 747–790. Some employ a descriptive lens to identify areas of increased opportunities for non-consensual law-making, noting State consent remains resilient elsewhere; see, for example, Nico Krisch, 'The Decay of Consent: International Law in an Age of Global Public Goods' (2014) 108(1) *American Journal of International Law* 1–40. Others defend consent's continuing value (and vitality); see, for example, Eva Kassoti, 'Beyond State Consent? International Legal Scholarship and the Challenge of Informal International Law-Making' (2016) 63(2) *Netherlands International Law Review* 99–131; Duncan B. Hollis, 'Why State Consent Still Matters: Non-State Actors, Treaties, and the Changing Sources of International Law' (2005) 23(1) *Berkeley Journal of International Law* 137–174.

[2] Krisch, fn. 1, at 26: 'Treaty law does not seem to have come under significant pressure at all; the key role of consent in creating new rules via treaties, though obviously impeding efforts at lawmaking, continues to be firmly anchored.' At the same time, however, the popularity of the treaty instrument itself may be under strain, or perhaps, even in decline: see Duncan B. Hollis, 'Preface to the Second Edition', *The Oxford Guide to Treaties*, 2nd ed. (Oxford: Oxford University Press, 2020), pp. vii–xi.

[3] International legal scholarship has long recognized that *pacta sunt servanda* must rest on a basis other than consent to avoid circular reasoning or an infinite regress of consenting to consent: see Thomas M. Franck, *The Power of Legitimacy among Nations* (Oxford: Oxford University Press, 1990), p. 187: '"Why are treaties binding?" is a question usually answered by the superficial assertion that "treaties are binding because states have agreed to be bound" . . . But the binding force . . . cannot emanate solely from the agreement of the parties. It must come from some ultimate unwritten rule of recognition, the existence of which may be inferred from the conduct and belief . . . of states'; Samantha Besson, 'State Consent and Disagreement in International Law-Making: Dissolving the Paradox' (2016) 29(2) *Leiden Journal of International Law* 289–316, at 299; Alfred P. Rubin, *Ethics and Authority in*

does function as the vehicle by which *pacta sunt servanda* assigns treaties their binding force. As every student of international law learns, States create their treaties via consent while treaties only bind consenting States.[4]

Despite its (deservedly) prominent role, consent's contribution to treaty-making understates just how many functions consent may serve for international agreements more generally. Consent operates to elaborate various aspects of an international agreement, including its *commitment, content* and *constitution*. Beyond establishing the existence of a treaty itself, consent is necessary to establish the (social) fact of any *commitment*. Consent thus constructs all forms of international agreement, not just those governed by international law (treaties), but those governed by national law (contracts) and even those not governed by law at all (political commitments). At the same time, consent delineates more than an agreement's existence; it also elucidates its *contents* – what the agreement 'is' in terms of both its substance and scope. Consent may even reach beyond establishing commitments and scoping their contents to function as a *constitution* of sorts for treaties. To use the language of H. L. A. Hart, consent may delimit not only the 'primary' rules encapsulated via a treaty's existence and its contents, but also the 'secondary rules' that determine who can make treaties, how they must do so, and the way a treaty is recognized, adjusted and ended.[5] All told, consent's functions for international agreements appear ubiquitous.

This chapter aims to foreground consent's multitude of functions for international agreements. Doing so begs two related questions. First, what elements comprise consent? Second, what are its rules of recognition in international agreements? At present, neither international law nor international relations appear well equipped to answer such inquiries. Consent remains an under-examined and polysemous concept – oscillating between elements that are subjective (i.e. consent as a manifestation of will) and objective (i.e. consent as acceptance of some 'thing') – that leaves ample room for diverging views on its presence (or absence) in particular

International Law (Cambridge: Cambridge University Press, 1997), p. 15; Gerald Fitzmaurice, 'Some Problems Regarding the Formal Sources of International Law', in Frederik M. van Asbeck (ed.), *Symbolae Verzijl* (Leiden: Martinus Nijhoff, 1958), pp. 153–176, p. 164.

4 See, for example, Arts. 11, 26, 34 of the Vienna Convention on the Law of Treaties (hereafter VCLT), 1155 UNTS 331 (adopted 23 May 1969, entered into force 27 January 1980).

5 Herbert L. A. Hart, *The Concept of Law*, 2nd ed. (Oxford: Oxford University Press/Clarendon Press, 1994), p. 79. Hart himself questioned the existence of secondary rules in international law to the consternation of international lawyers; Mehrdad Payandeh, 'The Concept of International Law in the Jurisprudence of HLA Hart' (2010) 21(4) *European Journal of International Law* 967–995, at 982.

circumstances.[6] Consent is, moreover, largely undifferentiated. To be sure, some formalities offer aid in recognizing consent's purpose; an instrument of ratification, for example, will almost always embody a State's consent to be bound.[7] Overall, however, international law does not mandate formalities for consent's particular functions nor methodologies for identifying it in their absence. Today, almost any of consent's functions can be established by almost any formal or informal means.

Such flexibility may be a feature when considering a function in isolation (e.g. making it easier to recognize the existence of a treaty). Consent's flexibility becomes more problematic, however, in recognizing what consent does among multiple possibilities.[8] If, for example, any measure of consent establishes the existence of a treaty commitment, how do we know when consent establishes the existence of a political commitment instead? That challenge has rising importance as States increase their use of political commitments and 'multistakeholder' agreements instead of multilateral ones.[9]

This chapter asks if having such an underdeveloped concept doing so much is a problem for international agreements. Difficulties in recognizing consent and differentiating among its functions risk inconsistent understandings, unaligned expectations and disputes about the existence of treaties or other forms of international agreements, their contents and the relevant constitutive rules. Those problems in turn hinder exogenous inquiries into the effectiveness of international agreements – an inability to differentiate among commitments, contents and capacities precludes assessments of whether and how agreements' actual operations align with their object and purpose. Consent's polysemy may even create perverse incentives to label as consent instances where the decision-maker recognizes that it is manifestly

6 Besson, fn. 3, at 295: 'Defining consent is by no means easy as most international legal scholars do not explain what they mean by it. A cursory survey of the use of the term "consent" in international law reveals that consent is used to refer both to the "free will" of states and to their "acceptance" of international law.'

7 Art. 14 VCLT.

8 Accord Matthew Craven, 'The Ends of Consent', in Michael Bowman and Dino Kritsiotis (eds.), *Conceptual and Contextual Perspectives on the Modern Law of Treaties* (Cambridge: Cambridge University Press, 2018), pp. 103–135, p. 103: 'very ubiquity of consent as an analytic – governing everything from the underpinnings of treaty obligation (*pacta sunt servanda* and good faith), to processural dimensions (competence, signature, ratification, accession and approval), conditions of validity (capacity, error, fraud, mistake, coercion), interpretation (*travaux préparatoires*) and effect (*pacta tertiis* etc.) – is such as to make it very much more difficult to isolate what consent actually means in this context'.

9 See, for example, Curtis A. Bradley, Jack Goldsmith and Oona A. Hathaway, 'The Rise of Nonbinding International Agreements: An Empirical, Comparative, and Normative Analysis' (in press, 2023) 90 *University of Chicago Law Review*.

absent 'in fact' but proceeds to construct consent's existence by operation of 'law' instead.[10]

Thus, the time is ripe for opening a broader research agenda on the problems consent poses not just for treaties but international agreements more generally.[11] International law scholarship could catalogue whether and when consent's capacities manifest in practice. More normative work could address whether and in what ways to reconcile consent's ambiguities for better differentiation of its different functions.[12] Various candidates already exist for doing so (e.g. presumptions/defaults, content-based criteria). I add here a modest suggestion: following Louis Sullivan's famous idea that 'form follows function',[13] international law might explore mandating different formalities for consent's different functions. Whether as complements or substitutes, using formalities to differentiate consent's functions could improve their efficacy. In turn, we might create new pathways to improve the efficacy of international agreements themselves.

6.2 CONSENT AS COMMITMENT

Consent's most recognized role in international agreements undoubtedly lies in its expression of a party's commitment to be bound. Simply put, States must consent to be legally bound to a treaty.[14] Of course, a treaty will not bind a State by virtue of consent alone. Like all agreements, treaties require not just the *commitment* consent represents but also its *mutuality* – two or more States (or other subjects of international law) making overlapping commitments,

[10] Of course, one could argue that consent is always socially constructed, collapsing any distinction between consent 'in law' and consent 'in fact'. I am suggesting here, however, a distinction drawn from the common law tradition differentiating decision-makers' recognition of consent via some objective manifestation of subjective will versus cases where the consent label attaches because the law (or values underpinning it) support doing so.

[11] Throughout this chapter, I will use the term international agreements as an umbrella category that includes non-binding 'political commitments' as well as binding agreements whether governed by international law (treaties) or domestic law (contracts).

[12] Although my own focus here lies in improving the determinacy and (presumed) efficacy of consent's different functions, broader assessments of consent's utility overall or in particular functional spaces deserve attention as well.

[13] Mario Manieri-Elia, *Louis H. Sullivan* (New York: Princeton Architectural Press, 1996), p. 126.

[14] Jutta Brunnée, 'Consent' (last updated January 2022), in Rüdiger Wolfrum (ed.), *Max Planck Encyclopedia of Public International Law* (Oxford: Oxford University Press, 2008). Available at: https://opil.ouplaw.com/display/10.1093/law:epil/9780199231690/law-9780199231690-e1388, last accessed 13 December 2022, para. 5; International Law Commission (hereafter ILC), 'Fourth Report on the Law of Treaties, by Gerald Fitzmaurice, Special Rapporteur', *Yearbook of the International Law Commission* (1959) Vol. II, UN Doc. A/CN.4/120, pp. 37–81, p. 42.

whether bilaterally or in more multilateral arrangements.[15] Thus, consent does not automatically render the treaty into existence for a consenting State; it does so only if the treaty is already in force or if/when it subsequently does so.[16] In other words, consent is a required – but not sufficient – condition to trigger the principle of *pacta sunt servanda*.[17]

Consent to be bound may be the paradigmatic example of consent in treaty-formation. But it is not the only one.[18] The adoption of treaty texts (which form the basis for any ensuing consent to be bound) primarily 'takes place by the consent of all the States participating in its drawing up'.[19] Likewise, treaty authentication occurs via shared consensual means.[20] Binding third parties to a treaty prominently depends on consent as well – both the consent of the treaty parties to grant/hold third parties to rights/obligations as well as the consent of the third party to such an arrangement.[21] Moreover, just as it brings the treaty into existence, mutuality of consent can produce its end.[22] Parties

[15] Duncan B. Hollis, 'Defining Treaties', in Hollis, *The Oxford Guide*, fn. 2, pp. 11–45, pp. 19–21; Besson, fn. 3, at 297: '[VCLT defines an agreement] as the mutuality of expressed consents to be bound by a treaty'; Jan Klabbers, *The Concept of Treaty in International Law* (The Hague: Kluwer, 1996), pp. 51–53; Paul Reuter, *Introduction to the Law of Treaties*, translated by Jose Mico and Peter Haggenmacher (London: Pinter, 1989), para. 65. Mutuality distinguishes consent to a treaty commitment from binding unilateral acts, even as sources divide over whether the law binds a State to unilateral commitments based on estoppel or expressions of intent to be bound: see *Nuclear Tests (Australia/New Zealand* v. *France)* [1974] ICJ Rep. 253, at 267–268, paras. 43–50; Eva Kassoti, 'Unilateral Legal Acts Revisited: Common Law v. Civil Law Approaches and Lessons from the International Law Commission's (Failed) Attempt to Codify Unilateral Acts of States' (2013) 26 *Hague Yearbook of International Law* 168–200, at 199–200.

[16] Brunnée, fn. 14, para. 7.

[17] Craven, fn. 8, p. 120: '[VCLT] is overtly rigorous about the necessity of consent for purposes of the assumption of obligations under treaty ... so far as treaties are concerned, obligation follows ... consent (rather than the other way round)'; Besson, fn. 3, at 302: '[Treaty] epitomizes the understanding of consent *qua* agreement.'

[18] On the differentiation of consent to be bound from 'consent *simpliciter*' evident in other VCLT rules as well as consent to otherwise established or separate agreements, see Shabtai Rosenne, *An International Law Miscellany* (Leiden: Martinus Nijhoff, 1993), pp. 357, 369.

[19] Art. 9 VCLT. The VCLT provides an exception where two-thirds of the States present and voting adopt the treaty or apply a different rule. Ibid.

[20] Art. 10 VCLT: '[authentication occurs] (a) by such procedure as may be provided for in the text or agreed upon by the States participating in its drawing up; or (b) failing such procedure, by the signature, signature ad referendum or initialling by the representatives of those States of the text of the treaty or of the Final Act of a conference incorporating the text.'

[21] Art. 34 VCLT: 'A treaty does not create either rights or obligations for a third State without its consent'; Arts. 10, 35, 36 VCLT; Brunnée, fn. 14, para. 5.

[22] Art. 54 VCLT: 'The termination of a treaty or the withdrawal of a party may take place: (a) in conformity with the provisions of the treaty; or (b) at any time by consent of all the parties after consultation with the other contracting States'; Laurence R. Helfer, 'Terminating Treaties', in Hollis, *The Oxford Guide*, fn. 2, pp. 624–640, p. 627: 'States are the undisputed masters of

may consent to withdrawals/termination in the original treaty design or via their collective consent at any time thereafter.[23]

More importantly, consent's role is not limited to constructing the existence of a treaty – that is, an agreement governed by international law.[24] Consent is a prerequisite for *any* agreement.[25] It is obviously central to a contract's formation – an agreement governed by national law(s) – such that States or their institutions must consent to form contracts with other international actors.[26] Consent is just as essential to the formation of political commitments – agreements that derive their normative force not from any basis of legal obligation but from moral or political expectations.[27] Political

treaty exit rules'; ILC, 'Second Report on the Law of Treaties, by Gerald Fitzmaurice, Special Rapporteur', *Yearbook of the International Law Commission* (1957) Vol. II, UN Doc. A/CN.4/107, pp. 16–70, p. 22. Along with its validity rules, VCLT Part V provides additional grounds for termination independent of *mutual* consent (e.g. breach, *rebus sic stantibus*, impossibility) even as each presupposes the unilateral consent of the invoking party.

23 Art. 54 VCLT; ILC, 'Draft Articles on the Law of Treaties', *Yearbook of the International Law Commission* (1966) Vol. II, pp. 177–274, p. 249, para. 3: 'Commission considered that, whatever may be the provisions of a treaty regarding its own termination, it is always possible for all the Parties to agree together to put an end to the treaty'; Vincent Chapaux, 'Article 54 Convention of 1969', in Olivier Corten and Pierre Klein (eds.), *The Vienna Convention on the Law Treaties: A Commentary*, Vol. 2 (Oxford: Oxford University Press, 2011), pp. 1236–1246, p. 1243. Although it leaves the treaty's existence unaffected, mutual consent is also the driving force behind a treaty's suspension per Art. 57 VCLT; Mark F. Villiger, *Commentary on the 1969 Vienna Convention on the Law of Treaties* (Leiden: Martinus Nijhoff, 2009), p. 710.

24 Even if all treaties are agreements, it does not follow that all agreements are treaties: see Hollis, fn. 15, p. 19; Villiger, fn. 23, p. 77; ILC, 'Fourth Report on the Law of Treaties, by Humphrey Waldock, Special Rapporteur', *Yearbook of the International Law Commission* (1965) Vol. II, UN Doc. A/CN.4/177 and Add.1 and 2, pp. 3–72, p. 11, para. 1; *Yearbook of the International Law Commission* (1965) Vol. I, UN Doc. A/CN.4/SER.A, p. 10, para. 10; ILC, 'First Report on the Law of Treaties, by James L. Brierly, Special Rapporteur', *Yearbook of the International Law Commission* (1950) Vol. II, UN Doc. A/CN.4/23, pp. 222–248, p. 227, para. 19.

25 Organization of American States, 'Guidelines of the Inter-American Juridical Committee on Binding and Non-Binding Agreements' (hereafter IAJC Guidelines) (2020). Available at: www.oas.org/en/sla/iajc/docs/Guidelines_on_Binding_and_Non-Binding_Agreements_publication.pdf, last accessed 29 September 2022, Guideline 1.1, p. 24: 'Although its usage in a text is often indicative of a treaty, the concept [of agreement] may be defined more broadly to encompass mutual consent by participants to a commitment regarding future behavior.'

26 See, for example, Randy Barnett, 'A Consent Theory of Contract' (1986) 86 *Columbia Law Review* 269–321. Contracting parties (or adjudicators) may also select non-State law (for example, *lex mercatoria*) to govern contracts in lieu of – or in addition to – national legal systems: see IAJC Guidelines, fn. 25, p. 55.

27 IAJC Guidelines, fn. 25, Guideline 1.3, p. 25: '[A Political commitment is a] non-legally binding agreement between States, State institutions, or other actors intended to establish commitments of an exclusively political or moral nature'; accord Anthony Aust, *Modern Treaty Law and Practice*, 3rd ed. (Cambridge: Cambridge University Press, 2013), pp. 28–29, pp. 35–39; Michael Bothe, 'Legal and Non-Legal Norms – A Meaningful Distinction in

commitments have existed in international relations for well over a century in various guises (e.g. gentlemen's agreements, informal agreements and non-binding agreements).[28] They have, however, taken on heightened prominence and prevalence in recent years.[29]

Unfortunately, the necessity of consent has not translated into mandatory formalities or methodologies for establishing its existence, let alone differentiating to what type of agreement it pertains. International law has largely left the concept of agreement undefined, which leaves unresolved whether consent only constructs the fact of agreement or if it also dictates specific types of agreements.[30] The International Court of Justice's (hereafter ICJ) jurisprudence has done little to qualify matters. In *Aegean Sea*, for example, the ICJ never explained if it declined jurisdiction because Greece and Turkey's Prime Ministers had not reached a *binding* agreement in their Joint Communiqué or if they had never consented to *any* agreement at all.[31] Similar ambiguity is evident in the International Tribunal for the Law of the Sea's (hereafter ITLOS) *Bay of Bengal* decision denying a 'conditional understanding' reflected in the parties' Agreed Minutes constituted an agreement contemplated under an earlier treaty.[32] In practice, however, there may be real value in just identifying the existence of an agreement *per se* as all agreements set collective expectations for participants' proper behaviour (albeit under varying logics of appropriateness).[33]

International Relations' (1980) 11 *Netherlands Yearbook of International Law* 65–95, at 66; Oscar Schachter, 'Twilight Existence of Nonbinding International Agreements' (1977) 71(2) *American Journal of International Law* 296–304.

28 Duncan B. Hollis and Joshua J. Newcomer, '"Political" Commitments and the Constitution' (2009) 49(3) *Virginia Journal of International Law* 507–584, at 516–524; Klabbers, fn. 15, p. 18.

29 Council of Europe, 'Non-Legally Binding Agreements in International Law' (26 March 2021). Available at: www.coe.int/fr/web/cahdi/non-legally-binding-agreements-in-international-law, last accessed 29 September 2022; Canada, Finland, Germany, Israel, Japan, Korea, Mexico, and Spain agree on the increasing frequency and significance of political commitments: see Treaty Law Division, Global Affairs Canada, 'Working Group on Treaty Practice. Survey on Binding and Non-Binding International Instruments' (18 September 2019), pp. 13, 31; IAJC Guidelines, fn. 25, Final Report, para. 1; Kassoti, fn. 1, at 101.

30 Hollis, fn. 15, p. 19.

31 *Aegean Sea Continental Shelf Case (Greece* v. *Turkey)* (Judgment) [1978] ICJ Rep. 3, para. 107.

32 *Dispute concerning Delimitation of the Maritime Boundary between Bangladesh and Myanmar in the Bay of Bengal (Bangladesh/Myanmar)* (Judgment of 14 March 2012) Case No. 16, 2012 ITLOS Rep. 4, para. 92.

33 Accord Alan Boyle, 'Reflections on the Treaty as a Law-Making Instrument', in Alexander Orakhelashvili and Sarah Williams (eds.), 40 *Years of the Vienna Convention on the Law of Treaties* (London: BIICL, 2010), pp. 1–28, p. 28: '[A]t this point, the status of an agreement as a treaty is less important than its status as an agreement between States, whether binding in international law or not.'

In terms of identifying consent to be bound to a treaty, States usually express it via some concrete act that manifests a willingness to accept the international legal commitment. Article 11 of the Vienna Convention on the Law of Treaties (hereafter VCLT) identifies five vehicles for doing so: (i) definitive signature; (ii) an exchange of instruments constituting a treaty; (iii) ratification; (iv) acceptance or approval; and (v) accession.[34] Negotiators may select one or more of these options in individual cases, but the VCLT declined to mandate any of them. Article 11 of the VCLT provides that consent may also occur 'by any other means if so agreed'.[35] This has left room for an array of additional (and often creative) methods for expressing consent to bound, including the completion of domestic approval procedures,[36] initialling,[37] collateral documents,[38] or adoption of a 'resolution of approval'.[39] At the same time, the VCLT does not purport to capture all the forms of treaty-making; it leaves open, for example, the possibility of 'oral' treaties.[40]

International courts and tribunals have endorsed such flexibility. As Eva Kassoti notes, the ICJ's practice 'evidences the irrelevance of considerations of form and the importance attached to the "reality of consent"'.[41] The Court has found treaties to exist in various written instruments, including agreed minutes,[42] an understanding[43] and a declaration.[44] In its 2014 *Venezuelan*

[34] Arts. 2(1)(b), 11 VCLT. The 1986 Vienna Convention adds a sixth vehicle: the (little used) 'act of formal confirmation': see Art. 11(2) of the Vienna Convention on the Law of Treaties between States and International Organizations or between International Organizations, 25 ILM 543 (adopted 21 March 1986, not yet in force) (hereafter 1986 VCLT).

[35] Art. 11 VCLT; Art. 11 1986 VCLT.

[36] UN Conference on the Law of Treaties, 'Official Records: Documents of the Conference', UN Doc. A/CONF.39/11/Add.2, p. 84, paras. 47–48 (referencing the 1955 agreement on Austria's permanent neutrality).

[37] For example, Agreement on Initialling the General Framework Agreement for Peace in Bosnia and Herzegovina (hereafter Dayton Agreement), 35 ILM 91 (14 December 1995), Arts. I, II.

[38] For example, Iran–United States: Settlement of the Hostage Crisis (hereafter Algiers Accords) (19 January 1981), 20 ILM 223.

[39] For example, Text on the Establishment of a Preparatory Commission for the Comprehensive Test-Ban Organization (1996) [1999] UKTS 46.

[40] Art. 3 VCLT: 'The fact that the present Convention does not apply ... to international agreements not in written form, shall not affect: (a) the legal force of such agreements'; Hollis, fn. 15, p. 24; Reuter, fn. 15, para. 66.

[41] Kassoti, fn. 1, at 112–113.

[42] *Maritime Delimitation and Territorial Questions (Qatar* v. *Bahrain)* (Jurisdiction and Admissibility) [1994] ICJ Rep. 112, paras. 21–25: '[agreed minutes were] not a simple record of a meeting ... They enumerate the commitments to which the Parties have consented'.

[43] *Case concerning Pulp Mills on the River Uruguay (Argentina* v. *Uruguay)* (Judgment) [2010] ICJ Rep. 14, para. 128.

[44] *Case concerning the Land and Maritime Boundary between Cameroon and Nigeria (Cameroon/Nigeria)* (Judgment) [2002] ICJ Rep. 303, para. 264.

Fisheries Judgment, the Court of Justice of the European Union (hereafter CJEU) found that the European Union (hereafter EU) and Venezuela had consented to an agreement where (i) the EU made a declaration offering Venezuela use of its surplus catch allowances in a fishery subject to certain conditions and (ii) Venezuela, after notice of that declaration, had formally applied to the EU for fishing authorizations, which the Court regarded as acceptance of the EU's offer.[45]

Thus, today States have 'unlimited freedom as far as the methods of expressing consent to be bound are concerned'.[46] That same freedom persists in executing other forms of consent relating to the commitment's existence. There is, for example, no *acte contraire* doctrine in international law requiring the same form of consent to terminate a treaty as used to create it originally.[47]

If anything can denote consent to a treaty (or its end), how can consent denote other forms of international agreement? National laws may provide separate rules of recognition to delimit whether and when consent creates a contract. But political commitments have no such directives. As such, it can be difficult to differentiate cases of consent to a treaty commitment from cases of consent to a political commitment. Ratification, acceptance, approval and

45 CJEU, *European Parliament & European Commission* v. *Council of the European Union* (Joined Cases C-103/12 and C-165/12) ECLI:EU:C:2014:334 [2014], OJC 26, 26.1.2015, p. 2, paras. 68–73; Kassoti, fn. 1, at 113.

46 Klabbers, fn. 15, p. 72; Jean d'Aspremont, 'Formalism versus Flexibility in the Law of Treaties', in Christian J. Tams, Antonios Tzanakopoulos, Andreas Zimmermann and Athene E. Richford (eds.), *Research Handbook on the Law of Treaties* (Cheltenham: Edward Elgar, 2016), pp. 257–284, p. 261: 'the expression of individual consent and the meeting of all individual consents can generate a valid treaty ... irrespective of the process of their expression'; Besson, fn. 3, at 297. In contrast, many States' domestic laws impose mandatory procedures for forming such consent. Rosenne suggests that the existence of domestic approval procedures helps explain the international law of treaties' flexibility on the forms of consenting to be bound: see Rosenne, fn. 18, p. 366.

47 Robert Kolb, *The Law of Treaties: An Introduction* (Cheltenham: Edward Elgar, 2016), p. 209: 'There is no rule of parallelism of form in international law; a treaty concluded in the most formal way can be terminated (abrogated) by an informal consent. Any type of consent suffices: express or implied'; ILC, 'Summary Records of the Eighteenth Session', *Yearbook of the International Law Commission* (1966) Vol. I, Part Two, UN Doc. A/CN.4/SER.A/1966, p. 225, para. 94: 'The new wording of article 38, sub-paragraph (*b*), had been chosen deliberately and the phrase "by consent of all the parties", which had been substituted for "by agreement of all the parties" was intended to take account of tacit consent to terminate.' In contrast, domestic legal systems exhibit a mix of approaches including some that do follow the *acte contraire* principle for purposes of internal approval procedures (e.g. if Parliament approves the original treaty, it must also be involved in its amendment). China, Germany and Switzerland treat amendments as subject to the same procedure as original treaty-making: see Duncan B. Hollis, Merritt R. Blakeslee and L. Benjamin Ederington (eds.), *National Treaty Law and Practice* (Leiden: Martinus Nijhoff, 2005), pp. 163, 326, 657.

accession all usually indicate consent to be legally bound to a treaty. Yet, the lack of ratification (or acceptance, etc.) will not deprive consent of its treaty-making function.[48] Other consent mechanisms are more multifunctional. When a State affixes its signature to an agreement, for example, it may qualify as (i) 'definitive signature', reflecting the signer's consent to be bound, (ii) 'simple signature', indicating that the State will consider consenting to be bound by ratification at some future date or (iii) consent to the terms of a political commitment.

In some cases, parties may mutually agree on the particular function their consents serve. In the *Iron Rhine ('Ijzeren Rijn') Railway* arbitration, Belgium and the Netherlands acknowledged they had consented to an agreement in a Memorandum of Understanding (MOU) *and* that this MOU was not a 'binding instrument'.[49] In other cases, contracting parties differ on what their consent represents. In *Pulp Mills*, for example, neither Argentina nor Uruguay disputed that their presidents had consented to an agreement via a 31 May 2005 press release; their dispute revolved around whether that agreement was a binding treaty or not.[50]

Efforts to resolve such disputes have bifurcated into two approaches for evaluating agreements reached – a subjective test and an objective test – each of which traces back to the polysemy of the consent concept itself. On the one hand, the International Law Commission (hereafter ILC), the Vienna Conference, many States and several international courts and tribunals have endorsed differentiating treaties from political commitments based on the parties' *intentions*.[51] The *South China Sea* Tribunal, for example, emphasized that '[t]o constitute a binding agreement, an instrument must evince a clear

48 Klabbers, fn. 15, p. 74.

49 *Award in the Arbitration regarding the Iron Rhine ('Ijzeren Rijn') Railway between the Kingdom of Belgium and the Kingdom of the Netherlands* (2005) 27 RIAA 35, para. 156.

50 See *Pulp Mills*, fn. 43, paras. 132–133.

51 On the support for the intent test, see IAJC Guidelines, fn. 25, Guideline 3.2 and accompanying commentary, pp. 77–83; Brazil, Colombia, Mexico, Peru, and the United States invoked 'intent' as deciding criterion for identifying a treaty. Ibid.; see also *Pulp Mills*, fn. 43, p. 79, footnote 126; Switzerland, Federal Department of Foreign Affairs, 'Practice Guide to International Treaties' (2015). Available at: www.eda.admin.ch/dam/eda/en/documents/publications/Voelkerrecht/Praxisleitfaden-Voelkerrechtliche-Vertraege_en.pdf, last accessed 30 September 2022, p. 4: 'establishing whether the parties wish to make their agreement legally binding is essential. If this is not the intention, it is not a treaty'; CJEU, *France* v. *Commission* (C-233/02) EU:C:2004:173 (2004) ECR I-02759, para. 42: 'intention of the parties must in principle be the decisive criterion for the purpose of determining whether or not the Guidelines are binding'; accord Aust, fn. 27, pp. 20–22; United Nations Conference on the Law of Treaties, 'Summary Records of Second Session', UN Doc. A/CONF.39/11, Add.1, 225, para. 13; ILC, fn. 23, p. 189, para. 6.

intention to establish rights and obligations between the parties'.[52] States similarly believe that a political commitment flows from its participants' intentions to elaborate commitments independent of a legal basis.[53] These searches for intentions necessarily emphasize consent as the parties' manifestation of will, focusing on what they understood their consent to do and assessing the extent of any resulting inter-subjectivity.[54]

In contrast, the ICJ, among others, emphasizes a more objective approach, using the *object* of the parties' consent to catalogue its legal (or non-legal) status. In *Qatar* v. *Bahrain*, the Court found that the parties had concluded a legally binding agreement accepting ICJ jurisdiction in the form of Agreed Minutes, notwithstanding protestations by Bahrain's Foreign Minister that he had not intended to do so.[55] The Court viewed the Agreed Minutes as a treaty based on the 'terms of the instrument itself and the circumstances of its conclusion, not from what the parties say afterwards was their intention'.[56] The parties' consent to a treaty followed, therefore, from objective criteria – for example, the language and types of clauses included in the instrument (and perhaps even its very subject-matter). Thus, the character of the agreement could be inferred from its object in lieu of deducing that character from the parties' own manifestations of will/intent.[57] The *Chagos* Arbitration Tribunal evinced a similar approach, emphasizing the need for an 'objective determination' in sorting binding from non-binding agreements.[58] Member States of the Organization of American States have likewise emphasized the structure and language used in a text to determine its status.[59]

The intent and objective tests are not the only means for demarcating consent to be bound by an agreement as a treaty; other criteria may include surrounding circumstances (e.g. was the agreement subjected to domestic

52 *An Arbitral Tribunal Constituted under Annex VII to the 1982 United Nations Convention on the Law of the Sea (Philippines* v. *People's Republic of China)*, PCA, Award on Jurisdiction (29 October 2015), Case No. 2013-19, para. 213.

53 See, for example, IAJC Guidelines, fn. 25, p. 79, footnote 126: 'political commitments involve "instruments that the participants *intend* to be non-legally binding"' (emphasis added).

54 Reuter, fn. 15, para. 65: 'parties have to manifest their will by "expressing" it'. For an effort to distinguish consent from manifestations of will, see Pellet, Chapter 1 in this volume.

55 *Maritime Delimitation and Territorial Questions (Qatar* v. *Bahrain)* (Jurisdiction and Admissibility) [1994] ICJ Rep. 112, para. 27.

56 Ibid.

57 The ICJ has continued this approach in recent cases: see *Maritime Delimitation in the Indian Ocean (Somalia* v. *Kenya)* (Judgment) [2017] ICJ Rep. 3, para. 42; *Pulp Mills*, fn. 43, para. 128.

58 *Chagos Marine Protected Area Arbitration (Mauritius* v. *United Kingdom)*, PCA, Award (18 March 2015), Case No. 2011-03 (18 March 2015), p. 168, para. 426.

59 On the views of Jamaica and The Dominican Republic, see IAJC Guidelines, fn. 25, p. 81.

approval procedures required for treaties?) and subsequent practice (e.g. how have parties/participants characterized the agreement?).[60] It is also possible that the agreement or its surrounding circumstances may obviate confusion over what the consent created. Nonetheless, the rising use of political commitments, which complicate consent's ability to establish the existence of particular international agreements, suggests that future disputes can – and will – occur.

If there is so much doubt about how to identify and evaluate active forms of consent, can more passive behaviours ever comprise the requisite consent? Paul Reuter had his doubts (as did James Leslie Brierly).[61] Nico Krisch, moreover, was careful to differentiate consent from cases of consensus, suggesting that the availability of acquiescence to some States in reaching consensus differentiates consensus from the more active manifestations of will represented by consent.[62] Acquiescence *has* traditionally been excluded from situations calling for affirmative consent, which would include the formation of agreements.[63] But Samantha Besson's observation that consent in

60 *Delimitation of the Maritime Boundary in the Bay of Bengal*, fn. 32, paras. 93–97: 'the circumstances ... do not suggest that [the Agreed Minutes] were intended to create legal obligations'. In this case, Myanmar was clear in its intention to only agree to a comprehensive agreement and neither State submitted the Agreed Minutes to their constitutional procedures for binding international agreements; but failure to follow domestic treaty-making procedures will not deny an agreement of its treaty status. Ibid.; see also *Somalia* v. *Kenya*, fn. 57, paras. 48–50; *South China Sea Arbitration*, fn. 52, para. 216. The South China Sea Tribunal emphasized how China had repeatedly labelled the agreement at issue as a 'political document'. Ibid. The ICJ appears particularly committed to prioritizing finding consent as a matter of international law independent of whether national approval procedures were followed, as witnessed by its repeated denial of attempts to invoke Art. 46 VCLT to void consent to be bound. See, for example, *Land and Maritime Boundary between Cameroon and Nigeria (Cameroon* v. *Nigeria)* [2002] ICJ Rep. 303, paras. 265–266; Art. 46 VCLT: 'A State may not invoke the fact that its consent to be bound by a treaty has been expressed in violation of a provision of its internal law regarding competence to conclude treaties as invalidating its consent unless that violation was manifest and concerned a rule of its internal law of fundamental importance.'

61 Reuter, fn. 15, para. 66: '*any* conduct of the parties may express a will, especially active conduct, such as performance of an obligation or departure from an earlier attitude. Does the same hold good for *passive* consent ... Such an extension of the treaty mechanism is debatable ... although an obligation may indeed arise ... it could perhaps be explained otherwise than as resulting from an agreement' such as via unilateral acts, acquiescence, estoppel, preclusion or custom; James Leslie Brierly and Andrew Clapham, *The Law of Nations: An Introduction to the International Law of Peace*, 7th ed. (Oxford: Clarendon, 1963), p. 50: '[T]he theory of implied consent is a fiction invented by the theorist.'

62 Krisch, fn. 1, at 17. Although different definitions exist, I define consensus as the absence of any formal objection: see 1982 UN Convention on the Law of the Sea, 1833 UNTS 3 (opened for signature 10 December 1982, entered into force 16 November 1994), Art. 161(8)(e).

63 Iain C. MacGibbon, 'The Scope of Acquiescence in International Law' (1954) 31 *British Yearbook of International Law* 143–186, at 143: 'Acquiescence is essentially a negative

international law necessarily involves an 'agreement to disagree' suggests that the delta between consent and consensus might not be so significant.[64] That said, if consensus is declared over the overt protests of one or more States, it becomes harder to qualify it as consent *per se*.[65] Cases where a court or tribunal implies consent may be subject to similar challenges. The ICJ and the ITLOS have identified 'tacit agreements' without explaining their methodology for identifying the parties' consent other than to note evidence of such agreements must be 'compelling'.[66] These cases beg the question of whether consent arising by operation of law actually more often involves circumstances where adjudicators believe consent *should have* been forthcoming than those where the decision-maker recognizes that consent *in fact* occurred.

6.3 CONSENT AS CONTENT

Consent to an agreement does more than elaborate the fact of a commitment; it also delineates its contents. An agreement's mutual commitments involve shared expectations for future behaviour, such that consent to the fact of these mutual commitments also necessarily establishes their substance.[67] When two States consent to an extradition treaty, for example, their consent not only contributes to the treaty's formation, but also delineates its contents – the substantive rights and obligations expected of each State party.[68] Similarly, consent to a political commitment simultaneously signals the agreement's

concept . . . used to describe the inaction of a State which is faced with a situation constituting a threat to or infringement of its rights: it is not intended to connote the forms in which a State may signify its consent or approval in a positive fashion'; Irina Buga, *Modification of Treaties by Subsequent Practice* (Oxford: Oxford University Press, 2018), p. 68.

64 Besson, fn. 3, at 313: 'if it is true that treaties are the expressions of mutual consent and cannot be concluded without consent, consent need not imply complete agreement . . . treaties are arguably best approached as incompletely theorized agreements, or at least as agreements to disagree'.

65 For cases of quasi-consensus declared over objection of a State see Krisch, fn. 1, at 17.

66 *Case concerning Territorial and Maritime Dispute in the Caribbean Sea (Nicaragua v. Honduras)* [2007] ICJ Rep. 659, para. 253; *Maritime Dispute (Peru v. Chile)* (Judgment) [2014] ICJ Rep. 3, para. 91; *Dispute concerning Delimitation of the Maritime Boundary between Ghana and Côte d'Ivoire in the Atlantic Ocean (Ghana v. Côte d'Ivoire)* (Judgment) Case No. 23 (23 September 2017) ITLOS Rep. 4, para. 212.

67 In the same vein, interpreting an agreement necessarily involves affirming its existence: see Duncan B. Hollis, 'The Existential Function of Interpretation in International Law', in Andrea Bianchi, Daniel Peat and Matthew Windsor (eds.), *Interpretation in International Law* (Oxford: Oxford University Press, 2015), pp. 78–110.

68 Of course, the substance of agreements is not limited to rights/obligations; agreements can also set expectations of affirmative conduct, prohibited acts, permissions, and constitute new actors/processes.

existence and what expectations that agreement sets. Thus, discerning any agreement's contents by asking what it means (interpretation) and how it operates (its material, temporal and spatial application) necessarily touches on the substance and scope of the consent offered to join the agreement itself. In doing so, the difficulties described above in identifying and differentiating among consent as commitment will necessarily extend into any process of using consent for content-determination.

Consent's contributions to questions of content are not bounded, however, solely by the original commitment. Agreements' contours can depend on consent in other ways. Reservations allow a party to condition its consent to be bound by a treaty unilaterally, excluding or modifying the treaty provisions the reserving State would otherwise be bound to perform.[69] A reservation's admissibility depends on the parties' mutual consent, whether directly (i.e. where the treaty specifies whether and which reservations are allowed) or indirectly (i.e. via the treaty's object and purpose).[70] Consent also undergirds non-reserving States' responses. They may accept (i.e. consent to) the reservation operating as the reserving State intended or deny their consent and with it the application of the provisions to which the reservation relates, or even the treaty as a whole.[71]

Consent can also construct treaty interpretations beyond the text itself. A treaty's context includes 'any agreement relating to the treaty' to which all the parties consented 'in connection with the conclusion of the treaty'.[72] Interpreters must also 'take into account ... any subsequent agreement between the parties regarding the interpretation of the treaty or the application of its provisions'.[73] Unlike the treaty itself, the ILC has concluded that such subsequent agreements may be binding or non-binding, suggesting consent to a political commitment can assist in giving a treaty commitment meaning.[74] In such cases, the question is whether the parties consented to an interpretative agreement at all. In the *Case Concerning Kasikili/Sedudu Island*, for

69 Brunnée, fn. 14, para. 8.
70 Art. 19 VCLT.
71 Arts. 20, 21 VCLT.
72 Art. 31(2)(a)–(b) VCLT.
73 Art. 31(3)(a) VCLT.
74 ILC, 'Draft Conclusions on Subsequent Agreements and Subsequent Practice in Relation to the Interpretation of Treaties, with Commentaries', in ILC, 'Report of the International Law Commission on the Work of Its Seventieth Session', UN Doc. A/73/10 (2018), pp. 11–116, p. 15: 'An agreement under article 31, paragraph 3 (*a*) and (*b*), requires a common understanding regarding the interpretation of a treaty which the parties are aware of and accept. Such an agreement may, but need not, be legally binding for it to be taken into account.'

example, the ICJ read the varying views contained in exchanges between South Africa and Bechuanaland and concluded that they 'demonstrate[d] the absence of agreement' on the underlying treaty's interpretation and application.[75]

Of course, consent can do more than reserve to or interpret treaties; it can also amend them. As a general rule, amendments only bind consenting parties and, like all treaties, only when the amendment has entered into force.[76] Various processes exist for producing amendments. Some, like the UN Charter, provide for amendment by majority consent instead of the consent of all Member States.[77] Others provide more attenuated or 'tacit' consent procedures, most often with respect to a treaty's technical annexes. Among many multilateral environmental treaties, for example, in consenting to the treaty, the parties agree to the presumption of consent to certain subsequently adopted amendments (States may override this presumption by opting out of the amendment).[78]

In emphasizing the role of consent in delimiting an agreement's contours and contents, I do not mean to suggest that treaty changes can never occur without consent, but I believe that the prevalence of non-consensual mechanisms may be overestimated. As Jutta Brunnée explained in her survey of conferences of the parties (COPs) and multilateral environmental agreements:

> [S]tates are bound not by the decision of COPs, but through their consent, be it actual (for example, protocols and amendments), presumed (for example, opt-out procedures for annexes and their amendments), or 'general' (for example, adjustments). From the standpoint of a formal analysis, COPs can be said to play a legislative role only in the latter, rather limited, range of cases, in which they adopt decisions that are formally binding upon states.[79]

75 *Case concerning Kasikili/Sedudu Island (Botswana* v. *Namibia)* (Judgment) [1999] ICJ Rep. 1045, para. 63.

76 Art. 40(4)–(5) VCLT.

77 Charter of the United Nations, 1 UNTS XVI (signed 26 June 1945, entered into force 24 October 1945), Arts. 108, 109.

78 Rotterdam Convention on the Prior Informed Consent Procedure for Certain Hazardous Chemicals and Pesticides in International Trade, 2244 UNTS 337 (adopted 10 September 1998, entered into force 24 February 2004), Art. 22(2)–(4). Some treaties authorize consenting parties to opt out of 'tacit' amendment procedures entirely. International Convention on the Control of Harmful Antifouling Systems on Ships, IMO Doc AFS/CONF/26 (adopted 5 October 2001, entered into force 17 September 2008), Art. 16(2)(e)(ii), Art. 16 (2)(f)(ii).

79 Jutta Brunnée, 'COPing with Consent: Law-Making under Multilateral Environmental Agreements' (2002) *Leiden Journal of International Law* 1–52, at 32; Martins Paparinskis, 'Regulating Treaties: A Comparative Perspective', in Tams *et al.*, fn. 46, pp. 39–53, pp. 45–51.

It is worth noting, moreover, that in practice States have proven reluctant to embrace non-consent-based changes to their treaty commitments even where they originally consented to doing so. The Montreal Protocol on Substances that Deplete the Ozone Layer is among the most well-known examples where parties consenting to the treaty consent to authorize a supermajority vote of the Meeting of the Parties (MOP) to adjust for all parties control measures with respect to the consumption and production of ozone-depleting substances.[80] That provision has not, however, ever been used; the parties have always made their decisions by consensus instead.[81] This raises the question of how often States rely on consensual means despite the availability/authority afforded to non-consensual ones.

Like consent *qua* commitment, international law and international relations have done little to structure how States should manifest consent as content. Formalities are few and far between. Reservations arise by their purported effect on the treaty, not the form employed.[82] Subsequent agreements, as noted, can arise by consent that is either binding or non-binding. Amendments, in contrast, depend on a binding manifestation of consent to be bound, but that consent can be anterior to the amendment itself (e.g. via the primary treaty's amendment procedure) or contemporaneous (e.g. an amending agreement governed by international law). So long as there is mutual consent to an agreement to amend, international law does not impose any requirements of form. There is no requirement, for example, to follow the formalities observed to create the underlying treaty.[83] As Mark Villiger explained, an amendment agreement 'need not be in writing; it may – notwithstanding constitutional difficulties – be oral or even tacit, and can occur, for instance, by means of subsequent practice'.[84] Consenting to the contents of political commitments, meanwhile, has garnered little attention.

80 Montreal Protocol on Substances that Deplete the Ozone Layer, 1522 UNTS 3 (concluded 16 September 1987, entered into force 1 January 1989), Art. 2.

81 Brunnée, fn. 14, para. 11.

82 Philippe Gautier, 'Article 2 Convention of 1969', in Corten and Klein, fn. 23, Vol. 1, pp. 33–65, p. 49: '[VCLT definition of a reservation] underlies the lack of formalism of the law of treaties. Any declaration, whatever its title, made when signing or expressing the consent to be bound by the treaty, may constitute a reservation.'

83 ILC, 'Draft Conclusions on Subsequent Agreements', fn. 74, p. 58; Kerstin von der Decken, 'Article 39', in Oliver Dörr and Kirsten Schmalenbach (eds.), *Vienna Convention on the Law of Treaties: A Commentary*, 2nd ed. (Berlin: Springer, 2018), pp. 757–766, p. 761.

84 Villiger, fn. 23, p. 513. The ILC was less sanguine on amendments via subsequent practice, although it did not conclusively rule them out: see ILC, 'Draft Conclusions on Subsequent Agreements', fn. 74, p. 14, Conclusion 7(3).

States and stakeholders have rarely discussed – let alone agreed on – formalities or methodologies for discerning their contours and contents.

Such vagaries create challenges in constructing the contents of agreements. I have already noted how many of the difficulties with consent as commitment implicate content-determination exercises. The manifestations of consent as content raise additional issues. At what point does anterior consent become so attenuated from adjustments to a treaty's contents that the subsequent treaty alteration no longer warrants being deemed consented to at all? And where there is consent, how can we accurately differentiate its construction of a subsequent agreement on interpretation from an amendment to the treaty?[85] The ILC's work on subsequent agreements signalled the need for more attention to this topic, but did so for one set of interpretative questions, not the overall role of consent in treaty interpretation and application, let alone its implications for the meaning and operation of international agreements generally.

6.4 CONSENT AS CONSTITUTION

Beyond commitment and content, consent features prominently in constitution-like roles for international agreements, that is, setting out the constitutive rules as to who can make international agreements and the rules by which agreement-makers may do so.[86] Consider treaty-making. All States have the capacity to enter into treaties by virtue of their sovereignty.[87] Consent, however, frequently mediates this capacity in individual cases. When one State consents to form a treaty with another State, that consent concurrently signals each State's acceptance of the other's Statehood and the treaty-making status accompanying it.[88] Multilateral treaty consent may have similar constitutive functions for the consenting State, even as the effect of

[85] Brunnée, fn. 14, para. 12: 'it can be difficult to separate the realm of interpretation from the terrain that would normally require formal amendment'.

[86] I use the term 'constitution' here loosely to reflect consent's role in constructing constitutive rules, not a broader claim for any 'constitutionalism' in international agreements as a class. For more on constitutionalism, see Jeffery L. Dunoff and Joel Trachtman, *Ruling the World? Constitutionalism, International Law and Global Governance* (Cambridge: Cambridge University Press, 2009).

[87] *Case of the S.S. "Wimbledon" (Great Britain* v. *Germany)* [1923] PCIJ Ser. A No. 1, Annual Digest of Public International Law Cases, Vol. II, 1933, pp. 393–394, para. 35.

[88] Where States consent to non-treaty agreements (like a political commitment) with non-State actors, consent will not constitute the agreement-makers' *legal* status so much as their political valiance as appropriate interlocutors in international relations. Such agreements are, however, no less consensual; consent just serves a different constitutive function in such contexts.

consent's denial by objecting States is less clear.[89] Nor is consent's constitution of a treaty-making capacity limited to States. Treaty-making capacities of international organizations (hereafter IOs) depend not just on the IO's competence over a treaty's subject-matter, but also authority to engage in treaty-making on that subject, an authority that will usually derive from the consent of the States who constituted the IO, and always via the authority of its potential future treaty partners.[90] Consent similarly conditions treaty-making by other subjects of international law, for example, sub-national territorial units, supranational entities, and extra-national actors.[91] In the investment context, it even appears that States may consent to authorize at least one form of treaty commitment with individual investors – agreements to arbitrate.[92]

If anything, consent plays an even more prominent role in establishing who can conclude political commitments. Since political commitments do not depend on international (or national) law for their authority, they are not constrained by any legal rules on capacity.[93] This has allowed States to consent to political commitments *inter se* but also with other actors. Political commitments include agreement with or among sub-national territorial units, firms, civil society organizations, academic institutions and individuals, including broad-based 'multistakeholder' agreements like the 1000-plus signatories to the 2018 *Paris Call for Trust and Security in Cyberspace*.[94] Here again, however, the multiple manifestations of consent complicate matters. Absent an ability to differentiate among consent's various forms, it becomes difficult to discern if a State's consent to an international agreement

89 For example, following the 2012 UN General Assembly's resolution according Palestine 'non-Member observer State' status, Palestine consented to be bound to various multilateral treaties where the UN served as depositary. Several States indicated that their own consent to be bound should not extend to Palestine: see, for example, Canada, Communication, 'Depositary Notification, Rome Statute of the International Criminal Court, 23 January 2015', UN Doc. C.N.57.2015.TREATIES-XVIII.10: '[The Treaty] does not enter into force or have an effect on Canada's treaty relations, with respect to the "State of Palestine"').

90 Treaty-making capacity depends on the IO's relevant rules: see, for example, Art. 6 1986 VCLT; Olufemi Elias, 'Who Can Make Treaties? International Organizations', in Hollis, *The Oxford Guide*, fn. 2, pp. 97–116, p. 111: 'The types of treaties IOs actually conclude are a function of their competence to act *and* the acceptance of that competence by the other contracting parties.'

91 Hollis, fn. 1, pp. 147, 157, 163.

92 Tom Grant, 'Who Can Make Treaties? Other Subjects of International Law', in Hollis, *The Oxford Guide*, fn. 2, pp. 150–172, pp. 167–168.

93 IAJC Guidelines, fn. 25, Guideline 2.4 and accompanying commentary, pp. 69–70.

94 Paris Call for Trust and Security in Cyberspace, 'The Supporters' (12 November 2018). Available at: https://pariscall.international/en/supporters, last accessed 30 September 2022.

with a non-State actor confirms that actor's capacity to engage in treaty-making or to form a political commitment instead.[95]

In addition to constituting the capacity to conclude agreements, consent operates broadly in constituting the rules 'for' treaties themselves.[96] Indeed, notwithstanding its claim to customary international law status, we should not overlook how the VCLT's rules are the by-product of its 116 States parties' consent. Its rules on validity, moreover, centre almost entirely on consent. As Jan Klabbers explains:

> [T]he rules on validity and invalidity of treaties [are] laid down in VCLT Articles 46 through 53. In essence, most of these (Articles 46 through 52) deal with defects in the consent of a State to be bound, underlining the point ... that consent is practically speaking the most relevant general validity requirement when it comes to treaties. Such defects can have three broad sources: they can (i) be based on improper procedure or authorization; (ii) be the result of something misleading; or (iii) be the result of coercion. In all cases, the underlying rationale is that the consent to be bound has been affected: but for the affecting circumstance, the State concerned would not (or would most likely not) have expressed its consent to be bound.[97]

Of the treaty validity rules, therefore, only *jus cogens* does not look to a State's consent, even if manifestations of *jus cogens* as an actual validity rule remain elusive in practice.[98]

Beyond validity rules, the role of consent in many of the other secondary rules on the law of treaties has already been discussed. It is the VCLT, after all, that authorizes the use of consensual means for adoption, authentication, consent to be bound, reservations, subsequent agreements, amendments and termination. In other words, consent constitutes almost all the rules by which a treaty operates.

95 As Professors Besson and Martí note in their own contribution to this volume, answers to questions about the validity of international law lie in the law's legitimacy *and* who has the ability to claim legitimate authority. As such, it may matter not only what type of consent is given but who is giving it. A more defined theory of international law's sources might clarify matters but doing so requires markers of differentiation that have yet to be reconciled with the rising use of political commitments in practice: see Besson and Martí, Chapter 14 in this volume.

96 Craven, fn. 8, p. 105: 'consent appears, most visibly, as a structuring feature of treaty law'.

97 Jan Klabbers, 'The Validity and Invalidity of Treaties', in Hollis, *The Oxford Guide*, fn. 2, pp. 545–567, p. 550; Craven, fn. 8, p. 131; Arts. 53, 64 VCLT.

98 Even as it has come to serve as a yardstick for the general legality of State behaviour, *jus cogens* does not appear to have actually voided a treaty pursuant to Art. 53 VCLT. Aust, fn. 27, p. 279. Similarly, there are few examples of a fundamental change of circumstances justifying a State's non-performance of its obligations: see Art. 62 VCLT. On the relationship between consent and *rebus sic stantibus*, see Craven, fn. 8, p. 134.

Of course, the VCLT does include certain rules that do not depend on consent. It often does so, however, in a residual capacity; treaty parties may, by their mutual consent, vary such rules. Sometimes, the VCLT does this by endorsing whatever rule the parties consent to, via what the treaty itself provides (e.g. Articles 10, 12–17, 19–20, 22, 24–25, 28–31, 33, 40–41, 44, 54–58, 72, 76–78). Thus, the parties can dispense with principles like non-retroactivity or territorial application by consent, just as they can use consent to delineate specific rules for successive treaties.[99] In other instances, the VCLT provides for consent by authorizing the parties to 'otherwise agree' (e.g. Articles 11, 22, 25, 37, 44, 70, 72, 77, 79) or to establish a different intention varying a rule's application (e.g. Articles 7, 12–15, 28–29, 37, 39, 44, 59).

In practice, consent may even supplant secondary rules that make no accommodation for doing so. For example, the VCLT appears to require that States make reservations only in concert with their consent to be bound.[100] In practice, however, the United Nations has permitted reservations filed at a later time 'subject to the condition that ... no state party objects to it within a specified period of time', an approach based 'on the premise that any modification of existing treaty obligations is valid only with the unanimous consent of all the other parties to the treaty'.[101] Nor is this an isolated example; similar evolutions towards more consent-based outcomes are evident in issues around who can represent a State and bilateral treaty succession questions.[102] Such practices suggest that consent might not just infuse the existing secondary rules in the law of treaties but operate as a 'tertiary' rule of sorts, identifying – and adjusting – the secondary rules.[103] Such potential, however, revives jurisprudential questions of where consent ends. The logical challenges of

99 See, for example, Arts. 28–30 VCLT; on the residual character of Art. 30 VCLT, see Alexander Orakhelashvili, 'Article 30 of the 1969 VCLT', in Corten and Klein, fn. 23, Vol. 1, pp. 764–803, p. 774.

100 Art. 19 VCLT.

101 Palitha T. B. Kohona, 'Some Notable Developments in the Practice of the UN Secretary-General as Depositary of Multilateral Treaties: Reservations and Declarations' (2005) 99(2) *American Journal of International Law* 433–450.

102 On the contrast between flexibility in practice and the VCLT rules on full powers see d'Aspremont, fn. 46, pp. 262–263; The 1978 Vienna Convention automatic treaty succession rule was supplanted, in practice, by States' consent to bilateral treaty succession: see Patrick Dumberry, 'State Succession to Bilateral Treaties' (2015) 28 *Leiden Journal of International Law* 13–30, at 22.

103 Bruno Simma, 'Consent: Strains in the Treaty System', in Ronald St. J. Macdonald and Douglas M. Johnston (eds.), *The Structure and Process of International Law: Essays in Legal Philosophy Doctrine and Theory* (Leiden: Martinus Nijhoff, 1983), pp. 485–512, p. 503: '[VCLT] largely leaves untouched the freedom of the parties to contract out of the general mechanisms working for the integrity and continuance of treaties'.

'consenting to consent' suggest the basis for international agreements must involve more than consent, but it remains unclear whether consent-based rules run all the way to *pacta sunt servanda*, or if there are some intermediary brake points at which non-consent-based secondary rules emerge.

In terms of their constitutive rules, contracts differ from treaties in that the governing law – usually a specific nation's domestic law – addresses capacity questions and other secondary rules (nominally) independent of the contracting parties' consent.[104] The constitutive rules of political commitments, in contrast, are remarkably unclear. Even as States and other stakeholders admit the existence of these instruments (and increasingly employ them), there has been little discussion of what, if any, secondary rules the political context provides, let alone how these are formed or changed. The absence of such rules may prove increasingly problematic the more States and other stakeholders come to rely on international agreements not governed by international law.

6.5 REDRESSING PROBLEMS OF CONSENT FOR INTERNATIONAL AGREEMENTS?

The foregoing survey shows that consent is both (i) prevalent across many – if not most – functions associated with international agreements; and (ii) polysemous, with a core meaning that may prioritize manifestations of will or the object consent accepts. That combination provides flexibility to support the construction of commitments, content and constitutive rules. But it also poses problems for international agreements. Consent may construct all forms of international commitment, but it does not offer much assistance in differentiating among them. Indeed, as States diversify their use of commitments other than treaties, consent's role may actually cloud efforts to know when States are making a treaty or a political commitment and how adjudicators and other decision-makers may differentiate among international agreements once made.

However, consent's problems are not limited to separating treaties and political commitments. Consent may serve to interpret or amend, but States and other international actors have long struggled to divide such exercises notwithstanding the importance of doing so for various reasons (e.g. international institutional law, domestic approval procedures). These difficulties complicate our ability to evaluate the efficacy of the agreements themselves since knowing what the agreement 'is' or 'does' is a necessary prerequisite for assessing if it achieves its object and purpose. More broadly still, when it

104 I say this while noting that, at least in democratic States, the domestic private law that governs contracts itself emanates from the people's (collective) consent to domestic law.

comes to consent's constitutive functions, it is difficult to know how far consent goes. When do legal limits arise on the capacity of State consent to constitute new treaty-makers? Such problems are absent from the political commitment context, not because they do not exist, but because States and scholars have largely ignored questions about how consent constructs political commitments beyond establishing the commitment and its contents.

How can international law (and, for political commitments, international relations) address these challenges? For some, like Jan Klabbers, the problem lies not in consent but in the very idea of political commitments. Klabbers denies that States can consent out of international law and suggests, at a minimum, international law should adopt a presumption of treaty-making whenever States consent to an agreement.[105] Klabbers' rejection of political commitments would not, however, differentiate States' consent to treaties from consent to contracts (and the fact that States can usually choose their contracts' governing law suggests that legal regimes may be more optional than Klabbers' thesis suggests). Nor would it offer much aid in differentiating among different forms of consent *within* the law of treaties. The problem of distinguishing subsequent agreements from amendments would remain even if we were to deny using consent to a political commitment to produce the former. There is, moreover, the problem of State practice to consider. Today, States clearly understand themselves authorized to consent to construct different types of international agreements, rather than treaties alone.[106]

The idea of using presumptions (or default rules) to clarify consent's functions has more appeal. In the commitment context, establishing a presumption that State consent involves a treaty could ease existing confusion over identifying and differentiating among international agreement forms.[107]

[105] See generally Klabbers, fn. 15; Jan Klabbers, 'Not Re-visiting The Concept of Treaty', in Orakhelashvili and Williams, fn. 33, pp. 29–40, p. 29. Such views parallel long-standing questions about party-choice in private law settings with respect to how autonomous 'choice of law' clauses can be and whether domestic 'public' law can be the subject of forum shopping given competing and concurrent claims to prescriptive jurisdiction.

[106] See fn. 29; Kassoti, fn. 1, at 111. Klabbers himself has acknowledged this practice: Klabbers, 'Not Re-visiting', fn. 105, p. 30: 'it cannot be denied that many States have adopted the habit of concluding non-legally binding agreements'.

[107] Jan Klabbers, 'Governance by Academics: The Invention of Memoranda of Understanding' (2020) 80(1) *Zeitschrift für ausländisches öffentliches Recht und Völkerrecht* 35–72; Anthony Aust, 'The Theory and Practice of Informal International Instruments' (1986) 35(4) *International & Comparative Law Quarterly* 787–812, at 798; Kelvin Widdows, 'What Is an Agreement in International Law?' (1979) 50(1) *British Yearbook of International Law* 117–149. A few scholars have favoured a presumption against consent as treaty-making: see Schachter, fn. 27, at 297; James E. S. Fawcett, 'The Legal Character of International Agreements' (1953) 30 *British Yearbook of International Law* 381–400.

Doing so would not dispense with the possibility of States consenting to political commitments or contracts since countervailing evidence could rebut the presumption.[108] More discussion is needed, however, to assess which way any presumptions should point and how many are needed. We might, for example, want different presumptions about consent for agreements involving States *inter se* and those involving non-State actors. And if presumptions could work to reconcile consent as commitment, might they not offer similar utility to consent as content? Default rules already provide most of the constitutive rules for treaties, suggesting the issue there would be more of an empirical one – that is, how often do States and other treaty-makers employ a VCLT default rule versus employing their own *ad hoc*, consensual, solutions? It is also worth asking what presumptions could do *within* the realm of political commitments (recognizing that contract law is already fairly well developed in this regard, mitigating the necessity for similar inquiries there).[109] Of course, doing so via legal presumptions would undermine the informality on which much of political commitments' appeal lies, suggesting attention should focus on other forms of presumptions (e.g. moral ones).

Alternatively, we might flip the script between consent and content and use the latter to delineate the former. In 1962, Roberto Ago suggested that international law might regard agreements on certain subjects (e.g. boundaries, territorial seas) as treaties independent of party intent.[110] That approach might help explain the ICJ and ITLOS's willingness to find 'tacit' consent to agreements on various maritime boundaries.[111] Could such an approach help differentiate consent for international agreements? The answer may depend on whether this approach would use content as a complement to clarify consent's meaning or, instead, act as a substitute for it. Once content dictates consent and not vice versa, it may become easier for international courts to find consent 'at law' independent of recognizing its existence 'in fact'. And the more the idea of 'constructed' consent persists, the greater the chance that consent's pervasiveness could lead to its own demise – to a world where constructed consent fulfils the very functions that States and other subjects of international law previously directed via their own manifested acts of consent. In any case, instead of juxtaposing the rise of non-consensual law and international

[108] Barnett, fn. 26, at 309.

[109] In saying fairly well developed, I do not mean to suggest it is completely developed, as questions of conflict of laws remain, with the broader question as to why such choices/elections should be made at all.

[110] ILC, 'Summary and Records of the Fourteenth Session', *Yearbook of the International Law Commission* (1962) Vol. I, UN Doc. A/CN.4/Ser.A/1962, p. 52, para. 19.

[111] See fn. 66.

agreements (as existing scholarship so often does), it may already be more accurate to view the two phenomena as interrelated if not integrated.

To these two possibilities, I would add a third – directing specific formalities for each of consent's many functions. Instead of recognizing consent to be bound in any formal or informal means of consent, international law could delimit specific formalities for doing so. Reducing flexibility, however, need not eliminate it. The VCLT already offers five concrete vehicles for expressing consent to be bound, suggesting 'any other means if so agreed' may not actually be necessary or that it might be worthwhile to cabin a fuller list in ways that avoid future doubts as to the type of consent offered. Alternatively, formalities could be situated in the content of the commitment itself. At present, State practice suggests various linguistic markers (e.g. the use of 'shall' in a binding agreement and 'will' in political commitments) and clauses (e.g. an entry into force clause for treaties versus giving 'effect' to political commitments) are *indicative* of an international agreement's status.[112] Shifting from indicative to determinative criteria by mandating some of the current indicators could ease identification of treaty-making and political commitments in the wild. Nor must formalities always track existing practice. For example, a new solution to identifying consent to political commitments would be for international relations to come to expect participants to delineate that status explicitly.[113] The key challenge will be shifting social (and legal) expectations for States to understand the linkage between formalities and the particular manifestations of consent they aim to produce.

Nearly a century ago, Lord Arnold Duncan McNair noted the many functions treaties perform and called for different laws for different treaty types.[114] Neither the VCLT nor customary international law have executed on this idea to date. But it bears asking whether the many functions of consent to international agreements might provide an apt opportunity to do so.[115]

[112] IAJC Guidelines, fn. 25, Guideline 3.4 and accompanying commentary, pp. 87–93.

[113] For proposed language doing so, see IAJC Guidelines, fn. 25, Guideline 3.3 and accompanying commentary, pp. 84–86.

[114] For a categorization of treaties based on whether they involve (a) conveyances; (b) contracts; (c) law-making (whether constitutional or ordinary); and (d) incorporation, see Arnold McNair, 'The Functions and Differing Legal Character of Treaties' (1930) 11 *British Yearbook of International Law* 100–118. McNair envisioned different rules for each category such as treaties involving conveyances would survive war; *travaux préparatoires* would be more relevant for contractual treaties than law-making ones.

[115] Brölmann suggests this was because Humphrey Waldock and the ILC focused on treaty form over functions. Catherine Brölmann, 'Law-Making Treaties: Form and Function in International Law' (2005) 74 *Nordic Journal of International Law* 383–403, at 390. As this chapter has shown, however, any ILC focus on form did not result in the VCLT requiring any particular types/methods for assessing it.

International law might start, for example, employing different formalities to establish – and differentiate – among consent as commitment, content and constitution. The ILC's work on subsequent agreements and subsequent practice already shows the value in increasing formalism for at least some aspects of consent's role in constructing a treaty's contents.[116] Differentiating commitment from content would also track existing jurisprudence's acknowledgement of different processes for establishing law's existence (law ascertainment) from its meaning (content-determination).[117] It may make sense, therefore, for international law to vary whether and what formalities must accompany consent to make an international agreement from those for differentiating its contents. In the same vein, differentiating formalities for when consent operates as the law of treaties' secondary rules (or even as the means for their adjustment) would help clarify what functions international law permits it to perform and where that law becomes non-derogable beyond cases of *jus cogens* itself.

6.6 CONCLUSION

Consent may be, as Andrew Guzman charged, a 'slow, difficult, and cumbersome process' but it is also an ubiquitous one.[118] For international agreements, consent is not 'simply an instrumental medium by which other things are to be achieved (as a vehicle for social transactions of one kind or another)' but a vehicle to achieve 'a legal world configured around the idea that it is the systematic outcome of acts of collective free will rather than of coercion'.[119] The recent emphasis on supposedly non-consensual law-making may thus have important implications for the future of the international legal order. But it would be a mistake to equate claims of the treaty's decline with the decline of all international agreements and the consent that accompanies them.

Rather than focusing attention away from treaties and other forms of international agreements, this chapter has argued that States and scholars should spend as much time studying how consent constructs an agreement's commitment, contents and constitution as has been devoted to non-consensual alternatives in

[116] d'Aspremont, fn. 46, p. 278.

[117] See generally Jean d'Aspremont, *Formalism and the Sources of International Law: A Theory of the Ascertainment of Legal Rules* (Oxford: Oxford University Press, 2011), p. 157; Hollis, fn. 67.

[118] Guzman, fn. 1, at 751: '[Consent] creates endless bottlenecks, provides many veto points, and invites strategic holdout behavior, all of which make agreement more difficult. Even when it is achieved, consent is often reached only by weakening the content of an agreement.'

[119] Craven, fn. 8, p. 104.

the law of treaties and international law more generally.[120] Such a project will require both descriptive and normative elements. On the descriptive front, Jean d'Aspremont has posited a 'constant oscillation' in the law of treaties between formalism and flexibility.[121] The many functions of consent detailed here beg the question of whether that oscillation has ended, landing now firmly on the flexibility side of the equation. At present, we do not actually know how often States and other stakeholders employ contemporaneous consent to constitute the relevant rules for an international agreement in lieu of the VCLT's existing legal rules. More work is thus needed to understand when contemplated roles for consent (whether as commitment, content or constitutive rules) manifest in practice. Similarly, it is important to identify the frequency with which non-consensual rules like those for adjusting the Montreal Protocol are displaced by consent or consensus. Scholarship could thus map when and how often States or third-party decision-makers defer to consent, construct it or embrace non-consent-based tools to discern an international agreement's contents or commitments.

Assessing consent in practice would pair well with normative questions about what functions it should perform and how it can best do so. In lieu of consent's current polysemy, international law (and international relations more broadly) might benefit from deeper inquiries into consent's different functions and the means for differentiating among them. I have proposed here three categories of functions – commitment, content and constitutive rules – where consent's different operations could warrant different formalities. But I acknowledge that more research and dialogue is needed to assess whether these are the right categories, and whether other alternatives like presumptions or contents themselves could better direct consent's operations when it comes to international agreements.

At a minimum, sorting out different formalities for consent's different functions can add much needed certainty and transparency to a concept that is so prevalent across all forms of international agreement. Such certainty and transparency are necessary, moreover, to evaluating the efficacy of international agreements themselves – their capacity to perform the functions for which they are created by States and other international stakeholders, whether in terms of improving cooperation, reducing conflicts or providing the necessary means of coordination for issues warranting global governance. Thus, solving the problems of consent in all its forms and functions for international agreements could open up a new way to better understand international law itself.

[120] Indeed, I think it is yet to be decided if we are witnessing a decline in agreement-making even if formal treaty-making consensual structures are, as Krisch suggests, 'being increasingly sidelined by less consensual ones': Krisch, fn. 1, at 36.

[121] d'Aspremont, fn. 46, p. 257.

7

Consenting to Treaty Commitments

Endorsing Rules or Endorsing a Regime of Discursive Commitments?

FUAD ZARBIYEV

7.1 INTRODUCTION

International law is often described as a legal system having significant connections with State consent. Traditionally, consent was seen 'as the central engine which drives the great machine of international law'.[1] Even today, consent is sometimes described as 'constitutive of the international legal order',[2] and for many international lawyers, the often-quoted statement of the Permanent Court of International Justice in *The S.S. "Lotus"* that '[t]he rules of law binding upon States ... emanate from their own free will'[3] still remains an accurate description of international law.[4]

Others offer a more nuanced picture, but nonetheless accept that 'most of international law's deep structure is related to the consent of states'.[5] Still others point to the limitations of the consent paradigm and describe it as a 'foundational myth' rather than a helpful analytical device to understand contemporary international law.[6] What is often highlighted is that

1 Stephen C. Neff, 'Consent', in Jean d'Aspremont and Sahib Singh (eds.), *Concepts for International Law: Contributions to Disciplinary Thought* (Cheltenham: Edward Elgar, 2019), pp. 127–140.

2 Catherine Sweetser, 'Humanity as the A and Ω of International Law: Four Replies to Anne Peters' (2009) 20(3) *European Journal of International Law* 549–555, at 550.

3 *The Case of S.S. "Lotus" (France* v. *Turkey)* (Judgment) [1927] PCIJ Ser. A No. 10, p. 18.

4 See, for example, Anthony Aust, *Handbook of International Law*, 1st ed. (Cambridge: Cambridge University Press, 2005), p. 4 (stating that international law 'is based on the consent (express or implied) of states').

5 Nico Krisch, 'The Decay of Consent: International Law in an Age of Global Public Goods' (2014) 108(1) *American Journal of International Law* 1–40, at 3.

6 Wouter G. Werner, 'State Consent as Foundational Myth', in Catherine Brölmann and Yannick Radi (eds.), *Research Handbook on the Theory and Practice of International Lawmaking* (Cheltenham: Edward Elgar, 2016), pp. 13–31.

the consent paradigm is singularly ill-suited to account for customary international law.[7]

Despite these perennial controversies, one thing that is generally agreed upon is that the law of treaties is the 'bastion of consensualism'[8] and that consent is 'the cornerstone of all international treaty commitments'.[9] Treaty is described as '[t]he source of international law that epitomizes the understanding of consent *qua* agreement';[10] treaty law is said to 'most readily [reflect] the idea of consensual international law'.[11]

What consensualism means, however, is less straightforward. Consensualism can mean 'threshold consensualism', the fundamental notion that a State is not bound by a treaty without its consent to be bound by it. It cannot be disputed that consensualism at the very least means this 'comprehensive', 'all-embracing notion of consent'.[12] But consensualism cannot be limited to that understanding, excluding consent to specific commitments.[13] Just imagine a system where only the threshold consensualism exists with respect to treaties: that would mean that a State cannot be bound by a treaty without its consent, but what it is bound by would not be a matter of consent. This other side of consensualism – which I would call 'substantive consensualism' – is rarely discussed in the literature, but it remains indisputable as a logical premise of the law of treaties. As the International Court of Justice

7 Neff, fn. 1, pp. 127–140.

8 Hubert Thierry, 'L'évolution du droit international' (Volume 220) *Collected Course of the Hague Academy* of *International*, 1990, pp. 9–185, p. 36.

9 *Daimler Financial Services AG* v. *Argentine Republic*, ICSID, Award (22 August 2012) Case No. ARB/05/1, 51 ILM 1226, para. 168: 'Consent is . . . the cornerstone of all international treaty commitments . . . The primacy of the principle of consent runs through all types of treaty commitments entered into by states.'

10 Samantha Besson, 'State Consent and Disagreement in International Law-Making: Dissolving the Paradox' (2016) 29(2) *Leiden Journal of International Law* 289–316, at 297.

11 Jutta Brunnée, 'Consent' (last updated January 2022), in Rüdiger Wolfrum (ed.), *Max Planck Encyclopedia of Public International Law* (Oxford: Oxford University Press, 2008). Available at: https://opil.ouplaw.com/display/10.1093/law:epil/9780199231690/law-9780199231690-e1388, last accessed 30 December 2022; Duncan B. Hollis, 'Why State Consent Still Matters: Non-State Actors, Treaties and the Changing Sources of International Law' (2005) 23(1) *Berkeley Journal of International Law* 137–174, at 140: 'the treaty paradigm generally continues to be pre-conditioned on the presence of state consent'; Shabtai Rosenne, 'Consent and Related Words in the Codified Law of Treaties', in *Mélanges offerts à Charles Rousseau* (Paris: Pedone, 1974), pp. 229–248, pp. 230–231: 'by definition the law of treaties is itself concerned with "consent"'.

12 Rosenne, fn. 11, pp. 230–231.

13 Besson, fn. 10, p. 294: 'A lot of the difficulties with the notion of consent in international law stem from its polysemy. It is used to mean different things that may then related very differently to the validity or legitimacy of international law.'

(hereafter ICJ) clarified, a treaty is 'an instrument which derives its binding force and *content* from the consent of the contracting States'.[14]

The focus of this chapter is on substantive consensualism. Section 7.2 will attempt to show that the current law of treaties is premised on a theory of meaning that is inhospitable to substantive consensualism, a situation that can be traced back to the increasing marginalization of the intentionalist approach to treaty interpretation. Section 7.3 will argue that one consequence of this situation is that consent has become a discursive construction rather than an empirical reality in treaty interpretation.

7.2 MARGINALIZATION OF THE INTENTION OF THE PARTIES IN TREATY INTERPRETATION

The conventional wisdom about intentionalism in treaty interpretation is that treaty interpretation does not turn on the intention of the parties, but on what the meaning of the text that the parties negotiated and agreed on is. This view is generally associated with the International Law Commission's (hereafter ILC) work on a draft convention on the law of treaties and the Vienna Convention on the Law of Treaties (hereafter VCLT)[15] that came out of it. A recent publication makes the point forcefully:

> Party 'intent' is not one of the tools that the Vienna Convention on the Law of Treaties (VCLT) gives to treaty interpreters. To be sure, party intent is presumably reflected in the 'object and purpose' of the treaty, but it is not a separate criterion; in fact, the VCLT implicitly excludes party intent from playing an interpretive role.[16]

The notion that the VCLT 'implicitly excludes party intent from playing an interpretive role' might seem surprising given that to the naked eye the VCLT seems to be doing the exact opposite. Far from disregarding the intention of the parties or implicitly excluding it from the process of treaty interpretation, the VCLT explicitly includes it in that process, recognizing that the parties' intention could even displace the ordinary meaning of treaty terms in some

[14] *Request for Interpretation of the Judgment of 15 June 1962 in the Case Concerning the Temple of Preah Vihear (Cambodia* v. *Thailand)* (Judgment) [2013] ICJ Rep. 281, para. 75 (emphasis added).

[15] Vienna Convention on the Law of Treaties, 1155 UNTS 331 (adopted 23 May 1969, entered into force 27 January 1980).

[16] Andrea Bjorklund, 'The Enduring but Unwelcome Role of Party Intent in Treaty Interpretation' (2018) 112 *American Journal of International Law Unbound* 44–48, at 44.

circumstances.[17] But the fact that the VCLT can be mobilized for the proposition that intention has no independent role to play in treaty interpretation is reflective of a broader ambivalence of international lawyers about intentionalism in treaty interpretation. The latter do not approach treaty interpretation with naked eyes, but with a series of rarely articulated premises, presuppositions and normative projects that make the above-cited assertion not merely discursively available, but also rhetorically compelling.

7.2.1 *Intentionalism in the Intellectual History of Treaty Interpretation*

The ambivalence of international lawyers about the role of intention in treaty interpretation has deep roots in the intellectual history of the discipline. Consider Hugo Grotius' position in this regard. Referring to Cicero, Grotius notes that interpretation turns on what is meant, not on what is said.[18] But he also makes clear his view that what is meant cannot be understood without what is said:

> [I]f the intent could be understood by us without speech we should not use words at all. Because it cannot be so understood, words were invented, not to hinder, but to express the intent.[19]

For Grotius, this was by necessity so not only 'because internal acts are not of themselves perceivable', but also because

> some degree of certainty must be established, lest there should fail to be any binding obligation, in case every one could free himself by inventing whatever meaning he might wish, natural reason itself demands that the one to whom the promise has been made should have the right to compel the promisor to do what the correct interpretation suggests.[20]

Hence the importance to ensure that treaty interpretation proceeds 'without wicked deceit'.[21] Even though 'the inference of intent' remains for Grotius '[t]he measure of correct interpretation', that inference should be based on 'the most probable indications' in the form of 'words and implications'.[22]

[17] Art. 31(4) VCLT: 'A special meaning shall be given to a term if it is established that the parties so intended.'
[18] Hugo Grotius, *De Jure Belli ac Pacis* (Oxford: Oxford University Press, Clarendon Press, 1925), p. 409.
[19] Ibid., p. 422.
[20] Ibid., p. 409.
[21] Ibid.
[22] Ibid.

Those indications should act as public guarantees against unilateral manipulations of commitments. For instance, words cannot be made to mean what the author of a promise wants them to mean, but should be understood 'in their ordinary sense ... according to current usage'.[23] Grotius gives several examples showing the danger of deviating from such 'public meaning':

> The Locrians ... availed themselves of a stupid evasion in their perfidy; for they took oath that they would keep the agreement as long as they should stand on that ground and should bear heads on their shoulders; then they threw away the earth which they had placed in their shoes, and the heads of garlic which they had laid on their shoulders, as if in that manner they could free themselves from the religious obligation ... Similar is the fact that the Boeotians, having promised to restore a city, restored it not unharmed, but destroyed ... Likewise the Sultan Mahomet, after capturing Euboea, cut in two the man whose head he had promised should be safe.[24]

A similar reasoning was offered by Samuel Pufendorf[25] and Christian Wolff.[26] While Emer de Vattel's theory of interpretation remains largely similar to his predecessors', it also stands out for its clearer articulation of the reasons why a party's intention cannot control treaty interpretation. Like his predecessors, Vattel recognizes the importance of intention in treaty interpretation.[27] But he also makes clear that this is not a license to override the 'natural' meaning of treaty provisions:

> When a deed is worded in clear and precise terms, – when its meaning is evident, and leads to no absurd conclusion, – there can be no reason for refusing to admit the meaning which such deed naturally presents. To go elsewhere in search of conjectures, in order to restrict or extend it, is but an attempt to elude it. If this dangerous method be once admitted, there will be no deed which it will not render useless. However luminous each clause may be, – however clear and precise the terms in which the deed is couched, – all this will be of no avail, if it be allowed to go in quest of extraneous arguments,

23 Ibid.

24 Ibid., p. 410.

25 Samuel Pufendorf, *De Jure Naturae et Gentium* (Oxford: Oxford University Press/Clarendon Press, 1934), p. 301.

26 Christian Wolff, *Principes du droit de la nature et des gens* (Amsterdam: Marc Michel Rey, 1758), Vol. 2, Book IV, Chapter III, pp. 327–328.

27 Emer de Vattel, *Law of Nations* (Philadelphia: T. & J. W. Johnson, 1853), Book II, Chapter XVII, para. 274: 'The intention, sufficiently known, furnishes the true matter of the convention, – what is promised and accepted, demanded and granted'; ibid., Book II, Chapter XVII, para. 283: '[I]n all interpretations, the question is, to give the words that sense which ought to be presumed most conformable to the intention of the parties speaking.'

to prove that it is not to be understood in the sense which it naturally presents.[28]

Vattel states in no uncertain terms that intention is among such 'extraneous arguments':

> Those cavillers who dispute the sense of a clear and determinate article, are accustomed to seek their frivolous subterfuges in the pretended intentions and views which they attribute to its author. It would be very often dangerous to enter with them into the discussion of those supposed views that are not pointed out in the piece itself. There will be no security in conventions, no stability in grants or concessions, if they may be rendered nugatory by subsequent limitations, which ought to have been originally specified in the deed, if they were in the contemplation of the contracting parties.[29]

Vattel's first interpretive maxim – 'it is not allowable to interpret what has no need of interpretation' – was precisely designed to discourage attempts to go to 'extraneous arguments' such as the intention in the face of a clear text.[30]

The works that the Institute of International Law dedicated to treaty interpretation also constitute an important chapter in the intellectual history of treaty interpretation. Those works started with a report prepared by the first Rapporteur of the Institute on treaty interpretation Hersch Lauterpacht. In that report, Lauterpacht described the identification of the intention of the parties as 'the law of the judge', 'a fundamental factor in the matter of treaty interpretation' or 'the primary object of interpretation'.[31] For Lauterpacht, 'in the interest of good faith and stability of international transactions', it is 'essential' to take the natural meaning of the terms as the starting point in treaty interpretation and place on the party relying on a different meaning the burden of proof that the parties have departed from the natural meaning or that the natural meaning is not the one that appears at first sight.[32] However, he also highlighted that the objective of treaty interpretation being the identification of the intention of the parties, it should be borne in mind that the natural meaning is only the point of departure, which may or may not be confirmed as the final outcome.

Lauterpacht's philosophy of interpretation emphasizing the central role of the intention of the parties did not meet the consensus of the members. While

28 Ibid., para. 263.

29 Ibid., para. 264.

30 Ibid., para. 263.

31 Hersch Lauterpacht, 'De l'interprétation des traités' (1950) 43(1) *Annuaire de l'Institut de Droit International* 366–460, 420–423 (my translation).

32 Ibid., pp. 387, 433 (my translation).

some members agreed with his approach, others criticized it, finding it normatively undesirable or empirically misguided. Consequently, Maurice Bourquin proposed that Lauterpacht's first rule be reformulated as follows:

> The agreement of the parties having been embodied in the text of the treaty, it is necessary to take the natural and ordinary meaning of the terms of this text as the basis of interpretation.[33]

This proposition was adopted by the Institute without opposition. It made it into the draft text prepared by Gerald Fitzmaurice who replaced Lauterpacht after the election of the latter to the ICJ. Fitzmaurice never hid his radical disagreement with Lauterpacht's approach to treaty interpretation. While the draft articles prepared by Lauterpacht contained five express mentions of intention, the text prepared by Fitzmaurice and finally adopted by the Institute contained none.[34]

7.2.2 *Drafting History of the Interpretation Rules of the VCLT*

Even though the last Special Rapporteur of the ILC on the law of treaties Sir Humphrey Waldock insisted that the Commission did not try to resolve 'a doctrinal controversy',[35] there can be little doubt that the Commission made it a point to take a firm position about the place of intentionalism in treaty interpretation. In fact, the Special Rapporteur specifically pointed out that 'the Commission should take a clear position in regard to the role of the text in treaty interpretation' given that 'doctrinal differences concerning the methods of interpretation have tended to weaken the significance of the text as the expression of the will of the parties'.[36]

Waldock's approach was thus shaped and informed by his conviction that the Commission should emphasize 'the primacy of the text as evidence of the intention of the parties' and make clear the text's status as 'the dominant factor

33 Institut de Droit International, 'Délibération: De l'interprétation des traités' (1952) 44(2) *Annuaire de l'Institut de Droit International* 359–406, 380 (my translation).

34 Institut de Droit International, 'Délibérations: De l'interprétation des traités' (1956) 46 *Annuaire de l'Institut de Droit International* 317–349, 346.

35 United Nations Conference on the Law of Treaties, 'Summary Records of the Plenary Meetings and of the Meetings of the Committee of the Whole' (1968), UN Doc. A/CONF.39/C.1, p. 184.

36 ILC, 'Third Report on the Law of Treaties by Sir Humphrey Waldock, Special Rapporteur', *Yearbook of the International Law Commission* (1964) Vol. II, UN Doc. A/CN.4/167, pp. 5–66, p. 54; ILC, 'Draft Articles on the Law of Treaties with Commentaries', *Yearbook of the International Law Commission* (1966) Vol. II, UN Doc. A/CN.4/SER.A/1966/Add.1, pp. 187–274, p. 219.

in the interpretation of the treaty'.[37] For Waldock, one reason why it was important for the Commission to include rules of interpretation in the draft Convention was that a number of draft articles adopted by the Commission that referred to the intention of the parties could not properly be implemented without further clarification as to whether this intention was to be established by reference to the text or other evidence was admissible.[38] While Waldock never excluded the relevance of intention in treaty interpretation, he was adamant that the latter should not be given 'too large a place ... as an independent basis of interpretation'.[39] In this approach, elucidating the meaning of the text was presented as 'the starting point and purpose of interpretation', on the assumption that 'the text must be presumed to be the authentic expression of the intention of the parties'.[40] 'The general rules' of interpretation formulated in the third report of the Special Rapporteur made in fact no reference to the intention of the parties.[41] However, another draft article titled 'Application of the general rules' presented the context, the object and purpose of the treaty, the preparatory work, the circumstances surrounding the treaty's conclusion as well as the subsequent practice of the parties in the application of the treaty as 'other evidence or indications of the intention of the parties'.[42] In keeping with the theory that the text is the primary evidence of the intention of the parties, such 'other evidence or indications' could only be used to confirm the interpretation based on the natural and ordinary meaning rule, in case of ambiguity or obscurity of a term, if the natural and ordinary meaning leads to a manifestly absurd or unreasonable interpretation or to establish the special meaning in which the parties employed a term.[43]

This limited role of the intention of the parties was largely shared within the Commission.[44] While several members explicitly recognized the relevance of the intention of the parties, they agreed with the Special Rapporteur that the

37 ILC, 'Third Report on the Law of Treaties', fn. 36, p. 56.
38 Ibid., p. 54.
39 Ibid., p. 56.
40 Ibid.
41 Ibid., p. 52.
42 Ibid.
43 Ibid.
44 Only two members of the Commission disagreed with Waldock's approach in this regard. For Mr Tabibi, the intention of the parties should receive 'greater weight', since it was 'the most important element of any general rule [of treaty interpretation]': see ILC, 'Summary Records of the Sixteenth Session', *Yearbook of the International Law Commission* (1964) Vol. I, UN Doc. A/CN.4/SER.A/1964, p. 276, para. 25. Emphasizing the paramount importance of 'the autonomy of the will of the parties', Mr Bartos was of the view that '[w]hat the parties had intended was more important than what they had actually said in the treaty': see ibid., p. 279, para. 64.

intention was to be sought in the text agreed by the parties.[45] Only three governments criticized the Commission's choice in this regard.[46]

The most vigorous objection to the ILC's approach came from the United States (hereafter US) at the Vienna Conference on the Law of Treaties. The US Government represented by Professor Myres McDougal strongly criticized the Commission for its rejection of the 'common intent as the goal of interpretation' and for establishing an unnecessarily rigid system in the search of the common intention of the parties with its 'primacy of the text' approach.[47] For McDougal, while the text was important, it was only 'one important index among many of the common intent of the parties' and the search of the latter could include all factors that might prove relevant 'in a particular set of circumstances' without *a priori* exclusion or without establishing a 'fixed hierarchy' for all circumstances.[48] However, the amendment presented by the US was rejected, with several delegations finding the proposed lack of a hierarchy with the primacy of the text dangerous for the stability of treaty relations.[49]

7.2.3 *The Regime of Treaty Interpretation under the VCLT*

The regime of treaty interpretation set forth in the VCLT is often described as making room for all principal interpretive approaches without making a clear choice in favour of any of them. This seems to be the case with regard to intentionalism as well. Despite the ILC's attempts to marginalize the place of intention in treaty interpretation, Article 31 of the VCLT appears to be a good example of *praeteritio*, since Article 31 prominently calls attention to intention while seemingly excluding it. As pointed out at the beginning of Section 7.2, paragraph 4 of Article 31 states that, 'A special meaning shall be given to a term if it is established that the parties so intended.' This paragraph is

45 See, for example, ILC, 'Summary Records of the Eighteenth Session', *Yearbook of the International Law Commission* (1966) Vol. I, Part Two, UN Doc. A/CN.4/SER.A/1966, p. 188, para. 38: 'of course, the intention of the parties must be sought but it could only be found in the text'; ibid., p. 185, para. 7: 'Since the parties had chosen to express their will in written form, it was the terms used by them, in their context, which must be presumed to reflect their real intentions'; see also the interventions by Mr Tounkine (ibid., p. 189, para. 61) and by Mr Yasseen (ibid., p. 197, para. 50).

46 ILC, 'Summary Records on the Eighteenth Session', *Yearbook of the International Law Commission* (1966) Vol. II, Part Two, UN Doc. A/CN.4/SER.A/1966/Add. 1 (Part.2), pp. 99–101.

47 United Nations Conference on the Law of Treaties, fn. 35, pp. 167–168.

48 Ibid., p. 168.

49 Ibid., p. 174.

supposed to introduce an exception to the principle of the ordinary meaning set forth in paragraph 1. But its logical implications undermine this rule-exception dynamic: if a special meaning is to be given to a term when the parties so intended, it can only be so because a term is to be given whatever meaning the parties intended to give it. If this is so, both paragraph 1 and paragraph 4 are particular applications of such a general rule: paragraph 1 is based on the presumption that the parties normally intend to use treaty terms in their ordinary meaning; and paragraph 4 covers situations where it is established that the presumption of ordinary meaning is to be displaced.

Although the foregoing reasoning seems logically unassailable, it does not reflect how the treaty interpretation regime of the VCLT is generally understood. Most commentators writing today assume that the intention only comes into the picture under the limited circumstances contemplated in paragraph 4 of Article 31 without taking the pain to think about the logical implications of that provision.[50] As pointed out in Section 7.2.2, elucidating the meaning of the text rather than finding out the common intention of the parties was presented by the Commission as the goal of treaty interpretation. While the Commission highlighted that Article 31 titled 'General Rule of Interpretation' was not meant to introduce any hierarchy, there is little doubt that paragraph 4 of Article 31 was seen differently from the rest of that Article. For instance, in response to the proposition to place the content of paragraph 4 immediately after paragraph 1,[51] a member of the Drafting Committee appointed by the Commission responded that such a change would undermine 'the importance of paragraph 1' that he qualified as 'the golden rule of interpretation'.[52] He added that the Drafting Committee even considered deleting that paragraph completely, given that '[it] dealt with a minor point which was of limited application'.[53] Even though the ILC promoted the holistic approach to treaty interpretation, it was thus reluctant to subscribe to the view that meaning is a function of an intending agent's intention. The very definition of the starting point of treaty interpretation as 'the elucidation of the meaning of the text, not an investigation *ab initio* into the intentions of the parties'[54] assumes that the meaning of the text can, at least as a preliminary matter, be identified in an intention-free manner following the 'natural' or usual meaning of the words used in the text.

50 Robert Kolb, *Interprétation et création du droit international: Esquisse d'une herméneutique juridique moderne pour le droit international public* (Brussels: Bruylant, 2006), p. 607.

51 ILC, fn. 45, p. 267, para. 97.

52 Ibid., p. 269, para. 9.

53 Ibid.

54 ILC, 'Draft Articles with Commentaries', fn. 36, p. 220.

7.3 CONSENT TO TREATY COMMITMENTS: FROM 'RULE CONSENT' TO 'REGIME CONSENT'

In a system in which the common intention of the parties is an important parameter in treaty interpretation, the parties to the treaty would be best positioned to articulate that intention, as any third party pretending to know the common intention of the parties better than the parties themselves would face 'the paradox of knowing better'.[55] But as explained in Section 7.2, the official regime of treaty interpretation in international law has moved away from the intentionalist paradigm. While references to the common intention of the parties are still understandably present in the treaty interpretation discourse, the regime set forth in the VCLT is premised on the assumption that treaty interpretation is not 'an investigation *ab initio* into the intentions of the parties', but an exercise primarily based on the text, the latter being considered as the virtually exclusive medium used by the parties to express those intentions.[56] Arguably, this change in the object of interpretation has important consequences for the authority dynamics in treaty interpretation. The parties to a treaty may be said to be best positioned to know and expose their common intention, but they can claim no such exclusivity when elucidating the meaning of the text is considered to be 'the starting point and purpose of interpretation'.[57] In other words, State consent is likely to be less compelling in a regime in which the text is regarded as a primary object of treaty interpretation.

One consequence of this shift is that treaty interpretation is not an empirical investigation directed to finding out *what the parties meant*, but a discursive practice governed by 'linguistic rationalism' where the overarching question is *what the text means*.[58] What this entails for consent to the normative content of treaties is that one moves from what Stephen Neff calls 'rule consent' – 'consent to a rule or standard according to which future, unspecified acts will be judged' – to the 'regime consent', which refers to consent to 'participation in a system or regime which determines the manner in which rules are [interpreted]'.[59] As the

[55] Guy de Lacharrière, *La politique juridique extérieure* (Paris: Economica, 1983), p. 172; Martti Koskenniemi, *From Apology to Utopia: The Structure of International Legal Argument* (Cambridge: Cambridge University Press, 2005), p. 347.

[56] ILC, 'Draft Articles with Commentaries', fn. 36, p. 220, para. 11.

[57] ILC, 'Third Report on the Law of Treaties', fn. 36, p. 56.

[58] While I borrow the phrase 'linguistic rationalism' from Brandom, my use of it is not limited to the linguistic realm: see Robert Brandom, *Articulating Reasons: An Introduction to Inferentialism* (Cambridge, MA: Harvard University Press, 2000), p. 189.

[59] Neff, fn. 1, p. 128. While I make use of the terminology introduced by Neff, it should be noted that for him, rule consent 'underpins the whole of treaty law, virtually by definition'.

Iran–US Claims Tribunal (hereafter USCT) candidly articulated, 'the Vienna Convention does not require any demonstration of a "converging will" or of a conscious acceptance by each Party of all implications of the terms to which it has agreed'.[60] By expressing its consent to be bound by a treaty, a State in fact accepts a regime in which its rights and obligations are discursively articulated. In this regime, consent does not vanish, but it is a discursive construction rather than an empirical reality. To show how this regime operates, the rest of the chapter will focus on some of the most prominent doctrines that have been developed to justify expansive readings of treaty commitments.[61]

7.3.1 *The Doctrine of Implied Powers*

The conventional doctrine governing the powers of international organizations (hereafter IOs) is the principle of attributed powers; IOs only have the powers that have been conferred upon them by the Member States. While those powers are 'normally the subject of an express statement in [the] constituent instruments',[62] it is commonly accepted that IOs can also have implied powers 'which are not expressly provided for in the basic instruments which govern their activities'.[63] The foundational decision in which the doctrine of implied powers was clearly articulated is the advisory opinion of the ICJ in the *Reparations* Case.[64] The main issue in that case was whether the United Nations (hereafter UN) had the power to bring international claims for reparation on behalf of its agents for damages suffered in the exercise of the functions of the UN. The Court clarified that the governing principle was that 'the Organization must be deemed to have those powers which, though not expressly provided in the Charter, are conferred upon it by necessary implication as being essential to the performance of its duties'.[65]

60 *Iran* v. *United States*, IUSCT, Decision (6 April 1984) Case No. DEC-32-A18, p. 497. The Tribunal went on to add: 'It is the "terms of the treaty in their context and in the light of its object and purpose" with which the Tribunal is to be concerned, not the subjective understanding or intent of either of the Parties.' Ibid.

61 For the purposes of my argument, what is important is not the specific details of these doctrines, but the broad argumentative structure underpinning each of them.

62 *Legality of the Use by a State of Nuclear Weapons in Armed Conflict* (Advisory Opinion) [1996] ICJ Rep. 66, para. 25.

63 Ibid.

64 *Reparation for Injuries Suffered in the Service of the United Nations* (Advisory Opinion) [1949] ICJ Rep. 174; Viljam Engström, 'Implied Powers of International Organizations: On the Character of a Legal Doctrine' (2003) 14 *Finnish Yearbook of International Law* 129–158, at 133 (describing it as 'the milestone').

65 *Reparation for Injuries*, fn. 64, p. 182.

The Court first established a connection between the UN's purposes, functions and its agents, by noting that '[h]aving regard to its purposes and functions . . . the Organization may find it necessary, and has in fact found it necessary, to entrust its agents with important missions to be performed in disturbed parts of the world'.[66] It then explained why the capacity to protect its agents through claims for reparation for damages caused to them in the exercise of the UN's missions was necessary for the UN 'to ensure the efficient and independent performance of these missions and to afford effective support to its agents':[67]

> In order that the agent may perform his duties satisfactorily, he must feel that this protection is assured to him by the Organization, and that he may count on it. To ensure the independence of the agent, and, consequently, the independent action of the Organization itself, it is essential that in performing his duties he need not have to rely on any other protection than that of the Organization (save of course for the more direct and immediate protection due from the State in whose territory he may be). In particular, he should not have to rely on the protection of his own State. If he had to rely on that State, his independence might well be compromised, contrary to the principle applied by Article 100 of the Charter. And lastly, it is essential that – whether the agent belongs to a powerful or to a weak State; to one more affected or less affected, by the complications of international life; to one in sympathy or not in sympathy with the mission of the agent – he should know that in the performance of his duties he is under the protection of the Organization. This assurance is even more necessary when the agent is stateless.[68]

Finally, the Court made clear that the UN's capacity to bring international claims on behalf of its agents was a logical consequence of specific commitments that the Member States had entered into in the UN Charter and complementary agreements, referring in particular to the obligation to render to the UN 'every assistance' under Article 2, paragraph 5 of the Charter and to the principle of independence of the agents of the Secretariat set forth in Article 100 of the Charter.

This reasoning in several sequences enabled the Court to conclude that 'the capacity of the Organization to exercise a measure of functional protection of its agents arises by *necessary intendment* out of the Charter'.[69]

66 Ibid., p. 183.
67 Ibid.
68 Ibid., pp. 183–184.
69 Ibid., p. 184 (emphasis added).

7.3.2 *The Doctrine of Positive Obligations*

Classic civil and political rights are generally described as entailing 'negative obligations', whereby 'a State is required to abstain from interference with, and thereby respect, human rights'.[70] But the European Court of Human Rights (hereafter ECtHR) has long clarified that those rights also implicate 'positive obligations' requiring a State 'to take action to secure human rights'.[71] Such obligations are characterized as being 'inherent in an effective respect' for the rights set forth in the European Convention on Human Rights (hereafter ECHR).[72] This connection between the requirement of effective respect for human rights and the positive obligations is made explicit in cases in which the Court has made clear that many substantive rights recognized in the ECHR imply procedural obligations. For instance, the right to life has been read as requiring 'by implication' that 'there should be some form of effective official investigation when individuals have been killed as a result of the use of force by, *inter alias*, agents of the State'.[73] According to the Court, 'a general legal prohibition of arbitrary killing by the agents of the State would be ineffective, in practice, if there existed no procedure for reviewing the lawfulness of the use of lethal force by State authorities'.[74]

7.3.3 *Evolutive Treaty Interpretation*

The practice of evolutive interpretation developed by the ICJ can be analysed in similar terms. According to the Court, the use of non 'static', 'by definition evolutionary' or 'generic' terms or concepts leads to the conclusion that the parties must be presumed to have intended or accepted that the interpretation of those terms or concepts would be affected by relevant subsequent developments.[75] In *Navigational and Related Rights*, the Court offered the clearest articulation of this doctrine:

[70] David Harris, Michael O'Boyle, Ed Bates and Carla Buckley, *Law of the European Convention on Human Rights*, 2nd ed. (Oxford: Oxford University Press, 2009), p. 18.

[71] Ibid.

[72] *Marckx* v. *Belgium* (No. 6833/74) (1979) 2 EHRR 330, para. 31.

[73] *McCann and Others* v. *United Kingdom* (No. 18984/91) (1996) 21 EHRR 97, para. 161.

[74] Ibid.

[75] *Legal Consequences for States of the Continued Presence of South Africa in Namibia (South West Africa) notwithstanding Security Council Resolution 276 (1970)* (Advisory Opinion) [1971] ICJ Rep. 16, para. 53; *Aegean Sea Continental Shelf Case (Greece* v. *Turkey)* (Judgment) [1978] ICJ Rep. 3, para. 77; *Dispute regarding Navigational and Related Rights (Costa Rica* v. *Nicaragua)* (Judgment) [2009] ICJ Rep. 213, para. 66.

> [W]here the parties have used generic terms in a treaty, the parties necessarily having been aware that the meaning of the terms was likely to evolve over time, and where the treaty has been entered into for a very long period or is 'of continuing duration', the parties must be presumed, as a general rule, to have intended those terms to have an evolving meaning.[76]

In the context of human rights, evolutive interpretation is justified by reference to the 'living' nature of human rights treaties, which, pursuant to the dominant theory, calls for their interpretation 'in the light of present-day conditions'.[77]

7.3.4 *Discussion*

Using the theory of inferentialism introduced by Robert Brandom, one can characterize the examples described above as a practice in which linguistic rationalism gives rise to discursive commitments. As Brandom explains, the hallmark of such a practice is that making an assertion means 'taking up a particular sort of normative stance toward an inferentially articulated content: it is *endorsing* it, taking *responsibility* for it, *committing* oneself to it'.[78] According to Brandom, each move in the practice of discursive commitments takes the form of an assertion that can be assessed in terms of its correctness or appropriateness and every such assertion can be consequentially related to other potential assertions; it can commit the asserter to the consequences of the assertion and can serve as premises for new assertions by creating entitlements. As Brandom highlights, the participants in the practice keep score of their respective deontic statuses by treating each other as having various commitments and entitlements:

> If one asserts, '[t]he swatch is red,' one *ought* to add to one's score also '[t]he swatch is colored.' Making the one move *obliges* one to be prepared to make the other as well ... [A]ssertional games must have rules of this sort: rules of *consequential commitment*. Why? Because to be recognizable as assertional, a move must not be idle, it must make a difference, it must have consequences for what else it is appropriate to do, according to the rules of the game. Assertions express judgments or beliefs. Putting a sentence on one's list of

76 Ibid., para. 66.

77 *Tyrer* v. *The United Kingdom* (No. 5856/72) (1978–1980) 2 EHRR 1, para. 31; *The Right to Information on Consular Assistance in the Framework of the Guarantees of the Due Process of Law*, Inter-Am. Ct. H. R. (Advisory Opinion OC-16/99) [1999], para. 114.

78 Brandom, fn. 58, p. 192.

judgments, putting it in one's belief box, has consequences for how one ought, rationally, to act, judge, and believe.[79]

I submit that the treaty interpretation regime currently prevailing in international law largely operates as the inferential game described by Robert Brandom. In this regime, consent is not excluded, but rather than being a content-specific consent, it is a discursively constructed consent that States must be presumed to have given.[80] The 'must' here is not a logical 'must', but something dictated by legal discursive rationality prevailing in international legal discourse. For instance, in the case of an interpretive recognition of an implied power, an organization might not lose its effectiveness or sacrifice its objectives completely if that particular power is not recognized. Similarly, the doctrine of positive obligations is premised on the discursive assumption that the parties must have wanted their 'negative' obligations to remain effective. In the same vein, the principle of evolutive interpretation entails that the States must be presumed to have accepted that certain terms are to be interpreted in an evolutive way because they are 'generic' or 'by definition evolutionary' or because of the 'living' nature of the instrument in which they appear. In all these examples, the respective premises could potentially be challenged empirically, but that alternative is simply not discursively available: for instance, it would be difficult for States to defend the view that they wanted anything less than a fully effective organization[81] or that they wanted their commitments to remain ineffective. The 'civilizing force of hypocrisy' is certainly at work here, making it difficult to hold unprincipled positions publicly.[82] There is no expectation that each interpretive outcome should be traced back to specific State consent. However, because the consent paradigm is so fundamental in the international legal order, third-party treaty interpreters are expected, as a matter of treaty interpretation discipline, to rationally articulate interpretive outcomes as *consequences* of formally

79 Ibid.

80 For a similar analysis, see Werner, fn. 6, p. 18.

81 *Competence of the ILO to Regulate Incidentally the Personal Work of the Employer* (Advisory Opinion) [1926] PCIJ Ser. B No. 13, p. 18: 'It is not conceivable that they intended to prevent the Organization from drawing up and proposing measures essential to the accomplishment of that end.'

82 Jon Elster, 'Deliberation and Constitution Making', in Jon Elster (ed.), *Deliberative Democracy* (Cambridge: Cambridge University Press, 1998), pp. 97–122; Michel Foucault, *The Archeology of Knowledge and the Discourse on Language* (New York: Pantheon Books, 1972), pp. 118–119; Michel Foucault, 'The Order of Discourse', in Robert Young (ed.), *Untying the Text* (London: Routledge, 1981), p. 52.

undertaken commitments, which explains that they rarely acknowledge that they are creating new obligations even when they seem to be doing so.[83]

In sum, State consent can never control treaty commitments completely, because the parties have no complete mastery over the interpretation of their commitments. Building on Michel Foucault's famous statement, one can conclude that when undertaking commitments, States 'know what they do; they frequently know why they do what they do; but what they do not know is what what they do does'.[84]

[83] A telling example is the judgment of the ECtHR in the *Golder* v. *United Kingdom* case in which the Court found that the right of access to court constitutes an element that is inherent in the right to fair trial but hastened to add that '[t]his is not an extensive interpretation forcing new obligations on the Contracting States: it is based on the very terms of the first sentence of Article 6 para. 1 (art. 6–1) read in its context and having regard to the object and purpose of the Convention, a lawmaking treaty ... and to general principles of law': see *Golder* v. *United Kingdom* (No. 4451/70) (1979–1980) 1 EHRR 524, para. 36. The role of the consent paradigm also explains why outcomes that in theory can be construed as inferential consequences of a formal commitment are systematically dismissed when there is evidence that they have been excluded by the parties. Relevant examples include the refusal of the ECtHR to recognize the right to divorce (*Johnston* v. *Ireland* (No. 9697/82) (1987) 9 EHRR 203.

[84] Hubert Dreyfus and Paul Rabinow, *Michel Foucault: Beyond Structuralism and Hermeneutics* (Chicago: University of Chicago Press, 1982), p. 187. For a similar point in the specific context of discursive commitments, see Robert Brandom, 'From a Critique of Cognitive Internalism to a Conception of Objective Spirit: Reflections on Descombes' Anthopological Holism' (2004) 47(3) *Inquiry* 236–253, at 250.

8

State Consent in the Evolving Climate Regime

Individual and Collective Aspects

JUTTA BRUNNÉE

8.1 INTRODUCTION

Treaties, in particular multilateral treaties, have been the main anchors, and engines, for international law-making and cooperation in the environmental field. In the context of such multilateral agreements, State consent not only has individual effects, but also feeds into a collective process. Individual States cannot be obligated by a treaty, or an amendment to it, unless they express their consent to be so bound. But the treaty-making process can progress, and the treaty or amendment take effect, only when a collectivity of States so agrees.

The interplay between individual and collective aspects is, for example, evident, in the typically highly formalized multilateral treaty-making and amendment processes. States first adopt the text,[1] marking the end of the negotiations and fixing the terms of the treaty or amendment. Following adoption, multilateral treaties tend to be open for signature for a specified period of time.[2] Through their signatures, States commit not to defeat the object and purpose of the treaty.[3] Finally, once States submit their instruments

[1] Arts. 9, 40 of the Vienna Convention on the Law of Treaties (hereafter VCLT), 1155 UNTS 331 (adopted 23 May 1969, entered into force 27 January 1980).

[2] Multilateral environmental agreements (hereafter MEAs) have stipulated signature periods of varying lengths: see, for example, Art. 14 of the Convention on Long-Range Transboundary Air Pollution (hereafter LRTAP Convention), 1302 UNTS 217 (adopted 13 November 1979, entered into force 16 March 1983) (stipulating four days); Art. 12 of the Vienna Convention for the Protection of the Ozone Layer, 1513 UNTS 293 (adopted 22 March 1985, entered into force 22 September 1988) (stipulating six months); Art. 20 of the United Nations Framework Convention on Climate Change (hereafter UNFCCC), 1771 UNTS 107 (adopted 9 May 1992, entered into force 21 March 1994) (stipulating one year).

[3] Art. 18 VCLT.

of ratification (or accession, if they were not among the signatories),[4] they express their consent to be bound by the terms of the treaty or amendment. At each of these stages in the treaty-making process, States' individual acts also have a collective dimension.[5] First, the negotiating States must collectively agree to adopt the treaty text. Second, individual signatures show the level of support for the treaty to other States. Finally, unless the stipulated number of States ratify, the instrument will not enter into force.[6]

This choreography of individual and collective action gives States leverage not only in shaping their own obligations, but also in influencing the overall thrust of the agreement and the obligations others take on. Ideally, the interplay between the individual and collective aspects of the process creates the foundation for a viable treaty (or amendment). Adoption serves to crystallize terms acceptable to a large number of negotiating States. Signature and ratification ensure that individual States control whether and when to commit. The agreed entry into force threshold both underscores the importance of collective action and reassures individual States that their commitments will be matched by a meaningful number of other States.

However, as this chapter will illustrate, the intertwining of individual and collective action also has a darker side. One that is particularly troublesome in the context of environmental problems that require urgent action: it can slow the progress of a regime towards more ambitious requirements, or even result in a standstill. And so, unsurprisingly, the individual–collective dynamics of treaty-based law-making processes take centre-stage in international environmental law. The enduring challenge for the field is to guide States with diverse priorities and circumstances towards collective action. While this challenge is by no means unique to international environmental law, it

4 For simplicity's sake, this chapter uses the term 'ratification' to signify the expression of formal consent to be bound. It is the most common mode of formal consent, but of course there are other modes and terms: see Art. 11 VCLT.

5 Of course, the interplay between individual and collective action is not unique to treaty law. In customary law too, international law-making has individual and collective dimensions. Arguably, the collective dimension dominates in that context, since all States are bound once a sufficient number of individual actions converge to generate custom. For present purposes, however, the key point is that the treaty-based law-making process is distinctive because of its highly formalized nature, and the identification of specific expressions of consent and specific thresholds for the creation of legal effects: see Brölmann, Chapter 4 in this volume. She distinguishes 'three facets' of consent: 'consent as an intentional state, consent as an agreed (often symbolic) expression of that intentional state ... and consent as the activation of a particular obligation binding the subject'. In this chapter, I focus on the second and third of these facets, with an emphasis, in the case of the latter, not merely on effects for individual States, but on the collective action required to produce legal effects at all.

6 Art. 24 VCLT.

presents itself in a particularly stark fashion in the field, since problem-solving necessitates coordinated, collective action, which in turn requires the consent of a large number of States to the requisite commitments.

All told, international environmental law has been quite successful in supporting such collective action. Since the 1970s, States have negotiated a large number of multilateral environmental agreements (hereafter MEAs), dealing with regional as well as global issues.[7] The framework-protocol model, premised upon the incremental development of commitments over time, quickly emerged as the treaty design most conducive to promoting State consent to collective action.[8]

An initial framework treaty sets out a common concern and agreed objective, basic principles for and commitments to action, procedural obligations designed to promote information sharing and engagement, as well as rules and institutions for decision-making and subsequent treaty development. Supplementary treaties, usually referred to as protocols, allow for an overarching problem to be broken down into more manageable sub-issues. Early examples include regional agreements, tackling different aspects of marine environmental and resource protection through individual protocols,[9] or long-range transboundary air pollution on a pollutant-by-pollutant basis.[10]

Protocols are related to the underlying framework in that they adopt its basic goals, principles and decision-making rules. At the same time, they are separate from the framework since they have their own sets of parties and therefore entail commitments only for those parties.[11] It is precisely by

[7] Ronald B. Mitchell, 'International Environmental Agreements Database Project, 2002–2022 (Version 2020.1)', University of Oregon. Available at: http://iea.uoregon.edu/, last accessed 5 September 2022. The article identifies over 1,300 multilateral environmental agreements, a count that includes amendments and adjustments to existing agreements, adopted between 1800 and 2020, and illustrates the rise of environmental treaty-making activity after 1970 using a chart.

[8] For an overview see Jutta Brunnée, 'Environment, Multilateral Agreements', in Rüdiger Wolfrum (ed.), *Max Planck Encyclopedia of Public International Law* (Oxford: Oxford University Press, 2008). Available at: https://opil.ouplaw.com/display/10.1093/law:epil/9780199231690/law-9780199231690-e1388, last accessed 13 December 2022.

[9] See, for example, Convention for the Protection of the Marine Environment and the Coastal Region of the Mediterranean, 1102 UNTS 27 (adopted 16 February 1976 and entered into force 15 April 1988; amended 10 June 1995). On the related protocols, see United Nations Environment Programme (UNEP), 'Barcelona Convention and Protocols'. Available at: www.unep.org/unepmap/who-we-are/barcelona-convention-and-protocols, last accessed 5 September 2022.

[10] LRTAP Convention. For the related protocols, see UN Economic Commission for Europe (hereafter UNECE), 'Protocols'. Available at: https://unece.org/protocols, last accessed 5 September 2022.

[11] Daniel Bodansky, Jutta Brunnée and Lavanya Rajamani, *International Climate Change Law* (Oxford: Oxford University Press, 2017), pp. 86–88.

enabling individual States to decide which protocols to join, rather than requiring sweeping commitments by all in a single instrument, that framework-protocol regimes facilitate progress towards their overall objective.

In addition to reliance on protocols, and in order to facilitate collective standard-setting, MEAs also provide for a variety of decision-making processes that deviate from the highly formal approach described above for treaty-making and amendments. For example, rather than require explicit consent to be bound, MEAs often allow for technical standards to be changed or even expanded with effect for all parties, except those that explicitly opt out.[12] Furthermore, a good deal of treaty-based standard-setting is effected not through amendments or protocols, whereby adoption of an instrument would be followed by a formal expression of consent to be bound by individual States, but through the adoption of decisions by plenary bodies, without subsequent formal consent by individual States. These decisions take effect upon adoption and they commonly contain detailed standards or procedural requirements and even mandatory language, notwithstanding the fact that they are not legally binding.[13] In the adoption of such plenary body decisions, the emphasis is on collective action more than individual consent. This is particularly evident when decisions are adopted by consensus, such that States' consent is assumed, unless they take the relatively unusual step of breaking consensus, with the result that the decision is not adopted at all.[14]

The framework-protocol model and variegated consent approaches have also been deployed in the context of issues requiring global cooperation. In the case of ozone depletion, for example, these design features facilitated the development of what is widely considered to be the most successful environmental regime of all times, with universal participation in the phasing out of ozone-depleting substances.[15]

[12] Jutta Brunnée, 'Procedure and Substance in International Environmental Law' (Volume 405) *Collected Courses of the Hague Academy of International Law*, 2020, pp. 75–240, p. 210.

[13] Jutta Brunnée, 'COPing with Consent: Lawmaking under Multilateral Environmental Agreements' (2002) 15(1) *Leiden Journal of International Law* 1–52, at 32.

[14] On the role and challenges of consensus decision-making in the climate regime, see text accompanying fn. 44–48.

[15] VCLT; Montreal Protocol on Substances that Deplete the Ozone Layer (hereafter Montreal Protocol), 1522 UNTS 3 (adopted 16 September 1987 and entered into force 1 January 1989). On the regime's success see Frederike Albrecht and Charles F. Parker, 'Healing the Ozone Layer: The Montreal Protocol and the Lessons and Limits of a Global Governance Success Story', in Paul 't Hart and Mallory Compton (eds.), *Great Policy Successes* (Oxford: Oxford University Press, 2019), pp. 304–322; and World Meteorological Organization, 'Ozone Layer Recovery Is an Environmental Success Story' (15 September 2021). Available at: https://public.wmo.int/en/media/news/ozone-layer-recovery-environmental-success-story, last accessed 5 September 2022.

Against the backdrop of the experience with the ozone regime, States again resorted to the framework-protocol approach, and a range of approaches to consent, to tackle climate change. Alas, the complexity of the climate challenge and its many interlocking dimensions,[16] the need for ambitious actions with profound implications for economic development, and the attendant disagreements about appropriate burden-sharing, exceeded the capacity of previously successful approaches to facilitate collective action. The burden-sharing debate has been especially fraught as between developed and developing countries,[17] embedded as it is in larger tensions around international law's colonial history and the efforts of developing countries to decolonize international law.[18] As a result, many developing countries distrusted global climate politics, perceiving calls for emission reductions as encumbering their development or even as a green variant of neocolonialism[19] Industrialized States, in turn, demanded that developing nations cooperate to protect the global environment,[20] while at the same time resisting recognition of historical or differentiated responsibility greenhouse gas emission reductions.[21] Hence, since its inception, the climate regime has wrestled with the challenges of reconciling starkly different positions, and enabling progress towards more ambitious commitments in a consent-based system.

A broad spectrum of approaches to regime development can be found in the climate regime, ranging from formal consent to its component treaties (i.e. the UN Framework Convention on Climate Change (hereafter UNFCCC), the Kyoto Protocol and the Paris Agreement)[22] or amendments to these

[16] On the multifaceted nature of the climate challenge, see Bodansky *et al.*, fn. 11, pp. 2–10.

[17] Ibid., pp. 99–117.

[18] Usha Natarajan and Kishan Khoday, 'Environment', in Jean d'Aspremont and John Haskell (eds.), *Tipping Points in International Law: Commitment and Critique* (Cambridge: Cambridge University Press, 2021), pp. 132–148, pp. 137–138; Malavika Rao, 'A TWAIL Perspective on Loss and Damage from Climate Change: Reflections from Indira Gandhi's Speech at Stockholm' (2022) 12 *Asian Journal of International Law* 63–81, at 65–66.

[19] Natarajan and Khoday, fn. 18, p. 138; Rao, fn. 18, at 68; Sumudu Atapattu, 'The Significance of International Environmental Law Principles in Reinforcing or Dismantling the North–South Divide', in Shawkat Alam, Sumudu Atapattu, Carmen G. Gonzalez and Jona Razzaque (eds.), *International Environmental Law and the Global South* (Cambridge: Cambridge University Press, 2015), pp. 74–108, p. 82.

[20] Bodansky *et al.*, fn. 11, p. 109.

[21] For a discussion of the debate on differentiation in the climate regime, see Jutta Brunnée and Stephen J. Toope, *Legitimacy and Legality in International Law: An Interactional Account* (Cambridge: Cambridge University Press, 2010), pp. 151–166.

[22] Art. 17 UNFCCC; Kyoto Protocol to the United Nations Framework Convention on Climate Change (hereafter Kyoto Protocol), 2303 UNTS 162 (adopted 10 December 1997 and entered into force 16 February 2005); Paris Agreement, 3156 UNTS (adopted 12 December 2015, entered into force 4 November 2016).

treaties,[23] to standard-setting by plenary bodies, to recourse to non-binding commitments, notably in the Paris Agreement. I begin by exploring the UNFCCC and the Kyoto Protocol. I then turn to the Paris Agreement and consider the shift to what has been described as a 'bottom-up' approach.[24] The perhaps most striking feature of this approach is its reliance on non-binding, 'nationally determined contributions' (hereafter NDCs) that each party must 'prepare, communicate and maintain'.[25] Another aspect of the approach consists in a shift from binding to non-binding substantive standards, and a shift in emphasis from substantive to procedural obligations.[26] My focus in examining these features of the Paris Agreement is on their implications for the role of State consent and the interplay between the individual and collective dimensions of treaty-based law-making and standard-setting processes. To explore this interplay, I consider, on the one hand, the modes of expression of consent (including tacit or presumed) stipulated in the regime and, on the other hand, the thresholds (voting rules and entry into force requirements) it establishes in order for a given instrument to become binding or a set of standards to take effect.[27] I argue that the most significant consequence of the Paris Agreement's NDC approach in this context is a shift away from the anchoring of State consent to climate action in treaty-based processes, and hence from the linkages that adoption and entry into force requirements establish between multiple parties' individual expressions of consent.

8.2 THE UNFCCC

The text of the UNFCCC envisages a range of approaches to consent, emphasizing formal consent in relation to treaty terms, but allowing for simplified consent in relation to annexes on technical matters, and empowering the treaty's plenary body, the Conference of the Parties (hereafter COP) to adopt certain decisions.

[23] See, for example, the Doha Amendment to the Kyoto Protocol (hereafter Doha Amendment), UNFCCC Doc. FCCC/KP/CMP/2012/13/Add.1, Decision 1/CMP.8 (adopted 8 December 2012 and entered into force 31 December 2020). Available at: https://treaties.un.org/Pages/ViewDetails.aspx?src=TREATY&mtdsg_no=XXVII-7-c&chapter=27&clang=_en, last accessed 5 September 2022.

[24] See, for example, Bodansky *et al.*, fn. 11, pp. 23–25.

[25] Art. 4.2 Paris Agreement.

[26] Brunnée, fn. 12, pp. 194–208.

[27] Brölmann, Chapter 4 in this volume, identifying 'three facets' of consent. See fn. 5, noting that this chapter explores the interplay between Brölmann's second facet (expression of consent) and third facet (activation of obligation), with an emphasis not so much on individual effects but on the collective action required to produce an obligation or non-binding standard at all.

8.2.1 *Formal Consent*

The UNFCCC outlines a standard process for signature, ratification and entry into force of its original terms. The convention was open for signature for a year,[28] enabling States to signal support for the treaty while allowing them ample time to prepare for formal consent, which, in many constitutional systems, requires legislative approval.[29] Instruments of ratification were to be submitted to the United Nations (hereafter UN) Secretary-General as the convention's Depositary.[30] States as well as 'regional economic integration organizations' – a phrase designed to accommodate the European Union (hereafter EU) – were eligible to become parties to the convention.[31] The convention required fifty ratifications to enter into force,[32] a threshold meant to strike a balance between the need for substantial buy-in into what was intended to be a global treaty, and the desire to see reasonably speedy entry into force.[33] The UNFCCC garnered relatively rapid support: 165 States signed the convention while it was open for signature and it received the ratifications required for entry into force in less than two years.[34] To round out the terms of consent to the UNFCCC itself, the convention does not permit reservations, but does allow withdrawal after three years from the date of entry into force for the relevant party.[35] To date, there have been no withdrawals from the convention, which has succeeded in providing a lasting framework for global climate cooperation, and for managing disagreement,[36] with 196 States and the EU as parties.[37]

Since environmental concerns like climate change are not only complex but also evolving challenges, they require long-term cooperative schemes like the UNFCCC. Such regimes allow for standards to be adopted, expanded and revised, as the underlying issue, the parties' understanding of it or their

[28] Art. 20 UNFCCC.
[29] Bodansky *et al.*, fn. 11, p. 83.
[30] Arts. 19, 22 UNFCCC.
[31] Art. 22.1 UNFCCC.
[32] Art. 23.1 UNFCCC. Art. 23.3 stipulates that any ratification by a regional economic integration organization was not to be counted as additional to ratifications by its Member States.
[33] Bodansky *et al.*, fn. 11, p. 157.
[34] United Nations Treaty Collection (hereafter UNTC), 'United Nations Framework Convention on Climate Change'. Available at: https://treaties.un.org/Pages/ViewDetailsIII.aspx?src=IND&mtdsg_no=XXVII-7&chapter=27&Temp=mtdsg3&clang=_en, last accessed 5 September 2022.
[35] Art. 24 (Reservations) and Art. 25 (Withdrawal) UNFCCC.
[36] See generally Samantha Besson, 'State Consent and Disagreement in International Law-Making: Dissolving the Paradox' (2016) 29(2) *Leiden Journal of International Law* 289–316.
[37] UNTC, fn. 34.

capacity to address it evolve. Furthermore, in order to facilitate such long-term interaction, MEAs generally entail a significant degree of institutionalization.[38] Hence, whereas the UNFCCC itself was agreed upon by an Intergovernmental Negotiating Committee,[39] the convention established that its COP would be the forum for regular interaction between the parties, and negotiation, and adoption of all key decisions in the regime, including decisions related to regime development.[40]

The UNFCCC sets out different avenues for the further development of the climate regime. All of them have been hampered by the inability of the parties to agree upon the voting rule in its Rules of Procedure.[41] Given this disagreement, the COP never adopted the Rules of Procedure drafted in 1996,[42] but rather agrees at the beginning of each session to apply the draft rules,[43] with the exception of the rule on voting.[44] Since its inception, therefore, the COP has operated on the basis of a general agreement that decisions be taken by consensus.[45] As only an explicit objection will break consensus, consent in some sense is presumed in this process. Alternatively, one might say that, when the parties agree to a consensus process, they agree

38 Brunnée, fn. 8, paras. 24–30; Brölmann, Chapter 4 in this volume, who argues that different aspects of consent (intention, expression of intention, and obligatory effect) are 'disaggregated' in an institutionalized context. While Brölmann is correct in this diagnosis and in her assessment that the resultant flexibility is helpful in the 'engagement with "common concerns"', it is equally important to explore the linkages between individual expressions of consent and the collective action required to generate legal effects. These linkages reveal the challenges that can arise in the engagement with common concerns in a consent-based system.

39 Bodansky *et al.*, fn. 11, pp. 102–105.

40 Art. 7 UNFCCC; Brunnée, fn. 8, paras. 24–30. For comments on the institutionalization of law-making in the climate regime see Nico Krisch, 'The Decay of Consent: International Law in an Age of Global Public Goods' (2014) 108(1) *American Journal of International Law* 1–40, at 17.

41 Proposals to amend the decision-making rules in the convention itself to allow for majority voting have similarly failed to gain traction: see Luke Kemp, 'Framework for the Future? Exploring the Possibility of Majority Voting in the Climate Negotiations' (2016) 16(5) *International Environmental Agreements* 757–779, at 758.

42 UNFCCC, 'Draft Rules of Procedure of the Conference of the Parties and its Subsidiary Bodies' (22 May 1996), FCCC/CP1996/2.

43 Leonardo Massai, 'Dealing with "Consensus" at the UN Climate Talks', Climalia. Available at: www.climalia.eu/dealing-consensus-un-climate-talks/, last accessed 29 May 2022.

44 UNFCCC, fn. 42, at 2 (Rule 42, outlining two decision-making options, once allowing for decision by two-thirds majority of parties present and voting, provided that all efforts at consensus was exhausted, the other requiring consensus, except in the context of decisions on financial matters).

45 Antto Vihma, 'Climate of Consensus: Managing Decision Making in the UN Climate Change Negotiations' (2015) 24(1) *Review of European Community & International Environmental Law* 58–68, at 62; Kemp, fn. 41.

that silence will signify consent.[46] At the same time, individual parties or small groups of parties effectively have the option to veto decisions.[47] While actual consensus breaking has occurred on only a handful of occasions, the prospect of such a 'veto' has cast a long shadow. The spectre of a negative vote often suffices to prevent a decision from being put forward in the first place, or prompts compromises at a lower level of ambition.[48]

In principle, new or more ambitious substantive commitments could be enshrined in the convention by amendment. Amendments are adopted during a session of the COP.[49] The UNFCCC envisages that, '[i]f all efforts at consensus have been exhausted', an amendment can 'as a last resort be adopted by a three-fourths majority' of the parties present and voting.[50] Yet, notwithstanding this explicit decision rule for the adoption of amendments, the practice of the regime has been to seek consensus.[51] If adopted, an amendment enters into force once at least three-fourths of all convention parties submitted instruments of acceptance, but only for those parties that have accepted it.[52]

Due to the climate regime's consensus practice, treaty development through amendments may be hamstrung at the very outset, since the parties may even be unable to adopt the relevant text. From the vantage point of regime development, the amendment process also poses a number of other challenges. The parties must opt into an amendment through formal consent and, even for those parties that do, the new terms take effect only once the high threshold of required acceptances (148 parties) has been met. As a result, amendments may never enter into force, or do so only very slowly. Another inherent feature of the process is that the new terms brought about by an amendment may end up binding only a subset of the parties. In short,

46 Nico Krisch notes that consensus is 'somewhat softer than consent since it counts acquiescence as agreement': Krisch, fn. 40, at 17; on whether and when passive behaviours can signify consent see Hollis, Chapter 6 in this volume.

47 Note that there is some ambiguity as to what constitutes consensus in the climate regime. On some occasions, the COP President gaveled decisions through notwithstanding the objection of an individual party: Massai, fn. 43. Luke Kemp notes that, in the practice of the UNFCCC, presiding officers enjoy a 'great deal of interpretative power in determining whether there is a consensus among the parties': Kemp, fn. 41, at 760. Nico Krish refers to the resultant decision-making formula as 'quasi-consensus' or 'general agreement': Krisch, fn. 40, at 17.

48 Bodansky *et al.*, fn. 11, pp. 75–76.

49 Art. 15.1 UNFCCC.

50 Art. 15.2 UNFCCC.

51 Bodansky *et al.*, fn. 11, p. 89.

52 Art. 15.4 UNFCCC.

amendments are ill-suited to developing new commitments, like ambitious emission reduction commitments.

8.2.2 *Simplified Consent*

The UNFCCC stipulates a modified process for the adoption and amendment of annexes to the convention. Like other MEAs, the convention requires that annexes be 'restricted to lists, forms and other material of a descriptive nature that is of a scientific, technical, procedural or administrative character'.[53] Annexes or amendments to them must be adopted according to the same procedure as an amendment to the convention,[54] meaning in practice that consensus is required. It is the next step in the process that differs from the standard process: annexes and amendments to them enter into force for *all* parties, except those that provide written notification of their non-acceptance within six months from adoption.[55] In other words, in light of the primarily technical nature of the relevant terms, the convention facilitates enactment or amendment of annexes by replacing the standard 'opt-in' process with an 'opt-out' process. Whereas, in the case of the former, explicit consent by a specified number of States is required for consenting States to be bound, in the case of the latter, there is no threshold and consent is presumed unless a party explicitly declines. Or, perhaps more accurately, when the parties establish an opt-out decision-making process, they agree that silence will signify consent.[56]

And, yet, in the climate regime, even the apparently anodyne terms of an annex can be highly political, such that the consensus practice makes adoption impossible. For example, Annex I to the UNFCCC lists industrialized parties and countries with economies in transition, and Annex II industrialized parties only.[57] The convention, in turn, stipulates that Annex I and Annex II parties have emissions-related or financial commitments, respectively, that other parties (i.e. developing countries) do not have.[58] Over the years, it has proven to be impossible to amend notably Annex I so as to add countries whose economies had grown such that, arguably, they were no longer 'developing' countries.[59] Indeed, developing countries' desire to maintain a

53 Art. 16.1 UNFCCC.
54 Arts. 16.2, 16.4 UNFCCC.
55 Arts. 16.3, 16.4 UNFCCC.
56 Danae Azaria, 'Not All Silences "Speak": A Theory of (Non-)Communicative State Silence', unpublished manuscript, 2022.
57 Annex I and II UNFCCC.
58 Arts. 4.2, 4.3 UNFCCC.
59 Bodansky *et al.*, fn. 11, p. 123.

strict distinction between Annex I and non-Annex I States prompted them to oppose even an attempt by Kazakhstan to voluntarily join Annex I.[60]

This brief overview of the amendment process illustrates that, in addition to the reasons previously mentioned,[61] consent-related considerations account for the fact that supplementary treaties like protocols turned out to be preferable vehicles for the development of new climate commitments. Although protocols too must be adopted by the UNFCCC COP,[62] the requirements for entry into force can then be set by the new instrument.[63] In other words, the entry into force threshold can be tailored to the terms of the new instrument, allowing it to deviate both from the relatively moderate threshold for entry into force of the convention and the very high threshold stipulated for amendments. Similarly, although protocols typically draw on the procedural rules contained in the framework that anchors them, they can stipulate decision-making rules specific to them. The UNFCCC parties adopted two supplementary treaties, the Kyoto Protocol and the Paris Agreement, discussed in Sections 8.3 and 8.4.

8.2.3 *COP Decisions*

While both amendments and supplemental treaties are adopted by consensus in the COP, the parties retain full control over their commitments. A subsequent decision by each party, be it explicit consent to a treaty amendment or a supplemental treaty or refraining from opting-out of an annex or annex amendment, is required for new terms to become binding on them. By contrast, when the treaty empowers the COP to adopt particular decisions, these decisions take effect for all parties, without subsequent formal consent by individual States.

Generally speaking, the resulting standards are not legally binding.[64] Nonetheless, such formally non-binding decisions often contain mandatory language and have significant practical effect. For example, the UNFCCC empowers the COP to define methodologies for calculating national greenhouse gas emissions,[65] adopt its Rules of Procedure,[66] adopt criteria for the

[60] Joanna Depledge, 'The Road Less Travelled: Difficulties in Moving between Annexes in the Climate Change Regime' (2009) 9(3) *Climate Policy* 273–287, at 279.
[61] See fn. 11 and accompanying text.
[62] Art. 17.1 UNFCCC.
[63] Art. 17.3 UNFCCC.
[64] Brunnée, fn. 13, at 32. The underlying treaty may of course provide for binding decision-making, although this has remained exceptional: see Art. 2.9 Montreal Protocol.
[65] Art. 4.1(a) UNFCCC.
[66] Art. 7.3 UNFCCC.

joint implementation of certain commitments[67] and agree upon modalities for the operation of the convention's financial mechanism.[68]

Although, as discussed in Section 8.3, recourse to COP decisions assumed increasing importance under the auspices of the Kyoto Protocol, the slow evolution of the climate regime shows that even formally non-binding standards are subject to difficult negotiations and, given the regime's consensus practice, can be difficult to adopt. The aforementioned fate of the COP's Rules of Procedure is a case in point. Nonetheless, non-binding decision-making by the COP allows, at least in principle, speedier regime development and adjustment than processes that involve subsequent ratification by individual States. Equally important is that non-binding decisions enable the adoption of standards that are applicable to all parties – an important feature for efforts to address collective action issues like climate change.

8.3 THE KYOTO PROTOCOL

The Kyoto Protocol was adopted in 1997, a mere two years after the entry into force of the UNFCCC. Part of the explanation for its swift negotiation can be found in the fact that the negotiating mandate adopted by the COP specifically excluded new commitments for developing countries,[69] thus largely bracketing the question of burden-sharing between industrialized and developing countries for the purposes of the protocol negotiations.[70] Furthermore, the protocol too was in some respects akin to a framework treaty – its text left the details of many of its core elements to be adopted by the Meeting of the Parties (hereafter MOP) upon entry into force.

In respect of burden-sharing, the Kyoto Protocol's features reflected the convention's proposition that 'developed country Parties should take the lead in combating climate change',[71] and the insistence of developing countries that their commitments ought to be differentiated from those of developed countries.[72] The protocol thus enshrined emission reduction targets only for the parties listed in Annex I to the convention (i.e. developed countries and

[67] Art. 4.2(d) UNFCCC.

[68] Art. 11.3 UNFCCC.

[69] UNFCCC, 'The Berlin Mandate: Review of the Adequacy of Article 4, paragraph 2(a) and (b), of the Convention, Including Proposals related to a Protocol and Decisions on Follow-Up', FCCC/CP/1995/7/Add.1, 4 (6 June 1995).

[70] Bodansky *et al.*, fn. 11, pp. 105–109.

[71] Art. 3.1 UNFCCC.

[72] Ibid. For a discussion, see Bodansky *et al.*, fn.11, pp. 26–30.

countries with economies in transition).[73] Each party's target was set out in an Annex B to the protocol, enabling the parties to take on differentiated commitments to reduce or limit emissions.[74]

However, in agreeing to this approach and to binding emission reduction commitments, Annex I parties negotiated a number of safeguards into the protocol. Three of these safeguard features are significant for the purposes of this exploration of consent in the climate regime.

First, the protocol stipulated a five-year commitment period (2008–2012), and that an amendment to Annex B would be required to establish commitments for subsequent periods.[75] In other words, Annex I parties did not consent to long-term emission targets, but rather ensured that there would be another decision point.

Second, the protocol contained a range of flexibility elements, such as allowing the parties to pool and jointly meet commitments, or to engage in trade emissions trading.[76] In order to both backstop the emissions targets and ensure the integrity of the flexibility elements, the parties also agreed to develop stringent emissions inventory and reporting requirements,[77] and to create a compliance mechanism for the protocol.[78] Since each of these elements required detailed rules in order to be operable, the protocol empowered its MOP to adopt decisions to flesh out these key parts of the protocol.[79]

Third, while the protocol was open to signature and ratification by all convention parties,[80] its commitment structure called for a tailored entry into force formula. On the one hand, the protocol would not have had practical impact unless ratified by the parties for which it set out emission reduction commitments – Annex I parties. On the other hand, these parties sought to ensure that other major Annex I emitters were similarly obligated. Both considerations militated against a simple numerical threshold for ratifications and prompted the protocol's 'double-trigger' formula. It premised entry into force of the protocol upon ratification by at least fifty-five parties to the

[73] Art. 3.1 Kyoto Protocol.
[74] Art. 3.1 and Annex B Kyoto Protocol.
[75] Art. 3.9 Kyoto Protocol; fn. 107–111 and accompanying text.
[76] Arts. 3.10–3.12, Art. 6 (Joint Implementation), Art. 12 (Clean Development Mechanism), Art. 17 (Emissions Trading) Kyoto Protocol.
[77] Arts. 5, 7, 8 Kyoto Protocol.
[78] Art. 18 Kyoto Protocol.
[79] Arts. 6.2, 7.4, 8.4, 12.7, 17, 18 Kyoto Protocol.
[80] Art. 24.1 Kyoto Protocol.

convention, including Annex I parties accounting for at least 55 per cent of these parties' total carbon emissions.[81]

The Kyoto Protocol took much longer than the convention to enter into force, for interconnected reasons, involving the need to elaborate on major parts of the regime and its entry into force formula. Both the industrialized parties that would take on emission reduction commitments and the developing States that would not, needed to know the precise degrees of flexibility, transparency and oversight that would obtain under the protocol before deciding whether or not to ratify it. The bundle of decisions, dubbed the Marrakesh Accords, which put the required flesh on the protocol bones, took several years to negotiate and was adopted in 2001.[82] But the need to first hammer out the details of the protocol's operation was not the only cause for delay in its entry into force. Reaching the emissions share threshold of the entry into force formula proved challenging since the United States (hereafter US), accounting for more than 30 per cent of the relevant emissions, indicated, also in 2001, that it would not ratify the protocol.[83] The US withdrawal meant that every other Annex I party had to join the protocol for it to enter into force. The emissions share threshold was finally crossed in February 2005.[84] Today, the Kyoto Protocol has 192 parties.[85] While the protocol was successful insofar as all of its Annex I parties met their emissions targets,[86] its overall impact was limited in that it ultimately accounted for only 24 per cent of global greenhouse gas emissions,[87] Canada having withdrawn just before the end of the first commitment period, in 2012.[88]

Operating under the auspices of the UNFCCC, the Kyoto Protocol deployed the same range of approaches to consent as its parent treaty, with some notable variations. We already considered the formula for the protocol's initial entry into force. We also saw that the protocol specifically provided for much more extensive use of simple decisions of the parties than did the

[81] Art. 25.1 Kyoto Protocol (focusing on total emissions in 1990, which was also the reference year for emission reduction obligations under Art. 3.1).

[82] UNFCCC, 'The Marrakesh Accords', Decisions 2-24/CP.7, FCCC/CP/2001/13/Add.1-3 (21 January 2002).

[83] Bodansky *et al.*, fn. 11, p. 107.

[84] UNTC, 'Kyoto Protocol to the United Nations Framework Convention on Climate Change'. Available at: https://treaties.un.org/Pages/ViewDetails.aspx?src=TREATY&mtdsg_no=XXVII-7-a&chapter=27&clang=_en, last accessed 5 September 2022.

[85] Ibid.

[86] Michael Grubb, 'Full Legal Compliance with the Kyoto Protocol's First Commitment Period – Some Lessons' (2016) 16(6) *Climate Policy* 673–681.

[87] Bodansky *et al.*, fn. 11, pp. 108, 173.

[88] UNTC, fn. 84.

UNFCCC. Notably, the Marrakesh Accords provided the rule-book for key parts of the Kyoto Protocol, containing detailed standards and mandatory terms, notwithstanding their non-binding nature.

As part of the Marrakesh Accords, the parties adopted a compliance mechanism, the declared goals of which were to 'facilitate, promote and enforce compliance' with the protocol,[89] and that envisaged certain consequences that the compliance committee could apply to non-complying parties.[90] The adoption of this mechanism through a simple MOP decision is of some interest for present purposes. Since the protocol stipulated that any mechanism 'entailing binding consequences' had to be adopted by amendment,[91] the result of this approach was that the agreed upon consequences were not binding in a formal legal sense. However, an amendment would have required individual parties to consent to the compliance mechanism, casting doubt on whether the mechanism would enter into force, and which parties would be subject to it.[92] By contrast, adoption through a consensus decision ensured immediate applicability of the mechanism to all parties. In practice, the mechanism's non-binding nature does not appear to have undercut its operation – the parties engaged with the mechanism and brought their conduct in line with its findings.[93] It stands to reason that the absence of a compliance mechanism, or its selective applicability, would have been considerably more problematic for the protocol, such that adoption of the mechanism by consensus decision rather than through formal amendment had significant advantages.

The key challenge for the protocol parties, however, was the need to plan beyond the protocol's first commitment period and develop a post-2012 emission reduction regime. In these negotiations, which commenced immediately upon the protocol's entry into force,[94] the parties were confronted with the full force of the difficult burden-sharing issues raised by global climate action.[95] In view of the emissions trajectories of major developing countries,

89 UNFCCC, 'Procedures and Mechanisms Relating to Compliance under the Kyoto Protocol', Decision 27/CMP.1, FCCC/KP/CMP/2005/8/Add.3 (30 March 2006).

90 Ibid., ss. XIV–XV.

91 Art. 18 Kyoto Protocol.

92 Krisch, fn. 40, at 17.

93 For a discussion see Brunnée and Toope, fn. 21, pp. 201–204.

94 Art. 3.9 Kyoto Protocol (stipulating that the consideration of new commitments was to commence 'at least seven years before the end of the first commitment period', that is, in 2005).

95 Bodansky *et al.*, fn. 11, p. 109.

such as China and India,[96] industrialized countries insisted that any post-2012 emissions regime had to include commitments by developing countries. In turn, developing countries insisted that the Kyoto Protocol, with its focus on binding emissions commitments for only industrialized countries ought to be extended for an additional commitment period.[97]

It is in this context that the terms of the Kyoto Protocol, combined with the configuration of consent requirements in the climate regime, turned from facilitators of global climate action into shackles.[98] The terms of the protocol, as noted, limited binding emission reduction commitments to a five-year period, and for Annex I countries only.

Adding non-Annex I parties into the commitment regime would, therefore, have required amendments to the protocol. The process for amendments to the protocol, in turn, matches that for amendments to the convention: given the regime's practice, consensus would be required for adoption,[99] and a three-fourths majority of protocol parties for entry into force.[100]

Similarly, new commitments for existing Annex I parties required amendments to the protocol's Annex B.[101] Recall that the UNFCCC provided for a simplified process for amendments to its annexes, on account of their primarily technical nature.[102] In this simplified process, amendments require consensus for adoption, but then enter into force for all parties except those that opt out. The Kyoto Protocol's provisions on the adoption or amendment of annexes mirror those of the convention.[103] However, amendments to the protocol's Annex A (listing greenhouse gases subject to emission limitations) and Annex B (listing each party's emission target) are excluded from the simplified process and subjected to the entry into force requirements for amendments to the provisions of the protocol.[104] As a result, amendments to Annexes A and B enter into force only for the ratifying parties, and only upon

[96] By 2005 China, for example, had overtaken the US as the single largest national emitter of greenhouse gases: see Bodansky *et al.*, fn. 11, pp. 8, 354.

[97] Ibid., p. 108.

[98] See generally, Joost Pauwelyn, Ramses A. Wessel and Jan Wouters, 'When Structures Become Shackles: Stagnation and Dynamics in International Lawmaking' (2014) 25(3) *European Journal of International Law* 733–763, at 748–749. For comments on the burdensome nature of the UNFCCC's consensual approach, see Krisch, fn. 40, at 18.

[99] Art. 13.5 Kyoto Protocol (stipulating that the UNFCCC COP's Rules of Procedure apply *mutatis mutandis* under the Kyoto Protocol, except as otherwise decided by consensus by the protocol's MOP).

[100] Art. 20 Kyoto Protocol.

[101] See fn. 75 and accompanying text.

[102] See fn. 54–55 and accompanying text.

[103] Art. 21 Kyoto Protocol.

[104] Arts. 21.5, 21.7 Kyoto Protocol.

acceptance by three-fourths of the protocol parties. What is more, an amendment to Annex B can be adopted only with the written consent of the party in question.[105] In other words, the protocol reverts to and indeed augments the standard consent process for Annexes A and B because these annexes bear directly upon the scope of parties' emission targets.

Unsurprisingly, given the entrenched positions, it proved politically impossible to amend the protocol to include all States.[106] As part of a multi-pronged effort to break the logjam in the climate negotiations, the parties did adopt an amendment to the Kyoto Protocol in 2012 – the Doha Amendment. However, it was confined to the creation of a new commitment period for the protocol's industrialized parties.[107] Furthermore, because Canada had withdrawn from the protocol and Japan and Russia declined to accept new emissions targets, the Doha Amendment ended up applying to the parties representing less than 12 per cent of global emissions.[108]

The reasons why it proved impossible to turn the Kyoto Protocol into a long-term, global emissions reduction regime were first and foremost political, of course. For developing countries, the Kyoto Protocol encapsulated how the burdens of climate action ought to be allocated – through binding emission reduction commitments for industrialized but not developing countries. In turn, this very feature of the protocol was an insurmountable obstacle to re-engaging the US.[109] Furthermore, any agreement containing binding emission reduction commitments would be hard-pressed to garner the two-thirds majority in the Senate required for US ratification of a treaty.[110] Thus, although the adoption and entry into force of the Doha Amendment shows that a formal consent process need not be an obstacle to the development of new commitments, such a process could not deliver a genuinely global commitment regime. By the time the Doha Amendment finally entered into force in 2020,[111] the UNFCCC parties had adopted the Paris Agreement.

[105] Art. 21.7 Kyoto Protocol.

[106] For an overview, see Bodansky *et al.*, fn. 11, pp. 108–115.

[107] Doha Amendment.

[108] Bodansky *et al.*, fn. 11, p. 114.

[109] Office of the Press Secretary, The White House, 'Text of a Letter from the President to Senators Hagel, Helms, Craig, and Roberts' (13 March 2001). Available at: https://georgewbush-whitehouse.archives.gov/news/releases/2001/03/20010314.html, last accessed 5 September 2022. For a detailed discussion, see Luke Kemp, 'Bypassing the "Ratification Straitjacket": Reviewing US Legal Participation in a Climate Agreement' (2015) 16(8) *Climate Policy* 1011–1028.

[110] Bodansky *et al.*, fn. 11, p. 224.

[111] UNTC, 'Doha Amendment to the Kyoto Protocol'. Available at: https://treaties.un.org/Pages/ViewDetails.aspx?src=TREATY&mtdsg_no=XXVII-7-c&chapter=27&clang=_en, last accessed 5 September 2022.

8.4 THE PARIS AGREEMENT

Much like the Kyoto Protocol, which, practically speaking, it has supplanted, the Paris Agreement operates under the umbrella of the UNFCCC.[112] Recourse to a new treaty enabled the parties to deviate from the approach of the Kyoto Protocol and to develop a commitment regime with a very different mix of substantive and procedural, and binding and non-binding requirements. This new approach enabled the Paris Agreement to establish a commitment regime applicable to all convention parties, including both developed and developing countries.[113]

Briefly put, the Paris Agreement calls upon the parties to strengthen the global response to climate change, by mitigating emissions with a view to holding global temperature increases 'to well below 2 °C above pre-industrial levels and pursuing efforts to limit the temperature increase to 1.5 °C'.[114] To this end, all States are to undertake progressively more ambitious efforts.[115] However, States' contributions to the global response to climate change are to be 'nationally determined'.[116] Thus, while the parties are obligated to 'prepare, communicate and maintain successive nationally determined contributions' (NDCs),[117] these NDCs are not legally binding under international law. Nonetheless, the parties are subject to detailed procedural requirements designed to ensure the transparency and accountability with respect to their NDCs, and their performance in implementing them.[118]

From the vantage point of consent, the Paris Agreement combines a range of approaches to maximize the potential for increasingly ambitious climate action: formal consent, simplified consent, decisions of the agreement's MOP, and NDCs.

The Paris Agreement itself is a binding treaty, and so subject to the standard formal process involving adoption, signature,[119] ratification and entry into force.[120] The agreement's entry into force formula is a variation on that of the Kyoto Protocol, requiring ratification by at least fifty-five convention

[112] Preamble and Art. 2.1(a) Paris Agreement.

[113] While the Paris Agreement does differentiate between developed and developing countries in some respects, its emissions related provisions apply to '[e]ach Party'. See Arts. 4.2, 4.3 Paris Agreement.

[114] Art. 2.1(a) Paris Agreement.

[115] Art. 4.3 Paris Agreement.

[116] Art. 3 Paris Agreement.

[117] Art. 4.2 Paris Agreement.

[118] For an overview, see Brunnée, fn. 12, pp. 203–206.

[119] Art. 12 Paris Agreement.

[120] Art. 21 Paris Agreement.

parties 'accounting for at least an estimated 55 per cent of the total global greenhouse gas emissions'.[121] The formula balances the Paris Agreement's global reach and the desire to ensure effectiveness and inclusion of major emitters. A record 175 convention parties signed the agreement on the day it opened for signature, and it entered into force in less than a year.[122] The coordinated announcement of ratification by the world's largest emitters, China and the US,[123] sent a strong signal to other States. There was also a shared sense of urgency, not only concerning climate change, but also in view of the pending US elections and the prospect of a less sympathetic new administration.[124]

However, while the Paris Agreement entered into force for the US in 2016,[125] the Trump Administration took advantage of the fact that consent to the climate treaties can be undone. The Paris Agreement's withdrawal provision limits the parties' ability to 'unconsent', but only by barring them from notifying their withdrawal sooner than three years after the agreement's entry into force (for them), and by stipulating that the withdrawal takes effect one year after notification.[126] As a result, although the US withdrawal from the Paris Agreement took effect in November 2020, another change in administration saw the US rejoin the Paris Agreement shortly after, in January 2021.[127]

With respect to amendments to the Paris Agreement itself, the agreement imports *mutatis mutandis* the UNFCCC's formal consent approach (i.e. the adoption by consensus, the acceptance and entry into force upon acceptance by three-fourths of the parties to the agreement).[128] In turn, for the adoption and amendment of Annexes, the Paris Agreement imports the UNFCCC's simplified consent process (i.e. the adoption by consensus and the entry into force for all parties, except those that opt-out in writing).[129] Finally, like the UNFCCC and the Kyoto Protocol, the Paris Agreement envisages a

[121] Art. 21.1 Paris Agreement.

[122] UNTC, 'Paris Agreement'. Available at: https://treaties.un.org/Pages/ViewDetails.aspx?src=TREATY&mtdsg_no=XXVII-7-d&chapter=27&clang=_en, last accessed 5 September 2022.

[123] Tom Phillips, Fiona Harvey and Alan Yuhas, 'Breakthrough as US and China Agree to Ratify Paris Climate Deal', *The Guardian*, 3 September 2016. Available at: www.theguardian.com/environment/2016/sep/03/breakthrough-us-china-agree-ratify-paris-climate-change-deal, last accessed 5 September 2022.

[124] Bodansky *et al.*, fn. 11, p. 247.

[125] UNTC, fn. 122.

[126] Art. 28 Paris Agreement.

[127] UNTC, fn. 122, footnote 5.

[128] Art. 22 Paris Agreement; fn. 49–52 and accompanying text.

[129] Art. 23 Paris Agreement; fn. 53–55 and accompanying text.

significant role for standard-setting by simple decision of the plenary body. In fact, the decision of the UNFCCC COP that adopted the text of the Paris Agreement (for subsequent signature and ratification by the parties) also supplements the treaty text in many key respects.[130] Furthermore, much like the Kyoto Protocol, the text of the Paris Agreement stipulates that the agreement's MOP is to adopt the modalities, procedures and guidance required for the operation of the agreement. Thus, the 'Rulebook' adopted at the first meeting of the Paris Agreement MOP consists of a set of COP decisions that flesh out primary obligations and other terms, such as those related to transparency and oversight.[131]

The most experimental aspect of the Paris Agreement's approach is that, instead of enshrining binding emission reduction obligations, it relies on the parties' non-legally binding NDCs. Since they are nationally determined, the NDCs are not part of the agreement but 'housed' outside of the agreement; they are recorded in a public registry, accessible at the UNFCCC website.[132] It is this feature of the Paris Agreement that has prompted many observers to describe its approach as 'bottom-up', in contrast to the Kyoto Protocol's 'top-down' reliance on binding targets enshrined in the treaty.[133] Of course, as other commentators have pointed out, the Kyoto targets too were ultimately nationally determined, as individual parties decided which targets to put

130 Paris Agreement; UNFCCC, 'Adoption of the Paris Agreement', Decision 1/CP.21, FCCC/CP/2015/10/Add.1 (29 January 2016).

131 UNFCCC, 'Further Guidance in Relation to the Mitigation Section of Decision 1/CP.21', Draft Decision -/CMA.1, UN Doc. FCCC/CP/2018/L.22 (14 December 2018); UNFCCC, 'Modalities, Procedures and Guidelines for the Transparency Framework for Action and Support Referred to in Article 13 of the Paris Agreement', Draft Decision -/CMA.1, UN Doc. FCCC/CP/2018/L.23 (14 December 2018); UNFCCC, 'Matters relating to Article 14 of the Paris Agreement and paragraphs 99–101 of Decision 1/CP.21', Draft Decision -/CMA.1, UN Doc. FCCC/CP/2018.L.16 (14 December 2018); UNFCCC, 'Modalities and Procedures for the Effective Operation of the Committee to Facilitate Implementation and Promote Compliance Referred to in Article 15, paragraph 2 of the Paris Agreement', Draft Decision -/CMA.1, UN Doc. FCCC/CP/2018/L.5 (14 December 2018). The full set of decisions agreed to in Katowice is available at United Nations Climate Change, 'Katowice Climate Conference', December 2018. Available at: https://unfccc.int/process-and-meetings/the-paris-agreement/katowice-climate-package#eq-1, last accessed 5 September 2022. For a discussion see Lavanya Rajamani and Daniel Bodansky, 'The Paris Rulebook: Balancing International Prescriptiveness with National Discretion' (2019) 68(4) *International & Comparative Law Quarterly* 1023–1040.

132 Art. 4.12 Paris Agreement; UNFCCC, 'NDC Registry'. Available at: www4.unfccc.int/sites/NDCStaging/Pages/Home.aspx, last accessed 5 September 2022.

133 See, for example, Jessica F. Green, Thomas Sterner and Gernot Wagner, 'A Balance of Bottom-Up and Top-Down in Linking Climate Policies' (2014) 4(12) *Nature Climate Change* 1064–1067.

forward for inclusion in the Protocol's Annex B.[134] The main difference between the Kyoto targets and the Paris Agreement's NDCs is that compliance with the former was owed to the other protocol parties, whereas the Paris Agreement limits itself to obligating the parties to 'prepare, communicate and maintain successive' NDCs. While the parties, therefore, are free to determine the content of their NDCs, the Paris Agreement does provide for certain normative expectations, including that each successive NDC 'will represent a progression beyond' the party's current NDC and will 'reflect its highest possible ambition', as well as 'its common but differentiated responsibilities and respective capabilities, in the light of different national circumstances'.[135] The parties' NDCs are also to be pursued 'with a view to achieving the purpose' of the Paris Agreement, including notably the temperature goals it sets out.[136] Furthermore, individual parties 'shall pursue mitigation measures, with the aim of achieving the objectives' of their NDCs.[137]

However, for the purposes of this chapter, it is not the legal status of the NDCs that is of greatest interest. Rather, it is that the NDC approach represents yet another variation of consent in the climate regime. After all, States do consent to climate action, but they do so, not in the context of an international negotiation, but through their respective domestic decision-making processes. This shift merits unpacking. One might say that NDCs do not represent international law at all, and that the consent involved, is, therefore, not consent in the sense explored in this volume. Strictly speaking, this reading is of course correct. However, it seems fair to say that the lines between the international and the national realms, in terms of deliberation, decision-making and commitments, are blurrier than they may appear on the surface.

First, in joining the Paris Agreement, States consent to maintaining consecutive NDCs. Second, each party's NDC is to be guided by the Paris Agreement's normative expectations (highest possible ambition, progression over time and common but differentiated responsibilities and respective capabilities).[138] Third, the parties are subject to a range of reporting and other procedural requirements, feeding into the Paris Agreement's transparency

[134] Joanna Depledge, 'The "Top-Down" Kyoto Protocol? Exploring Caricature and Misrepresentation in Literature on Global Climate Change Governance' (2022) *International Environmental Agreements: Politics, Law and Economics*. Available at: https://doi.org/10.1007/s10784-022-09580-9, last accessed 5 September 2022.

[135] Art. 4.3 Paris Agreement.

[136] Arts. 2, 3, 4.1 Paris Agreement.

[137] Art. 4.2 Paris Agreement.

[138] See text accompanying fn. 135.

framework which, although not formally assessing compliance with NDCs, will provide for a publicly accessible tracking of the parties' progress in the achievement of NDCs.[139] Finally, while individual parties 'may at any time adjust' their existing NDCs, the Paris Agreement specifies that an NDC may be adjusted 'with a view to enhancing its level of ambition, in accordance with the guidance adopted by the [MOP]'.[140]

In short, although a State adopting an NDC through its national process is not consenting to international law in the conventional sense, it stands to reason that its domestic decision-making is encumbered by the collective expectations and requirements developed under the auspices of the Paris Agreement. Another way of thinking about the NDC process is that it inverts the standard notion that, once a State consents to obligations under an international agreement, it is obligated to adopt the national decisions required for their implementation – the 'top-down' approach. Under the Paris Agreement, national action is determined through domestic deliberation and decision-making, but rather than as entirely 'bottom-up' decision-making is perhaps better understood as occurring in dialogue with the international process. At the same time, notwithstanding this important dialogic dimension, the fact that NDCs are adopted at the national level has an important benefit: it bypasses the delays and blockages that can result from both the formal amendment process and the climate regime's consensus practice. Individual parties can unilaterally make more ambitious, albeit internationally non-binding, commitments.

8.5 CONCLUSION

Given the challenges of navigating the interplay between the individual and collective dimensions of the treaty-based law-making process, it is perhaps a miracle that the UNFCCC came into being at all. Two factors help explain that feat. First, the convention was adopted at the 1992 UN Conference on Environment and Development, following the new world order then seen by many to have been ushered in by the fall of the Berlin Wall, and in hindsight widely seen as the peak of enthusiasm for environmental treaty-making.[141]

[139] UNFCCC, 'Introduction to Transparency'. Available at: https://unfccc.int/Transparency, last accessed 5 September 2022.

[140] Art. 4.11 Paris Agreement. For a detailed assessment, see Lavanya Rajamani and Jutta Brunnée, 'The Legality of Downgrading Nationally Determined Contributions under the Paris Agreement: Lessons from the US Disengagement' (2017) 29(3) *Journal of Environmental Law* 537–551.

[141] Stacy D. VanDeveer, 'Green Fatigue' (2003) 27 *Wilson Quarterly* 55–59.

Second, as a framework convention, the UNFCCC entailed relatively limited commitments, thereby facilitating States' participation.[142]

By contrast, as the exploration of the Kyoto Protocol has shown, progressing towards more ambitious commitments in a consent-based system is a delicate task, especially in a treaty with global reach. Arriving at ambitious terms applicable to all parties is especially challenging, given the interconnected individual and collective aspects of the process: a sufficient number of States must be willing to bind themselves for new terms to take legal effect. It stands to reason that, given States' starkly different circumstances, outlooks and priorities, the individual-collective dynamics of formal consent processes render them ill-suited to the development of a global greenhouse gas reduction regime, let alone an ambitious one, or one that could increase ambition rapidly enough to keep pace with the accelerating climate crisis. A quirk of the climate regime – its consensus practice – presents an additional hurdle, complicating the adoption of amendments or supplementary treaties, and even the adoption of non-legally binding decisions of the COP.

The Paris Agreement was intended to transcend the constraints of the previous approaches. The resultant design of the Paris Agreement might appear to contain something of a paradox. On the one hand, it entails that consent – be it formal or simplified consent, or consensus decision-making – plays a much more limited role in treaty development than it does under the UNFCCC and the Kyoto Protocol. On the other hand, NDCs, by definition, leave individual parties in control.

The most significant shift inherent in the Paris Agreement's bottom-up approach, then, is not so much the move away from State consent, but its location at the national level. The result is a shift away from the anchoring of individual consent in treaty-based law-making processes, and hence from the linkages that adoption and entry into force requirements establish between multiple parties' individual acts of consent. In other words, while domestic decision-making occurs in the context of collective expectations and processes, the NDC approach disentangles the individual and collective dimensions of consent to climate action under the auspices of the Paris Agreement. This disentangling entails a major benefit, precisely because it unshackles States' pursuit of more ambitious climate action from the formal treaty development process that has constrained progress in the climate regime for more than two decades, or even allowed individual States to block collective action.

[142] See text accompanying fn. 8.

So far, it appears that such a blend of law-making and standard-setting approaches may have more potential to promote genuinely global climate action than the binding emission reduction regime enshrined in the Kyoto Protocol.[143] Optimistically, the Paris Agreement's NDC approach might even result in deeper and more authentic national engagement with the goals and requirements of an international regime, while also going some way to addressing concerns about international law's legitimacy deficits and overreach into sovereign spheres.[144] Still, it is too soon to know whether the Paris model will succeed, such that it progressively generates more ambitious commitments – sufficiently ambitious to meet the Paris Agreement's temperature targets. The key question for the climate regime is whether it will be able to provide a robust and durable normative and procedural context that ties States' policy choices into a collective process, notwithstanding the decoupling of individual commitments from the formal treaty-based law-making process.

[143] Gabriela Iacobuta, Navroz K. Dubash, Prabhat Upadhaya, Mekdelawit Deribe and Niklas Höhne, 'National Climate Change Mitigation Legislation, Strategy and Targets: A Global Update' (2018) 18(9) *Climate Policy* 1114–1132, at 1123 (showing that NDCs now cover 90 per cent of the global population and 89 per cent of global GHG emissions).

[144] For a discussion of the rise of such concerns, see Mattias Kumm, 'The Legitimacy of International Law: A Constitutionalist Framework of Analysis' (2004) 15(5) *European Journal of International Law* 907–931. On the claim that international law has become overly invasive of States' sovereign spheres, see Eric A. Posner, 'Liberal Internationalism and the Populist Backlash' (2017) 49 *Arizona State Law Journal* 795–819.

9

Consent and Sources

The European Court of Human Rights and the International Law Commission

GEORG NOLTE*

9.1 INTRODUCTION

The European Court of Human Rights (hereafter ECtHR) stated in *Demir and Baykara* that:

> [I]n searching for common ground among the norms of international law it [the Court] has never distinguished between sources of law according to whether or not they have been signed or ratified by the respondent State.[1]

This statement may be read as expressing either a triviality or a challenge. It would be trivial if it merely expressed the fact that some sources of international law – customary international law and general principles of law – do not require signature or ratification by a State for a legally binding rule to come into existence. After all, State practice and *opinio juris* as the elements of customary international law as well as domestic legislation as a basis for general principles of law do not usually come in the form of signature or ratification. But if the Court's dictum in *Demir and Baykara* was not intended to express a triviality, may it then be expressing a challenge to the role which

* This contribution is an expanded and updated version of a presentation given in 2020 to the Council of Europe's Committee of Legal Advisers on Public International Law. The views expressed here are my own. I thank Helmut Aust, Freie Universität Berlin, and Janina Barkholdt, International Court of Justice (hereafter ICJ), for their helpful comments; Keilin Anderson, ICJ, for her excellent editorial support; and Victoria McHale, ICJ, for her fine linguistic review.

[1] *Demir and Baykara* v. *Turkey* (No. 34503/97) (2009) 48 EHRR 54, GC, para. 78; Samantha Besson, 'Community Interests in the Identification of International Law', in Eyal Benvenisti and Georg Nolte (eds.), *Community Interests in International Law* (Oxford: Oxford University Press, 2018), pp. 50–69, p. 61.

consent has traditionally played for the sources of international law?[2] Does it indicate a 'decay of consent'[3] or lend support to those who are criticizing 'voluntarism'?[4]

It is well known that the modern debate on the sources of international law started in 1920 when the Advisory Committee of Jurists prepared a Draft Statute for the Permanent Court of International Justice (hereafter PCIJ).[5] One of the most controversial questions addressed during the Committee's deliberations concerned the law that the Court would be authorized to apply. The Committee settled on three sources: treaties, customary international law and general principles of law, all of which were listed in what later became Article 38 of the Statute of the PCIJ (and subsequently Article 38 of the International Court of Justice's (hereafter ICJ) Statute).[6]

The exchanges on the applicable law in 1920 were controversial because the members of the Advisory Committee disagreed about the role and the powers of the future court. On one side there were members such as Baron Édouard Descamps from Belgium, who maintained that if there was no specific treaty or customary rule, the Court should decide according to 'the legal conscience of civilized nations'.[7] On the other side there were members such as Elihu Root from the United States, who insisted that the Court must decide on the basis of clear rules of international law and that such rules could not be invented by judges.[8] The compromise reached by the Committee consisted in proposing that general principles of law should be '*recognized* by civilized nations'.[9] Thus, such principles were not supposed to simply result from the legal conscience of enlightened judges; rather, they needed to be

2 A modernization of the role of consent in legal theory is proposed by Samantha Besson, 'State Consent and Disagreement in International Law-Making: Dissolving the Paradox' (2016) 29 (2) *Leiden Journal of International Law* 289–316.

3 Nico Krisch, 'The Decay of Consent: International Law in an Age of Global Public Goods' (2014) 108(1) *American Journal of International Law* 1–40; Prosper Weil, 'Towards Relative Normativity in International Law' (1983) 77(3) *American Journal of international Law* 413–442.

4 See, for example, Pellet, Chapter 1 in this volume.

5 Advisory Committee of Jurists, 'Draft Statute', *Procès-verbaux of the Proceedings of the Committee June 16th–July 24th, 1920 with Annexes* (The Hague: Van Langenhuysen Brothers, 1920), Annex I, pp. 698–746.

6 Ibid., pp. 730–731.

7 Ibid., pp. 306, 310–311, 318–319, 322–325.

8 Ibid., pp. 308–310; 317–318.

9 Ibid., pp. 730–731 (emphasis added); Alain Pellet and Daniel Müller, 'Article 38', in Andreas Zimmermann, Christian Tams, Karin Oellers-Frahm and Christian Tomuschat (eds.), *The Statute of the International Court of Justice: A Commentary*, 3rd ed. (Oxford: Oxford University Press, 2019), paras. 17–41.

actually recognized, primarily in the domestic legal orders of 'civilized nations', as the relevant subjects were called at the time.

The debate within the Advisory Committee of Jurists made clear that the three sources identified in Article 38 of the Statute of the ICJ were the result of different forms of consent given by States: treaties expressing explicit and relatively specific consent, customary international law expressing implicit and relatively diffuse consent through practice and *opinio juris*, and general principles of law expressing consent resulting primarily from transposable parallel legal domestic principles. Thus, in that sense the doctrine of sources of international law has also become a doctrine of variations of consent. And these variations of consent were taken seriously, since the legitimacy and the *modus operandi* of the new permanent court depended on their respect. For the members of the Advisory Committee of Jurists this concern was particularly acute because they envisaged a court with a broad compulsory jurisdiction. Their concern remained valid even after that ambition for the scope of the Court's jurisdiction was later abandoned.

Today, we are still discussing the foundations and the limits of the powers of international courts, including those of the ECtHR. We still aim to achieve legal certainty, to ensure legitimacy and justice, and to avoid conflicting obligations that may emanate from different regimes of international law.[10] But are we pursuing these aims by arguing about the sources of international law and are we continuing to conceive consent as the common basis of the sources of international law? Or are we calling such classical approaches into question, as the dictum of the ECtHR might suggest?[11]

9.2 THE WORK OF THE INTERNATIONAL LAW COMMISSION ON THE SOURCES OF INTERNATIONAL LAW

Statements like the one in *Demir and Baykara* have sometimes been understood as implying that the European Convention on Human Rights (hereafter

[10] Council of Europe, 'The Place of the European Convention on Human Rights in the European and International Legal Order: Reports of the Steering Committee for Human Rights (CDDH) adopted at Its 92nd meeting (26–29 November 2019)' (2020). Available at: https://rm.coe.int/place-of-the-echr-in-the-european-and-international-legal-order/1680a05155, last accessed 21 October 2022, p. 7, para. 2: 'The key motivation of the report has been the importance of avoiding the dangers of conflicting obligations and the fragmentation of international law in particular with a view to strengthen legal certainty for the State Parties.'

[11] More recent decisions which follow the *Demir and Baykara* approach include *Shirkanyan* v. *Armenia*, no. 54547/16, para. 200, ECHR 22 February 2022; *Genovese* v. *Malta* (No. 53124/09) (2014) 58 EHRR 25, para. 44.

ECHR) has a special human rights character that is in tension with general international law, including with its methodological rules on sources.[12] It was this perceived tension that contributed to the decision by the International Law Commission (hereafter ILC) in 2002 to create a Study Group on 'Fragmentation of International Law'.[13]

The 2006 report of the Study Group (hereafter the Fragmentation Report)[14] can still be regarded as framing the debate. As far as the ECtHR is concerned,[15] the Fragmentation Report comes to the conclusion that the Court, when interpreting the ECHR in the light of other rules of international law, applies the customary rules on treaty interpretation as they are reflected in Articles 31 and 32 of the Vienna Convention on the Law of Treaties (hereafter VCLT).[16] The 2020 report of the Steering Committee for Human Rights 'on the place of the European Convention of Human Rights in the European and international legal order' has confirmed this finding.[17]

Thus, is the Strasbourg Court more faithful to a traditional understanding of the sources of international law than the dictum in *Demir and Baykara* might suggest? Or does the Court's jurisprudence provide impulses for innovation of the doctrine of sources at the international level that dilutes or leaves the consent element behind? The ILC has in recent years addressed such questions when working on restatements of the three classical sources of international law, as well as on peremptory norms of general international law (*jus cogens*).[18] The most important reason why the ILC has worked on

[12] *The Republic of Ireland* v. *the United Kingdom* (No. 5310/71) (1979–1980) 2 EHRR 25, para. 239; *Loizidou* v. *Turkey* (Preliminary Objections) (No. 15318/89) (1995) 20 EHRR 99, para. 70; William Schabas, *The European Convention on Human Rights: A Commentary* (Oxford: Oxford University Press, 2015), pp. 640, 735.

[13] ILC, 'Report of the International Law Commission on the Work of Its Fifty-Fourth Session', *Yearbook of the International Law Commission* (2002) Vol. II, Part Two, UN Doc. A/57/10, p. 97, paras. 492–493.

[14] ILC, 'Report of the Study Group of the International Law Commission on Fragmentation of International Law, Finalized by Martti Koskenniemi' (2006), UN Doc. A/CN.4/L.682/ Add.1.

[15] The report is based on a multitude of references to the Strasbourg Court: see ibid., p. 18, paras. 53–54 (on reservations to treaties); ibid., pp. 21–22, 25–26, 27, paras. 71–73, 90–94, 101 (on *lex specialis*); ibid., p. 32, paras. 130–131 (on teleological interpretation); ibid., pp. 38–39, 41, paras. 161–164, 174 (on special regimes); ibid., p. 54, paras. 246–249 (on *lex posterior*); ibid., pp. 76–77, paras. 372–373 (on *jus cogens*); ibid., p. 89, paras. 435–438 (on systemic integration).

[16] ILC, fn. 14, pp. 92, 119, paras. 174, 435.

[17] Council of Europe, fn. 10, pp. 13–14; however, the report also provides examples of the Court emphasizing the special character of the Convention as a human rights treaty.

[18] ILC, 'Report of the International Law Commission on the Work of Its Seventieth Session', UN Doc. A/73/10 (2018), ch. IV (on subsequent agreements and subsequent practice in relation to the interpretation of treaties), pp. 11–116, and ch. V (on identification of customary

those sources and fundamental norms is to provide more legal certainty with respect to the identification of international law by States, as well as by courts at the national, regional and universal levels.[19] In the course of its work, the ILC has, to a certain extent, identified the contribution of the ECtHR to the general rules on the sources of international law. In the following, I will briefly look at the Strasbourg Court's jurisprudence regarding treaties (Section 9.3), customary international law (Section 9.4) and general principles of law (Section 9.5) from the perspective of the work of the Commission, before concluding with a few general reflections (Section 9.6).

9.3 TREATIES

As far as treaties are concerned, the clearest example of an innovative contribution by the ECtHR to their understanding as a source of international law is without doubt its well-known jurisprudence regarding the effects of invalid reservations. This jurisprudence has been read as a challenge to the consent element in the law of treaties.[20] The ILC, in its subsequent work on reservations to treaties carried out under Special Rapporteur Alain Pellet, has, however, considered this jurisprudence to be compatible with the requirement of consent, going even so far as to say that '[t]he "Strasbourg approach" thus consists of acting on the reserving State's will to be bound by the treaty

international law), pp. 117–156; ILC, 'General Principles of Law', in ILC, 'Report of the International Law Commission on the Work of Its Seventy-First Session', UN Doc. A/74/10 (2019), ch. IX, pp. 329–339; ILC, 'Peremptory Norms of General International Law (*jus cogens*)', in ILC, 'Report of the International Law Commission on the Work of Its Seventy-Third Session', UN Doc. A/77/10 (2022), ch. IV, pp. 10–89, pp. 51–52.

19 ILC, 'Annex I: Treaties over Time in Particular: Subsequent Agreement and Practice', in ILC, 'Report of the International Law Commission on the Work of Its Sixtieth Session', *Yearbook of the International Law Commission* (2008) Vol. II, Part Two, UN Doc. A/63/10, pp. 152–169, p. 156, para. 22; ILC, 'Annex A: Formation and Evidence of Customary International Law', in ILC, 'Report of the International Law Commission on the Work of Its Sixty-Third Session', *Yearbook of the International Law Commission* (2011) Vol. II, Part Two, UN Doc. A/66/10, pp. 183–188, p. 183, para. 4; ILC, 'Annex A: General Principles of Law', in 'Report of the International Law Commission on the Work of Its Sixty-Ninth Session', *Yearbook of the International Law Commission* (2007) Vol. II, Part Two, UN Doc. A/72/10, pp. 155–167, p. 162, para. 35.

20 *Belilos* v. *Switzerland* (No. 10328/83) (1988) 10 EHRR 466, para. 50; *Loizidou* v. *Turkey*, fn. 12, paras. 70–77; ILC, 'Text of the Guide to Practice, Comprising an Introduction, the Guidelines and Commentaries Thereto, an Annex on the Reservations and Dialogue and a Bibliography', *Yearbook of the International Law Commission* (2011) Vol. II, Part Three, UN Doc. A/66/10/Add.1, pp. 35–351, pp. 229–231.

even if its reservation is invalid'.[21] The Commission subsequently reaffirmed the principle of consent in this context, observing that '[t]he status of the author of an invalid reservation in relation to a treaty depends on the intention expressed by the reserving State or international organization on whether it intends to be bound by the treaty with the benefit of the reservation or whether it considers that it is not bound by the treaty'[22] and that, notwithstanding any prior expressions of its intention to be bound regardless of the validity of a reservation, a State author of an invalid reservation 'may express at any time its intention not to be bound to the treaty without the benefit of the reservation'.[23]

The Commission has thus re-emphasized the role and the importance of consent, even using 'voluntarist' terms such as 'will'[24] and 'intention'.[25] At the same time, the Commission has recognized that consent can come in many forms and shades and that much depends on the proper interpretation of relevant acts, particularly by the body that is called to interpret the act. Thus, the way in which the Strasbourg Court and other human rights bodies, on the one hand, and the ILC, on the other hand, have dealt with the question of the legal effect of invalid reservations demonstrates that international courts and other bodies cannot escape their dependence on what, under the circumstances, may plausibly be called consent.

[21] ILC, fn. 20, pp. 311–312, paras. 24–26: '(24) In its judgment in the *Belilos* case, the European Court of Human Rights paid particular attention to Switzerland's position with regard to the European Convention. It expressly noted: "At the same time, Switzerland was, and regarded itself as, bound by the Convention irrespective of validity of the declaration." Thus, the Court clearly took into consideration the fact that Switzerland itself – the author of the invalid "reservation" – considered itself to be bound by the treaty despite the nullity of this reservation and had behaved accordingly. (25) In the *Loizidou* case, the European Court of Human Rights also based its judgment, if not on the will of the Turkish Government – which had maintained during the proceedings before the Court that "if the restrictions attached to the Articles 25 and 46 (art. 25, art. 46) declarations were not recognized to be valid, as a whole, the declarations were to be considered null and void in their entirety" – then on the fact that Turkey had knowingly run the risk that the restrictions resulting from its reservation would be declared invalid: That she, against this background, subsequently filed declarations under both Articles 25 and 46 (art. 25, art. 46) – the latter subsequent to the statements by the Contracting Parties referred to above – indicates a willingness on her part to run the risk that the limitation clauses at issue would be declared invalid by the Convention institutions without affecting the validity of the declarations themselves. (26) The "Strasbourg approach" thus consists of acting on the reserving State's will to be bound by the treaty even if its reservation is invalid.'

[22] ILC, fn. 20, Guideline 4.5.3, pp. 306–315, p. 306, para. 1.

[23] Ibid., para. 3.

[24] Ibid., p. 310.

[25] Ibid., p. 311.

The Court also makes a less specific contribution to treaties as a source of international law, and to the corresponding role of consent, through its method of treaty interpretation.[26]

One of the main reasons why the ILC has worked on treaty interpretation in recent years consists in the challenge that the ECtHR appeared to pose to the general Vienna rules on treaty interpretation.[27] Since the 1970s, the Strasbourg Court has been well known for its occasionally evolutive approach to the interpretation of Convention rights.[28] The Court has justified this approach by referring to the specific character of the ECHR as a human rights treaty.[29] The ILC has, however, indicated that evolutive approaches to treaty interpretation are neither specific to human rights treaties nor a separate method of treaty interpretation.[30] For example, the Commission has pointed to the 2009 *Costa Rica* v. *Nicaragua* Judgment, in which the ICJ applied a form of evolutive interpretation to a nineteenth-century bilateral border treaty.[31]

Evolutive interpretation should not, however, be undertaken lightly. Other international courts and tribunals have engaged in such interpretations to varying degrees.[32] The World Trade Organization (WTO) Appellate Body, for example, has remained rather reluctant in that respect, and for good reasons. It is perhaps possible to say that the Strasbourg Court has contributed to establishing more legitimacy at the universal level for evolutive approaches to interpretation. The work of the ILC nevertheless suggests that evolutive approaches to treaty interpretation need to be pursued with some caution so as

[26] Photini Pazartis, Geir Ulfstein, Panos Merkouris and Daniel Peat, 'Final Report of the ILA Study Group on the Content and Evolution of the Rules of Interpretation' (ILA, 79th Biennial Conference, Kyoto, 2020). Available at: https://papers.ssrn.com/sol3/papers.cfm?abstract_id=3757730, last accessed 27 October 2022; Linos-Alexander Sicilianos, 'Interpretation of the European Convention on Human Rights: Remarks on the Court's Approach' (Speech delivered 5 May 2020). Available at: https://rm.coe.int/interpretation-of-the-european-convention-on-human-rights-remarks-on-t/1680a05732, last accessed 27 October 2022.

[27] ILC, 'Subsequent Agreements and Subsequent Practice in Relation to the Interpretation of Treaties', in ILC, 'Report of Its Seventieth Session' (2018), fn. 18, ch. IV, pp. 11–116, pp. 66, 68, paras. 7, 14; ILC, 'Annex I: Treaties over Time in Particular', fn. 19, p. 158, para. 35; Council of Europe, fn. 10, pp. 6, 14, 17.

[28] See, for example, *Tyrer* v. *The United Kingdom* (No. 5856/72) (1979–1980) 2 EHRR 1, para. 31; *Dudgeon* v. *The United Kingdom* (No. 7252/76) (1982) 4. EHRR 149, para. 60; *Chapman* v. *the United Kingdom* (No. 27238/95) (2001) 33 EHRR 18, paras. 70 and 93.

[29] See, for example, *Magyar Helsinki Bizottság* v. *Hungary* (No. 18030/11) (2020) 71 EHRR 2, para. 138; *Biao* v. *Denmark* (No. 38590/10) (2017) 64 EHRR 1, GC, para. 131.

[30] ILC, 'Subsequent Agreements', fn. 27, pp. 66–67, 68, paras. 8, 9, 14; Council of Europe, fn. 10, p. 19.

[31] *Dispute regarding Navigational and Related Rights (Costa Rica* v. *Nicaragua)* (Judgment) [2009] ICJ Rep. 213, pp. 242–244, paras. 64–70.

[32] ILC, 'Subsequent Agreements', fn. 27, pp. 65–66, para. 7.

to maintain the necessary connection with the required consent of the parties to a treaty. This connection is referred to in conclusion 8 of the relevant ILC work, which reads:

> Subsequent agreements and subsequent practice under articles 31 and 32 may assist in determining whether or not the presumed intention of the parties upon the conclusion of the treaty was to give a term used a meaning which is capable of evolving over time.[33]

According to the commentaries, conclusion 8:

> (9) . . . by using the phrase 'presumed intention', refers to the intention of the parties as determined through the application of the various means of interpretation that are recognized in articles 31 and 32. The 'presumed intention' is thus not a separately identifiable original will, and the travaux préparatoires are not the primary basis for determining the presumed intention of the parties, but they are only, as article 32 indicates, a supplementary means of interpretation. And although interpretation must seek to identify the intention of the parties, this must be done by the interpreter on the basis of the means of interpretation that are available at the time of the act of interpretation and that include subsequent agreements and subsequent practice of parties to the treaty. The interpreter thus has to answer the question of whether parties can be presumed to have intended, upon the conclusion of the treaty, to give a term used a meaning that is capable of evolving over time.
>
> (10) Draft conclusion 8 does not take a position regarding the question of the appropriateness of a more contemporaneous or a more evolutive approach to treaty interpretation in general . . . The conclusion should, however, be understood as indicating the need for some caution with regard to arriving at a conclusion in a specific case whether to adopt an evolutive approach. For this purpose, draft conclusion 8 points to subsequent agreements and subsequent practice as means of interpretation that may provide useful indications to the interpreter for assessing, as part of the ordinary process of treaty interpretation, whether the meaning of a term is capable of evolving over time.[34]

Thus, evolutive interpretation should, as far as possible, be supported by a broad practice of the parties to a treaty, so as to ensure the necessary degree of legal certainty and legitimacy.[35] By emphasizing the element of practice in

[33] Ibid., p. 14.
[34] Ibid., pp. 66–67.
[35] Ibid., Commentary to conclusions 7 and 8, pp. 63, 67.

the context of evolutive interpretation, the ILC and the Strasbourg Court are maintaining the classical doctrine of sources and consent.

9.4 CUSTOMARY INTERNATIONAL LAW

The contribution of the ECtHR to the understanding of the second classical source, customary international law, is less pronounced than its contribution to the law of treaties. Neither the reports of the Special Rapporteur on identification of customary international law,[36] Sir Michael Wood, nor the commentaries to the 2018 conclusions of the ILC on this topic[37] contain many references to the jurisprudence of the ECtHR. This may be due to the emphasis given by the Special Rapporteur to the jurisprudence of the ICJ.

The ILC has elaborated on the role of consent for the identification of customary international law by noting that:

> [t]he Latin term *opinio juris* has been retained in the draft conclusions and commentaries alongside 'acceptance as law' because of its prevalence in legal discourse (including in the case law of the International Court of Justice), and also because it may capture better the particular nature of the subjective element of customary international law as referring to legal conviction and not to formal consent.[38]

Thus, as in the context of the law of treaties, the Commission has chosen to circumscribe the required consent in relatively voluntarist terminology. In that sense, the term 'conviction' (for *opinio juris*) corresponds to the terms 'will'

[36] ILC, 'First Report on Formation and Evidence of Customary International Law, by Sir Michael Wood, Special Rapporteur', UN Doc. A/CN.4/663, in ILC, 'Report of the International Law Commission of the Work of Its Sixty-Fifth Session', *Yearbook of the International Law Commission* (2013) Vol. II, Part Two, UN Doc. A/68/10, pp. 64–68; ILC, 'Second Report on Identification of Customary International Law by Sir Michael Wood, Special Rapporteur', UN Doc. A/CN.4/672, in ILC, 'Report of the International Law Commission on the Work of Its Sixty-Sixth Session', *Yearbook of the International Law Commission* (2014) Vol. II, Part Two, UN Doc. A/69/10, pp. 147–153; ILC, 'Third Report on Identification of Customary International Law by Sir Michael Wood, Special Rapporteur', UN Doc. A/CN.4/682, in ILC, 'Report of the International Law Commission on the Work of Its Sixty-Seventh Session', *Yearbook of the International Law Commission* (2015) Vol. II, Part Two, UN Doc. A/70/10, pp. 28–32; ILC, 'Fourth Report on Identification of Customary International Law by Sir Michael Wood, Special Rapporteur', UN Doc. A/CN.4/695 (2016); ILC, 'Fifth Report on Identification of Customary International Law by Sir Michael Wood, Special Rapporteur', UN Doc. A/CN.4/717 (2018).

[37] ILC, 'Identification of Customary International Law', in ILC, 'Report of Its Seventieth Session' (2018), fn. 18, ch. V, pp. 117–156.

[38] Ibid., p. 123, footnote 665.

(reservations to treaties)[39] and 'intention' (interpretation of treaties).[40] Although this choice of words appears to disregard the criticism of 'voluntarism', the reason for it may not simply be an automatic continuation of dated terminology, but rather an insistence on a thorough examination of the available evidence in the light of the prerogative of States to determine the coming into existence and the content of treaties and rules of customary international law. This is particularly important when it comes to the identification of rules of customary international law through non-binding instruments (which have not 'been signed or ratified by the respondent State'[41]), such as resolutions by political or other non-judicial organs of international organizations. The ILC has articulated this point most specifically with respect to resolutions of the United Nations General Assembly:

> As the International Court of Justice has observed, resolutions 'even if they are not binding … can, in certain circumstances, provide evidence important for establishing the existence of a rule or the emergence of an *opinio juris*'. This is particularly so when a resolution purports to be declaratory of an existing rule of customary international law, in which case it may serve as evidence of the acceptance as law of such a rule by those States supporting the resolution. In other words, '[t]he effect of consent to the text of such resolutions … may be understood as an acceptance of the validity of the rule or set of rules declared by the resolution …
>
> (6) Because the attitude of States towards a given resolution (or a particular rule set forth in a resolution), expressed by vote or otherwise, is often motivated by political or other non-legal considerations, ascertaining acceptance as law (*opinio juris*) from such resolutions must be done 'with all due caution' … In each case, a careful assessment of various factors is required in order to verify whether indeed the States concerned intended to acknowledge the existence of a rule of customary international law. As the International Court of Justice indicated in *Legality of the Threat or Use of Nuclear Weapons*, 'it is necessary to look at [the resolution's] content and the conditions of its adoption; it is also necessary to see whether an *opinio juris* exists as to its normative character. Or a series of resolutions may show the gradual evolution of the *opinio juris* required for the establishment of a new rule.[42]

The Commission has also elaborated on the role of silence, or inaction, as a means of expressing consent:

[39] ILC, fn. 20, p. 310.

[40] Ibid., p. 311.

[41] *Demir and Baykara* v. *Turkey*, fn. 1.

[42] ILC, 'Identification of Customary International Law', fn. 37, p. 148.

3. Failure to react over time to a practice may serve as evidence of acceptance as law (*opinio juris*), provided that States were in a position to react and the circumstances called for some reaction.[43]

The Strasbourg Court, when identifying a rule of customary international law, seems generally to have followed the methodology outlined by the ICJ and the ILC. This approach of the Court cannot be taken for granted, given the emphasis some authors place on the – generously interpreted and generously applied – *opinio juris* aspect of customary international law, at the expense of the State practice element. The Court, when called to identify a rule of customary international law, has mostly made efforts to carefully identify the relevant *opinio juris* and State practice, particularly in its case law relating to questions of State immunity, such as *Al-Adsani* v. *United Kingdom*,[44] *Jones* v. *United Kingdom*[45] and *Cudak* v. *Lithuania*.[46] However, it is also worth mentioning that former Judge Ineta Ziemele has recommended that the Court improve its identification of relevant State practice when determining a rule of customary international law.[47] While this is indeed good advice, my impression is that the Court usually does take seriously the requirements for the identification of rules of customary international law. In so doing, it is methodologically contributing to legal certainty and to maintaining the importance of State consent.

9.5 GENERAL PRINCIPLES OF LAW

General principles of law, the third source under Article 38 of the ICJ Statute, have only very exceptionally been referred to by the ECtHR.[48] This lack of

43 Ibid., Conclusion 10, p. 140, para. 3.

44 *Al-Adsani* v. *the United Kingdom* (No. 35763/97) (2002) 34 EHRR 11, GC, paras. 60–66.

45 *Jones* v. *United Kingdom* (Nos. 34356/06 and 40528/06) (2014) 59 EHRR 1, paras. 110–215.

46 *Cudak* v. *Lithuania* (No. 15869/02) (2010) 51 EHRR 15, GC, paras. 29–33, 64–69. The ICJ, for its part, has relied on the Strasbourg Court when identifying a rule of customary international law in *Jurisdictional Immunities of the State* (*Germany* v. *Italy*) (Judgment) [2012] ICJ Rep. 99, paras. 78, 90.

47 Ineta Ziemele, 'European Consensus and International Law', in Anne van Aaken and Iulia Motoc (eds.), *The European Convention on Human Rights and General International Law* (Oxford: Oxford University Press, 2018), p. 36.

48 *Golder* v. *The United Kingdom* (No. 4451/70) (1979) 1 EHRR 524, para. 35: 'Article 31 para. 3 (c) of the Vienna Convention indicates that account is to be taken, together with the context, of "any relevant rules of international law applicable in the relations between the parties". Among those rules are general principles of law and especially "general principles of law recognized by civilized nations" (Art. 38 para. 1 (c) of the Statute of the International Court of Justice). Incidentally, the Legal Committee of the Consultative Assembly of the Council of Europe foresaw in August 1950 that "the Commission and the Court must necessarily apply

practice may have to do with the fact that general principles of law in the sense of Article 38 have, so far, not played an important role at the universal level[49] – one of the reasons for this being the now discredited requirement that they must be 'recognized by civilized nations'. Yet this explanation for the lack of references to general principles of law in the jurisprudence of the Strasbourg Court may not be sufficient.

If we look at the reasons why general principles of law were accepted in 1920 as the third source of international law, we see that they are used to 'fill gaps' and to prevent a denial of justice.[50] The need for these functions also exists, *mutatis mutandis*, in the context of the ECHR. In fact, during the drafting of the ECHR in 1950, its founders envisaged the adoption of a provision pursuant to which the supervisory organs would determine the conformity of the legislation or laws of Member States with the ECHR on the basis of 'the general principles of law recognized by civilized nations referred to in Article 38 of the Permanent Court of International Justice'. This proposal was ultimately *not* included in the ECHR, but 'for one reason only[:] [w]e on the Committee could not contemplate the organs or the machinery doing anything else'.[51]

It is well known that the Court would later do something else, at least terminologically. Indeed, to determine the conformity of acts of Member

such principles" in the execution of their duties and thus considered it to be "unnecessary" to insert a specific clause to this effect in the Convention (Documents of the Consultative Assembly, working papers of the 1950 session, Vol. III, No. 93, p. 982, para. 5).' Apart from this decision, reference has been made to 'general principles of law recognised by civilised nations' mainly when interpreting Art. 7(2) of the Convention; see, for example, *Maktouf* v. *Bosnia and Herzegovina* (Nos. 2312/08 and 34179/08) (2014) 58 EHRR 11, GC, paras. 66, 72; *Kolk and Kislyiy* v. *Estonia* (Decision on Admissibility), nos. 23052/04 and 24018/04, para. 126, ECHR 2006-I.

49 Statement of Abdulqawi Ahmed Yusuf, President of the International Court of Justice before the Sixth Committee of the UN General Assembly, New York (1 November 2019). Available at: http://statements.unmeetings.org/media2/23328836/president-icj-e.pdf, last accessed 27 October 2022, para. 27: 'Neither the PCIJ nor the ICJ has ever explicitly based a decision on a rule or principle derived from the "general principles of law recognized by civilized nations".' The only explicit reference to Art. 38(1) (c) of the ICJ-Statute has been made in the controversial *South West Africa Cases (Ethiopia v. South Africa; Liberia v. South Africa)* (Second Phase) (Judgment) [1966] ICJ Rep. 6, pp. 6, 47, para. 88.

50 See the debate on this issue in the Advisory Committee of Jurists, fn. 5, pp. 307–319.

51 Special Rapporteur Sir David Maxwell-Fyfe, 'Report presented by Sir D. Maxwell Fyfe', in Council of Europe, 'References to the notion of the "general principles of law recognised by the civilised nations" contained in the travaux préparatoires of the Convention', CDH(74)37, p. 16. Available at: www.echr.coe.int/LibraryDocs/Travaux/ECHRTravaux-PGD-CDH(74)37-BIL1678846.pdf, last accessed 27 October 2022; Council of Europe, *Collected Edition of the "Travaux Préparatoires" of the European Convention on Human Rights, Volume VI, Consultative Assembly* (Leiden: Brill, 1985), p. 78.

States with the ECHR, the Court examines whether the interpretation and any restrictions of Convention rights are supported by a 'European consensus'.[52] European consensus is found by comparing the laws of the different Member States and by determining whether there is a sufficient commonality among them. Regardless of whether 'European consensus' is a particular method of treaty interpretation, a form of regional customary law, or a regional general principle of law,[53] the approach it pursues has certain similarities to what the Advisory Committee of Jurists envisaged in 1920 when conceiving general principles of law for the Statute of the PCIJ, and what the founders of the European Convention envisaged in 1950.

However, one important difference between the original approach to the identification of general principles of law, as envisaged in 1920 and 1950, and the method by which the ECtHR today determines the existence of a 'European consensus' consists in the relatively detailed inquiry that the European Court usually undertakes when searching for such consensus. In contrast, the traditional approach to the identification of general principles of law in international law consists in a relatively generous grouping of various legal systems into 'legal families', in which commonalities can more easily be found than by using a more rigorous approach such as the one chiefly used by the ECtHR to identify a European consensus. A commentary on Article 38 of the ICJ Statute by Alain Pellet and Daniel Müller reflects the approach of many international lawyers when they discuss:

> the method to be employed for discovering the principles *in foro domestico*. In the abstract, it would seem that recourse to comparative law is essential; but it is not and such a requirement would in any case be unrealistic; the material is hardly available to the parties or to the judges who, moreover, are lawyers trained in international law (or national law) but who, with all due respect, usually can hardly be seen as comparatists. In any case, this would be unnecessary: all modern domestic laws can be gathered into a few families or systems of law which, insofar as general principles are concerned, are coherent enough to be considered as 'legal systems', and, since only very general rules are to be taken into consideration in any event, it is enough to ascertain that such principles are present in any (or some) of the laws belonging to these various systems.[54]

[52] *Magyar Helsinki Bizottság* v. *Hungary* (No. 18030/11) (2020) 71 EHRR 2, para. 148; Ziemele, fn. 47.

[53] *Lalmahomed* v. *The Netherlands* (Concurring Opinion of Judge Ziemele), no. 26036/08, ECHR, 22 February 2011.

[54] Pellet and Müller, fn. 9, p. 928, para. 264.

Such a generous approach possesses a certain intuitive plausibility, given that it is more difficult to ascertain and appropriately compare the more heterogeneous legal systems of 193 States than it is to compare the more homogeneous ones of forty-six States. On the other hand, one is tempted to ask why general principles of law have gained such little importance in the jurisprudence of international courts and tribunals, if it is so much easier, methodologically speaking, to determine their existence than it is to determine the existence of a European consensus. Is it simply because Article 38 of the ICJ Statute speaks of general principles recognized by 'civilized' nations and that this problematic term constitutes an additional obstacle to the acceptability of this third source of international law? Or is it because international courts and tribunals have felt uncertain about the basis from which to determine general principles of law, and thus about the subjects and the kind of 'recognition', or consent, that are required?

While these questions are difficult to answer with respect to the past, it is likely that they will be easier to answer in the future. This is because, in 2019, the ILC, under its Special Rapporteur Marcelo Vazquez-Bermudez, began work on the topic of 'General principles of law'. Although in 2022 this work is still at a provisional stage, the ILC has embarked on a course which is likely to lead to a different setting for the discussion and identification of general principles of law as the third source of international law.

In a first step, the ILC has clearly disavowed the major intellectual obstacle to the acceptance and use of general principles of law, that is the requirement that they be recognized by 'civilized nations': in its draft conclusion 2, provisionally adopted in 2021, the ILC states: 'For a general principle of law to exist, it must be recognized by the community of nations.' The ILC goes on to explain in the commentary:

> Draft conclusion 2 employs the term 'community of nations' as a substitute for the term 'civilized nations' found in Article 38, paragraph 1 (c), of the Statute of the International Court of Justice, because the latter term is anachronistic. The term 'community of nations' is found in article 15, paragraph 2, of the International Covenant on Civil and Political Rights, a treaty to which 173 States are parties and which is thus widely accepted.[55]

On this basis it should now be possible to overcome most reservations towards general principles of law which result from the use of the term

[55] ILC, 'General Principles of Law', in ILC, 'Report of the International Law Commission on the Work of Its Seventy-Second Session' (2021), UN Doc. A/76/10, ch. VIII, pp. 150–163, p. 162, para. 3.

'civilized' in Article 38. The removal of this obstacle will enable courts and scholars to concentrate on the main methodological issue for the identification of general principles of law derived from national legal systems and possibly also others that are formed within the international legal system. Both forms of general principles of law raise questions about the subjects and the kind of 'recognition', or consent, that are required.

In this respect, the ILC has, in a second step, in its draft conclusion 5, provisionally adopted, in 2022, a rather demanding, consent-oriented approach for the identification of general principles of law derived from national legal systems:

> *Determination of the existence of a principle common to the various legal systems of the world*
>
> 1. To determine the existence of a principle common to the various legal systems of the world, a comparative analysis of national legal systems is required.
> 2. The comparative analysis must be wide and representative, including the different regions of the world.
> 3. The comparative analysis includes an assessment of national laws and decisions of national courts, and other relevant materials.[56]

This draft conclusion explicitly states that 'the various legal systems of the world' are the 'national legal systems'. Does this mean that the ILC is thus discarding the more generous and approximate 'legal families' approach, as outlined, for example, by Pellet and Müller?[57] The commentary suggests that this is indeed the case:

> This description is aimed at clarifying that, while it is not necessary to assess every single legal system of the world to identify a general principle of law, the comparative analysis must nonetheless be sufficiently comprehensive to take into account the legal systems of States in accordance with the principle of sovereign equality of States. The term 'different regions of the world' was included to emphasize that it does not suffice to show that a legal principle exists in legal systems representing certain legal families (such as civil law, common law and Islamic law), but that it is also necessary to show that the principle has been recognized widely in the various regions of the world or, as the International Court of Justice indicated in the *Barcelona Traction* case, that a principle has been 'generally accepted by municipal legal systems.[58]

[56] ILC, 'Report of the International Law Commission on the Work of Its Seventy-Third Session' (2022), UN Doc. A/77/10, p. 319.

[57] Pellet and Müller, fn. 9.

[58] ILC, 'Report of Its Seventy-Third Session' (2022), fn. 56, pp. 320–321.

Even if the ILC has not, so far, recognized a distinct contribution of the Strasbourg Court to the identification of general principles of law, it appears to follow the methodology of the European Court in identifying a European consensus. It remains to be seen whether this approach is sufficiently pragmatic and practicable at the universal level to be used by international courts and tribunals to identify, more than was the case before, general principles of law.[59] What is clear, however, is that the ILC emphasizes the consent element of general principles of law by requiring their 'recognition' to be identified in a relatively granular way through a comparative analysis of national legal systems.

As far as general principles of law formed within the international legal system are concerned, the ILC has provisionally adopted a draft conclusion 7:

> *Identification of general principles of law formed within the international legal system*
>
> 1. To determine the existence and content of a general principle of law that may be formed within the international legal system, it is necessary to ascertain that the community of nations has recognized the principle as intrinsic to the international legal system.[60]

It is a matter of controversy within the ILC whether this second means of identifying general principles of law should be recognized. The main reason for the disagreement seems to lie in the question of how specific a consent must be for a binding rule of international law to come into existence. However, the members of the ILC appear to agree, at a high level of abstraction, that

> (3) [a]s regards the methodology for the identification of general principles of law formed within the international legal system, the Commission considered that it is similar to that applicable to general principles of law derived from national legal systems.

Some members of the ILC considered that:

> the distinction between customary international law and general principles of law formed within the international legal system, within the meaning given

[59] Council of Europe, fn. 10, p. 21: 'based on a comprehensive analysis of the practice and specific circumstances of the States Parties in line with the consensual nature of State obligations under international law'; *Case concerning Application of the Convention on the Prevention and Punishment of the Crime of Genocide (Bosnia and Herzegovina* v. *Serbia and Montenegro)* (Merits) [2007] ICJ Rep. 43, para. 119.

[60] ILC, 'Report of Its Seventy-Third Session' (2022), fn. 56, p. 320.

> in draft conclusion 7, was not clear, and that the Commission should be cautious not to put forward a methodology for the identification of those general principles of law that could overlap with the conditions for the emergence of rules of customary international law.[61]

In other words, some members are concerned that the conditions for the identification of general principles of law formed within the international legal system would undermine the more specific requirements of consent that are contained in the State practice and *opinio juris* elements of customary international law, thereby allowing for the possibility of a 'custom lite'.[62]

9.6 CONCLUSION

So, does the observation of the ECtHR in *Demir and Baykara*, according to which '[the Court] has never distinguished between sources of law according to whether or not they have been signed or ratified by the respondent State',[63] mean that the Court takes lightly the rules on the sources of international law and that it mainly contributes a specialist perspective to general international law? This does not appear to be the case. To the contrary, the Strasbourg Court has, it seems, taken seriously the rules on the sources of international law and has been careful to specifically identify consent – except perhaps in its jurisprudence on reservations. In addition, the Court has contributed certain innovative elements that have been noted by the ILC and found to be broadly compatible with general international law.

This leads me to the conclusion that the observation of the Court in *Demir and Baykara* should simply be read as referring to the classical rules on the sources of international law that, to a certain extent, do permit taking acts or pronouncements into account that are not binding as such. The interpretation of treaties may be influenced by the subsequent conduct of the parties or by the recommendations of treaty bodies. The identification of customary international law requires to examine rather specifically State practice and *opinio juris*. And general principles of law may derive from domestic legal systems, or they might be recognized within the international legal system. All these acts

61 Ibid., p. 323.

62 See, for example, Sir Michael Wood, in ILC, 'Provisional Summary of Record of the 3539th Meeting' (2021), UN Doc. A/CN.4/SR.3539, p. 13; Mathias Forteau in ILC, 'Provisional Summary of Record of the 3538th Meeting' (2021), UN A/CN.4/SR.3538, p. 12; Eduardo Valencia Ospina, in ILC, 'Provisional Summary of Record of the 3538th Meeting' (2021), UN/A/CN.4/SR.3538, p. 8; ILC, 'Third Report on General Principles of Law by Marcelo Vázquez-Bermúdez, Special Rapporteur' (2022), UN Doc. A/CN.4/753, p. 9, para. 20.

63 See fn. 1.

or pronouncements are not binding under international law as such, but they are forms of expressing or identifying consent. The ICJ, by recognizing in the *Diallo* case 'that it should ascribe great weight to the interpretation adopted by' the Human Rights Committee, has adopted a similar approach in a particular context.[64] If its jurisprudence is understood in this sense, the Strasbourg Court can be seen as playing the role of a constructive stakeholder in general international law. Thus, when taking such acts or pronouncements into account, the Court does not fail to distinguish between hard law and soft law, nor does it take the requirement of consent lightly.[65]

However, the rules on the sources of international law represent a never-ending challenge. The character of this challenge becomes clear if one looks back to one hundred years ago and to the reasons why these rules, or categories, were formulated. They were not formulated merely to provide a point of departure for the teaching of law students. Rather they were formulated for the purpose of establishing, and placing limits on, the power of a court to declare the law.[66] This concern for the sustained legitimacy of international courts and for legal certainty is a primary reason why the ILC, following the Fragmentation report of its Study Group, embarked on restatements of the rules on the sources of international law. These restatements have come about primarily by comparing the methodological approaches of different international courts and tribunals. The draft conclusions of the Commission have re-emphasized the importance of the forms of consent laid down in the doctrine of sources of international law. This is also true of the most recent restatement of the methodology for identifying peremptory norms of general international law (*jus cogens*), which was adopted on second reading by the Commission in 2022 and whose commentaries make various references to the jurisprudence of the Strasbourg Court.[67] The Commission may, in the future, further refine the role of consent for the sources of international law by including on its agenda a proposal by Mathias Forteau to work on the topic

64 *Ahmadou Sadio Diallo (Republic of Guinea* v. *Democratic Republic of the Congo)* (Merits) [2010] ICJ Rep. 639, para. 66. The ICJ had already confirmed that treaty rules may be 'open to adapt to emerging norms of international law': *Gabčíkovo-Nagymaros Project (Hungary* v. *Slovakia)* (Judgment) [1997] ICJ Rep. 7, para. 111.

65 Angelika Nussberger, 'Hard Law or Soft Law – Does It Matter?: Distinction between Different Sources of International Law in the Jurisprudence of the ECtHR', in van Aaken and Motoc, fn. 47, pp. 48–52. She refers to *National Union of Rail, Maritime and Transport Workers* v. *United Kingdom* (No. 31045/10) (2015) 60 EHRR 10.

66 See fn. 8; the same sentiment was expressed during the elaboration of the European Convention in 1950 by Mr Charles Chaumont when he said that 'the Court is not intended to create new law *ex cathedra*': see, Council of Europe, 'References to the Notion', fn. 51, p. 10.

67 ILC, 'Peremptory Norms of General International Law', fn. 18, pp. 29–39.

of 'Non-legally binding international agreements (Les accords internationaux juridiquement non-contraignants)'.[68] It would thus look at the topic 'from the other side', while also examining the 'potential legal effects'[69] of such non-binding agreements, and thereby give flesh to what the ECtHR expressed in its dictum in *Demir and Baykara*.[70]

The ECtHR has so far played a role that is both sensitive to the basic requirements of general international law and moderately innovative. The Court appears to have coped relatively well in the face of certain challenges, including those mounted since 2010 in the context of the Interlaken process,[71] not least because it has been respectful of the methodological rules regarding the sources of international law, particularly in so far as they serve to ensure the necessary degree of consent. It is true that these rules do not place strict limits on the competence of the Court to pronounce the law. But they do provide standards for arriving at and explaining decisions, particularly when these decisions may be perceived as innovative.[72] The rules regarding the sources of international law, specifically those regarding the forms of consent, thus contribute to legal certainty and to the accountability of the ECtHR and other international courts.[73]

68 ILC, 'Annex I: Non-legally Binding International Agreements', in ILC, 'Report on the Work of the Seventy-Third Session', fn. 18, pp. 352–365, pp. 353–362.
69 Ibid., pp. 355–357.
70 See fn. 1.
71 Council of Europe, fn. 10, p. 9.
72 Ziemele, fn. 47, pp. 23–40.
73 Council of Europe, fn. 10, p. 21, para. 96.

10

Variations around the Notion of Consent in Investment Arbitration

LAURENCE BOISSON DE CHAZOURNES*

10.1 INTRODUCTION

In the early twentieth century, the Permanent Court of International Justice (hereafter PCIJ) in the *Status of Eastern Carelia* held that '[i]t is well established in international law that no State can, without its consent, be compelled to submit its disputes with other States either to mediation or to arbitration, or to any other kind of pacific settlement'.[1] Over the years, this principle has been reaffirmed consistently by international courts and tribunals[2] – whether permanent or *ad hoc* – in various cases, including both contentious and advisory matters.[3]

In the absence of a centralized power at the international level, all 'international adjudicatory bodies' are based on 'the consent and agreement of the subjects (i.e. the litigants, *les justiciables*)'.[4] The arbitral tribunal in the *Chevron* v. *Ecuador* case, while discussing the principle of consent, remarked that:

* The author wishes to thank Aditya Laddha for his very helpful assistance in the preparation of this chapter. This chapter was written in the framework of the project: *The International Judicial Function under Pressure: Do Courts and Tribunals Go Off the Rails?*, funded by the Swiss National Foundation.

1 *Status of Eastern Carelia* (Advisory Opinion) [1923] PCIJ Ser. B No. 5, p. 27.

2 Clément Marquet, *Le consentement étatique à la compétence des juridictions internationales* (Paris: Pedone, 2022); Tams, Chapter 3 in this volume.

3 *East Timor (Portugal* v. *Australia)* [1995] ICJ Rep. 90, para. 34; *Interpretation of Peace Treaties with Bulgaria, Hungary and Romania* (Advisory Opinion) (first phase) [1950] ICJ Rep. 65, p. 71.

4 *Abaclat and Others (Case formerly known as Giovanna A. Beccara and Others)* v. *Argentine Republic*, ICSID, Decision on Jurisdiction and Admissibility (4 August 2011) Case No. ARB/07/5, 52 ILM 667, Dissenting Opinion of Georges Abi-Saab (28 October 2011), para. 7.

> [N]o international tribunal may exercise jurisdiction over a State without the consent of that State; and, by analogy, *no arbitration tribunal has jurisdiction over any person unless they have consented*. That may be called the 'consent' principle, and it goes to the question of the tribunal's jurisdiction.[5]

One would assume that given the clear terms in which international courts and tribunals have formulated and upheld the principle of consent, it would not evoke confusion or extensive discussion. The steady rise of varied international disputes, however, has generated significant debate about the interpretation and application of the principle of consent. In investor–State arbitration in particular (although not limited to it), the nature of consent is heavily discussed. International courts and tribunals are being increasingly criticized by States for committing jurisdictional overreach. The underlying problem may well be whether the contours of consent to arbitration are clear.

Investment arbitral tribunals, while dealing with the question of State consent have shown sharp divisions on the notion of consent. A stock-taking of the varied approaches taken by arbitral tribunals to State consent highlights the indeterminacy of the contours of consent in practice. This chapter begins by exploring consent in the context of arbitration under the Convention on the Settlement of Investment Disputes between States and nationals of other States (hereafter ICSID Convention),[6] which accounts for the majority of investor–State arbitrations, and the different means of expression of consent of a State and investor to arbitration contemplated in the ICSID regime (Section 10.2). It then deals with the theoretical underpinnings of the notion of consent to investment arbitration and the jurisprudential debates that surround it (Section 10.3). To illustrate the multiplicity of thoughts and varied techniques deployed in interpreting the notion of consent, possibly leading to the expansion of arbitral jurisdiction, the chapter will analyse the issue of State consent in the context of most-favoured nation (hereafter MFN) clauses as a case study (Section 10.4).

This chapter seeks to reveal that, when it comes to consent, its understanding and interpretation raise a fundamental question: Do we really know what

5 *Chevron Corporation and Texaco Petroleum Company* v. *The Republic of Ecuador (II)*, PCA, Third Interim Award on Jurisdiction and Admissibility (27 Février 2012) Case No. 2009-23, para. 4.61 (emphasis added); Rejla Radović, *Beyond Consent: Revisiting Jurisdiction in Investment Treaty Arbitration* (Leiden: Brill, 2022), p. 13; *Fisheries Jurisdiction (Spain* v. *Canada)* (Jurisdiction of the Court: Judgment) [1998] ICJ Rep. 432, para. 37.

6 Other issues relating to consent in investment arbitration are not covered in this contribution. They include, *inter alia*, issues relating to consent in non-ICSID arbitration, and issues of consent arising out of questions relating to mass claims, umbrella clauses, jurisdiction *ratione materiae*, jurisdiction *ratione personae* or jurisdiction *ratione temporis*.

it means? Throughout this chapter, it will be demonstrated that there are a number of uncertainties around the notion of consent, which are yet to be dealt with.

10.2 EXPRESSION OF STATE CONSENT TO INTERNATIONAL INVESTMENT ARBITRATION UNDER THE ICSID CONVENTION

Article 25(1) of the ICSID Convention sets out the jurisdictional requirements that must be satisfied to bring a claim before the International Centre for Settlement of Investment Disputes (hereafter the Centre). The jurisdiction of the Centre extends to 'any legal dispute arising directly out of an investment between a Contracting State (or any constituent subdivision or agency of a Contracting State designated to the Centre by that State) and a national of another Contracting State'.[7] Moreover, 'when the parties have given their consent, no party may withdraw its consent unilaterally'.[8]

Article 25(1) of the Convention underpins the idea of mutuality of consent. The investor must perform a reciprocal act of consent.[9] ICSID does not impose any technical requirements regarding how consent should be expressed. Consent to arbitration can be manifested by States in multiple ways.[10] However, in the framework of the ICSID Convention, 'parties to the dispute' must 'consent in writing to submit to the ICSID Centre'.[11]

Before turning to the issue of expression and interpretation of consent, it is necessary to outline how consent to arbitration should be determined. Consent can never be presumed by an arbitral tribunal. Consent to jurisdiction of international arbitral tribunals must always be established. Consent must be certain.[12] For arbitral tribunals, the interpretation of consent is fundamental as the principle of *compétence de la compétence* requires an

7 Convention on the Settlement of Investment Disputes between States and Nationals of Other States (adopted on 18 March 1965, entered into force 14 October 1966), 575 UNTS 159, Art. 25(1).

8 Ibid.

9 Yas Banifatemi and Elise Edson, 'Jurisdiction of the Centre', in Julien Fouret, Rémy Gerbay and Gloria M. Alvarez (eds.), *The ICSID Convention, Regulations and Rules: A Practical Commentary* (Cheltenham: Edward Elgar, 2019), pp. 102–255, p. 146.

10 *Brandes Investment Partners, LP* v. *The Bolivarian Republic of Venezuela*, ICSID, Award (2 August 2011) Case No. ARB/08/3, para. 34.

11 *Southern Pacific Properties (Middle East) Limited* v. *Arab Republic of Egypt*, ICSID, Decision on Jurisdiction (14 April 1988) Case No. ARB/84/3, para. 99.

12 *Certain Questions of Mutual Assistance in Criminal Matters (Djibouti* v. *France)* (Judgment) [2008] ICJ Rep. 177, paras. 60–62.

international court or a tribunal to establish the jurisdiction and its limits objectively, based on the title of jurisdiction, and should not go beyond it.[13]

Many arbitral tribunals have considered that the agreement to arbitrate between the parties should be 'clear and unambiguous'.[14] A few tribunals have embarked on the debate concerning the expansive or restrictive interpretation of consent.[15] But as rightly observed by Judge Rosalyn Higgins, 'there is no rule that requires a restrictive interpretation of compromissory clauses'.[16] She added that there is no doubt that the International Court of Justice (hereafter ICJ) 'has no judicial policy of being either liberal or strict in deciding the scope of compromissory clauses; they are judicial decisions like any other'.[17]

Under the ICSID regime, States enjoy flexibility regarding freedom of expression of consent to arbitration. Consent can be expressed either before or after the dispute has arisen. In the latter case, consent to arbitration could be expressed through a *compromis*, that is an agreement to arbitrate after the dispute between the host State and investor has arisen. Although such a means is not common in investment arbitration, it nevertheless remains a way to express consent.[18] This chapter, however, will primarily focus on the expression of consent prior to the materialization of the dispute between the host State and investor through State contracts (Section 10.2.1), national legislation on foreign investment (Section 10.2.2), and investment treaties (Section 10.2.3), and the issues arising therefrom.

[13] *Case concerning Armed Activities on the Territory of the Congo (New Application: 2002) (Democratic Republic of the Congo* v. *Rwanda)* (Jurisdiction and Admissibility) (Judgment) [2006] ICJ Rep. 6, para. 88.

[14] *Plama Consortium Limited* v. *Republic of Bulgaria*, ICSID, Decision on Jurisdiction (8 February 2005) Case No. ARB/03/24, 44 ILM 717, para. 198; *Ambiente Ufficio S.P.A. and Others (formerly Giordano Alpi and Others)* v. *Argentine Republic*, ICSID, Decision on Jurisdiction and Admissibility (8 February 2013) Case No. ARB/08/9, Dissenting Opinion of Santiago Torres Bernárdez (2 May 2013), para. 346.

[15] *Mondev International Ltd.* v. *United States of America*, ICSID, Award (11 October 2002) Case No. ARB(AF)/99/2, 42 ILM 85, para. 43.

[16] *Oil Platforms (Islamic Republic of Iran* v. *United States of America)* (Separate Opinion of Judge Higgins) [1996] ICJ Rep. 857, para. 35.

[17] Ibid.

[18] *Compañia del Desarrollo de Santa Elena S.A.* v. *Republic of Costa Rica*, ICSID, Award (17 February 2000) Case No. ARB/96/1, para. 26. Additionally, it is controversial if the consent of the parties and jurisdiction of the tribunals can be established through the principle of *forum prorogatum*. On this point, see *Klöckner Industrie-Anlagen GmbH and Others* v. *United Republic of Cameroon and Société Camerounaise des Engrais*, ICSID, Decision of the *ad hoc* Committee (3 May 1985) Case No. ARB/81/2, para. 9 (I translate).

10.2.1 *State Contracts*

Before the 1990s, investment arbitrations arising under contracts between States and investors dominated the workload of the ICSID.[19] Consent may be expressed by the host State and investor through a contract relating to the operation of investment between the host State and investor. In reality, an investment to a host State could involve negotiation and the conclusion of multiple complex contracts. In such cases, not every investment-related contract would contain a dispute resolution clause referring to arbitration. The arbitral tribunals, in practice, have not considered such contracts isolated from each other.[20] State contracts differ from national legislation on foreign investment and investment treaties in one aspect: there is a direct agreement to arbitrate between the State and investor as contracting parties. Moreover, such contracts raise different questions of interpretation.[21]

10.2.2 *National Legislation on Foreign Investment*

Another basis of consent may be through national legislation, which usually regulates foreign investment in the host State. However, in practice, reference to investment arbitration under national law may not always be clear or mandatory. By way of example, the Investment Code of Seychelles Act (2005) provides that:

> Disputes which cannot be resolved by the parties themselves *may be* [as opposed to shall be] settled: a) by an arbitration procedure whether local or international that is based on a previous agreement between the parties; or b) by legal proceedings in accordance with the Law of Seychelles.[22]

[19] ICSID, 'The ICSID Case Load – Statistics Issues 2022-1' (2022). Available at: https://icsid.worldbank.org/sites/default/files/documents/The_ICSID_Caseload_Statistics.1_Edition_ENG.pdf, last accessed 15 September 2022, p. 11 (in 2021, however, only around 15 per cent of cases submitted to the ICSID Centre for arbitration were based on such contracts); James Crawford, 'Treaty and Contract in Investment Arbitration' (2008) 24(3) *Arbitration International* 351–374.

[20] Christoph Schreuer, 'Consent to Arbitration', in Peter T. Muchlinski, Federico Ortino and Christoph Schreuer (eds.) *The Oxford Handbook of International Investment Law* (Oxford: Oxford University Press, 2008), pp. 830–867.

[21] Laurence Boisson de Chazournes, 'The Blurring of the Line between Contract-Based and Treaty-Based Investment Arbitration' (2019) 1(2) *The Journal of the Institute of Transnational Arbitration* 98–106.

[22] Art. 13.2 of the Investment Code of Seychelles Act, 2005; Borzu Sabahi, Noah Rubins and Don Wallace Jr, *Investor-State Arbitration*, 2nd ed. (Oxford: Oxford University Press, 2019).

Another example is Article 8 of the Egyptian Law No. 43 of 1974, which provided various means, including the ICSID Convention, to settle investment disputes.[23] This provision was the basis of consent in the *SPP* v. *Egypt*, famously referred to as the *Pyramids* case. Egypt had *inter alia* argued that 'Article 8 contains no language expressly consenting to the jurisdiction ... [and] of Article 8 is nothing more than a non-limitative list of possible methods of dispute settlement which may be negotiated by the investor and the Egyptian Government on a case-by-case basis'.[24]

Consequently, according to Egypt, a separate *ad hoc* expression of consent was required to establish the jurisdiction of the Centre.[25]

The claimants, on the other hand, argued that Article 8 established 'a mandatory, hierarchic sequence of dispute resolution procedures'. They also contended that:

> [I]f the investor and the Government of Egypt have not agreed on a means of dispute settlement (the first method of dispute resolution mentioned in Article 8), and if there is no applicable bilateral treaty in force between Egypt and the investor's State (the second method of dispute resolution mentioned in Article 8), legal disputes arising directly out of investments must be settled by the procedures specified in the [ICSID Convention].[26]

The tribunal observed that 'in deciding whether in the circumstances of the present case Law No. 43 constitutes consent to the Centre's jurisdiction, the tribunal will apply general principles of statutory interpretation taking into consideration, where appropriate, relevant rules of treaty interpretation and principles of international law applicable to unilateral declarations'.[27] As a result, the tribunal *inter alia* held that the text of Article 8 'does not import into a treaty additional requirements that the treaty does not contain'. The Convention makes no mention of a separate *ad hoc* consent. It says only that there must be 'consent in writing'.[28] Ultimately, the tribunal held that a separate agreement of consent to arbitration is not required under the aforementioned Egyptian Law. This case has been said to be the 'tipping point'[29] in the history of the ICSID, as it opened the door to investment arbitration based

[23] The 1974 Egyptian legislation has been replaced by Law No. 72 Promulgating the Investment Law (2017).

[24] *SPP* v. *Egypt*, fn. 11, para. 73.

[25] Ibid.

[26] Ibid., para. 72.

[27] Ibid., para. 61.

[28] Ibid., para. 99.

[29] Jan Paulsson, 'The Tipping Point', in Meg Kinnear, Geraldine R. Fischer, Jara Minguez Almeida, Luisa Fernanda Torres and Mairée Uran Bidegain (eds.), *Building International*

on national legislation, and on investment treaties which are explored in Section 10.2.3. In the context of domestic legislation, the question of interpretation of consent also gives rise to a related issue of applicable law governing its interpretation.[30]

10.2.3 *Investment Treaties*

Since the late 1950s, the international legal order has witnessed a 'big bang' of bilateral investment treaties (hereafter BITs). As a result, the most contemporary means to express consent, in practice, has been through BITs, or multilateral treaties such as the Energy Charter Treaty (hereafter ECT).[31] In practice, the basic mechanism of expressing consent through treaties – albeit with some exceptions – is similar to consent expressed in national legislation. States parties to the investment treaties include a dispute resolution provision that offers arbitration to the investors of one State party (home State of the investor) against the other State party to the treaty (host State). Unlike national legislation, in which an offer to arbitration is given to investors of all States, treaties are limited to investors of the other State party. For instance, Article 8(1) of the United Kingdom-Sri Lanka BIT, provided, as follows: 'Each contracting Party hereby consents to submit to [ICSID] … for settlement by conciliation or arbitration under the [ICSID Convention] any legal disputes arising between [the State and an investor concerning investment].'[32]

The dispute settlement provisions in many BITs also provide for a range of forums for arbitration with ICSID being one of them. Other possibilities could range from settlement of disputes through the domestic courts of the host State, to arbitration under the International Chamber of Commerce (hereafter ICC) rules, the London Court of International Arbitration (LCIA) rules or under the United Nations Commission on International Trade Law (hereafter UNCITRAL) rules.

Investment Law: The First 50 Years of ICSID (The Hague: Kluwer Law International, 2015), pp. 85–96, p. 86.

30 Laurence Boisson de Chazournes, 'Rules of Interpretation and Investment Arbitration', in Kinnear *et al.*, fn. 29, pp. 13–25, p. 18; Michele Potestà, 'The Interpretation of Consent to ICSID Arbitration Contained in Domestic Investment Laws' (2011) 27(2) *Arbitration International* 149–170.

31 According to the ICSID Statistics report, 60 per cent of the cases instituted in 2021 were based on the BITs: see ICSID, fn. 19, p. 11.

32 *Asian Agricultural Products Ltd. (AAPL)* v. *Republic of Sri Lanka*, ICSID, Award (27 June 1990) Case No. ARB/87/3, 30 ILM 577, para. 2.

Moreover, BITs can contain clauses that offer unequivocal consent to arbitration. For instance, the wording of the clauses stipulates that parties 'hereby consents' or the dispute 'shall be submitted to arbitration'.[33] Other clauses, such as 'all disputes concerning investments' or 'any legal dispute concerning investments',[34] have seen the arbitral jurisprudence split on their interpretation.

The arbitral tribunal in *Salini* v. *Morocco*, while interpreting the clause – 'all disputes concerning investments' – held that not only claims concerning violations of the BITs fall within the jurisdiction of the tribunal but also claims based on contracts.[35] The arbitral tribunal, in *SGS* v. *Pakistan*, however, reached a different conclusion in its interpretation of a similar clause. The tribunal held that the expression 'disputes with respect to investments' does not necessarily imply that 'both BIT and purely contract claims are intended to be covered by the Contracting Parties'.[36] This shows that the drafting of jurisdictional clauses in BITs can open the door to multiple objections to jurisdiction.

These varied means of expressing consent to investment arbitration have in practice given rise to several questions, which, at the heart, remain questions of interpretation of the boundaries or confines of State consent. It also shows how the issue of interpretation of consent is a never-ending debate and in constant flux in investor–State arbitration. At times, the arbitral decisions are in contrast with each other, as the tribunals concerned do not agree on the canons of interpretation. On other occasions, the tribunals reach different conclusions on similarly worded provisions, despite applying the same rules of treaty interpretation.

10.3 PERSPECTIVES ON THE NOTION OF CONSENT

10.3.1 *'Arbitration without Privity'*

Consent to arbitration between host State and investor in a BIT is asymmetrical in nature as a BIT is a treaty concluded between States, and not between a State and an investor. Similarly, consent to arbitration in national legislation can be considered as a unilateral act by a State. On the contrary, in State

33 Schreuer, fn. 20.

34 Ibid.

35 *Salini Construttori S.P.A.* v. *Kingdom of Morocco*, ICC Case No. 16550/ND, Award, 5 December 2011.

36 *SGS Société Générale de Surveillance S.A.* v. *Islamic Republic of Pakistan*, ICSID, Decision on Jurisdiction (6 August 2003) Case No. ARB/01/13, 42 ILM 1285.

contracts or *compromis*, the dispute resolution clauses are symmetrical, operating directly between an investor and a host State. This has led to an evolution of a distinct conceptual understanding of an arbitration agreement in investment arbitration, which is generally referred to as 'arbitration without privity'[37] or 'offer-acceptance theory'.[38] In the 1990s, the investment arbitration regime – based on treaties and legislation – was not regarded as a 'subgenre of an existing discipline' but as 'dramatically different from anything previously known in the international sphere'.[39]

According to the theory of 'arbitration without privity', consent of a State in national legislation or a treaty is merely an 'offer to agree to arbitration, rather than a full contractual *compromis* as one would find in an investment contract'.[40] An expression of consent by a State is insufficient to bestow jurisdiction on a tribunal as a reciprocal act on part of an investor is required. The unilateral offer of the State is 'consummated as a binding obligation to arbitrate only with the investor's acceptance of that offer'.[41] When an investor accepts the State's open offer to arbitrate, a valid and binding agreement is created between the parties. This is 'a manifestation of the maxim "*pacta sunt servanda*" and applies to undertakings to arbitrate in general'.[42] The direct action of international arbitration, being initiated by an investor, 'allows the true complainant to face the true defendant'.[43] The offer-acceptance model is also explained as a legal fiction that was necessary to avail the 'procedures and institutions of commercial arbitration [which] would not have been available to the investment treaties'.[44]

This theory has been endorsed by arbitral tribunals. The arbitral tribunal in the *Generation Ukraine* v. *Ukraine* case observed that 'it is firmly established that an investor can accept a State's offer of ICSID arbitration contained in a bilateral investment treaty by instituting ICSID proceedings. There is nothing

37 Jan Paulson, 'Arbitration without Privity' (1995) 10(2) *ICSID Review – Foreign Investment Law Journal* 232–257.

38 Radović, fn. 5, p. 49.

39 Paulson, fn. 37, p. 256.

40 *Tradex Hellas SA* v. *Republic of Albania*, Award (29 April 1999), 5 ICSID Reports 70, at paras. 132–205; Sabahi *et al.*, fn. 22.

41 *Tradex Hellas SA* v. *Republic of Albania*, fn. 40.

42 Schreuer, fn. 20.

43 Paulson, fn. 37, p. 256.

44 Thomas W. Wälde, 'The Specific Nature of Investment Arbitration', in Philippe Kahn and Thomas W. Wälde (eds.), *New Aspects of International Investment Law* (Leiden: Brill, 2007), pp. 42–119, p. 60.

in the BIT to suggest that the investor must communicate its consent in a different form directly to the State'.[45]

If a dispute resolution clause in domestic law or a treaty is merely an offer to arbitrate, which in turn is to be accepted by the investor, should the perfected consent or perfected arbitration agreement be regarded as a treaty between the investor and the host State?[46] If it is a treaty, the rules of treaty interpretation and international law could be considered in determining the scope of State consent. On the other hand, if it is construed as a contract or unilateral declaration (see Sections 10.3.2 and 10.3.3), other rules of interpretation could be applicable.[47] While 'arbitration without privity' is a commonplace in investment arbitration nowadays, it is not uncontroversial. Some authors have suggested that rather than treating State consent in a BIT or national legislation as an 'offer', it should be regarded as an 'invitation to treat' or 'invitation to bargain'.[48] According to this approach, a conclusion of a separate arbitration agreement between the host State and investor is required to initiate arbitration either under a treaty or national legislation. This approach is partly based on the understanding that the ICSID Convention, for instance, was originally meant to adjudicate matters of settlement of contractual disputes between States and foreign investors.[49]

10.3.2 *Arbitration Agreements as Contracts?*

The theory of offer-acceptance, as discussed in Section 10.3.1, is not the only one that has been discussed in understanding State consent in investment arbitration regime. Another view stipulates treating the perfected arbitration agreement, arising out of a BIT or national law, as a contract and not a treaty.[50] The Court of Appeal of England and Wales in *Occidental* v. *Ecuador* held that 'the agreement to arbitrate which results by following

[45] *Generation Ukraine Inc.* v. *Ukraine*, ICSID, Award (16 September 2003) Case No. ARB/00/9, 44 ILM 404, para. 12.2.

[46] Schreuer, fn. 20.

[47] See discussion on the *CEMEX* v. *Venezuela* case (*CEMEX Caracas Investments B.V and CEMEX Caracas II Investments B.V* v. *Bolivarian Republic of Venezuela*, ICSID, Decision on Jurisdiction (3 December 2010) Case No. ARB/08/15, 49 ILM 1195) in Boisson de Chazournes, fn. 30, p. 18.

[48] Muthucumaraswamy Sornarajah, *Resistance and Change in the International Law on Foreign Investment* (Cambridge: Cambridge University Press, 2015), p. 141.

[49] José Enrique Alvarez, 'The Public International Law Regime Governing International Investment' (Volume 344) *Collected Courses of the Hague Academy of International Law*, 2011, pp. 282–283.

[50] Radović, fn. 5, p. 49; Crawford, fn. 19, p. 361.

the Treaty route is not itself a treaty' but 'an agreement between a private investor on the one side and the relevant State on the other'.[51]

It could be said that the framework of understanding an arbitration agreement as a contract is not significantly different from the 'arbitration without privity' or offer-acceptance model as in both approaches consent of both the State and investor is required to form an arbitration agreement.[52] The point here is not whether there is any difference between State consent and investor consent but rather the requirement of consent of both the parties to form an arbitration agreement. But there is one difference between 'arbitration without privity' and arbitration agreement as contract approaches. If the contract avenue is followed, by necessary implication, it raises the question of the law governing the arbitration agreement.

The Court of Appeal in *Occidental* v. *Ecuador* held that such an arbitration agreement should be governed by international law as 'it is closely connected with the international Treaty which contemplated its making, and which contains the provisions defining the scope of the arbitrators' jurisdiction'.[53] For Judge James Crawford, for pragmatic reasons, the approach in *Occidental* v. *Ecuador* was correct because if the arbitration agreement had been a treaty:

> it would have been unenforceable [under the New York Convention of 1958, which has no application to international law arbitrations, e.g. between states or other international legal persons] and issues arising under it would have been non-justiciable before an English court, which the Court of Appeal expressly denied. The investor has neither international legal personality nor treaty-making capacity, and it does not acquire either merely by accepting an offer to arbitrate made in a treaty.[54]

The two approaches – arbitration without privity and arbitration agreement as a contract – reveal that consent is indeterminate.

10.3.3 *Consent as a Unilateral Act?*

Another school of thought approaches the expression of State consent in BITs and national legislations as provisions constituting 'an agreement on their

[51] *Republic of Ecuador* v. *Occidental Exploration and Production Company* [2006] Q.B. 432, at 458.

[52] Radović, fn. 5, p. 49.

[53] Ibid.

[54] Crawford, fn. 19, p. 361.

own, usually with interrelated provisions'.[55] Unlike the aforementioned approaches, this could lead to a different conception of the investment arbitration regime. It has been suggested that theorizing the notion of State consent as a unilateral act would equate 'unilateral standing offers' stipulated in treaties and domestic law, to 'unilateral declarations recognising compulsory jurisdiction of the ICJ'.[56] The ICJ does not apply the rules of treaty interpretation codified in the Vienna Convention on Law of the Treaties to unilateral declarations or acts.[57] Accordingly, under this approach, it has been suggested that the 2006 Guiding Principles on Unilateral Acts of States of the International Law Commission (ILC) should be applied:

> [a] unilateral declaration entails obligations for the formulating State only if it is stated in clear and specific terms. In the case of doubt as to the scope of the obligations resulting from *such a declaration, such obligations must be interpreted in a restrictive manner.* In interpreting the content of such obligations, weight shall be given first and foremost to the text of the declaration, together with the context and the circumstances in which it was formulated.[58]

This approach is advanced to consider a restrictive approach to the interpretation of State consent and jurisdiction of the arbitral tribunal.

It has also been explained that unilateral jurisdictional undertakings operate as a 'direct obligation to submit to a readily available dispute resolution and permits the investor unilaterally to serve the consenting state'.[59] To avail the benefit of consent, the 'investor will also have to consent to ICSID jurisdiction and in that sense accept the offer of arbitration contained in a treaty'.[60] This, however, would not change the nature of international legal obligations

55 Yulia Andreeva, 'Interpreting Consent to Arbitration as a Unilateral Act of State: A Case Against Conventions' (2011) 27(2) *Arbitration International*, 129–148, at 138; Michael D. Nolan and Frédéric Sourgens, 'Limits of Consent – Arbitration without Privity and Beyond', in Miguel Angel Fernández Ballesteros and David Arias (eds.), *Liber Amicorum Bernardo Cremades* (The Hague: Kluwer Law International, 2010). Available at: https://papers.ssrn.com/sol3/papers.cfm?abstract_id=2180302, last accessed 15 September 2022, pp. 1–11.

56 Andreeva, fn. 55, p. 140.

57 *Land and Maritime Boundary between Cameroon and Nigeria (Cameroon* v. *Nigeria)* (Judgment) [1998] ICJ Rep. 275, para. 30: '[T]he regime for depositing and transmitting declarations of acceptance of compulsory jurisdiction is distinct from the regime envisaged for treaties by the Vienna Convention. Thus, the provisions of that Convention may only be applied to declarations by analogy.'

58 United Nations International Law Commission, 'Guiding Principles Applicable to Unilateral Declarations of States Capable of Creating Legal Obligations', *Yearbook of the International Law Commission* (2006) Vol. II, Part Two, UN Doc. A/61/10 (2006), pp. 160–166, p. 164, para. 7 (emphasis added).

59 Nolan and Sourgens, fn. 55, pp. 31–32.

60 Ibid.

stipulated in a BIT between two sovereign States, or under national law. State consent in investor–state arbitration, therefore 'must divorce itself from contemplating it from the investor's point of view. This point of view, important though it is in every practical regard, is not dogmatically relevant to the understanding of state consent, as such'.[61] In simple words, this approach would see acceptance of the State's offer as not relevant to establishing the consent as such, and only to the question of whether it has been triggered or invoked.[62] The investor's acceptance would allow the tribunal to resolve a specific dispute.

A specific practical consequence of this approach, however, has been identified. If State consent to arbitration is an independent legal obligation, and not dependent on any reciprocal act of acceptance by investors, a State is then not permitted to denounce such consent immediately by merely withdrawing from ICSID Convention.[63] Article 72 of the ICSID Convention provides that a denunciation notice by a State does not 'affect the rights or obligations of [a State or an investor] arising out of consent to the jurisdiction of the Centre given by one of them before such notice was received'. As a result, a State would be required to denounce the instrument of consent, that is national legislations or treaties separately which usually provides for a survival period of several years protecting the rights of foreign investors.[64]

As can be seen, there are different theoretical perspectives and ways of enquiry to understand consent. While each of these approaches touches upon the understanding of the notion of consent, it can have significantly different outcomes in arbitration when applied. For instance, if arbitral tribunals approach consent as unilateral acts that should be read restrictively, the jurisdiction of the arbitral tribunal could be constrained. Arbitration without privity, on the other hand, provides a different understanding of arbitration agreement between the host State and an investor, which can be said to be based on a functional necessity, allowing the arbitral tribunal to adjudicate the dispute by removing the asymmetry between the State and investor on the basis of 'perfected consent'.

61 Ibid.

62 Ibid.

63 Michael D. Nolan and Frédéric Sourgens, 'The Interplay between State Consent to ICSID Arbitration and Denunciation of the ICSID Convention: The (Possible) Venezuela Case Study' (2007) 5 *Transnational Dispute Management*. Available at: www.transnational-dispute-management.com/article.asp?key=1899, last accessed 15 September 2022.

64 Ibid.

10.4 DO MFN CLAUSES GIVE A NEW FLAVOUR TO A STATE'S CONSENT TO ARBITRATION?

MFN clauses in investment treaties typically prohibit nationality-based discrimination against investments and investors from host States. Such clauses ensure a level playing field between different investors of different countries by creating 'equality of competitive conditions'.[65] To this extent, MFN clauses extend the treatment of foreign investors that is more favourable under a BIT to the treatment of foreign investors that is less favourable under other BITs. Over the years, there has been a debate regarding the nature of treatment that should be extended to foreign investors. Since most of the MFN clauses are general in wording, varied and competing interpretations of such provisions are inevitable. Are investors entitled to enjoy only substantive benefits that might be imported from a third treaty by virtue of an MFN clause? Or, can MFN clauses be relied on by investors to also import favourable terms of dispute settlement resolution stipulated in another BIT between the host State and a third State? Taking a step back, one could even question if there exists a difference between substantive protection rights offered to investors and an option to settle disputes through arbitration.

The interpretation of MFN clauses has widespread implications for State consent, as it has been interpreted to allow the importation of investor-favourable dispute settlement terms from a third BIT (or the comparator BIT) to the BIT applicable in the dispute (or the base BIT). The right to bring an action against a State is not automatic; it is based on State consent. Thus, it is necessary to understand the ways MFN clauses are interpreted by arbitral tribunals to establish State consent. Moreover, the arbitral practice around the interpretation of MFN has been split between fundamentally contradicting approaches. Some consider that the arbitral practice has moved from a jurisprudential split to a jurisprudential schism with one camp belonging to *Maffezini* v. *Spain* (Section 10.4.1) and another belonging to *Plama* v. *Bulgaria* (Section 10.4.2).[66] Additionally, there is a noticeable trend

[65] United Nations Conference on Trade and Development (hereafter UNCTAD), 'Most Favoured Nation Treatment: UNCTAD Series on Issues in International Investment Agreements II' (New York and Geneva, 2010), UNCTAD/DIAE/IA/2010/1, p. 13.

[66] Stephan W. Schill, 'Maffezini v. Plama: Reflections on the Jurisprudential Schism in the Application of Most-Favored-Nation Clauses to Matters of Dispute Settlement', in Kinnear *et al.*, fn. 29, pp. 251–265; Julie Maupin, 'MFN-Based Jurisdiction in Investor–State Arbitration: Is there any Hope for a Consistent Approach?' (2011) 14(1) *Journal of International Economic Law* 157–190.

of 'consent shopping' in the interpretation of MFN clauses which allows investors to import investor–State arbitration into a treaty that does not have a valid investor–State arbitral provision (Section 10.4.3).

10.4.1 Maffezini *v.* Spain: *The Curtain-Raiser?*

The arbitral tribunal in *Maffezini* v. *Spain* caused a tectonic shift in the interpretation and application of MFN clauses, producing a strong debate on the scope of MFN clauses and the extent to which foreign investors could rely on favourable investor–State dispute settlement provisions from various distinct BITs. This has complicated not only the assessment of the true scope of consent but has also questioned the role of third-party adjudicators in international legal order on a more fundamental level. The approach of tribunals that have considered the applicability of MFN clauses to dispute resolution provisions can be divided into two issues: the use of MFN clauses to overcome procedural thresholds that are pre-conditions to arbitration, and the expansion of the jurisdiction of arbitral tribunals not in conformity with the consent expressed.

In *Maffezini* v. *Spain*, the arbitral tribunal allowed the claimant to dispense with a provision in the base BIT, that is, the Argentine-Spain BIT of 1991 requiring the investor to litigate any claims against Spain in Spanish courts during a certain period, before attempting to access investor–State arbitration. In essence, the arbitral tribunal permitted to import more favourable dispute settlement provisions of another BIT entered into by Spain with Chile that did not contain an eighteen-month waiting period requirement and, therefore, were less restrictive.[67] The MFN clause in the Argentine-Spain BIT stated: 'In *all matters* subject to this Agreement, this treatment shall not be less favourable than that extended by each Party to the investments made in its territory by investors of a third country.'[68]

While the clause itself was silent on its applicability to other BIT provisions, and if the dispute settlement provisions are covered by the MFN clause, the tribunal reached its conclusion by relying on the words 'all matters' in the MFN clause. Furthermore, the broad language was unique to the Argentine-Spain BIT and was not common in Spanish treaty practice, thereby according greater significance to the inclusion of such language.[69] The tribunal

[67] *Emilio Agustín Maffezini* v. *The Kingdom of Spain*, ICSID, Decision of the Tribunal on Objections to Jurisdiction (25 January 2000) Case No. ARB/97/7, 40 ILM 1129, para. 64.

[68] Ibid., para. 38 (emphasis added).

[69] Ibid., paras. 54–58.

regarded the dispute settlement arrangements in BITs to be 'inextricably related' to the protection of foreign investors.[70]

The tribunal, however, identified certain public policy considerations that would serve as limitations on the use of MFN clauses to import dispute settlement provisions.[71] These public policy considerations included, *inter alia*, a requirement to exhaust local remedies (considered by the tribunal to be a fundamental rule of public international law), and fork-in-the-road provisions that require investors to choose between domestic courts or international arbitration.[72] Additionally, the *Maffezini* v. *Spain* tribunal observed that 'if the agreement provides for a particular arbitration forum, such as ICSID, for example, this option cannot be changed by invoking the clause, in order to refer the dispute to a different system of arbitration'.[73] For some, the *Maffezini* v. *Spain* decision was the first decision to permit an investor to expand a tribunal's jurisdictional mandate by importing, through the MFN clause, more favourable dispute resolution provisions.[74]

After *Maffezini* v. *Spain*, tribunals have frequently resorted to MFN clauses to import dispute settlement terms favourable to investors from a third BIT. In *Siemens* v. *Argentina*, for instance, the tribunal had to consider the scope of the MFN clause in Germany–Argentina BIT. The dispute resolution provision, in this case, required disputes to be submitted to local courts for eighteen months before resorting to international arbitration. The tribunal held that the words 'treatment' and 'activities related to the investments' in the MFN clause were sufficiently wide to include settlement of disputes. As a result, it permitted the investor to invoke the wider dispute resolution clause in the Argentina–Chile BIT.[75] Similarly, in *Impregilo* v. *Argentina*, the Italy–Argentina BIT had required that investors should first pursue such local remedies for at least eighteen months. The majority found that the investor could rely on the MFN clause to avail benefit from a more favourable six-month consultation and waiting period found in the US–Argentina BIT.[76] Article 3(1) of the Argentina–Italy BIT provides that: 'Each Contracting Party

70 Ibid.

71 Ibid., para. 63.

72 Ibid., para. 64.

73 Ibid.

74 Zachary Douglas, 'The MFN Clause in Investment Arbitration: Treaty Interpretation Off the Rails' (2011) 2(1) *Journal of International Dispute Settlement* 97–113.

75 *Siemens A.G.* v. *The Argentine Republic*, ICSID, Decision on Jurisdiction (3 August 2004) Case No. ARB/02/8, 44 ILM 138, para. 103.

76 *Impregilo S.P.A.* v. *Argentine Republic (I)*, ICSID, Award (21 June 2011) Case No. ARB/07/17, para. 108.

shall, within its own territory, accord to investments made by investors … and to *all other matters* regulated by this Agreement, a *treatment* that is no less favorable than that accorded to its own investors or investors from third-party countries.'

According to the majority, the words 'treatment' and 'all other matters regulated by this Agreement' were wide enough to apply to procedural matters such as dispute settlement. The majority further held that 'the argument that the *ejusdem generis* principle would limit its application to matters similar to "investments" and "income and activities related to such investments" is not convincing, since the wording does not allow "all other matters" to be read as "all similar matters" or "all other matters of the same kind"'.[77] For the dissenting arbitrator, however, MFN clauses could not displace such pre-conditions to arbitration. The dissenting arbitrator further notes that 'a conditional right to ICSID cannot magically be transformed into an unconditional right by the grace of the MFN clause. The access to the right as provided in the basic treaty cannot be modified through an MFN clause'.[78] The explanation behind this position is that apart from conditions *ratione personae*, *ratione materiae* and *ratione temporis*, there is another condition to be fulfilled. It is a condition *ratione voluntatis* according to which:

> the State must have given its consent to such a procedure which allows a foreign investor to sue the State directly on the international level. This consent is expressed broadly or restrictively, with conditions of exhaustion of local remedies or waiting periods, as allowing all claims or only certain claims: in other words, the consent is given under certain conditions. Just as the conditions of nationality for example must be fulfilled before an investor can have access to all the rights granted by the BIT, the conditions shaping the State's consent to arbitration must be fulfilled before a right to arbitration can arise.[79]

Moreover, the dissenting opinion also noted that conceptually 'the substantive treatment and the jurisdictional treatment are to be treated differently under the *ejusdem generis* principle, precisely because the qualifying conditions in order to benefit from each of this type of treatment are not the same'.[80] A distinction should be made between 'rights' stipulated in the BIT and the

[77] Ibid., para. 99.

[78] *Impregilo S.P.A. v. Argentine Republic (I)*, fn. 76, Concurring and Dissenting Opinion of Professor Brigitte Stern (21 June 2011), para. 99.

[79] Ibid., para. 52.

[80] Ibid., para. 37.

'fundamental conditions for access to the rights'.[81] As a result, an MFN clause could only 'concern the rights that an investor can enjoy, it cannot modify the fundamental conditions for the enjoyment of such rights, in other words, the insuperable conditions of access to the rights granted in the BIT'.[82]

10.4.2 Plama *v.* Bulgaria *and Subsequent Cases: An Attempt to Restrict the* Maffezini *v.* Spain *Wave?*

Since *Maffezini* v. *Spain*, a number of tribunals have opposed the use of MFN clauses to incorporate more favourable clauses, such as expanding the scope of a dispute beyond a specific subject-matter[83] or expanding the jurisdiction of the tribunal to include both treaty and contract claims.[84]

In *Plama* v. *Bulgaria*, the applicable BIT between Bulgaria and Cyprus did not provide for investor–State arbitration. The MFN clause of the BIT, however, required to 'apply to the investments in its territory by investors of the other Contracting Party a treatment which is not less favourable than that accorded to investments by investors of third states'.[85]

Relying on the MFN clause, the claimant argued that 'the dispute resolution provisions of other Bulgarian BITs such as the Bulgaria–Finland BIT, which provides for the possibility of ICSID arbitration, are imported into the Bulgarian-Cyprus BIT'.[86] In essence, the reliance of the claimant on the MFN clause was not to remove any procedural hurdle before establishing the jurisdiction of the arbitral tribunal. Rather, it was to construct consent for investor–State arbitration which otherwise did not exist in the applicable BIT. The arbitral tribunal noted that 'the intention to incorporate dispute settlement provisions must be clearly and unambiguously expressed'.[87] The tribunal further held that the 'dispute resolution provisions in a specific treaty have been negotiated with a view to resolving disputes under that treaty. States cannot be presumed to have agreed that those provisions can be enlarged by incorporating dispute resolution provisions from other treaties negotiated in

[81] Ibid.

[82] Ibid., para. 47.

[83] *Vladimir Berschader and Moïse Berschader* v. *The Russian Federation*, Award (21 April 2006) SCC Case No. 080/2004; *Wintershall Aktiengesellschaft* v. *Argentine Republic*, ICSID, Award (8 December 2008) Case No. ARB/04/14; see *Austrian Airlines* v. *The Slovak Republic*, UNCITRAL, Final Award (9 October 2009).

[84] *Salini Costruttori S.P.A. and Italstrade S.P.A.* v. *Hashemite Kingdom of Jordan*, ICSID, Decision on Jurisdiction (29 November 2004) Case No. ARB/02/13, 44 ILM 569, para. 119.

[85] *Plama* v. *Bulgaria*, fn. 14, para. 187.

[86] Ibid., para. 79.

[87] Ibid., para. 204.

an entirely different context'.[88] The tribunal concluded that 'an MFN provision in a basic treaty does not incorporate by reference dispute settlement provisions in whole or in part set forth in another treaty, unless the MFN provision in the basic treaty leaves no doubt that the [States] intended to incorporate them'.[89]

Plama v. *Bulgaria*, however, is distinct from *Maffezini* v. *Spain* in one crucial aspect. In *Plama* v. *Bulgaria*, Bulgaria had never consented to the jurisdiction of the ICSID with respect to disputes between Bulgaria and investors from Cyprus. In *Maffezini* v. *Spain*, on the other hand, the question addressed by the tribunal was whether an investor had to comply with the domestic litigation requirement before the initiation of investment arbitration.

At this juncture, it is also important to illustrate how similarly worded MFN clauses, such as the ones at stake in *Maffezini* v. *Spain*, have been given competing interpretations. In *Daimler* v. *Argentina*, for instance, the question before the tribunal was whether the investor could rely on the MFN clause of the Argentina–Germany BIT to bypass the eighteen-month domestic court litigation requirement.

The tribunal in *Daimler* v. *Argentina* first observed that the eighteen-month domestic court requirement is a mandatory pre-requisite to commencing international arbitration. Subsequently, the tribunal interpreted the phrase 'treatment in [host State's] territory' in the MFN clause as a 'clearly expressed territorial limitation upon the scope of its MFN clauses' and held that '[States] did not intend for the Treaty's extra-territorial dispute resolution provisions to fall within the scope of those clauses'.[90] In other words, an international arbitration 'almost without exception takes place outside the territory of the Host State and [thus] per definition proceeds independently of any State control'.[91] As a result, *inter alia*, the majority held that the MFN clause in the BIT does not capture dispute settlement provisions.

In relation to the issue of circumvention of procedural pre-conditions to arbitration, consent is once again at stake. The query here is whether such conditions form part of the scope of consent to arbitral jurisdiction, or whether they are a matter of admissibility. There are two schools of thought on this approach. According to some, conditions to consent are a matter of admissibility and do not shape the limits of State consent to arbitration. For others,

88 Ibid., para. 207.

89 Ibid., para. 223.

90 *Daimler Financial Services AG* v. *Argentine Republic*, ICSID, Award (22 August 2012) Case No. ARB/05/1, 51 ILM 1226, para. 231.

91 Ibid., para. 228.

such 'conditions shaping the State's consent are considered jurisdictional prerequisites to the existence of a right to international arbitration' and as a result, 'an MFN clause will never be able to change the parameters of such consent to a mechanism of international arbitration'.[92]

10.4.3 '*Consent Shopping*': *Substituting Consent to Specific Arbitral Forums?*

Another issue that does not strictly fall in either the *Maffezini* v. *Spain* or the *Plama* v. *Bulgaria* factual and legal matrix, but concerns the role of the MFN clauses, is the importation of a different dispute settlement mechanism for arbitration from one BIT to another. At the heart of this issue is a fundamental enquiry: does an MFN clause of a base BIT permit an investor to invoke the third BIT to initiate arbitration before a dispute settlement mechanism that is either not contemplated or not applicable in the base treaty in the first place? In other words, does an MFN clause permit an investor to import from another treaty an arbitration forum that may be 'more favourable'? This is different from the mere importation of less stringent procedural conditions to arbitration as was at stake in *Maffezini* v. *Spain* or *Daimler* v. *Argentina*.

In *Garanti Koza* v. *Turkmenistan*, the arbitral tribunal for the first time allowed the investor to invoke the MFN clause and import the State's consent to a specific arbitral forum found in another BIT. The applicable base treaty, in this case, was between the United Kingdom (hereafter UK) and Turkmenistan. Article 8 of the BIT provided as follows:

> (1) Disputes between a national or company of one Contracting Party and the other Contracting Party concerning an obligation of the latter ... in relation to an investment of the former which have not been amicably settled shall, after a period of four [months] from written notification of a claim, be submitted to international arbitration if the national or company concerned so wishes.
> (2) Where the dispute is referred to international arbitration, the national or company and the Contracting Party concerned in the dispute may agree to refer the dispute either to: (a) the [ICSID]; or (b) the Court of Arbitration of the [ICC]; or (c) an international arbitrator or ad hoc arbitration tribunal to be appointed by a special agreement or established under the [UNCITRAL].

[92] *Impregilo S.P.A.* v. *Argentine Republic (I)*, fn. 76, Concurring and Dissenting Opinion of Professor Brigitte Stern (21 June 2011), para. 88; *Almasryia for Operating and Maintaining Touristic Construction Co L.L.C.* v. *State of Kuwait*, ICSID, Award on The Respondent's Application under Rule 41(5) Of The ICSID Arbitration Rules (1 November 2019) Case No. ARB/18/2, para. 39.

> If after a period of four months from written notification of the claim there is no agreement to one of the above alternative procedures, the dispute shall . . . be submitted to arbitration under [UNCITRAL].

As can be seen, the BIT required the investor and the State to agree on the specific arbitral forum – either ICSID, ICC or *ad hoc* international arbitration – to which the dispute would be referred. In the absence of an agreement, the default option would be to refer the dispute to UNCITRAL arbitration. Turkmenistan had not agreed to go to the ICSID arbitration but the investor argued that the MFN clause of the UK–Turkmenistan BIT should be used to permit the investor to import consent to ICSID arbitration provided by Turkmenistan in other BITs such as the Switzerland–Turkmenistan BIT.[93] The majority held that 'Article 8(1) establish[ed] unequivocally Turkmenistan's consent to submit disputes with UK investors to international arbitration. That consent satisfies the fundamental condition that the State must have consented to participate in arbitration before it may be required to do so.'[94] For the majority, Article 8(1) however, did not inform 'whether Turkmenistan has agreed to participate in ICSID Arbitration with a UK investor, because [it contained] no information about what kind of international arbitration Turkmenistan has consented to engage in'.[95] Article 8 (2) dealt with 'the arbitration systems that may be used if the conditions of Article 8(1) are met'.[96]

The majority subsequently turned to the analysis of the MFN clause of the BIT, which specifically provided for its applicability to the dispute settlement provisions of the BIT. It noted that 'Turkmenistan consented to international arbitration in Article 8(1)', and the BIT 'opened the door to a search by a UK investor for more favourable terms in treaties entered into by Turkmenistan with other states by choosing to make the MFN clause of the BIT applicable to the investor-state arbitration provisions'.[97] The majority found that since Turkmenistan had:

> provided investors of third States, specifically Switzerland, with an unrestricted choice between ICSID Arbitration and UNCITRAL Arbitration, there is no reason why Turkmenistan's consent to ICSID Arbitration in its BIT with Switzerland may not be relied upon by a U.K. investor, if the

93 *Garanti Koza LLP* v. *Turkmenistan*, ICSID, Decision on the Objection to Jurisdiction for Lack of Consent (3 July 2013) Case No. ARB/11/20, para. 15.

94 Ibid., para. 29.

95 Ibid.

96 Ibid., para. 25.

97 Ibid., para. 78.

> provision for ICSID Arbitration or an unrestricted choice between ICSID Arbitration and UNCITRAL Arbitration provides treatment more favorable to the investor than the treatment provided by the base treaty.[98]

The majority in clear terms observed that 'the effect of the MFN clause is not to satisfy the requirements of Article 8(2), but to replace those requirements with a more favourable provision from another treaty, in this case Article 8(2) of the Switzerland-Turkmenistan BIT, which does not require a separate agreement between the Claimant and Turkmenistan in order to commence an ICSID Arbitration'.[99]

The dissenting arbitrator, however, explained that the majority focused solely on Article 8(1) and not on Article 8(2). In fact:

> Articles 8(1) and 8(2) are two sides of the same coin. The coin – Article 8 – encompasses the provisions governing consent to international arbitration under the U.K.-Turkmenistan BIT. One side of the coin – Article 8(1) – shows the general precondition(s) under which a foreign investor can initiate international arbitration against the host state; the other side – Article 8(2) – fixes the strict conditions under which the foreign investor can pursue one specific venue of international arbitration (e.g., ICSID arbitration) rather than another (e.g., UNCITRAL arbitration).[100]

On the interpretation of the MFN clause, the dissenting arbitrator explained that it 'cannot bypass the requirement of consent to ICSID arbitration'.[101] If MFN clauses are permitted to allow for:

> consent to ICSID through incorporation by reference in the frame of a treaty that does not allow this, [it] would have the effect of 'replac[ing] a procedure specifically negotiated by parties with an entirely different mechanism'[102] or 'system of arbitration'. It would involve a forum-shopping attitude that bypasses the consent requirement of the Respondent while running against the fundamental principles of international adjudication.[103]

There are a few interrelated questions in such a case: *first*, whether consent can be imported from one treaty to another treaty? *Second*, what are the contours of State consent to arbitrate in the first place? *Third*, can the question

[98] Ibid., para. 79.
[99] Ibid., para. 77.
[100] *Garanti Koza* v. *Turkmenistan*, fn. 93, Dissenting Opinion by Laurence Boisson de Chazournes (3 July 2013), para. 19.
[101] Ibid., para. 62.
[102] As noted in *Plama* v. *Bulgaria*, fn. 14, para. 209.
[103] *Garanti Koza* v. *Turkmenistan*, fn. 93, Dissenting Opinion by Laurence Boisson de Chazournes (3 July 2013), para. 19.

of consent to arbitration be delinked from consent to a specific forum, for instance, the ICSID or the UNCITRAL?

For some, if consent is not established under the base treaty itself, it would be hardly reasonable to import consent from a treaty between a host State and a third State. This would mean if conditions to ICSID arbitration or UNCITRAL arbitration under the base treaty are not fulfilled, an MFN clause could not be invoked to have recourse to ICSID arbitration or UNCITRAL arbitration. This is so because such an approach would have the effect of substituting the negotiated conditions for an arbitral forum stipulated in the treaty and disregarding the consent States expressed in the treaty text.

For others, the question is if an MFN clause can be read together with a dispute resolution provision of another BIT between the host State and a third State to establish consent to arbitration. The focus is not on whether conditions of consent to a specific dispute settlement mechanism in this base treaty are fulfilled. Under this approach, it is considered that MFN clauses are not being used to import consent to arbitration but merely the favourable conditions to facilitate access to arbitration before a specific dispute settlement mechanism. Interestingly, the tribunal in *Maffezini* v. *Spain* had cautioned against the operation of the MFN clause in such a manner: '[I]f the agreement provides for a particular arbitration forum, such as ICSID, for example, this option cannot be changed by invoking the clause, in order to refer the dispute to a different system of arbitration.'[104]

At this juncture, an important distinction should be borne in mind. Consent to arbitration and consent to a specific dispute settlement are intrinsically linked. Consent to arbitration provides that a State has agreed to settle the dispute through arbitration, and defines the scope and limits of the jurisdiction of the arbitral tribunal. On the other hand, consent to a specific dispute settlement is consent to the jurisdiction of a specific dispute settlement mechanism such as arbitration under the ICSID Convention, or under UNCITRAL or any other arbitration rules. The question at stake is whether an MFN clause can have the effect of substituting consent to a specific dispute settlement mechanism with another dispute settlement mechanism.

Lastly, the importation of consent to a specific arbitral forum through an MFN clause raises the issue of the interplay of the *ejusdem generis* rule. In *Garanti Koza* v. *Turkmenistan*, the BIT in dispute stipulated 'non-consent' to ICSID arbitration in the absence of a mutual agreement between the parties. The subject matter of the dispute resolution clauses in such situations

[104] Ibid.

would be a conditional resort to arbitration before a specific dispute settlement mechanism. In light of this, should an MFN clause be used to invoke a dispute resolution clause that provides for automatic resort to ICSID arbitration or UNCITRAL arbitration? In this context, it is interesting to refer to the explanation of the *ejusdem generis* principle offered by the ILC, and especially in relation to the notion of substantial identity:

> [t]he effect of the most-favoured-nation process is, by means of the provisions of one treaty, to attract those of another. Unless this process is strictly confined to cases where there is a substantial identity between the subject-matter of the two sets of clauses concerned, the result in a number of cases may be to impose upon the granting State obligations it never contemplated.[105]

10.5 CONCLUSION

When courts and tribunals are faced with the issue of consent, which inevitably is also a question of jurisdiction, the task of judges and arbitrators can be primarily divided into two mutually inclusive parts. The first relates to determining the existence of consent and the second relates to ascertaining its scope. These conditions are a 'necessary prerequisite to the exercise of the international judicial function'.[106] When there is ambiguity or uncertainty about the existence and scope of State consent to arbitrate, there is a need to reflect on how a court or tribunal may exercise jurisdiction. Certainly, consent cannot be presumed in favour of jurisdiction. At the same time, a finding of lack of jurisdiction should not be considered as a defect in a treaty scheme that runs against its object and purpose of providing investment protection.[107]

The arbitral practice reveals that consenting to investment arbitration is a matter beyond a grant of authority to a court or tribunal to adjudicate the dispute between parties. What does a State mean when it gives consent to arbitration, or international adjudication generally? It is one thing to say that consent lays down the scope and limits of the jurisdiction of international

[105] United Nations, 'Draft Articles on Most-Favoured-Nation Clauses', Adopted by the International Law Commission at Its Thirtieth Session (20 July 1978), *Yearbook of the International Law Commission* (1978) Vol. II, Part Two, UN Doc. A/33/10, pp. 16–72, p. 30, paras. 10–11.

[106] *Garanti Koza LLP* v. *Turkmenistan*, fn. 93, Dissenting Opinion by Laurence Boisson de Chazournes (3 July 2013), para. 5.

[107] *ICS Inspection and Control Services Limited* v. *The Argentine Republic (I)*, PCA, Award on Jurisdiction (10 February 2012) Case No. 2010-09, para. 281.

courts and tribunals. But it is a different task altogether to determine the contours of consent. The importation of consent to arbitration under a specific dispute settlement mechanism through an MFN clause, for instance, shows that the importance of the role of State consent is seemingly being reduced in investment arbitration. It could be said that such 'consent shopping' is taking us farther away from the notion of 'privity' between disputing parties as investors covered under the base BIT are being permitted to import conditions favourable to establishing State consent from a comparator BIT to which they are strangers. In this context, is there a risk of 'a marginalisation of consent in international arbitration'?[108] The various ways and approaches of expression of consent and different interpretative techniques and understandings significantly shape the meaning and contours of consent. It also offers an explanation for the current state of the case law – which is often inconsistent – in investment arbitration. The notion of consent appears to be an inherently indeterminate concept in investment arbitration. While States could engage in clear and more precise drafting of dispute settlement provisions in a treaty or national legislation, the meaning of consent *per se* and its limits would anyhow, it seems, remain susceptible to being given different meanings and interpretations.

[108] Brigitte Stern, 'Un coup d'arrêt à la marginalisation du consentement dans l'arbitrage international (A propos de l'arrêt de la Cour d'appel de Paris du 1er juin 1999)' (2000) 3 *Revue de l'arbitrage* 403–427, at 403: 'marginalisation du consentement dans l'arbitrage international' (my translation); Brigitte Stern, 'ICSID Arbitration and the State's Increasingly Remote Consent: A Propos the Maffezini Case', in Steve Charnovitz, Debra P. Steger and Peter Van den Bossche (eds.), *Law in the Service of Human Dignity: Essays in Honour of Florentino Feliciano* (Cambridge: Cambridge University Press, 2005), pp. 246–260, pp. 259–260.

PART III

Subjects and Institutions of Consent

11

The Consent of International Organizations in the Making of General and Conventional Rules of International Law

FERNANDO LUSA BORDIN*

11.1 INTRODUCTION

In *The S.S. "Lotus"*, the Permanent Court of International Justice stated that because '[i]nternational law governs relations between independent States . . . [t]he rules of law binding upon States . . . emanate from their own free will as expressed in conventions or by usages generally accepted as expressing principles of law'.[1] While this is a proposition that needs to be unpacked and qualified, it roughly encapsulates a key element of the contemporary understanding of the sources of international law: in a decentralized legal system of sovereign equals, States have considerable agency in the making of the rules that bind them. Of course, the nature of that agency varies according to the nature of the rule being made. Treaty rights and obligations are created when States express their consent to be bound, whereas customary rules stem from the normative practices in which they partake. That means that while a strong form of State consent is required for the making of conventional rules, State consent features in the emergence of custom only in a heavily mediated sense.[2] When we turn to general principles of law shared by the different

* I would like to thank Samantha Besson and Jan Klabbers for their insightful comments on an earlier draft of this chapter. It goes without saying that all errors remain mine.

[1] *The Case of the S.S. "Lotus" (France* v. *Turkey)* (Judgment) [1927] PCIJ Ser. A No. 10, p. 18.

[2] While States need to accept the customary process as generative of legal rules, the rules themselves result from general practice accompanied by a sense of legal obligation. Custom no doubt presupposes a degree of State *consensus* implied in the adherence to certain practices. For this reason, I favour the phrase 'state/IO participation' over 'state/IO consent' when referring hereafter to customary international law. For a discussion of the relationship between consent and custom, see Fernando Lusa Bordin, 'A Glass Half Full? The Character, Functions and Value of the Two-Element Approach to Identifying Customary International Law' (2019) 21(3–4) *International Community Law Review* 283–306, at 291–293.

nations of the world,[3] State consent fades even further from view. Even so, the proposition that there is an element of State consent in the making of general and conventional rules of international law – the 'free will' to which the Permanent Court referred – is intelligible to the international lawyer.

But international law no longer governs 'relations between independent States' only. It also applies, to varying degrees, in relations between States and international organizations (hereafter IOs), between States and individuals, between IOs and individuals, and between all of these and other existing international legal persons. The diversification of the international community raises two related sets of questions. First, which of the rules of international law that apply to States can be extended to legal subjects that are not States? Second, to what extent are legal subjects other than States involved in the making of international law?

This chapter does not presume to conduct an exhaustive investigation of those questions, but rather, more modestly, to deal with one of the pieces of the puzzle: the role of the consent of IOs in the creation of rights and obligations that apply on the international plane.[4] Consent is broadly understood here as a form of 'legal agency', whereby the 'intentional state' expressed or implied in the conduct of a participant in the legal system produces effects in law, including law-making.[5] What I propose to do, therefore, is to offer a

3 In the sense of Art. 38(1)(c) of the Statute of the International Court of Justice (hereafter ICJ).

4 The emergence of IOs has had a game-changing effect on international law-making. IOs have greatly facilitated the conclusion of treaties by States (see, e.g., the International Labour Organization and the Organization for Economic Co-Operation and Development) and have catalysed the development of custom by providing forums where States can engage in concerted interactions (see, e.g., the United Nations (hereafter UN) General Assembly) and bodies that produce authoritative restatements of customary rules (e.g. the International Law Commission). Several universal and regional IOs have been likewise extremely active in creating forms of 'secondary law' that apply to their Member States and other entities (e.g. the World Health Organization's International Health Regulations and the European Union's regulations and directives). Those formidable contributions to international law-making are not covered in this chapter, which rather focuses on the much narrower question of how IOs can formally participate, *qua* subjects of international law, in the law-making processes resulting in treaty and customary rules. But for comprehensive studies of IOs' wider contributions to international law-making, see José E. Alvarez, *International Organizations as Law-Makers* (Oxford: Oxford University Press, 2005); José E. Alvarez, *The Impact of International Organizations on International Law* (Leiden: Brill, 2017).

5 I am borrowing from Catherine Brölmann, 'Capturing the Juridical Will', in Sufyan Droubi and Jean d'Aspremont (eds.), *International Organizations, Non-State Actors, and the Formation of Customary International Law* (Manchester: Manchester University Press, 2020), pp. 42–61. Ascribing a juridical will to legal constructs such as States and IOs is not without challenges, given that it requires one to anthropomorphize intellectual constructs, attributing

general account of the legal agency that IOs enjoy, *qua* subjects of international law, in the process of formation of general international law (Section 11.2) and in the acquisition of treaty rights and obligations (Section 11.3). In so doing, I make two claims. The first is that even though IO practice can and should be taken into account in the identification of customary rules, it is not a necessary element in the process of formation of those rules; the applicability of custom to IOs thus does not depend on their participation in the customary process. The second is that under the current law, IOs can only be bound by treaty rules to which they have consented, which may give rise to problematic gaps between the treaty obligations of IOs and the treaty obligations of their members. In pursuing those claims, I offer some reflections on the systemic and normative implications of the formal involvement of IOs in the making of rules of general and conventional international law.

11.2 IO PARTICIPATION IN CUSTOMARY INTERNATIONAL LAW

11.2.1 *Do IOs Need to Consent to Customary Rules in the Formation of Which They Did Not Participate?*

It is a common assumption that IOs are subject to the rules of general international law, that is, to customary international law (including *jus cogens*) and general principles of law.[6] That assumption finds support in the advisory opinion given by the International Court of Justice to the World Health Organization (WHO) in 1980, where the Court said that '[i]nternational organizations are subjects of international law and, as such, are bound by any obligations incumbent upon them under general rules of international law'.[7] The applicability of general international to IOs is not self-evident, however, and the Court's dictum itself raises a couple of pressing questions. First, should 'general rules of international law' – the somewhat odd phrase that the Court employs – be understood as comprising all rules of general

to them forms of action that are essentially human. For a discussion of the particular challenges of doing so in relation to IOs, see Brölmann, Chapter 4 in this volume.

6 See, for example, Henry G. Schermers, 'The Legal Bases of International Organization Action', in René-Jean Dupuy (ed.), *A Handbook on International Organizations* (Leiden: Brill, 1998), pp. 401–412, p. 402; Philippe Sands and Pierre Klein (eds.), *Bowett's Law of International Institutions*, 6th ed. (London: Sweet and Maxwell, 2009), pp. 463–464; Chittharanjan Félix Amerasinghe, *Principles of the Institutional Law of International Organizations*, 2nd ed. (Cambridge: Cambridge University Press, 2005), pp. 386–387.

7 *Interpretation of the Agreement of 25 March 1951 between the WHO and Egypt* (Advisory Opinion) [1980] ICJ Rep. 73, para. 37.

international law or only the relevant 'general' rules among them? Second, does 'any obligations incumbent upon them' mean, more generally, any obligation under general international law that happens to be relevant for the conduct of an IO or, more specifically, obligations that address themselves to IOs as a category of legal subjects?

It should come as no surprise, then, that some authors express doubts as to the wholesale applicability to IOs of the general international law of States. Dissecting the International Court's dictum, Jan Klabbers suggests that assuming 'customary international law generally speaking ..., created as it is by States, to bind also actors others than States, is difficult to reconcile with the very concept of customary law, contested as that concept may be'.[8] His argument, which provides a convenient gateway to the present analysis, merits to be considered in full:[9]

> Customary law, on any plausible conceptualization, is the law that results from the aggregate of activities of the members of a bounded political community. In international law, this is traditionally the community of States. Likewise, within States, the scope of customary law is often said to be limited to the members of the specific community (nation, tribe, people) who practice the custom concerned. Hence, claiming that the Court must have meant that customary international law is binding on international organizations ignores the circumstance that organizations are not part of the relevant political community. And if they are so considered, they should be treated on equal footing with the other members. If States can contract out by persistently objecting (in theory, at any rate), the same possibility should be open to international organizations, lest they be treated as 'second-class citizens'. In short, holding that organizations are bound by customary international law is difficult to reconcile with the very idea of custom; it would be tantamount to saying that a custom in force among the Masai in Kenya would also bind the nomadic Bedouin tribes of Mauritania, native American communities in the US and Canada, and Roma communities in Eastern Europe.

8 Jan Klabbers, 'Sources of International Organizations' Law: Reflections on Accountability', in Samantha Besson and Jean d'Aspremont (eds.), *The Oxford Handbook on the Sources of International Law* (Oxford: Oxford University Press, 2017), pp. 987–1006.

9 Klabbers is one of the most sophisticated contemporary commentators on the law of IOs, and, reading his piece, one has the impression that he is exploring an avenue of inquiry rather than purporting to offer a comprehensive or categorical claim on the applicability of general international law to IOs. Yet, the fact that his exploration is likely to influence other commentators (see, e.g., Christina Binder and Jane A. Hofbauer, 'Applicability of Customary International Law to the European Union as a *Sui Generis* International Organization', in Fernando Lusa Bordin, Andreas T. Müller and Francisco Pascual-Vives (eds.), *The European Union and Customary International Law* (Cambridge: Cambridge University Press, 2022), pp. 7–47, pp. 13–16) warrants subjecting it to a very close reading.

Klabbers' argument is essentially one about the link between customary law and participation in the corresponding normative practices. Custom is not normative because it is imposed: it is normative because it is shared and experienced as law in a political community.[10] Klabbers makes the related observation that IOs, whose opportunity to act is limited by constituent instruments and other internal rules, may have 'no legal possibility to help contribute to the formation of rules on customary law other than on issues related to their core functions'. That would be problematic because 'if one is to become bound by a customary rule, it is only fair that one is also able to contribute to its formation'.[11] Klabbers' argument, it must be clarified, focuses on 'primary rules' of customary international law, that is, rules that govern the conduct of States. For Klabbers is comfortable with the idea that 'secondary rules', such as those found in the law of treaties and the law of international responsibility, apply to States and IOs alike. That is because those rules are essential for the functioning of the international legal system and, as such, 'binding on the members of the international community regardless of their specific consent'. 'The system of international law (such as it is) could not function', he explains, if States or IOs 'could unilaterally decide to ignore any rules on responsibility, or if they could unilaterally de-activate the *pacta sunt servanda* norm, or give their own (unilateral) version of the *rebus sic stantibus* doctrine'.[12] Even so, in the end, he suggests that there may not be 'all that many rules of international law that are binding on international organizations', which entails that those organizations 'have *carte blanche* to do as they please, and are well-nigh uncontrollable'.[13]

In his thought-provoking analysis, Klabbers fails to consider a consequential distinction between the participants in any given legal system: that between legal subjects involved in law-making processes (law-makers) and other legal

[10] Klabbers, fn. 8.

[11] Ibid., p. 998.

[12] Ibid., p. 999. In some respects, Jan Klabbers' analysis is reminiscent of H. L. A. Hart's discussion of 'the minimum content of natural law', which suggests that a legal order can hardly exist without minimal rules limiting violence, protecting property, recognizing promises and imposing sanctions: *The Concept of Law*, 2nd ed. (Oxford: Oxford University Press, 1994), pp. 193–200. A qualification to be made, however, is that even if the functioning of a legal system may depend upon the existence of some version of those rules, their specific content is calibrated through contingent law-making processes and can vary widely. For example, different versions of the law of remedies or of the *res sic stantibus* doctrine are possible, and those that we find in contemporary international law are in large part a result of the customary process.

[13] Jan Klabbers, fn. 8, p. 1000. Klabbers then considers theories that apply 'ethical and moral standards' to fill the accountability gap that the law leaves.

subjects that do not get to play this role.[14] For example, the law-makers of domestic legal systems take the form of institutions such as parliaments that enact rules addressed at legal subjects that are not law-makers (individuals, corporations, etc.).[15] Granted, a legal system based on customary law is likely a system where there is a considerable overlap between law-makers and legal subjects. That is because that kind of system does indeed presuppose a 'bounded political community' of law-makers whose 'aggregate of activities' can result in law. But it does not follow that a system based on custom needs to comprise *only* legal subjects that are law-makers. In the case of international law, this proposition is neatly illustrated by the status of individuals as subjects of international law. It is nowadays well accepted that individuals can be addressed by rules of customary international law, in particular those stemming from international human rights law and international criminal law.[16] Yet, no one would suggest that the validity of those 'primary rules' of custom depend on the direct consent or participation of the individuals to whom they are addressed. Rather, the orthodox position is that individuals do not have the capacity to make international law *qua* individuals. That capacity is reserved to other law-makers.

Of course, individuals and IOs form very different categories of international legal subjects. Unlike individuals, IOs are created by States as entities endowed with the capacity to act on the international plane.[17] Though IOs are typically run by Member States sitting in political organs, they are self-governing in the sense that they are not subjected to the domestic jurisdiction of those States. Rather, they enjoy exclusive 'organic jurisdiction' over their

[14] As the ICJ itself held in 1951, '[t]he subjects of law in any legal system are not necessarily identical in their nature or in the extent of their rights, and their nature depends upon the needs of the community': *Reparation for Injuries Suffered in the Service of the United Nations* (Advisory Opinion) [1949] ICJ Rep. 174, p. 178. 'Legal subjects' are here understood, in a formal sense, as a synonym of 'legal persons'. Legal persons, in Kelsen's persuasive explanation, are 'personified unit[ies] of a set of legal norms', that is to say, centres of imputation of legal norms that the legal system itself constitutes: Hans Kelsen, *General Theory of Law and State*, translated by Anders Wedberg, 1st ed. (Cambridge, MA: Harvard University Press, 1945), p. 93.

[15] I am not considering, here, the senses in which individuals and corporations could be viewed as law-makers by making contracts or performing other legally relevant acts. Suffice it to say that individuals and corporations cannot be described as law-makers in the same way as parliaments can.

[16] For a thorough analysis, see Kate Parlett, *The Individual in the International Legal System: Continuity and Change in International Law* (Cambridge: Cambridge University Press, 2011), pp. 229–340.

[17] See, for example, the discussion in Manuel Rama-Montaldo, 'International Legal Personality and Implied Powers of International Organizations' (1970) 44 *British Yearbook of International Law* 111–155, at 138.

own internal affairs.[18] That IOs can engage in international relations as legally autonomous entities makes them much more similar to States than to other non-State entities, at least from the viewpoint of public international law. Does it follow that IOs 'should be treated on equal footing' with States when it comes to the making of customary international law? Is treating IOs as 'second-class citizens' by assuming that they are bound by custom created by States problematic?

It is often said that States are the 'original' subjects of international law, while IOs are merely 'derivative' subjects. This description must be treated with circumspection, as it has led members of the international legal profession to conflate issues of political status with issues of legal status.[19] Yet, the description is of assistance in examining the questions that Klabbers raises. The reason why IOs need not be treated on equal footing with States when it comes to the formation of custom is that international law remains a decentralized legal system formally committed to the principle of the sovereign equality of States. Sovereign equality justifies placing the 'original' subjects at the centre of the customary process. For if IOs were to be regarded as *necessary participants* in the customary process on par with States, that would alter the basic fabric of the system in two objectionable ways. First, it would allow a group of States to manipulate the process of custom formation by adding further necessary participants that could be deployed to artificially enhance that group's formal legal position. Second, it would allow that group of States to contract out from general international law to the detriment of third parties. Indeed, if an IO were not bound by the customary rules that bind their members, it would provide a convenient route for those members to circumvent obligations that they owe to other legal subjects individually. International law would allow States to set up organizations like the North Atlantic Treaty Organization (NATO) to circumvent the customary norms of the *jus ad bellum* and the *jus in bello*, or organizations such as the European Union (hereafter EU) to exercise unfettered jurisdiction over third States or individuals living abroad. When confronted by the State or individuals whose customary rights were being breached, the States setting up the IO would not

18 Finn Seyersted, *Common Law of International Organizations* (Leiden: Brill, 2008), pp. 70–72.

19 As noted by Seyersted, '[t]he general reluctance of legal writers to admit that the capacity for sovereign and international acts, rights and duties is inherent in intergovernmental organizations and that they basically have general and objective international personality, may be seen as a reminiscence of the ancient doctrine that only sovereign States are subjects of international law': see Finn Seyersted, 'Objective International Personality of Intergovernmental Organisations: Do Their Capacities Really Depend upon Their Constitutions?' (1964) 34(4) *Nordisk Tidsskrift for International Ret* 1–112, at 91.

only be able to rely on the separate legal personality of the organization, but also on the fact that the organization would not have committed an internationally wrongful act to begin with.[20] This would hardly be a principled way to incorporate IOs into the international legal system, or a solution that the international community of States would stand behind.

It is illuminating, in this connection, to revisit an argument that commentators have made in support of the proposition that general international law applies to IOs. The argument is based on an analogy between IOs and new States.[21] It is the mainstream position that a new State is bound by the customary rules existing at the time of its creation even if it did not have the opportunity to contribute to their formation. As stated in the ninth edition of Lassa Oppenheim's treatise:

> [N]ew states which come into existence and are admitted into the international community thereupon become subject to the body of rules for international conduct in force at the time of their admittance. No single state can say on its admittance into the community of nations that it desires to be subjected to such and such rules of international law, and not to others. The admittance includes the duty to submit to all the rules in force, with the sole exception of those which are binding upon such states only as are parties to a treaty creating the rules concerned.[22]

If the admittance of new States into the international community includes the duty to submit to the rules of general international law in force, the

[20] Art. 61 of the 2011 Articles on the Responsibility of International Organizations for Internationally Wrongful Acts (hereafter ARIO) was adopted by the ILC to cater for these situations. It provides that '[a] State member of an international organization incurs international responsibility if, by taking advantage of the fact that the organization has competence in relation to the subject-matter of one of the State's international obligations, it circumvents that obligation by causing the organization to commit an act that, if committed by the State, would have constituted a breach of the obligation', 'whether or not the act in question is internationally wrongful for the international organization' itself. But the use of the phrases 'take advantage' and 'cause' may make the provision too narrow a ground for Member State responsibility.

[21] See, for example, Guglielmo Verdirame, *The UN and Human Rights* (Cambridge: Cambridge University Press, 2011), p. 71; Lorenzo Gradoni, 'The Human Rights Dimension of International Criminal Procedure', in Goran Sluiter, Hakan Friman, Suzannah Linton, Salvatore Zappala and Sergey Vasiliev (eds.), *International Criminal Procedure: Principles and Rules* (Oxford: Oxford University Press, 2013), pp. 74–94, p. 81; Kristina Daugirdas, 'How and Why International Law Binds International Organizations' (2016) 57(2) *Harvard International Law Journal* 325–381, at 325, 357–358; August Reinisch, 'Sources of International Organizations' Law: Why Custom and General Principles Are Crucial', in Besson and d'Aspremont, fn. 8, pp. 1007–1024, pp. 1016–1018.

[22] Robert Jennings and Arthur Watts (eds.), *Oppenheim's International Law*, Vol. 1, 9th ed. (London: Longman, 1992), pp. 14–15.

argument goes, so must be the case with the admittance of IOs. Indeed, the comparison between IOs and new States is illuminating in that it shows the systemic implications of suggesting that IOs are not bound by general international law when they act on the international plane. Why would international law exempt IOs from the default obligations that it imposes on new States?[23] Yet, that comparison is not exact. In the case of new States, there is a tension between the principle of sovereign equality (which could arguably support a clean slate approach) and an implicit principle of stability of the legal system (which would require new States to take the system as they find it). The mainstream position is that stability must qualify sovereign equality, for too much disruption would be caused if new States were allowed to pick and choose which default rules to follow. While the application of custom to IOs can also be justified on grounds of stability, no tension with sovereign equality exists in this scenario. Quite the opposite, the application of custom to IOs is in line with sovereign equality because it protects the legal position of third parties when a group of States chooses to act through an IO. It thus finds justification in a much more powerful argument of coherence than is the case with the application of custom to new States.[24]

Sovereign equality, it must be conceded, is not an absolute value. The legal autonomy that comes with sovereign equality can be (and is often) used to justify action that does not benefit the peoples that States represent. Still, there is some value in adopting sovereign equality as a structural principle of the international legal system, both from a pragmatic and from a normative point of view. Pragmatically, as Benedict Kingsbury has argued, ‘normative inhibitions associated with sovereignty moderate existing inequalities of power between States, and provide a shield for weak States and weak institutions’.[25] Sovereign equality may be a blunt instrument, but it is hard to think of a practical alternative, not least because it has been relatively successful in

[23] The upshot of such ‘more favourable treatment’, it must be noted, is that IOs would not enjoy customary rights either.

[24] For an extended argument on the extent to which an analogy between States (old and new) and IOs can justify extending to IOs rules developed by/for States, see Fernando Lusa Bordin, *The Analogy between States and International Organizations* (Cambridge: Cambridge University Press, 2019).

[25] Benedict Kingsbury, ‘Sovereignty and Inequality’ (1998) 9(4) *European Journal of International Law* 599–625, at 601–602. The sentiment was recently expressed by the United Arab Emirates at an open debate at the United Nations (hereafter UN) Security Council, where its delegation said the following: ‘For small states, the multilateral rules-based system and international law are vital because they ensure us equal rights as part of the community of nations and protect us all from the abuse of power and hegemony of a few’: UN Doc. S/PV.8262, p. 85.

providing a modicum of order and stability. Normatively, the principle reflects an ideal of equality among the various self-governing political communities of the world, 'notwithstanding differences of an economic, social, political or other nature'.[26] In the absence of an international community that can support a world government, there is merit to a system that allows for pluralism, where peoples can define and pursue their own political, social and economic development.[27] To be clear, even when we say that sovereignty is vested in the State, it is in the representation of human communities that it finds its moral justification. As Jeremy Waldron puts it, 'states are not the bearers of ultimate value' (they 'exist for the sake of human individuals'), and 'a state's sovereignty is an artificial construct, not something whose value – like that of the human individual – is to be assumed as a first principle of normative analysis'.[28] That is why it can be misleading to think about either States or IOs as the 'citizens' of an international political community to begin with.[29] Both are better conceptualized as 'officials' of the international legal system, the 'proxy-subjects' to whom various competences are ascribed because of their status of 'trustees for the people committed to their care'.[30] But for all that it conceals, the principle of sovereign equality helps us see that States and IOs are not necessarily equivalent or interchangeable 'proxy-subjects'. For as long as States remain the main representatives of human communities,[31] their prerogative to make the default rules that apply to other categories of legal subjects on the international plane is justified.

[26] Art. 2(1), UN Charter and UNGA Res. 2625/XXV (24 October 1970).

[27] In this sense, the principle of equal rights and self-determination of peoples is the corollary of sovereign equality. For a thoughtful discussion of sovereignty as an instrument for personal and collective self-determination, and of how to make sense of those principles in a context of growing global interdependencies, see Eyal Benvenisti, 'Sovereigns as Trustees of Humanity: On the Accountability of States to Foreign Stakeholders' (2013) 107(2) *American Journal of International Law* 295–333, at 302–305.

[28] Jeremy Waldron, 'Are Sovereigns Entitled to the Benefit of the International Rule of Law?' (2011) 22(2) *European Journal of International Law* 315–343, at 325, 328. The term 'proxy-subjects' is borrowed from Samantha Besson, 'The Authority of International Law: Lifting the State Veil' (2009) 31(3) *The Sydney Law Review* 343–380. She subscribes to a similar line of reasoning.

[29] As Jeremy Waldron notes, if States are entitled to respect as the 'basic unit of international law', that is not the respect owed to 'an anarchic individual, dragged kicking and screaming under the umbrella of law for the first time by some sort of international social contract', but rather the respect owed to 'a law-constituted and law-governed entity': see Waldron, fn. 28, at 343.

[30] Ibid., at 325; for a discussion not only on the moral foundations of the idea of sovereigns as trustees but also on how it can be translated into legal prescriptions, see Benvenisti, fn. 27.

[31] For a discussion of the connection between State sovereignty and individual liberty, and the 'deficit of liberty' that befalls 'supranational sovereignty', see Guglielmo Verdirame,

As I make those broad-stroke remarks, two caveats seem in order. First, I do not mean to suggest that autonomy, pluralism or a formal notion of representation can offer a full justification for sovereign equality and the primacy of States in the customary process. Samantha Besson has thoughtfully argued that though 'there is a normative argument to be made for the role of state consent in international law-making', that argument ultimately rests in democracy within States: 'the equality of each democratic state *qua* states people'.[32] The upshot is that the normative argument is tied to a substantive notion of representation and does not apply to non-democratic States in quite the same way. Second, the discussion here concerns the respective roles of IOs and States in the creation of default rules from which, with the exception of *jus cogens*, Member States can derogate in their mutual relations and in their relations with the organizations they establish (i.e. when one moves from the 'international plane' to the 'institutional plane'). In the case of IOs with universal or quasi-universal membership like the United Nations (hereafter UN), the boundaries between the international plane and the institutional plane are blurry, because the internal law of the organization binds all (or almost all) States. That may provide the IO with the occasion to contract out of customary rules through the 'secondary law' adopted by its political organs. For example, by virtue of Articles 25 and 103 of the UN Charter, the votes of nine States in the Security Council may result in decisions that exempt the UN and/or its members from the application of ordinary rules of general international law. That is no doubt a striking departure from the principle of sovereign equality, enshrined in a treaty provision and explained by the UN's unique standing in the international community. Surely, the same possibility is not open to regional IOs such as the EU or the Community of Andean States when they relate with third States or other IOs.

11.2.2 *The Relevance of IO Participation in the Customary Process*

I have argued in the preceding section that the participation of IOs in the customary process is not a pre-condition for the applicability of customary international law to them. Does it follow, however, that IOs may not be participants in the customary process in their own right? Is the practice of IOs *qua* IOs irrelevant for the formation of customary rules?

'A Normative Theory of Sovereign Transfers' (2013) 49(2) *Stanford Journal of International Law* 371–424, at 414–422.

32 Samantha Besson, 'State Consent and Disagreement in International Law-Making: Dissolving the Paradox' (2016) 29(2) *Leiden Journal of International Law* 289–316, at 302–306.

In its study on the identification of customary international law, the International Law Commission (hereafter ILC) concluded that '[i]n certain cases, the practice of international organizations also contributes to the formation, or expression, of rules of customary international law' (Conclusion 4 (2)).[33] The Commission identified three such cases. First, if 'member States have transferred exclusive competences to the international organization … the practice of the organization may be equated with the practice of those States'.[34] Second, IO practice is relevant whenever an IO exercises powers that are 'functionally equivalent to the powers exercised by States', such as serving as depositories for treaties or engaging in military operations.[35] Third, IO practice may contribute to the emergence of rules 'addressed specifically to [IOs] (such as those on their international responsibility or relating to treaties to which international organizations may be parties)'.[36] In the first two scenarios, IO practice may contribute to the formation of customary rules that apply to any subject of international law; in the third, IO practice gives rise to rules that are specific to IOs as a category of international legal subjects.[37] According to the ILC, the *opinio juris* of IOs is to be demonstrated in the same ways as the *opinio juris* of States.[38]

The position taken by the ILC was not uncontroversial. Some delegations at the Sixth Committee of the UN General Assembly expressed concern that the Commission had gone too far in equating IO practice with State practice. The most vocal detractor of the Commission's approach was the United States (hereafter US), which described Conclusion 4(2) as 'an inaccurate statement of the current state of the law to the extent that it suggests that the practice of entities other than States contributes to the formation of customary international law'.[39] The US argued, in particular, that 'even when States provide broad State like powers or exclusive competences to an international

33 ILC, 'Report of the International Law Commission on the Work of Its Seventieth Session', UN Doc. A/73/10 (2018), pp. 122–156, p. 130.

34 Ibid., p. 131, para. 6.

35 Ibid., p. 131.

36 Ibid., p. 131, para. 5.

37 For an assessment of potential contributions that IOs may make to custom, see Kristina Daugirdas, 'International Organizations and the Creation of Customary International Law' (2020) 31(1) *European Journal of International Law* 201–233.

38 ILC, fn. 33, p. 131 (clarifying that the forms of evidence of the *opinio juris* of States – 'public statements made on behalf of States; official publications; government legal opinions; diplomatic correspondence; decisions of national courts; treaty provisions; and conduct in connection with resolutions adopted by an international organization or at an intergovernmental conference' – apply '*mutatis mutandis*' to IOs).

39 ILC, 'Identification of Customary International Law', UN Doc. A/CN.4/716 (2018), at 18–19.

organization, it is rarely, if ever, with the express authorization that the organization exercise the powers of the member States to generate practice for the purpose of customary international law'. It expressed concern over 'a novel interpretation of international law that would implicitly and retroactively expand the mandates of international organizations in this unclear way'.[40]

The US was in essence suggesting that States should not be presumed to have consented to delegating to IOs the prerogative to partake in custom-generating normative practices. This position is unpersuasive, however, because discarding IO practice would be tantamount to discarding the practice of the States that have chosen to act through a separate legal person instead of acting individually. That is evident in the case of transfer of exclusive competences to 'supranational' regional IOs such as the EU: if IO practice in the exercise of exclusive competences were not equated with the practice of Member States, the latter 'would themselves be deprived of or reduced in their ability to contribute to State practice'.[41] But even in the trickier cases where the delegation of competences is not exclusive, and Member States retain the option to take action alongside the IO, dismissing IO practice would penalize States that favour collective action. The resulting paradox would be that the more States act together through an IO, the less influence they can have on the development of custom.

Crucially, the Commission's approach is compatible with sovereign equality as a structural principle of international law. The Commission observes that 'the more directly a practice of an international organization is carried out on behalf of its member States or endorsed by them, and the larger the number of such member States, the greater weight it may have in relation to the formation, or expression, of rules of customary international law'.[42] I take the Commission to mean that, while the practice of IOs *qua* IOs is relevant for the identification of custom, the weight of that practice can be no greater than the weight of what could otherwise have been the aggregate practice of the Member States. For example, in an analysis of the generality of a practice – of how widespread and representative that practice is – the contribution of an IO with five Member States would be no greater than the contribution that those five Member States could have made had they acted

40 Ibid., at 20.

41 ILC, 'Third Report on Identification of Customary International Law by Sir Michael Wood, Special Rapporteur', *Yearbook of the International Law Commission* (2015) Vol. II, Part One, UN Doc. A/CN.4/682, pp. 93–134, pp. 53, 126.

42 ILC, fn. 33, p. 131, para. 7.

individually.[43] Rather than treating IOs as fully additional participants in the customary process, which might allow States to benefit from over-representation contrary to the principle of sovereign equality, the ILC thus treats IOs as proxies for Member States. That is implied in the Commission's acknowledgement that discrepancies between IO practice and the practice of Member States affect the weight to be accorded to IO practice. That weight is to be determined by considering factors such as 'the nature of the organization; the nature of the organ whose conduct is under consideration; whether the conduct is *ultra vires* the organization or organ; and whether the conduct is consonant with that of the member States of the organization'.[44]

The Commission thus succeeds in proposing a nuanced approach. On the one hand, it would be neither principled nor realistic to exclude IO practice from the customary process when States act collectively through an IO. On the other hand, 'the primacy of States as subjects of international law' and their 'pre-eminent role' in the customary process is done justice once it is recognized that IO practice can only complement or replace State practice within certain bounds. Acknowledging the relevance of IO practice for the formation of custom also goes some way towards dealing with Klabbers' concern that 'if one is to become bound by a customary rule, it is only fair that one is also able to contribute to its formation'. Even if IOs are not *necessary* participants in the customary process, once they start acting as legally autonomous subjects they become *contingent* participants whose practice matters.[45] By acting collectively through IOs, States may even enhance their

[43] That is not to suggest that a strict quantitative or mathematical test is applied in, or appropriate for, the identification of custom. Quite the opposite, the practice of international courts and tribunals has been to look for 'general' or 'settled' practice that is widespread and representative, an analytical framework which, in the words of the ILC, 'does not lend itself to exact formulations, as circumstances may vary greatly from one case to another': ibid., p. 136. Still, '[i]t is important that [States participating in the practice] are representative, which needs to be assessed in light of all the circumstances, including the various interests at stake and/or the various geographical regions': ibid., p. 136. It is for this kind of assessment that a quantitative sensibility may be helpful, within reason, especially when the practice of IOs with limited membership is considered.

[44] Ibid., p. 136.

[45] In an insightful study on the applicability of customary international law to the EU, Christina Binder and Jane Hofbauer suggest a 'tiered approach' along the following lines: 'a newly founded IO will be bound to the customary international law which existed at the moment of its creation. With regard to newly emerging customary international law, the IO – particularly one with considerable independence and autonomy from its member states – will need to express its consent to be bound in some way or another': Binder and Hofbauer, fn. 9, p. 16. While their analysis may take the analogy with new States too far, overstating the role of 'IO consent', it captures the reality that once an IO is created its practice will have an influence, one way or another, on the rules that have a bearing on its conduct.

prospects of pulling their weight in the development of customary rules: the EU is in a much stronger position to influence the consolidation of certain normative practices than any of its Member States on its own.[46]

While viewing IOs as proxies for Member States can shed light on the nature and weight of their normative practices, it does not follow that there is a substantive identity between IO practice and what would otherwise have been the aggregate of the practice of members. After all, IOs are separate legal persons that express a 'distinct will' with a degree of autonomy from their members. Sometimes that 'distinct will' is the result of compromises reached by States sitting in political organs; other times it is shaped or affected by the acts of organs where States do not sit, such as secretariats composed of international civil servants or dispute settlement bodies.[47] So, even if there are good reasons to postulate that an IO's contribution to custom cannot be greater than the contribution which its members could have made in a 'quantitative' sense, IO practice cannot be reduced to the practice of members in a 'qualitative' sense. To describe IOs as contingent participants in the customary process is not to deny their legal agency as autonomous entities or the fact that an IO may steer customary international law in directions that the practice of the members acting individually might not have. Those are dynamics that the ILC study barely touches, but which deserve to be carefully examined by stakeholders and observers.

The participation of IOs *qua* subjects of international law in the customary process gives rise to a couple of additional questions. The first concerns the contribution that IOs can make to the creation of rules of *jus cogens*. If the normative practice of IOs is relevant for the formation of ordinary rules of customary international law, the same should be true for the customary rules that acquire a peremptory character. That was not what the ILC has concluded, however, in its recent study on *jus cogens*. In the Commission's opinion, while '[a]cts and practice of international organizations may provide evidence for the acceptance and recognition by States when determining whether a norm has a peremptory character[,] the positions of entities other than States are not, of themselves, sufficient to establish the acceptance and recognition required for an elevation of a norm of general international law to peremptory status'.[48] The Commission thus favoured a literal reading of the

46 See generally Jed Odermatt, 'The European Union's Role in the Making and Confirmation of Customary International Law', in Bordin *et al.*, fn. 9, pp. 66–94.

47 Which, among other things, raises questions as to how the *opinio juris* of IOs is to be assessed.

48 ILC, 'Peremptory Norms of General International Law (*Jus Cogens*)', in ILC, 'Report of the International Law Commission on the Work of Its Seventy-Third Session', UN Doc. A/77/10 (2018), pp. 10–89, p. 39, para. 5.

definition of *jus cogens* found in Article 53 VCLT, according to which 'a peremptory norm of general international law is a norm accepted and recognized by the international community *of States* as a whole as a norm from which no derogation is permitted'.[49] This comes across as a needlessly rigid and exclusionary position, which stands in tension with the more nuanced approach the Commission took in the study on the identification of custom. IO participation need not be an essential element in the formation of *jus cogens*, but one should not exclude the possibility that States transfer to IOs competences relating to 'fundamental values of the international community' that *jus cogens* norms protect or may come to protect in the future.[50] The second question concerns the applicability to IOs of the persistent objector doctrine, according to which '[w]here a State has objected to a rule of customary international law while that rule was in the process of formation, the rule is not opposable to the State concerned for so long as it maintains its objection'.[51] Neither the ILC study on the identification of custom nor academic commentary specifically focusing on the doctrine[52] discusses whether an IO can avoid being bound by an emerging customary rule in such a manner. But accepting the proposition that IOs may contract out of emerging customary rules coheres with accepting the proposition that IOs may participate in the formation of those rules to begin with.[53] This may well be a question of greater academic than practical interest, for the objection of an IO of sizeable membership to a putative rule would likely have the effect of preventing that rule from becoming customary international law in the first place.

11.3 IO CONSENT IN THE ACQUISITION OF TREATY RIGHTS AND OBLIGATIONS

From the moment IOs started to conclude international agreements, it has never been in doubt that, as is the case with States, an IO must express its

49 Ibid. (emphasis added).

50 To borrow the Commission's own description of the nature of *jus cogens* rules: ILC, fn. 48, p. 18.

51 ILC, fn. 33, p. 152.

52 See, for example, James A. Green, 'The Persistent Objector Rule in the Work of the International Law Commission on the Identification of Customary International Law' (2018) 27(1) *Italian Yearbook of International Law* 175–188; Shelly Aviv Yeini, 'The Persistent Objector Doctrine: Identifying Contradictions' (2022) 22(2) *Chicago Journal of International Law* 581–620.

53 Daugirdas, fn. 21, at 368, fn. 235.

consent in order to become party to a treaty. The provisions in Articles 11 to 16 of the 1969 Vienna Convention on the Law of Treaties (hereafter VCLT 1969), specifying the means whereby consent to be bound by a treaty can be expressed, have been extended to IOs in the 1986 Vienna Convention on the Law of Treaties between States and International Organizations and between International Organizations (hereafter VCLT 1986). Special Rapporteur Paul Reuter justified the ILC's approach to the codification project that served as basis for VCLT 1986 by referring to the 'general principle of consensualism, which constitutes the basis of any treaty commitment and entails the legal equality of the parties'.[54] According to Reuter, 'since the Vienna Convention [is] based on the principle of consensus, international organizations in general should, with very rare exceptions, be assimilated to States'.[55] The only discrepancy between VCLT 1969 and VCLT 1986 when it comes to the means to express consent is cosmetic, resulting from a baffling debate about whether it would be appropriate to say that IOs may 'ratify' a treaty. The Commission concluded that the term ratification 'should be reserved for States, since in accordance with a long historical tradition it always denotes an act emanating from the highest organs of the States, generally the Head of State, and there are no corresponding organs in international organizations'.[56] It then invented the phrase 'act of formal confirmation' to use in its place. In a biting note, Willem Riphagen cited this terminological tweak as an example of one of those 'optical illusions so dear to politicians', quipping that '[e]ven a perfunctory knowledge of information theory could have saved our international legislators from such nonsense'.[57] The distinction between ratification of a treaty by a State and formal confirmation of a treaty by an IO is and remains of no legal consequence.

While the debate on IO consent in the conclusion of treaties was straightforward, the issue of how Member States acquire rights and obligations

[54] ILC, 'Report of the International Law Commission on the Work of Its Thirty-Third Session', *Yearbook of the International Law Commission* (1981) Vol. I, UN Doc. A/CN.4/SER.A/1981, pp. 45–46, para. 5.

[55] ILC, 'Report of the International Law Commission on the Work of Its Thirtieth Session', *Yearbook of the International Law Commission* (1978) Vol. I, UN Doc. A/CN.4/SER.A/1978, p. 185, para. 25.

[56] ILC, 'Report of the International Law Commission on the Work of Its Thirty-Fourth Session', *Yearbook of the International Law Commission* (1982) Vol. II, Part Two, UN Doc. A/CN.4/SER.A/1982/Add.1, p. 19, paras. 8–9.

[57] Willem Riphagen, 'The Second Round of Treaty Law', in Francesco Capotorti, Pierre Pescatore, Claus-Dieter Ehlermann, Jochen A. Forwein, René Joliet, Thijmen Koopmans and Robert Kovart (eds.), *Du droit international au droit de l'intégration* (Baden-Baden: Nomos Verlagsgesellschaft, 1987), pp. 565–582, p. 570.

provided in treaties concluded by an IO, and vice versa, proved much more complex. What is the legal position of IOs and their members vis-à-vis one another's treaties? Article 34 VCLT 1969 encapsulates the *pacta tertiis nec nocent nec prosunt* rule, according to which a treaty does not create obligations or rights for a third party without the consent of that third party. That rule is then fleshed out in Articles 35 and 36, which distinguish between treaty obligations and treaty rights: third parties are bound by treaty obligations only if they expressly assent in writing, but their assent is presumed in the case of treaty rights. It was felt that the flexible rule on acceptance of treaty rights could be maintained. In contrast, the rule requiring third parties to consent expressly in writing was deemed too strict; given the nature of the relations between IOs and their members, the general law of treaties should make it easier for members to accept obligations imposed by treaties concluded by IOs and vice versa.[58]

The Commission thus spent considerable time and energy discussing proposals to facilitate the giving of consent by Member States to obligations in treaties concluded by IOs, including the possibility of construing provisions in constituent instruments as expressing consent *ex ante*.[59] However, those proposals proved divisive, and delegations at the 1986 Vienna Conference declined to adopt the text proposed by the ILC, adding instead a saving clause to VCLT 1986 to clarify that the Convention 'shall not prejudge any question that may arise in regard to the establishment of obligations and rights for States members of an international organization under a treaty to which that organization is a party'.[60] The Commission gave much less attention to the converse

[58] See, for example, ILC, 'Tenth Report on the Question of Treaties Concluded between States and International Organizations or between Two or More Organizations, by Mr. Paul Reuter, Special Rapporteur', *Yearbook of the International Law Commission* (1981) Vol. II, Part One, UN Doc. A/CN.4/341, pp. 43–70, pp. 67–68, para. 99.

[59] The (rather rigid) final version of Art. 36 *bis* adopted by the ILC read as follows: 'Obligations and rights arise for States members of an international organization from the provisions of a treaty to which that organization is a party when the parties to the treaty intend those provisions to be the means of establishing such obligations and according such rights and have defined their conditions and effects in the treaty or have otherwise agreed thereon, and if: (a) the States members of the organization, by virtue of the constituent instrument of that organization or otherwise, have unanimously agreed to be bound by the said provisions of the treaty; and (b) the assent of the States members of the organization to be bound by the relevant provisions of the treaty has been duly brought to the knowledge of the negotiating States and negotiating organizations.'

[60] Art. 74(3) VCLT 1986. For a thorough recounting and discussion of the history of the ill-fated Art. 36*bis*, see Catherine Brölmann, 'The 1986 Vienna Convention on the Law of Treaties: The History of Draft Article 36*bis*', in Jan Klabbers and René Lefeber (eds.), *Essays on the Law of Treaties* (Leiden: Martinus Nijhoff, 1996), pp. 121–142.

issue of how IOs can express consent to obligations provided in treaties concluded by their members. Special Rapporteur Reuter proposed to replace the requirement of express assent in writing with the more flexible requirement that the IO accept the obligation 'in an unambiguous manner and in accordance with [its] rules'.[61] But his proposal fell on deaf ears in the Commission, which in the end chose to replicate the language found in Article 35 VCLT 1969.[62]

What is most puzzling about the ILC debates on the legal position of IOs and members vis-à-vis each other's treaties is that the applicability of the *pacta tertiis* rule – that is, the assumption that IOs and their Member States are in fact third parties in relation to one another's treaties – was never seriously questioned. In his Sixth Report, Special Rapporteur Reuter engaged with the foundations of the rule, referring to the Commission's previous work on the law of treaties between States. He identified two main rationales for the *pacta tertiis* rule: first, it 'represents the general law of all conventional regimes, and the entire [1969 Vienna Convention] is imbued with the spirit of conventional consensus'; second, 'the subjects of law that are parties to the agreements in question are equal and sovereign and, more than for other subjects of law, this sovereignty requires that they may not be legally committed by the will of a third party'.[63] Only the first rationale remained relevant once IOs were added to the equation. For one, Reuter observed, IOs were 'neither sovereign nor even equal; all their powers are strictly at the service of their member States; it is the function they assume that justifies and circumscribes their activities and their very being'.[64] Moreover, 'the appearance of international organizations on the scene of international legal relations [gave] rise to some exceptions to this relative effect of treaties',[65] so that Member States might occupy 'a position falling between that of a third State and that of a State party' to treaties concluded by the organization'.[66] Even so, Reuter

[61] ILC, 'Sixth Report on the Question of Treaties Concluded between States and International Organizations or between Two or More International Organizations, by Mr. Paul Reuter, Special Rapporteur', *Yearbook of the International Law Commission* (1977) Vol. II, Part One, Un Doc. A/CN.4/298, pp. 119–136, p. 127, para. 7.

[62] ILC, 'Report of the International Law Commission on the Work of Its Thirtieth Session', *Yearbook of the International Law Commission* (1978) Vol. I, Un Doc. A/CN.4/SER.A/1978, p. 190, para. 26.

[63] ILC, fn. 61, p. 120, para. 5.

[64] Ibid., pp. 120–121, para. 6.

[65] Ibid., p. 120, para. 5.

[66] ILC, 'Report of the International Law Commission on the Work of Its Thirty-Fourth Session', *Yearbook of the International Law Commission* (1982) Vol. I, UN Doc. A/CN.4/SER.A/1982, p. 26, para. 10.

stopped short of suggesting that the *pacta tertiis* rule should be rethought. '[T]here can be no revision', he said, 'but only adaptation, of the principles embodied in articles 34 to 38 of the Vienna Convention', which 'simply reflect the notion of consensus that prevails with respect to conventions in international relations as in private relations'.[67] At the Commission, only a couple of members expressed doubts about this assumption. Francis Vallat observed that, even accepting 'the fact that an international organization was an entity separate from its member States', the latter 'might not be complete strangers to the treaty-making process' of an IO 'negotiating on the basis of a mandate conferred' by them.[68] Similarly, Juan José Calle y Calle suggested that an IO represents 'the institutionalization of the collective will of its members', so that when members sitting in an organization's political organs authorize the conclusion of a treaty they themselves '[assume] the obligations which the organization had contracted on their collective behalf'.[69] But there was little appetite at the Commission – and even less at the Vienna Conference – to engage with these deeper challenges. As noted above, even the more accommodating approach proposed by the Special Rapporteur – to apply *pacta tertiis* while providing for more flexible ways to express consent – failed to attract the support of delegations at the conference.

Overall, the picture that emerges is one of a strict separation between IOs and Member States as subjects of international law. In the words of an ILC member who fought hard for this idea, the Soviet jurist Leonid Ushakov, an IO '[acts] as a subject of international law independently of its members', for its 'legal personality [is] its own and it [possesses] its own will, distinct from the will of its members taken separately or collectively'.[70] The upshot is that by concluding a treaty an IO '[binds] only itself' and not its members, which '[remain] third States in relation to the treaty'.[71] Is this a sound approach for all cases, though? There is some tension between the proposition that IOs only acquire treaty rights and obligations by consent and the proposition, discussed in Section 11.2.1, that IOs are bound by rules of general international law even when they did not participate in their formation. That tension can be explained away, at least in part, when we consider the difference between the default rules of custom, capable of applying to all legal subjects operating on the international

[67] ILC, fn. 61, p. 124, para. 125.

[68] ILC, fn. 66, p. 24, para. 46.

[69] ILC, 'Report of the International Law Commission on the Work of Its Twenty-Ninth Session', *Yearbook of the International Law Commission* (1977) Vol. 1977, UN Doc. A/CN.4/SER.A/1977, p. 126, para. 5.

[70] ILC, fn. 54, p. 173, para. 31.

[71] ILC, fn. 66, p. 23, para. 39.

plane, and the *lex specialis* of treaties, adopted to cater for specific (and often strictly transactional) circumstances. It would be indeed problematic if an IO were deemed bound by every treaty that a member or group of members happened to conclude *inter se* or with third parties. But, isn't the position somewhat different if the members transfer to the IO the competence to perform acts that fall under the scope of a treaty to which all of them are party but the IO is not? In this scenario, viewing the IO as a third party would seem artificial, leading to a pointlessly fragmented network of legal obligations.

The problem is compounded by the fact that IOs are seldom allowed to join key multilateral treaties that bind a significant proportion (if not the entirety) of their membership,[72] for reasons that have more to do with historical and political contingencies than with the content of those agreements.[73] The relations between the EU and the UN provide a sobering example. All EU members are bound by the UN Charter, and commit under Article 103 to give primacy to Charter obligations over obligations under other international agreements. The EU, however, is not a party to the UN Charter. That made it easier for the Court of Justice of the EU, in the *Kadi case*, to uphold EU law over the obligation of EU members to comply with resolutions of the UN Security Council.[74] More recently, the UN Secretariat has complained about the effects of the EU's General Data Protection Regulation (hereafter GDPR) on the operations of the organizations in the UN System. Among other things, the Secretariat observed that the GDPR is jeopardizing the relationship of UN System organizations with private parties that, apprehensive of the imposition

72 In great measure because most of them do not allow IOs to become party to them. Exceptions include Art. 305 of the UN Convention on the Law of the Sea (1833 UNTS 397 (adopted 12 October 1982, entered into force 16 November 1994)) and recent provisions such as Art. 44 of the 2006 Convention on the Rights of Persons with Disabilities (2515 UNTS 3 (adopted 13 December 2006, entered into force 3 May 2008)) and Art. 305 of the Paris Agreement to the UN Framework Convention on Climate Change (3156 UNTS (adopted 12 December 2015, entered into force 4 November 2016)). The formulation 'regional (economic) integration organizations' employed in recent treaties seems a bit restrictive, however.

73 It is important to acknowledge, in this connection, that there may be reasons not to extend to an IO certain treaty rules that bind the Member States *inter se*, even as regards the IO's relations with third parties. Evidently, legal obligations need not be applicable to all legal subjects at the same time: they are subject to as many qualifications *ratione personae, ratione loci, ratione temporis*, etc., as may be necessary for the goal being pursued to be achieved. The problem discussed in this section presents itself when no principled reasons would exist to exempt IOs from complying with key treaty regimes to which their members have made a strong commitment.

74 Observing that EU law forms the 'autonomous legal system' of a 'community based on the rule of law': CJEU, *Kadi and Al Barakaat International Foundation* v. *Council and Commission ('Kadi I')* (Joined Cases C-402/05 P and C-415/05 P) EU:C:2008:461 [2008] ECR I-635, 3 September 2008, GC, para. 316.

of penalties by the supervisory authorities of EU Member States, are reluctant to transfer personal data that is essential for those organizations to fulfil their functions.[75] The EU's exercise of jurisdiction over UN transactions arguably clashes with the immunity that the UN is owed under Article 105(1) of the Charter and the 1946 Convention on the Privileges and Immunities of the United Nations. Again, however, neither the Charter nor the 1946 Convention are binding on the EU *qua* treaties under public international law. As a result, in its exchanges with the EU, the UN is put in the awkward position of having to appeal to obligations of EU Member States (which are not binding on the EU *qua* IO) and to provisions of EU law (which the UN has no standing to invoke). By giving too much emphasis to the separate legal personality of IOs, making the applicability of all treaty norms subject to their consent, international law creates the occasion for the circumvention, intentional or unwitting, of international obligations.[76]

11.4 CONCLUSION

It is a mistake to suppose that the emergence of IOs on the international scene has had no impact on the structure of the international legal system. By creating entities with their own legal personality and the capacity to operate on the international plane, States have bestowed upon those entities a form of agency that is certain to affect international law-making processes. It is thus the case that IOs have been concluding treaties for decades, and that their capacity to contribute to the formation of customary international law through their own practice has been progressively recognized. In other words, the consent of IOs matters.

At the same time, as one appreciates the role of their legal agency in the making of general and conventional rules of international law, one must avoid the temptation to read too much into the fact that IOs enjoy separate personality and legal autonomy on the international plane.[77] For one, there is no

[75] United Nations, 'Impact of the European Union's Data Protection Regulations on the Activities of UN System Organizations' (14 May 2020). Available at: https://edpb.europa.eu/sites/default/files/webform/public_consultation_reply/2020.05.14_letter_to_edpb_chair_with_un_comments_on_guidelines_2-2020.pdf, last accessed 29 December 2022.

[76] But see fn. 20 on the role that Art. 61 ARIO might have in mitigating this.

[77] Samantha Besson has warned that instead of a 'discussion institutionnelle' about States and IOs, international lawyers have been somewhat stuck in a 'curieux débat sur la (véritable ou non) "personnalité" juridique internationale des uns et des autres': see Samantha Besson, *Reconstruire l'ordre institutionnel international* (Paris: Éditions du Collège de France, Fayard, 2021), para. 64. While legal personality is no doubt an important legal construct that needs to be carefully studied, an excessive focus on its formal aspects can cloud not only normative but also doctrinal analysis.

reason to presume that States, as the system's primary law-makers, cannot create rules that apply to IOs, or that customary rules originally developed for inter-State relations cannot be extended to IOs because IOs did not participate in their creation. Moreover, the contribution that IO practice can make to the customary process must be appraised in the light of the principle of sovereign equality.

It must be conceded, however, that a strong view of separate personality and legal autonomy has indeed seemed to prevail in the law of treaties, where the rules codified in VCLT 1986 indicate that IOs are only bound by the treaty rights or obligations to which they consent. Even so, one should not lose sight of the normative problems that this approach creates, as it makes it easier for States to circumvent obligations owed to third parties by acting through IOs.

12

Consent and Informal Law-Making

The View from the Court of Justice of the European Union

EVA KASSOTI

12.1 INTRODUCTION

State consent plays a central role in international treaty law-making;[1] the very assumption of obligations by means of a treaty is premised on the expression of consent by the parties. As the International Court of Justice (hereafter ICJ) stressed in its Advisory Opinion on the *International Status of South-West Africa*: 'An "agreement" implies consent of the parties concerned.... The parties must be free to accept or reject the terms of contemplated agreement. No party can impose its terms on the other party.'[2] At the same time, the diversification of instruments and the pluralization of actors involved in modern international law have accentuated the phenomenon of informal international law,[3] thereby raising questions about the practical value and relevance of consent, as a threshold criterion, in modern international treaty law. As shown in Section 12.2, different attempts in the literature to grapple with informal international law-making in its multiple manifestations have invariably led to abandoning consent as the normativity threshold, thereby muddling the distinction between law and non-law. Arguably, these attempts

1 Despite this, the concept remains polysemous. On this, see generally Samantha Besson, 'State Consent and Disagreement in International Law-Making: Dissolving the Paradox' (2016) 29 (2) *Leiden Journal of International Law* 289–316, at 294; Mathew Craven, 'The Ends of Consent', in Michael J. Bowman and Dino Kritsiotis (eds.), *Conceptual and Contextual Perspectives on the Modern Law of Treaties* (Cambridge: Cambridge University Press, 2018), pp. 103–135, p. 103.

2 *International Status of South-West Africa* (Advisory Opinion) [1950] ICJ Rep. 128, p. 139.

3 The chapter employs the term 'informal' to connote 'non-binding'. Note, however, that authors have used the term to connote the lack of formalities traditionally associated with international law – and not the lack of binding force of an instrument: see, for example, Joost Pauwelyn, 'Informal International Lawmaking: Framing the Concept and Research Questions', in Joost Pauwelyn, Ramses A. Wessel and Jan Wouters (eds.), *Informal International Lawmaking* (Oxford: Oxford University Press, 2012), pp. 13–34, pp. 15–16.

have failed to gain traction exactly because key functions of the international legal system, namely maintaining a high degree of legal certainty, stability, predictability and accountability in international relations, are contingent on the existence of a clear distinction between law and non-law. Authors who have resisted the trend of deformalization highlight the international legal system's mechanisms of coping with informality – and thus, its capacity to absorb informal prescriptions.[4]

However, proponents of a distinction between law and non-law tend to neglect, or pay little attention to, how the European Union (hereafter EU), a significant international legal actor, and more particularly its courts, cope with informality in its relations with the outside world. It is important to address this blind spot as informal arrangements form an essential part of the EU's external governance machinery. In this light, the present contribution purports to examine how the Court of Justice of the European Union (hereafter CJEU) deals with informal arrangements between the EU and third parties aimed at replacing international agreements. In turn, this assessment offers unique insights from practice that directly feed into the debate about the role and relevance of consent as a threshold criterion in international law.

The structure of the chapter is as follows: Section 12.2 will briefly sketch out the current debate on informality in international legal literature. Section 12.3 maps out the typology of informal agreements in the EU's external practice. Section 12.4 examines the CJEU's approach to informal agreements concluded between the EU and other recognized law-makers, whereas Section 12.5 focuses on the Court's practice in relation to issues of consent by non-State actors. Section 12.6 concludes by proffering some broader points for reflection on the basis of the previous analysis.

12.2 INFORMALITY IN INTERNATIONAL TREATY-MAKING: A LINGERING ISSUE

Writing in 2014, Joost Pauwelyn, Ramses A. Wessel and Jan Wouters noted a sharp decline in the conclusion of treaties and a concomitant rise of informal means of co-operation.[5] This trend has continued unabated and a recent study confirmed that informal agreements 'are not just an important part of the

[4] See Section 12.2.

[5] Joost Pauwelyn, Ramses A. Wessel and Jan Wouters, 'When Structures Become Shackles: Stagnation and Dynamics in International Lawmaking' (2014) 25(3) *European Journal of International Law* 733–763, at 734–735.

international agreement landscape; they are increasingly *the* dominant part'.[6] Flexibility is one of the main reasons underpinning the increased recourse to informal law-making.[7] Flexibility is linked to the fact that, in this context, non-compliance comes with reduced penalties (and costs) and to procedural flexibility; the conclusion of informal agreements entails that States do not have to face (the often formidable) hurdles of obtaining consent at the national level, thereby making them attractive alternatives to treaties proper.[8] Furthermore, the rise of informality reflects the range of actors participating in modern international law-creating processes. A wide array of entities such as non-governmental organizations (hereafter NGOs), business actors and standard-setting bodies have entered the scene and this has resulted into an unprecedented *ratione personae* pluralization of international norm-creation.[9] The proliferation of new actors and instruments that escape the traditional framework of international law in conjunction with the fact that international law never really paid any attention to form and formalities for the purpose of ascertaining the binding nature of an act[10] have accentuated the problem of locating the boundary between law and non-law.

The rise of informal international law has had a significant impact on the discipline and on the way it construes the threshold of normativity in international law. Although it would be beyond the scope of this chapter to discuss how international legal scholars have grappled with the phenomenon of

[6] Curtis A. Bradley, Jack Goldsmith and Oona A. Hathaway, 'The Rise of Nonbinding International Agreements: An Empirical, Comparative, and Normative Analysis' (in press, 2023) 90 *University of Chicago Law Review*. Available at: https://ssrn.com/abstract=4023641, last accessed 5 January 2023, at 7.

[7] Council of Europe, Committee of Legal Advisers on Public International Law, 'Expert Workshop on Non-Legally Binding Agreements in International Law' (2021). Available at: https://rm.coe.int/concept-note-workshop-non-legally-binding-agreements-in-international-/1680a2358d, last accessed 5 January 2023.

[8] Timothy Meyer, 'Alternatives to Treaty-Making – Informal Agreements', in Duncan B. Hollis (ed.), *The Oxford Guide to Treaties*, 2nd ed. (Oxford: Oxford University Press, 2020), pp. 59–81, pp. 67–73.

[9] Jean d'Aspremont, 'Introduction: Non-State Actors in International Law: Oscillating between Concept and Dynamics', in Jean d'Aspremont (ed.), *Participants in the International Legal System: Multiple Perspectives on Non-State Actors in International Law* (London: Routledge, 2011), pp. 1–21, p. 4.

[10] Jean d'Aspremont, 'Formalism versus Flexibility in the Law of Treaties', in Christian Tams, Antonios Tzanakopoulos and Andreas Zimmermann (eds.), *Research Handbook on the Law of Treaties* (Cheltenham: Edward Elgar, 2014), pp. 257–284, p. 261; see, for example, *Case concerning Maritime Delimitation and Territorial Questions (Qatar* v. *Bahrain)* (Judgment) (Jurisdiction and Admissibility) [1994] ICJ Rep. 112, paras. 25, 27.

informal law-making (in its multiple manifestations) in depth,[11] it suffices to mention here that, broadly speaking, two main schools of thought have emerged: the grey zone and the bright line theorists. Grey zone theorists, in an attempt to cast the net wide and capture manifestations of normativity that escape the traditional framework, have invariably done away with the binary distinction between law and non-law (and thus, with the consent of recognized law-makers as the threshold of bindingness) either by proffering different visions of international law,[12] or different means of gauging normativity that radically depart from existing ones.[13] Ultimately, arguably, the grey zone school of thought has failed to gain traction *exactly* because it muddles the distinction between law and non-law. At the end of the day, as bright line theorists have highlighted, the binary distinction between law and non-law is essential in order to maintain international law's identity *qua* law[14] – namely to provide a framework of legal certainty, predictability and stability for the conduct of international relations. As José E. Alvarez succinctly put it: 'If everything is law, nothing may have the characteristics that we associate with law – that is, rules that are accessible, intelligible, clear, predictable and equally applicable to everyone.'[15]

However, admitting the importance of keeping a clear distinction between *lex lata* and *lex ferenda* does not ameliorate the difficulties associated with consent as a trigger of commitment in a pluralized normative setting. More particularly, two sets of questions present themselves here. First, what exactly amounts to consent and how are we to identify it? In the treaty context, the

[11] This issue has been treated in detail in Eva Kassoti, 'Beyond State Consent? International Legal Scholarship and the Challenge of Informal International Law-Making' (2016) 63(2) *Netherlands International Law Review* 99–131; Jan Klabbers, 'Law-Making and Constitutionalism', in Jan Klabbers, Anne Peters and Geir Ulfstein (eds.), *The Constitutionalization of International Law* (Oxford: Oxford University Press, 2009), pp. 81–125, pp. 93–104; Jean d'Aspremont, 'From a Pluralization of International Norm-Making Processes to a Pluralization of the Concept of International Law', in Pauwelyn *et al.*, fn. 3, pp. 185–199.

[12] See, for example, Rosalyn Higgins, *Problems and Process: International Law and How We Use It* (Oxford: Oxford University Press/Clarendon Press, 1994), p. 39; Harold D. Lasswell and Myres S. McDougal, *Jurisprudence for a Free Society: Studies in Law, Science and Policy* (Leiden: Martinus Nijhoff, 1992), pp. 24–25.

[13] See, for example, Jose E. Alvarez, *International Organizations as Law-Makers* (Oxford: Oxford University Press, 2005), pp. 63–122; Benedict Kingsbury, Nico Krisch and Richard B. Stewart, 'The Emergence of Global Administrative Law' (2005) 68 *Law and Contemporary Problems* 15–61.

[14] Kassoti, fn. 11, at 109–110; Jan Klabbers, 'The Undesirability of Soft Law' (1998) 67 *Nordic Journal of International Law* 381–391, 387.

[15] Jose E. Alvarez, 'The Relativity Apocalypse Is Nigh' (2020) 114 *American Journal of International Law Unbound* 77–81, at 81.

identification of consent for the purpose of ascertaining whether treaty obligations have been undertaken, entails identifying the common intention of the parties as this was manifested outwardly on the basis of 'objective' criteria focusing on the text of the instrument and on the circumstances surrounding its making.[16] In this way, the quest for an inherently subjective criterion, namely intention, has been 'objectified' with reference to form and expectations.[17] The attempt at 'objectification' does not hide the fact that this exercise 'grounds the identification of international treaties on an often indiscernible psychological element, and makes treaty-identification a deeply speculative operation aimed at reconstructing the author(s) intent'.[18] To be sure, the result is not always satisfactory and questions regarding whether an instrument expresses its authors' consent to be bound thereby as a matter of treaty-law still abound in practice, as the recent disagreement between the United States (hereafter US) and Iran regarding the legal status of their 2015 nuclear deal attests to.[19] Second, what are we to do with normative utterances that emanate from entities that have traditionally been seen as law-bearers, namely as having the capacity to possess rights and obligations but not as law-makers?[20]

Bright line theorists have put forward different answers to these questions. Although I have addressed the persuasive force of these suggestions elsewhere,[21] a few general points are worth making here. Jan Klabbers, for instance, has floated the idea of 'presumptive law', which means that 'all normative utterances should be presumed to give rise to law unless and until the opposite can somehow be proven'.[22] Apart from other shortcomings, this proposition does not conform with current practice; States, in their practice,

[16] Jan Klabbers, *The Concept of Treaty in International Law* (The Hague: Kluwer Law International, 1996), p. 65; Malgosia Fitzmaurice, 'The Identification and Character of Treaties and Treaty Obligations between States in International Law' (2002) 73(1) *The British Yearbook of International Law* 141–185, at 165–168; see, for example, *Maritime Delimitation and Territorial Questions*, fn. 10, para. 27; *Maritime Delimitation in the Indian Ocean (Somalia* v. *Kenya)* (Judgment) [2017] ICJ Rep. 3, para. 128; *Chagos Marine Protected Area Arbitration (Mauritius* v. *United Kingdom)*, PCA, Final Award (18 March 2015), 162 ILR 1, p. 168, para. 426.

[17] Vassilis Pergantis, *The Paradigm of State Consent in the Law of Treaties: Challenges and Perspectives* (Cheltenham: Edward Elgar, Elgar International Law, 2017), pp. 22–23.

[18] d'Aspremont, fn. 10, p. 272.

[19] Bradley *et al.*, fn. 6, pp. 11–12.

[20] For this distinction and relevant case law see Ilias Plakokefalos, 'Treaties and Individuals: Of Beneficiaries, Duty-Bearers, Users and Participants', in Tams *et al.*, fn. 10, pp. 625–653, pp. 629–630.

[21] Kassoti, fn. 11, at 118–122.

[22] Klabbers, fn. 11, p. 115.

consider themselves free to conclude non-binding agreements.[23] Although Duncan B. Hollis rejects the 'presumptive law' thesis, he does find recourse to presumptions appealing – and suggests different presumptions of bindingness for agreements involving recognized law-makers and those involving non-State actors.[24] At the same time, it is perhaps a bit difficult to see how this tackles the problems underpinning the presumptive law thesis. If States consider themselves free to conclude informal instruments, a presumption of bindingness runs counter to that very freedom and to the fact that States consciously and purposefully wish to place certain normative activities outside the legal framework. Jean d'Aspremont has suggested having recourse to 'written linguistic indicators' in the making of treaties for the purpose of ensuring a clearer distinction between treaties and other informal instruments.[25] This, however, does not seem to be able to do the trick either. It is not uncommon for States to omit references to the legal status of an instrument.[26] Similarly, the use of mandatory terms such as 'shall' or 'agree' has always been indicative of an agreement's status as a binding one.[27] However if the gist of d'Aspremont's thesis is that linguistic markers should be used as *constitutive* rather than *indicative* criteria of the legal status of an agreement, this would require a leap of faith on behalf of States – which they have simply not taken thus far, as a matter of positive law. This proposition also does not take into account the fact that States sometimes are *deliberately* vague about the legal status of an instrument. Thus, for instance, the disagreement over the binding character of the 2019 US–Mexico Joint Declaration on Migration has been attributed to internal political considerations rather than to any sort of ambiguity in the instrument's terms.[28]

This brief exposition shows that consent, as the threshold of commitment in the law of treaties, presents serious practical challenges that cannot be theorized away very easily. At the same time, despite their shortcomings, the above theoretical propositions by bright light theorists (and particularly, the

[23] The same criticism has been voiced by Hollis: see Hollis, Chapter 6 in this volume.

[24] Ibid.

[25] Jean d'Aspremont, *Formalism and the Sources of International Law: A Theory of the Ascertainment of Legal Rules* (Oxford: Oxford University Press, 2011), pp. 185–192. It is worth noting that d'Aspremont does not explain *exactly* what 'written linguistic indicators' means. It seems to amount to a clear signal on behalf of the parties to be legally bound by a treaty. For a discussion of d'Aspremont's 'social thesis', namely his account of how to treat normative output by actors that are not recognized law-makers, see ibid., pp. 195–220.

[26] *Chagos Marine Protected Area Arbitration*, fn. 16, p. 168, paras. 426–427.

[27] Anthony Aust, *Modern Treaty Law and Practice*, 3rd ed. (Cambridge: Cambridge University Press, 2013), pp. 30–31.

[28] Bradley *et al.*, fn. 6, p. 76.

presumptive law thesis) reveal that, quite apart from practical, descriptive challenges, informal law poses significant normative challenges for the discipline. More particularly, it is difficult to see how classic international law – with its binary simplicity of binding/non-binding – can keep up with the new developments on the ground, namely the increased recourse to intentional informality on behalf of States and the rise of new participants in international norm-creation. Thus, constructs such as the presumptive law thesis seem to be driven by the need to reconcile the traditional framework (which inevitably requires some sort of threshold in order to maintain the identity of law *qua* law) with the current sociological reality.[29]

This renders enquiries into how international judicial bodies deal with informality and questions of consent, as a threshold criterion, in their actual practice even more poignant. Admittedly, the case law of such bodies, and particularly that of the CJEU, which is the focus of this contribution, may not be vast and thus, it may not illuminate every aspect of the debate. It does, however, have something of value to say about what is consent, how it is to be construed and how to deal with the consent of non-recognized law-makers. Against this background, the next section will briefly map out the typology of informal agreements in the EU's external practice in order to provide some background to the discussion that will unfold in the rest of the chapter.

12.3 INFORMALITY IN THE EU'S TREATY-MAKING PRACTICE: AN UNDER-EXPLORED TOPIC

EU law is anything but unfamiliar with informal instruments; internally, these instruments have become an important tool of EU governance and the phenomenon has received much scholarly attention.[30] In recent years, recourse to informal arrangements in the specific context of the EU's external relations has gained momentum and it has been observed that 'recourse to non-binding instruments governing the relations of the EU with the rest of the world is increasingly common'.[31] Internally, informal law is estimated to amount to 13 per cent of all EU law – and it is assumed that the percentage

[29] Klabbers, fn. 11, pp. 109–110, pp. 113–114.

[30] See, for example, Linda Senden, *Soft Law in European Community Law* (Oxford: Hart, 2004); Fabien Terpan, 'Soft Law in the European Union – The Changing Nature of EU Law' (2015) 21(1) *European law Journal* 68–96.

[31] Paula García Andrade, 'The Distribution of Powers between EU Institutions for Conducting External Affairs through Non-Binding Instruments' (2016) 1(1) *European Papers* 115–125, at 115.

is not lower in the field of EU external relations.[32] Taking stock of this trend, Ott has stressed that 'compared to binding international agreements, at least twice as many bilateral soft law tools are agreed between EU actors and international organizations or third countries'.[33] Despite this, it is widely acknowledged that the EU's practice of concluding informal international agreements is still largely an under-explored phenomenon.[34]

The reasons underpinning the increased recourse to non-binding agreements in the EU's external action are not dissimilar to those bolstering the same trend in international law. In this context, too, flexibility, efficiency and the enhanced margin of discretion in the fulfilment of non-binding commitments have been credited as the main reasons for resorting to informal agreements.[35] Furthermore, the complexity of the EU's governance system and the complications inherent in concluding mixed agreements should not be ignored as factors that further reinforce the turn to informality.[36] The procedure pertaining to the conclusion of these agreements is cumbersome and requires protracted negotiations both within the Union and with third States. Often, these treaties may end up before EU courts[37] – and thus, create delays in ratification.[38] The complex rules pertaining to the conclusion of binding agreements coupled with the long negotiations of (often) quite broad and comprehensive mixed agreements illustrate the structural weaknesses of the EU as a treaty-maker and entail that the Union cannot act very swiftly – by means of a treaty – at the international level, particularly in times of crisis.[39]

32 Ramses A. Wessel and Joris Larik, *EU External Relations Law: Text, Cases and Materials*, 2nd ed. (Oxford: Hart, 2020), p. 103.

33 Andrea Ott, 'Informalization of EU Bilateral Instruments: Categorization, Contestation and Challenges' (2020) 39 *Yearbook of European Law* 569–601, at 577.

34 Ibid., p. 576; Francesco Spera, 'The Employment of International Soft Bilateral Instruments by the European Union in Its External Relations' (2020) 25(1) *Austrian Review of International and European Law* 3–36, at 5.

35 Andrade, fn. 31, at 116.

36 Ibid.; Ramses A. Wessel, 'Normative Transformations in EU External Relations: The Phenomenon of 'Soft' International Agreements' (2021) 44(1) *West European Politics* 72–92, at 75.

37 See, for example, Opinion 2/15, EU:C:2017:376, 16 May 2017; Opinion 1/17, EU:C:2019:341, 30 April 2019.

38 See, for example, Opinion 1/19, EU:C:2021:198, 6 October 2021.

39 Andrea Ott, 'The "Contamination" of EU Law by Informalization? International Arrangements in EU Migration Law' (2020) *Verfassungsblog*. Available at: https://verfassungsblog.de/the-contamination-of-eu-law-by-informalization/, last accessed 6 January 2023.

There is a broad array of informal agreements concluded between the EU and third parties covering a wide range of issues.[40] The EU's migration policy is an area where informal agreements have been utilized quite extensively.[41] Prominent examples here are the 2016 EU-Turkey Statement[42] and the Joint Way Forward with Afghanistan.[43] In this context, different types of non-binding arrangements have been used, such as policy dialogues, Common Agendas on Migration and Mobility as well as mobility partnerships, in order to tackle different issues of migration – including visa facilitation, legal migration issues as well as combatting irregular migration and cooperation on readmission and return.[44] These instruments often expressly indicate that their authors do not wish to enter into legally binding commitments thereby.[45]

[40] See, for example, the Revised Memorandum of Understanding with the United States of America regarding the Importation of Beef from Animals not treated with Certain Growth-Promoting Hormones and Increased Duties Applied by the United States to Certain products of the European Union, OJ 2014 No. L027, 30 January 2014, p. 2; European Commission, 'Proposal for a Council Decision Authorizing the Conclusion, on behalf of the European Community, of a Memorandum of Understanding between the European Community and the Swiss Federal Council on a Contribution by the Swiss Confederation towards Reducing Economic and Social Disparities in the Enlarged European Union, and Authorizing Certain Member States to Conclude Individually Agreements with the Swiss Confederation on the Implementation of the Memorandum', 20 October 2005, COM (2005) 468 final; Memorandum of Understanding between the European External Action Service (EEAS) (and signed by the High Representative of the European Union for Foreign Affairs and Security Policy) and the General Secretariat of the League of Arab States of 19 January 2015, HR (2015) 14; for an overview, see Wessel, fn. 36, pp. 76–81.

[41] Federico Casolari, 'The Unbearable "Lightness" of Soft Law: On the European Union's Recourse to Informal Instruments in the Fight against Irregular Immigration', in Francesca Ippolito, Gianluca Bordoni and Federico Casolari (eds.), *Bilateral Relations in the Mediterranean: Prospects for Migration Issues* (Cheltenham: Edward Elgar, 2020), pp. 215–228.

[42] European Council, 'EU-Turkey Statement of 18 March 2016' (2016). Available at: www.consilium.europa.eu/en/press/press-releases/2016/03/18/eu-turkey-statement/, last accessed 6 January 2023. The exact legal status of the Statement has been controversial; see further Eva Kassoti and Alina Carrozzini, 'One Instrument in Search of an Author: Revisiting the Authorship and Legal Nature of the EU–Turkey Statement', in Eva Kassoti and Narin Idriz (eds.), *The Informalisation of the EU's External Action in the Field of Migration and Asylum* (Berlin: Springer, TMC Asser Press, 2022), pp. 237–254.

[43] Joint Way Forward on migration issues between Afghanistan and the EU (2 October 2016). Available at: www.eeas.europa.eu/sites/default/files/eu_afghanistan_joint_way_forward_on_migration_issues.pdf, last accessed 6 January 2023; Joint Declaration on Migration Cooperation between Afghanistan and the EU, Council Doc. 5223/21 ADD (13 January 2021). Available at: www.eeas.europa.eu/sites/default/files/jmcd_-_english_version_signed_26apr2021.pdf, last accessed 6 January 2023.

[44] For an overview see Sara Poli, 'The Integration of Migration Concerns into EU External Policies: Instruments, Techniques and Legal Problems' (2020) 5(1) *European Papers* 71–94.

[45] Wessel, fn. 36, p. 80.

Turning to agreements with non-State actors, the Union has concluded a number of treaties with entities or territories other than States, including the Palestine Liberation Organization (hereafter PLO),[46] Hong Kong,[47] Taiwan,[48] and Kosovo.[49] In EU law literature, little attention has been paid to the legal status of these agreements under international law[50] – and hence, to the thorny question of the role that the consent of non-State actors may play in the context of treaty-making.

Against this backdrop, the Section 12.4 will examine how the CJEU has tackled informal agreements in its practice.

12.4 THE CJEU AND INFORMAL INTERNATIONAL AGREEMENTS

From the outset, it needs to be mentioned that only a handful of cases pertaining to informal agreements have been scrutinized by the CJEU. Limited as this practice may be, it shows that the EU courts' case law aligns with international judicial practice when it comes to understanding what consent is and how to identify it in the context of treaty-making. In *Opinion 1/13*, the Court noted that a treaty expresses the 'convergence of intent on the part of two or more subjects of international law'[51] – thereby equating

46 Euro-Mediterranean Interim Association Agreement on trade and cooperation between the European Community, of the one part, and the Palestine Liberation Organization (PLO) for the benefit of the Palestinian Authority of the West Bank and the Gaza Strip, OJ 1997 No. L187, 16 July 1997, p. 3.

47 Council Decision 1999/400/EC of 11 May 1999 concerning the Conclusion of the Agreement between the European Community and Hong Kong, China on Cooperation and Mutual Administrative Assistance in Customs Matters, OJ 1999 No. L151, 18 June 1999, p. 20.

48 Council Decision 2006/445/EC of 22 May 2006 on the conclusion of an Agreement in the form of Exchange of Letters between the European Community and the Separate Customs Territory of Taiwan, Penghu, Kinmen, and Matsu pursuant to Article XXIV:6 and Article XXVIII of the General Agreement on Tariffs and Trade (GATT) 1994 relating to the modification of concessions in the schedules of the Czech Republic, the Republic of Estonia, the Republic of Cyprus, the Republic of Latvia, the Republic of Lithuania, the Republic of Hungary, the Republic of Malta, the Republic of Poland, the Republic of Slovenia, and the Slovak Republic in the course of their accession to the European Union, OJ 2006 No. L176, 30 June 2006, p. 100.

49 Council Decision (EU) 2016/342 of 12 February 2016 on the conclusion, on behalf of the Union, of the Stabilisation and Association Agreement between the European Union and the European Atomic Energy Community, of the one part, and Kosovo of the other part, OJ 2016 No. L71, 16 March 2016, p. 1.

50 A notable exception is Peter Van Elsuwege, 'The EU and Non-Recognized Territories: Lessons from the Case Law of the Court of Justice of the European Union', in Benedikt C. Harzl and Roman Petrov (eds.), *Unrecognized Entities: Perspectives in International, European and Constitutional Law* (Leiden: Brill, 2021), pp. 107–129.

51 Opinion 1/13, EU:C:2014:2303, 14 October 2014, GC, para. 37.

consent with the common intention of the parties – in line with relevant international case law.

Furthermore, in the same vein with international jurisprudence, the CJEU's case law attests to the irrelevance of form in which an instrument is clothed for the purpose of ascertaining its binding character. In *France* v. *Commission*, the Court indicated its broad understanding of the term 'agreement', which encompasses 'any undertaking entered into by entities subject to international law, *whatever its formal designation*'.[52] More recent case law bears out this proposition. In the 2004 *France* v. *Commission* case, the Court ruled that although the Guidelines on Regulatory Co-Operation and Transparency concluded between the Commission and the US are non-binding, this does not automatically give an institution the power to adopt them.[53] Importantly, in ascertaining the non-binding character of the instrument in question, the Court paid no heed to its designation as 'Guidelines'. Similarly, in the *Swiss MoU* case, the Court did not infer the non-binding character of the instrument in question, an addendum to a Memorandum of Understanding (hereafter MoU) with Switzerland, merely from its label.[54] Rather, it satisfied itself that the instrument did not evidence the consent of its authors to be bound thereby as a matter of international law – and emphasized that, even in this context, the principles of conferral and institutional balance continue to apply.[55]

The 2014 *Venezuelan Fisheries* case[56] attests to the Court's indifference to considerations of form and formalities as well as to its willingness to ascribe binding force to instruments that manifest consent – even if this may entail stretching the notion of 'treaty' to a breaking point. Here, the Court concluded that a Council decision authorizing Venezuelan fishing vessels to fish in EU waters off the coast of French Guiana resulted in the conclusion of a treaty between the EU and Venezuela – once the latter tacitly accepted it by

52 CJEU, *French Republic* v. *Commission of the European Communities* (Case C-327/91) EU:C:1994:305 [1994] ECR I-03641, 9 August 1994, para. 27 (emphasis added).

53 CJEU, *French Republic* v. *Commission of the European Communities* (Case C-233/02) EU:C:2004:173, 23 March 2004, para. 40.

54 CJEU, *Council of the European Union* v. *European Commission* (Case C-660/13) EU:C:2016:616, 28 July 2016, GC.

55 Ibid., paras. 4, 11. The question of the binding nature of the instrument was treated *in extenso* in the Advocate General's Opinion, see CJEU, *Council of the European Union* v. *European Commission* (Case C-660/13) EU:C:2015:787, Opinion of Advocate General Sharpston, 26 November 2015, paras. 57–68.

56 CJEU, *European Parliament and European Commission* v. *Council of the European Union* (Joined Cases C-103/12 and C-165/12) EU:C:2014:2400, 26 November 2014, GC.

applying for fishing authorizations.[57] The better view, however, seems to be that the decision was a unilateral act creating legal effects under international law – rather than an offer that culminated in a treaty once it was accepted.[58] The Court sidestepped the awkward question of the procedural basis of the conclusion of this treaty. Overall, Article 218 of the Treaty on the Functioning of the European Union (hereafter TFEU) envisages a number of procedural steps before the conclusion of a treaty – none of which was taken *in casu*. From a broader perspective, what matters for present purposes is that the CJEU did not hesitate to attribute legal effect to the reality of consent – even if the form in which that consent was manifested did not neatly fit the traditional sources doctrine or the relevant EU law framework.

Turning to the question of ascertaining the consent to be legally bound, the CJEU largely follows the 'objective approach' developed in international judicial practice.[59] Thus, the quest for consent amounts to an examination of whether the instrument at hand manifests the intention of its authors to be bound as a matter of international law – as this is evidenced in the text of the instrument and the circumstances surrounding its making. Admittedly, this examination is much more carefully conducted and clearly articulated in the Advocate Generals' Opinions rather than in the Court's judgments.

In the 2004 *France* v. *Commission* case, the Advocate General concluded that the Guidelines at hand did not constitute a binding act on the basis both of their wording and the context within which they were made.[60] The Advocate General did not merely rely on the statement to the effect that the parties intended to apply them 'on a voluntary basis' contained in the Guidelines, but also cited the use of non-mandatory language (such as 'should' and 'may' instead of 'shall') as well as the broader legal and factual context in order to substantiate his finding.[61] Although the Court reached the same conclusion, it considered it unnecessary to delve into the actual wording used; in its view, the parties' own statement in conjunction with the negotiating history of the Guidelines sufficed to deduce that the parties had no

57 Ibid., paras. 68–72.

58 CJEU, *European Parliament and European Commission* v. *Council of the European Union* (Joined Cases C-103/12 and C-165/12) EU:C:2014:334, Opinion of Advocate General Sharpston, 15 May 2014, paras. 69–101; Eva Kassoti and Mihail Vatsov, 'A Missed Opportunity? Unilateral Declarations by the European Union and the European Court of Justice's *Venezuelan Fisheries* Judgment' (2020) 35 *The International Journal of Marine and Coastal Law* 55–81, at 63–75.

59 See above the case law mentioned in fn. 16.

60 CJEU, *French Republic* v. *Commission of the European Communities* (Case C-233/02) EU:C:2003:503, Opinion of Advocate General Alber, 25 September 2003, paras. 56–61.

61 Ibid., paras. 56, 59.

intention to enter into legally binding commitments when they concluded the Guidelines.[62]

In the same vein with Advocate General Alber, Advocate General Sharpston examined carefully both the actual terms and the circumstances attending the making of the 2013 addendum to the MoU between the Union and Switzerland before concluding that it was an informal agreement – despite the fact that none of the parties contested its non-legally binding character.[63] In setting out the parameters of her enquiry into the legal nature of the instrument, Advocate General Sharpston cited the ICJ's *Qatar* v. *Bahrain* Judgment – thereby expressly endorsing the view that the parties' consent to a treaty is to be ascertained on the basis of objective criteria – and thus, on what was manifested outwardly, rather than what the authors actually had in mind at the time of the instrument's conclusion.[64] By way of contrast, the Court did not provide a detailed examination of the matter – although it did expressly refer to the fact that both parties had admitted its informal character.[65] In general, it seems that the Court relied on the fact that the non-binding character of the instrument was common ground among the parties and thus, it treated it as a point of departure for the analysis of the main question of the case, namely whether the Commission had the power to adopt the decision on the signature of the relevant instrument.

Overall, this line of case law shows that, although rather laconic in its analysis at times, the Court has implicitly recognized (and hence, legitimized) the EU's practice of concluding informal agreements – thereby, also acknowledging that expressions of consent on the international plane do not automatically lead to legally binding commitments. For the latter to arise, objective *indicia* of the consent to be bound need to exist – and, in this context, the terms in which an instrument is drafted and the circumstances surrounding its making are of decisive relevance.

In this light, the General Court's analysis of the 2016 EU-Turkey Statement in the context of its orders in cases *NF*, *NG* and *NM*[66] constitutes a marked

62 *French Republic* v. *Commission of the European Communities*, fn. 53, paras. 43–44.

63 *Council of the European Union* v. *European Commission*, Opinion of Advocate General Sharpston, fn. 55, paras. 66–68.

64 Ibid.

65 *Council of the European Union* v. *European Commission*, fn. 54, para. 4.

66 CJEU, *NF* v. *European Council* (Case T-192/16) EU:T:2017:128, 28 February 2017, Order of the Court, GC; CJEU, *NG* v. *European Council* (Case T-193/16) EU:T:2017:129, 28 February 2017, Order of the Court, GC; CJEU, *NM* v. *European Council* (Case T-257/16) EU:T:2017:130, 28 February 2017, Order of the Court, GC. On grounds of brevity, the chapter will only refer to Case T-192/16 since the other two Orders are virtually identical.

departure from a line of case law where the CJEU acted as a legal realist – attributing legal effect to expressions of consent to be legally bound that *in fact* occurred. The General Court in this case argued that the Statement was not authored by the EU, but, rather, by the Heads of State or Government of the Member States, and thus, it did not have jurisdiction to review the act in question – since it was attributable to the Member States, rather than the Union.[67] Although the General Court did not expressly pronounce on whether the Statement culminated into a treaty – other than noting that even if it were an agreement, this would have been concluded between the Member States and Turkey, and not between the EU and Turkey – in later case law the CJEU has referred to the Statement as a 'political commitment'.[68]

However, there are many reasons to support the proposition that the EU authored the Statement and that the Statement constituted a treaty between the Union and Turkey. Although I have expanded on these issues elsewhere,[69] a few general points are worth making here. In relation to the question of authorship of the act, the General Court relied almost exclusively on internal (EU) documentation.[70] However, the statement was the result of negotiations with a third State and thus, the legal context attending the making of the Statement was that of international – and not EU – law. Hence, the rules for ascertaining the author as well as the binding nature of the act should also be rules of international law.[71] Although, admittedly, it is rather rare that international judicial bodies have been confronted with the task of establishing the author of an act, the ICJ's *Advisory Opinion on Kosovo*[72] provides some useful guidance. In establishing the authorship of Kosovo's declaration of independence, the Court relied on the text of the declaration as well as on the context in which it was issued.[73] Both the text and the context within which the EU–Turkey Statement were made bear out the proposition that it was indeed the Union – and not the Member States – that concluded it alongside with Turkey. According to the text of the Statement it was the EU that agreed to

67 *NF* v. *European Council*, fn. 66, paras. 71–73.

68 CJEU, *Access Info Europe* v. *European Commission* (Case T-851/16) EU:T:2018:69, 7 February 2018, GC, para. 90.

69 Kassoti and Idriz, fn. 42.

70 *NF* v. *European Council*, fn. 66, paras. 64–65.

71 Enzo Cannizzaro, 'Denialism as the Supreme Expression of Realism: A Quick Comment on NF v. European Council' (2017) 2(1) *European Papers* 251–257, at 255.

72 *Accordance with International Law of the Unilateral Declaration of Independence in respect of Kosovo* (Advisory Opinion) [2010] ICJ Rep. 403.

73 Ibid., paras. 101–109.

undertake a number of obligations. Furthermore, the text of the Statement makes express reference to, and builds upon, other instruments issued by the EU and Turkey – thereby confirming that the instrument forms part of a series of bilateral instruments that clearly pertain to EU–Turkey relations.[74]

Similarly, there is strong textual evidence to suggest that the EU–Turkey Statement is a treaty under international law.[75] The statement includes several concrete commitments entered into by both parties, which arguably demonstrate the parties' willingness to create legally binding commitments, namely: (i) the return of all irregular migrants from the Greek islands to Turkey as from March 2016; (ii) the 1:1 scheme; (iii) the express commitment to disburse funds.[76] This conclusion is further bolstered by the subsequent clarification that the return of migrants would take place in accordance with the principle of non-refoulement and 'international and EU law'– that is, the applicable legal framework.[77] Importantly, the commitments undertaken thereby were new in relation to what the parties had been doing previously, and thus, they did not merely constitute a re-statement of previous obligations. The above point towards the conclusion that by issuing the Statement, the parties consented to be legally bound thereby.

In the light of the many flaws in the General Court's line of reasoning, it is difficult not to take into account the strong political overtones of the *NF* order. The General Court here did not show any of its usual flexibility – which in the

[74] Including the EU–Turkey Statement of 29 November 2015: see European Council, 'Meeting of Heads of State or Government with Turkey, EU-Turkey Statement, 29 November 2015' (2015). Available at: www.consilium.europa.eu/en/press/press-releases/2015/11/29/eu-turkey-meeting-statement/, last accessed 6 January 2023; EU-Turkey Joint Action Plan of 15 October 2015: European Commission, 'EU-Turkey Joint Action Plan' (2015). Available at: https://ec.europa.eu/commission/presscorner/detail/de/MEMO_15_5860, last accessed 6 January 2023.

[75] Kassoti and Idriz, fn. 42, pp. 246–254; Mauro Gatti and Andrea Ott, 'The EU-Turkey Statement: Legal Nature and Compatibility with EU Institutional Law', in Sergio Carrera, Juan Santos Vara and Tineke Strik (eds.), *Constitutionalising the External Dimension of EU Migration Policies in Times of Crisis: Legality, Rule of Law and Fundamental Rights Reconsidered* (Cheltenham: Edward Elgar, 2019), pp. 175–201, pp. 195–197.

[76] European Council, fn. 42. Point 1 of the Statement expresses the parties' decision to return 'all new irregular migrants to Turkey'. It then stresses that this measure was 'temporary and extraordinary which is necessary to end the human suffering and restore public order' as well as that it was to take place 'in full accordance with EU and international law'. The necessity to underline the 'temporary and extraordinary' character of the measure arguably shows the parties' awareness that legal effects would be produced thereby. Furthermore, while point 6 of the statement utilizes the verb 'will', it does so in order to clarify that the EU is to 'mobilise additional funding . . . of an additional 3 billion euros'.

[77] Spijkerboer also recognized the use of this formula as an expression of awareness of legal commitments: see Thomas Spijkerboer, 'Minimalist Reflections on Europe, Refugees and Law' (2016) 1(2) *European Papers* 533–558, at 554.

past, as it has been shown previously in this section, has not prevented it from ascribing legal force to instruments that manifested the consent to be legally bound irrespective of formalities. To the contrary, it seems that by tackling the question of authorship in a rather formalistic and one-sided manner, the General Court wished to sweep under the carpet the real problem of the EU–Turkey Statement – namely its compatibility with international and EU law.[78]

How does this overview of the CJEU's practice feed into the international law debate on consent? A few general remarks are worth canvassing here. It has been shown that, in a similar vein to international adjudicatory bodies, the CJEU pays little attention to the designation of an instrument for the purpose of ascertaining its binding force; what matters is whether it expresses the 'objectivised' consent to be legally bound – something that is to be determined on the basis of its text and the circumstances surrounding its making. In this light, the CJEU case law does not lend empirical support either to the presumptive law thesis or to the 'written linguistic indicators' thesis. The EU courts do not simply presume an instrument to be binding, nor do they simply rely on statements to the effect that their authors did not intend them to be legally binding as *constitutive* of their non-binding character, despite the fact that the analysis is perhaps inelegant and not extremely thorough at times. At the same time, the CJEU's insistence on observing the principles of conferral and institutional balance even in the case of informal arrangements – coupled with the fact that these instruments do not escape judicial review simply because they are not binding – means that the Court is not only well aware of the new sociological reality on the ground of practice but also willing to find tools to ensure (at least, some form of) accountability and legal certainty even in this context – while keeping the boundary between law and non-law intact. Importantly, the *NF* saga shows a blind spot in the debate on consent. The case highlighted the importance of the role of the decision-maker in translating whether consent 'in fact' also amounts to consent 'in law'. Ultimately, high political stakes and hence, extra-legal considerations may have a bearing on how the decision-maker, tasked with identifying the consent to be legally bound, approaches questions of threshold, and that is something we should not lose sight of.

[78] Cannizzaro, fn. 71, at 257; Sergio Carrera, Leonhard den Hertog and Marco Stefan, 'It Wasn't Me! The Luxembourg Court Orders on the EU-Turkey Refugee Deal' (2017) *CEPS Policy Insights*. Available at: www.ceps.eu/download/publication/?id=9981&pdf=EU-Turkey%20Deal.pdf, last accessed 6 January 2023.

Against this background, the following section will explore how the CJEU has tackled questions of consent by non-State actors in its practice.

12.5 THE CJEU AND ISSUES OF CONSENT BY NON-STATE ACTORS

Legal personality under international law is a concept that exists in a spectrum; while States are actors that 'possess the totality of international rights and duties recognized by international law',[79] other actors (such as insurgent groups, national liberation movements and non-self-governing territories) may enjoy a degree of legal personality that affords them the capacity to act on the international plane, including treaty-making capacity.[80] The ICJ's Advisory Opinion in *Reparation for Injuries* which refers to the United Nations (UN) as an entity possessing 'a large measure of legal personality'[81] corroborates this view. Furthermore, the decision of the International Law Commission (hereafter ILC) to limit the Vienna Convention on the Law of Treaties (hereafter VCLT)[82] to treaties between States implicitly acknowledges this. Article 3 VCLT excludes treaties involving 'other subjects of international law' – thereby confirming that although such treaties do not fall within the scope of the VCLT, they do exist as a matter of international law. Whether a particular entity possesses treaty-making capacity is a matter of recognition; other actors must recognize its treaty-making capacity.[83] In this sense, the consent of a State to enter into a treaty with a non-State actor is constitutive of the latter's treaty-making capacity. Thus, while treaty-making remains the prerogative of States and State-empowered bodies, modern international law does accept the position that other actors can also enter the circle of treaty-makers on an *ad hoc* basis.[84]

[79] *Reparation for Injuries Suffered in the Service of the United Nations* (Advisory Opinion) [1949] ICJ Rep. 174, p. 180.

[80] See generally Tom Grant, 'Who Can Make Treaties? Other Subjects of International Law', in Hollis, fn. 8, pp. 150–172.

[81] *Reparation for Injuries*, fn. 79, p. 179.

[82] Vienna Convention on the Law of Treaties, 1155 UNTS 331 (adopted 23 May 1969, entered into force 27 January 1980).

[83] Anne Peters, 'Treaty-Making Power' (last updated March 2009) in Rüdiger Wolfrum (ed.), *Max Planck Encyclopedia of Public International Law* (Oxford: Oxford University Press, 2009). Available at: https://opil.ouplaw.com/view/10.1093/law:epil/9780199231690/law-9780199231690-e1494?prd=EPIL, last accessed 6 January 2023.

[84] James Crawford, 'Chance, Order, Chaos: The Course of International Law' (Volume 365) *Collected Courses of The Hague Academy of International Law*, 2013, pp. 9–389, p. 159, para. 261. As Crawford highlights though: 'The international law of personality is no doubt more open today, but for key purposes it is still a law of exclusion, not participation': ibid., p. 159, para. 261.

The CJEU's position towards the question of consent to treaties by non-State actors seems to have shifted over time. In *Brita*, a case concerning, *inter alia*, the EU-PLO Association Agreement, the CJEU merely assumed the treaty-making capacity of PLO without more – thereby remaining largely agnostic towards the underlying issue of consent by the actor in question.[85] However, in its later case law, the Court seems to have adopted the 'spectral' understanding of international legal personality described above. In *Psagot*, the CJEU made a distinction between States, a term 'referring to a sovereign entity exercising, within its geographical boundaries, the full range of powers, recognized by international law' and 'territories' which, in the context of that particular case, referred to 'geographical spaces which … have a separate and distinct status … under international law'.[86] The General Court's 2020 *Kosovo* Judgment[87] manifests in more explicit terms the CJEU's understanding and espousal of the international law distinction between full international legal personality and limited legal personality (including treaty-making capacity) that some actors may enjoy *ad hoc* and on the basis of recognition by established law-makers. The case concerned a complaint by Spain to the effect that participation of Kosovo's National Regulatory Authority (NRA) in EU bodies is precluded since Kosovo is not a 'third country' within the meaning of EU secondary legislation. The General Court argued that the fact that the TFEU makes reference both to 'third States' and 'third countries' implies that the latter concept is broader and thus, that it is 'clearly intended to pave the way for the conclusion of international agreements with entities "other than States"'.[88] In reaching its conclusion, the General Court pointed out the EU's own practice of concluding treaties with entities other than sovereign States, including the PLO, Taiwan, Hong Kong and Macao,[89] before stressing that the Union has entered into several treaties with Kosovo 'thus *recognising its capacity* to conclude such agreements'.[90] After carefully noting that the Union has not taken a position regarding Kosovo's Statehood,[91] the General Court highlighted that a distinction needs to be

[85] CJEU, *Brita GmbH* v. *Hauptzollamt Hamburg-Hafen* (Case C-386/08) EU:C:2010:91 [2010] ECR I-10289, 25 February 2010, paras. 4–53.

[86] CJEU, *Organisation juive européenne and Vignoble Psagot* v. *Ministre de l'Économie et des Finances* (Case C-363/18) EU:C:2019:954, 12 November 2019, GC, paras. 29–31.

[87] CJEU, *Kingdom of Spain* v. *European Commission* (Case T-370/19) EU:T:2020:240, 23 September 2020, GC.

[88] Ibid., para. 30.

[89] Ibid., para. 31.

[90] Ibid., para. 32 (emphasis added).

[91] Ibid., para. 33.

made between the non-recognition of Kosovo's Statehood and its capacity to enter into treaties under international law.[92] The use of term 'third countries' in Article 218 TFEU – the provision governing treaty-making by the Union – entails that the EU can enter into treaties with entities 'which may have rights and obligations' but may not be sovereign States within the meaning of international law.[93] On appeal, although Advocate General Kokott upheld the distinction between 'third states' and 'third countries' propounded by the General Court, she clarified that this does not follow from the wording of the TFEU, but rather from an interpretation of the secondary legislation at hand.[94]

While the General Court's ruling and the Advocate General's Opinion in *Kosovo* attest to a large degree of alignment with international law considerations on the participation of non-State actors in treaty-making, the CJEU's case law on Western Sahara paints a different picture. Arguably, this line of case law attests to how political considerations may influence the way that the CJEU approaches consent by non-States actors. Western Sahara constitutes both a non-self-governing territory whose people have the right to self-determination[95] and a territory that is occupied by Morocco.[96] The EU has carefully avoided pronouncing on the exact legal status of Morocco vis-à-vis Western Sahara and it has entered into a number of treaties with Morocco that de facto extended to Western Sahara – the legality of which has come under judicial scrutiny in the context of the *Front Polisario*[97] and *Western Sahara Campaign UK*[98] cases. The Grand Chamber of the CJEU dealt with the two cases in 2016 and in 2018 with essentially the same line of reasoning. By eschewing engagement with the question of the legal status of Western Sahara as an occupied territory as well as with the international legal

[92] Ibid., para. 34.

[93] Ibid., para. 35. On the unclear legal status of Kosovo under international law, see Jure Vidmar, 'International Organizations and Non-State Territorial Entities', in Harzl and Petrov, fn. 50, pp. 30–53, pp. 43–44.

[94] CJEU, *Kingdom of Spain* v. *European Commission* (Case C-632/20 P) EU:C:2022:473, Opinion of Advocate General Kokott, 16 June 2022, paras. 48–49.

[95] *Western Sahara* (Advisory Opinion) [1975] ICJ Rep. 12, p. 68, para. 162.

[96] See, for example, *R. (on the application of Western Sahara Campaign UK)* v. *Revenue and Customs Commissioners* [2015] EWHC 2898, paras. 40, 43.

[97] CJEU, *Council of the European Union* v. *Front populaire pour la libération de la saguia-el-hamra et du rio de oro (Council* v. *Front Polisario)* (Case C-104/16 P) EU:C:2016:973, 21 December 2016, GC.

[98] CJEU, *The Queen, on the Application of Western Sahara Campaign UK* v. *Commissioners for Her Majesty's Revenue and Customs, Secretary of State, Food and Rural Affairs (Western Sahara Campaign UK)* (Case C-266/16) EU:C:2018:118, 27 February 2018, GC.

obligations incumbent upon the EU exactly because of this status,[99] the CJEU concluded that: (i) Western Sahara has a status separate and distinct to that of Morocco and as such, it was not legally included in the territorial scope of the EU-Morocco agreements; and (ii) that international law, nevertheless, allows the inclusion of Western Sahara in these agreements as long as the people of the territory in question have consented thereto.[100]

Against this background, the Commission entered into consultations with local stakeholders that culminated into the *express* inclusion of the territory and waters of Western Sahara in the territorial scope of the EU–Morocco agreements.[101] This resulted in renewed litigation before the CJEU and in the 2021 General Court's *Front Polisario* judgments.[102] The General Court found that the principles of self-determination and the relative effect of treaties mean that Western Sahara has a status separate and distinct to that of Morocco, and as such, it constitutes a third party to any international agreement between the Union and Morocco.[103] Thus, extending the territorial scope of any EU-Morocco agreement to the territory necessarily entails obtaining 'the consent of the people of Western Sahara'.[104] The Court found that the consultations carried out by EU institutions did not meet the requisite threshold since they merely involved obtaining the consent of the *local*

[99] For analysis of the *Front Polisario* and *Western Sahara Campaign* judgments, see Eva Kassoti, 'The Compatibility of EU International Agreements Extending to Occupied Territories with International Law: *Front Polisario* and *Western Sahara Campaign UK*', in Graham Butler and Ramses A. Wessel (eds.), *EU External Relations Law: The Cases in Context* (Oxford: Hart, 2022), pp. 817–829.

[100] *Council* v. *Front Polisario*, fn. 97, paras. 106–107, *Western Sahara Campaign UK*, fn. 98, paras. 63–64.

[101] Council Decision (EU) 2019/217 of 28 January 2019 on the conclusion in the form of an Exchange of Letters between the European Union and the Kingdom of Morocco on the amendment of Protocols 1 and 4 to the Euro-Mediterranean Agreement establishing an association between the European Communities and their Member States, of the one part, and the Kingdom of Morocco, of the other part, OJ 2019 No. L34, 6 February 2019, p. 1; Council Decision (EU) 2019/441 of 4 March 2019 on the conclusion of the Sustainable Fisheries Partnership Agreement between the European Union and the Kingdom of Morocco, the Implementation Protocol thereto and the Exchange of Letters accompanying the Agreement, OJ 2019 No. L77, 20 March 2019, p. 4.

[102] CJEU, *Front populaire pour la libération de la saguia-el-hamra et du rio de oro* v. *Council of the European Union* (Joined Cases T-344/19 and T-356/19) EU:T:2021:640, 29 September 2021, GC; CJEU, *Front populaire pour la libération de la saguia-el-hamra et du rio de oro* v. *Council of the European Union* (Case T-279/19) EU:T:2021:639, 29 September 2021, GC.

[103] Joined Cases T-344/19 and T-356/19, fn. 102, paras. 201–202; Case T-279/19, fn. 102, paras. 151–152.

[104] Joined Cases T-344/19 and T-356/19, fn. 102, paras. 322–364; Case T-279/19, fn. 102, paras. 336–391.

population, namely the people currently living in the territory, instead of *the people of the territory*, namely the Saharawi people.[105]

By failing to engage with the analytical framework of the law of occupation, the General Court essentially implied that the only obstacle to the conclusion of an agreement applicable to Western Sahara is obtaining the consent of the people of the territory. However, it is not impossible that on appeal the CJEU decides that EU institutions enjoy a wide margin of discretion regarding *how* this consent can be obtained. Again, it is difficult to ignore the politically laden context of the judgment. Morocco strongly denies its status as an occupying power of Western Sahara and addressing the dispute as one involving questions of occupation would mean that the CJEU would be confronted with questions of international responsibility of the EU for breaching its duties of non-recognition and non-assistance since it entered into agreements with an occupying power extending to an occupied territory – without those agreements expressly stipulating that the occupying power contracts on behalf of the territory in its capacity as such – and not as the territory's sovereign.[106] Thus, by framing the dispute exclusively in terms of consent of the people of the territory, the CJEU arguably shielded the Union from politically awkward questions of international responsibility.

To be sure, the Western Sahara saga before the CJEU does not add much to the debate on consent by non-State actors from a technical point of view. Remaining exclusively within the frame of self-determination and the law governing the status of non-self-governing territories, the General Court did acknowledge that the ways in which EU institutions sought to obtain the consent of the people of the territory were below par. It does, however, inform the overall debate on consent as a normative threshold and the propositions floated in theory by bright line scholars to overcome issues of consent in modern international law. This line of case law attests (again) to the power of the authority identifying or construing consent by legal operation in each case and to the extra-legal considerations that may have a (significant) bearing on such decisions. Unsurprisingly, in this debate, as seen in this section, a premium is placed on the decision-maker – either in terms of empirical support of one position or another, or in terms of reliance thereon for applying in practice a particular (theoretical) proposition. What is perhaps surprising in

[105] Joined Cases T-344/19 and T-356/19, fn. 102, para. 364; Case T-279/19, fn. 102, para. 391.

[106] On the EU's obligations as a third party towards Western Sahara, see Eva Kassoti, 'The Legality under International Law of the EU's Trade Agreements Covering Occupied Territories: A Comparative Study of Palestine and Western Sahara' (2017) (3) *CLEER Papers*. Available at: www.asser.nl/media/3934/cleer17-3_web.pdf, last accessed 6 January 2023.

this context is that the politics surrounding the task of construing consent in law have not been given much consideration. The Western Sahara saga shows that over-reliance on case law in making broad assumptions or propositions regarding the role of consent in international law could be perhaps misleading – as the broader political framework of a dispute may influence the judicial outcome.

12.6 CONCLUSION

This chapter explored consent as a trigger of commitment in the context of treaty-making by focusing on how the CJEU deals in its practice with informal agreements. It has been shown that to a large degree the CJEU follows the practice of international adjudicatory bodies. The consent to be legally bound entails the ascertainment of the 'objectivised' common intention of an instrument's authors to be legally bound thereby – a task that is carried out by examining the instrument's terms as well as the circumstances surrounding its making. When it comes to treaties with non-State actors, the Court's jurisprudence attests to its awareness of the constitutive function of consent by recognized law-makers in this context.

The examination of the CJEU's case law also shows an important blind spot in the current debate on consent. Efforts to highlight the international legal system's capacity to digest social reality that falls below the normativity threshold, have resulted in different theoretical constructions as to how this can be done more widely – without diluting the distinction between law and non-law. Invariably, their purchase depends largely on the decision-maker – tasked with identifying and attributing legal effect to consent in each case. The CJEU's case law illuminates an aspect of the debate that, thus far, has garnered little attention, namely the politics of construing consent in judicial practice. Thus, attempts at theorizing how international law can become more sociologically clever and keep pace with current developments on the ground should be cognizant of the danger of over-relying on judicial practice. International law already has a set of tools (limited as it may be) that allows it to absorb informal output while keeping the line between law and non-law intact. Judicial practice can offer us invaluable guidance and insights into *how* this is done or can be done better. However, we should remain aware of the fact that *whether* this is done in the context of a particular case is not exclusively a matter of law.

13

Consent as a Guarantee of the Democratic Legitimacy of International Law

MONIQUE CHEMILLIER-GENDREAU*

13.1 INTRODUCTION

By proposing the topic of consent to international law, Samantha Besson invites us to reach beyond formal legal analysis and address the central issue of the acceptance of constraints. Such an endeavour requires a fresh assessment of international law's relationship with the subjects to which it is meant to apply.

International law consists of statements, and, in that respect, it is no different than national law. But unlike everyday language, legal statements create obligations for their addressees. If the addressees disregard the obligations defined in these statements, liability attaches. Through this legal discourse, some particular wills – the wills of those representing power – are imposed upon, and place constraints upon, the wills of all the members of the group. Law is the demarcation that separates two types of violence, that of the person who breaks the law and that of the police officer who enforces the law.

In international law, the States gathered in San Francisco in 1945 attempted to establish a comparable distinction by adopting the United Nations (hereafter UN) Charter. The violence of a State invading another was to be countered with what amounts to another form of violence: international sanctions. Because these sanctions are imposed under the authority of the UN Security Council, they are imbued with the force of law and become in effect lawful violence against unlawful violence. Yet, the question of the acceptance of such constraints by those who will be subjected to them remains open. As a result, those who exercise power seek justification in the consent of those upon whom that power is imposed.

* This chapter was translated from French by Dr Sévrine Knuchel, LLM thanks to the financial support of the Fondation du Collège de France.

French doctrine, for example, sidesteps this question by appealing to the strength of the positivist approach to law. The positivist approach adheres to legal forms: if legal forms are respected, the corresponding legal constraints and the violence they may implicate are in turn legitimate. Yet, while it is possible to find traces of consent in law's formal elements, consent may not be reduced to such formal elements.[1] Obviously, every legal norm necessarily takes some form (a contract, a convention, a resolution, a statute, a verbal agreement, etc.), but adherence to form cannot sufficiently account for the complex reality of legal norms. This is so because legal norms articulate the result of the weighing of competing values reached at a given moment in time: they convey choices between life options and modes of relationships among subjects.

These choices do not result from a 'will'. They result from the interplay of social contradictions. As Charles Chaumont highlighted in the 1970s, the foundation of law's binding character (and what makes the specificity of the constraining character of legal statements) ultimately depends on the overcoming of contradictions.[2] Social realities are bursting with contradictions between interests, points of view and concrete opposite situations. A legal norm appears as a point at which these contradictions are overcome. But overcoming does not mean erasing, and contradictions continue to evolve notwithstanding the adopted norms, whether statutes or contracts under domestic law, or treaties or customs under international law. A first contradiction (which Charles Chaumont identifies as the initial or 'primitive' contradiction) gives rise to a particular legal norm, but social or material realities continue to evolve, generating successive contradictions. The norm's binding character subsists as long as the subsequent contradiction is not stronger than the initial one. If the contradiction is uncertain, so will the norm be.[3] If the

1 For a different view maintaining that consent is essentially formal, see the comments of Jean d'Aspremont, Chapter 5 in this volume.

2 On this question and on applying the dialectic method to law, see Charles Chaumont, 'Rapport sur l'institution fondamentale de l'accord entre États', in *Annales de la Faculté de Droit et des Sciences Économiques de Reims* (Reims: Association Régionales des Amis de l'Université et de l'Enseignement Supérieur pour la promotion de l'Étude et la Recherche Scientifiques en liaison avec le monde de l'Économie (hereafter ARES), 1973), pp. 241–265; Centre d'Études des Relations Internationales, Faculté de Droit de Reims, *À la recherche du fondement du caractère obligatoire du droit international (force obligatoire et sujets de droit)* (Reims: ARES, 1974), pp. 1–39.

3 In international law, the UN Resolutions on the 'New International Economic Order' adopted in the 1970s offer a concrete example. The contradictions between the interests of developing countries and those of developed capitalist countries had not been overcome to the latter's detriment. As a result, these resolutions remained declaratory and did not have binding effects: see, for example, United Nations General Assembly (UNGA) Res. 3201 (1 May 1974).

subsequent contradiction is more important than the initial contradiction, the norm falls into disuse and social disorder emerges.[4]

From that perspective, the legal norm, whatever its form, is the expression of the equilibrium reached between these social contradictions at a given moment. Consent to law is merely expressing that the contradiction has been overcome; in other words, it is a measure of the power relations to which the social group submits. Yet, power relations within a society or among societies are not only based on material forces, whether economic or military. Ideological or moral forces also play a role and impact these relations. At times, they may even squarely contradict material forces.

It is at this point that the consent to law in a democratic perspective comes into play. Pursuant to the democratic postulate, social actors participate (directly or indirectly) in the norm's elaboration, allowing for diverging interests to express themselves until they reach an equilibrium that gives rise to the norm. In such a configuration, the legal norm will win adherence from all those to whom it applies. Yet, while this may happen at the domestic level, at the international level, consent rarely amounts to genuine adherence from those who will be subjected to the effects of the norm's application.

In this chapter, I will first show how the question of consent to international law has rarely been addressed during the classical period. I will then recall how this question arose along with the notions of social contract and democracy starting from the nineteenth century under the influence of Enlightenment philosophy, albeit without overcoming the difficulty of identifying which subject must consent to the norm. Finally, I will underscore how the fact that international law only applies to a society comprised of a limited circle of subjects, that is to all recognized States and the inter-State organizations they create, is an impediment to international law's appropriation by the entire social body concerned by its norms.

13.2 THE PERIOD WHEN THE ISSUE OF CONSENT WAS IGNORED

In the pre-modern era, the quest for domination and expansion of imperial formations pervades international relations, as illustrated by the Roman Empire and its successor the Holy Roman Empire, as well as by more distant empires, such as the Inca, Persian and Chinese Empires. At this time, the

4 Samantha Besson addresses this phenomenon when she highlights the disagreements persisting under treaties' agreements: see Samantha Besson, 'State Consent and Disagreement in International Law-Making: Dissolving the Paradox' (2016) 29(2) *Leiden Journal of International Law* 289–316.

question of international law is absent, even if a number of diplomatic and commercial relations unfold in accordance with some accepted rules. It is important to recall that the notion of sovereignty was born out of an imperial matrix. In its initial meaning derived from these political formations, sovereignty refers to a power whose features can be divided into two elements: its original character, which does not depend on any temporal authority, and its claim to universal extension. Nothing stands above sovereignty: the only justification for the power of Princes is its divine origin. Nor is there anything beyond sovereignty, which fosters the claim that Empires are destined to extend their power to the whole word. In that logic, Rome will develop the notion of *terra nullius*, a term that characterizes the lands occupied by 'barbarians'. Because these lands were not administered by recognized powers, they were considered open for conquest.

It is at the end of the Middle Ages that a radically different configuration emerges in Europe: a plurality of States proclaim their sovereignty, signalling the beginning of sovereignty's aporia. When the European Princes emancipate themselves from both the Emperors of the Holy Roman Empire (whose power had become symbolic) and the Pope, and declare that they are 'Emperors in their Kingdoms', they adopt the vertical dimension of original sovereignty: no power is superior to theirs. At the same time, they also agree to coexist with other sovereignties,[5] and, in so doing, abandon the horizontal dimension of sovereignty. The mutable 'limes' of former Empires will be replaced by the borders of modern States, which must define their territory. Yet, no principle deriving its authority from reason governs the division of territories into States. These States are born, live (sometimes briefly) and die at the whims of royal marriages, territorial imbalances, wars and population displacements. Borders are arbitrarily drawn, and expansionist greed never ceases to fuel wars.[6] At the time, international law is a law of war, supplemented by a few rules on diplomacy or ocean navigation.

The notion of consent is absent at that period, especially since each political community is represented by the person of its sovereign conceived as a mystical body that doubles the concrete reality of the monarchs' powers, in accordance with the theory of the King's two bodies.[7] The mystical or political body of the King represents the universality of the group upon which

5 Jacques Krynen, *L'empire du roi: Idées et croyances politiques en France, XIIIe-XVe siècle* (Paris: Gallimard, 1993).

6 The current war waged by Russia against Ukraine represents a contemporary resurgence of that trend.

7 Ernst Kantorowicz, *The King's Two Bodies: A Study in Medieval Political Theology* (Princeton: Princeton University Press, Princeton Classics, 2016).

he reigns. This body never dies, ensuring the State's continuity. Yet, paradoxically, the notion of universality is applied to a limited group (that of a precise kingdom), and no political or legal thought arises to express the idea of an unlimited universality, that of all the peoples of the world. This doctrine applies to distinct, and even competing, powers, and does not allow for a conceptualization of a global community of peoples.

A European legal order is only sketched with the emergence of the Westphalian system in 1635. This order is durably grounded in States' sovereignty. Jean Bodin had elaborated the legal theory of sovereignty in France half a century earlier. Bodin makes sovereignty a defining feature of the State, both internally and externally. He defines sovereignty as a domination that dispenses with consent altogether, because, in his view, sovereignty amounts to the power of ruling without the subject's consent.[8] At the time, the European Monarchies rely upon divine law to legitimize their power. These powers, known as 'sovereign' powers, derive their unlimited nature from that of the Pope. The distinctive feature of sovereignty remains its unrestricted nature. It corresponds to the capacity of transforming violence into law, and the sovereign is in command of the wand that enables that alchemy. The doctrine of regalian powers – those powers which are by nature considered as the sovereign's monopolies, including the power to wage (aggressive) war – lays the foundation for sovereignty's structure and completes its theoretical construction.

From then on, each national society is considered unified under the monarch's authority, even if the populations and the lords convening under the king's authority and leadership appear to be fundamentally heterogeneous. Sovereignty absorbs all of a society's contradictions and appears as the one and only source of the binding character of domestic norms and of the State's commitments in the international sphere. Sovereignty is the source of States' power to solve international issues by resorting to war. This will last until the nineteenth century. The German *Kompetenz-Kompetenz* doctrine will further add to this doctrinal construction with Georg Jellinek's proposal to define State sovereignty as the capacity to determine its own legal order.[9] Under such an approach, the international society becomes a juxtaposition of distinct, rival and sometimes even adversary, societies.

8 Jean Bodin, 'Concerning Sovereignty', in Jean Bodin, *Six Books of the Commonwealth*, translated by Marian J. Tooley (Oxford: Blackwell, 1967), pp. 24–35.

9 Georg Jellinek, *L'état moderne et son droit*, Vols. 1, 2, translated by Georges Fardis, introduction by Olivier Jouanjan (Paris: Éditions Panthéon-Assas, Les Introuvables, 2005).

It must be acknowledged that this assessment only pertains to European societies. Yet, political and legal concepts coined in the West will also influence other societies through colonization, and, later, decolonization.

Even when it was flourishing, the absolutist conception of State sovereignty – which allows State leaders to exercise power and state the law without requiring anyone else's consent – was not without its detractors. In the middle of the sixteenth century and a few decades before Bodin's theory of sovereignty, Étienne de La Boétie understood the risk inherent to domination. La Boétie calls it tyranny, because domination is power governing through voluntary servitude. This tyranny is at the opposite of La Boétie's understanding of political power. In his view, political power is the communion of free wills, looking for each other in 'l'entreconnaissance', that is in mutual recognition and fellowship.[10] La Boétie highlights how servitude is established by the power of one man. But for La Boétie, this One who symbolizes the State is no one but the strange paradox by which a whole people recognizes itself in the power of One alone, the sovereign. Yet, the unity between that people and the power that personifies it is a mere façade, because of the division between those who command and those who obey. Power, no matter who holds it, organizes each nation hierarchically.

The great lesson taught by La Boétie's writings is the distinction between two types of consent. One type of consent is blindly given in acceptance of tyranny; this leads to servitude. The social contract fiction developed a few centuries later will only reinforce that servitude. For La Boétie, the consent that leads to freedom may only originate from the heart of the universally shared principle of reason, because we all come 'from the same mould'.[11] While the mould is the same, we are nonetheless all different. According to La Boétie, what is important is mutual recognition, and the tension between singularity and multiplicity, because there cannot be freedom without acceptance of otherness. As a result, consent may not be delegated. It is necessarily continuous and exercised by fully free subjects who build their consent attendant to the circumstances.

In the seventeenth century, Hugo Grotius develops a fulsome theory of international law. At first, Grotius embraces the view of sovereignty as grounded in divine law. From that approach, the sovereign's power to govern owes nothing to consent. But Grotius will admit that sovereignties are limited by natural law, which he associates with the principle of right reason. Grotius will distinguish this natural law from voluntary law. The latter arises from the

[10] Étienne de La Boétie, *Le discours de la servitude volontaire* (Paris: Payot, 1978).

[11] Ibid.

nations' will when they conclude treaties in accordance with the principle of *pacta sunt servanda*. This understanding introduces a first ground of consent into international law, one that is attached to the will of States. But in 1625, in *On the Law of War and Peace*, Grotius analyses the question of sovereignty in greater depth. The outcome is a slightly different type of consent. Grotius no longer only envisions the consent of sovereigns who reach an agreement, but also the consent of the associates who form the basis of the polity. In his view, sovereignty first belongs to the polity as an association. Yet, Grotius does not follow the path to freedom all the way. In his view, the people can entrust its sovereignty to a single person or to an assembly. As its custodian, may the sovereign then wield the sovereignty that the people entrusted to him or her? Grotius introduces a new distinction: if the people's consent has been forced by conquest, the sovereign may use it as a property. But Grotius also adds: '[b]ut as to Kingdoms which were originally established by the full and free Consent of the People, I confess it cannot be presumed, that it was ever their Design to allow the King to alienate the Sovereignty'.[12]

This analysis reveals that in the period before the diffusion of Enlightenment thinking, the notion of consent to international law surfaces in some authors' works, but only timidly.

13.3 'THE PEOPLE' STEPS ONTO THE STAGE

Prepared by the eighteenth-century philosophers, the emergence of the people as a political subject imposes itself in the West, particularly in the wake of the American and French revolutions. Democracy will progressively be considered as the foundation of the State's legitimacy and of the law that it enacts. But the term 'democracy' is not unequivocal, and the search for freedom's ways proceeds by trials and errors. Sovereignty will not disappear from the political landscape. Yet, because thinkers still ignore that sovereignty contradicts freedom – Hannah Arendt will, much later, admit to this viewpoint[13] – they strive to consider them ultimately compatible. The notion of sovereignty will meander, going from *the sovereignty of the monarch* to *the*

[12] Hugo Grotius, 'The Division of War into Public and Private: An Explication of the Supreme Power', in Hugo Grotius, *The Rights of War and Peace*, Vol. 1 (Indianapolis: Liberty Fund, 2005), pp. 240–335; Hugo Grotius, 'Of an Oath', in Grotius, *The Rights of War and Peace*, fn. 12, pp. 768–801.

[13] Hannah Arendt, *The Human Condition*, 2nd ed. (Chicago: The University of Chicago Press, 1998), p. 234: 'If it were true that sovereignty and freedom are the same, then indeed no man could be free, because sovereignty, the ideal of uncompromising self-sufficiency and mastership, is contradictory to the very condition of plurality.'

sovereignty of the people, and then *to the sovereignty of the nation*, eventually falling back in the sole rulers' hands with *State sovereignty*.

Along with Enlightenment philosophy, the understanding of internal sovereignty will evolve in States claiming to be democratic, but the question of consent to the law has yet to impose itself. In Thomas Hobbes' conception, the social contract implies no reduction in State power since the sovereign's rights remain unrestricted. And the people becomes a single entity through representation and the fiction of the general will. The people is the social substrate of the sovereign State, itself considered as a legal person. The assumption is that the consent of the members of the multitude builds a single will, which is the will of all.[14] Consent is blended in representation. Jean-Jacques Rousseau will take an important step forward by conceptualizing popular sovereignty as the only kind of sovereignty. From then on, Bodin's conception of sovereignty is inverted: there is no sovereignty *upon* the people, but only the sovereignty *of* the people. And the people, by means of association, opens the way to the general will.

But in political thought, the notion of a 'people' and its political identification elicit difficult questions that obscure a clear statement of which subject has to consent to law. Assuming that a people is a human group identified as homogenous, may democracy be preserved through representation mechanisms such as those developed and standardized in the vast majority of the States of the world, that is, through the mechanisms of parliamentary representation?[15] The 'people', whose general will the State purports to convey, expresses its will at distant intervals only, and according to the prescriptions of electoral laws. Depending on the society at issue, the State will be more or less Jacobinist, and most often displaying a vertical political power. Is it then possible to assert that there is identification between the people and the State? As is well known, direct democracy is the only form of democracy that allows for a full identification between those who govern and those who are governed, but it is only achievable in societies with a small number of members. As soon as there is representation, the risk exists that representatives 'derive towards a sovereignty position'.[16]

[14] Thomas Hobbes, *Leviathan*, edited by Michael Oakeshott (New York: Simon & Schuster, 1969), p. 127: 'A multitude of men, are made one person, when they are by one man, or one person, represented; so that it be done with the consent of every one of that multitude in particular.'

[15] On this issue, see Ernst-Wolfgang Böckenförde, *Le droit, l'État et la constitution démocratique: Essais de théorie juridique, politique et constitutionnelle*, translated and edited by Olivier Jouanjan (Brussels: Bruylant, LGDJ, 2000).

[16] Ibid., p. 302.

For the expression of the people's will to remain democratic in a representative system, it is necessary that the representatives be authorized not on a permanent basis, but rather as part of a renewing cycle of democratic expression. This is what Ernst-Wolfgang Böckenförde refers to as the material concept of representation, which he distinguishes from formal representation. Material representation presupposes that representation mechanisms be established so that the individuals concerned by a decision can identify with how representatives address their concerns and with the resulting decisions. The production of norms will then create obligations, but at the same time it will also produce consent to these norms, and, as a result, the willingness to follow them.[17]

Such interrogations of the relationship between democracy and representation remain largely absent from the analyses of international law. Despite the influence of Enlightenment ideas, the external exercise of sovereignty retains an absolute character. The effectiveness of international law depends on the expression of the consent of each State, especially because this law is essentially contractual in origin: any norm applicable to a State results from the expression of its will, and may cease to be applicable to it if, by the same will, it decides to withdraw from it. The submission of disputes to the international judge also depends on State consent, as demonstrated by the voluntarist character of international justice. The sovereign is subjected to international justice only if it has consented to that submission, and the peoples are not consulted on these choices.

The emergence of the notion of 'people' will occur much later in international law than in general political philosophy. It will emerge along with the international legal developments that followed the two world wars of the twentieth century, and as humanity had become aware of the risks posed if the society of States is not grounded on democratic law. In 1945, the UN Charter appears to be a new attempt at renewing the principles in this area. The peoples' consent surfaces in several respects.

On the one hand, consent is taken into account to guarantee the effectiveness of the principle of the right of peoples to self-determination. Yet, when international law considered that each State may not necessarily represent a homogenous people and included the term 'people' in its vocabulary, a singular historical experience guided that inclusion: that of colonization/decolonization. At the time, the term was most often used to refer to the populations who had been subjected to the colonial yoke of European powers.

[17] Ibid., p. 304.

When the question of the identification of a people was raised outside of that historical context, international law remained opaque about the definition of a people, leading to endless conflicts. As a result, the fictional identification people/State has remained the formal solution to that fundamental question. The consent to norms remains reduced to the consent of States. At the time, few in the international sphere were concerned about whether each State's will would actually represent the will of its people – assuming that the expression 'a people's will' has a meaning, a question to which I will return.

On the other hand, the goals of the UN include respect for human rights and fundamental freedoms for all. Given that the first of such freedoms is that of participating in an electoral process for designating those who will be in charge of making the law, there seems to be a basis for a universal doctrine of consent to law. The resulting conception of law is, consequently, very formalistic. Once States' representatives have been elected, each people is supposed to have given its consent to those who will represent them. These representatives have a mandate to consent to international law through their adhesion to treaties, or by the mechanism of custom formation.

One must add that the UN Charter elides a number of contradictions that have led that institution to the stalemate in which it languishes today. On the one hand, the UN Charter promotes the development of international law, which will only thrive if it imposes itself on States. On the other hand, the UN Charter guarantees State sovereignty, allowing States to shelter behind their 'consent' to international law to select the norms to which they adhere. Admittedly, what the UN Charter guarantees is 'the sovereign equality' of States (Article 2, para. 1). But no sooner was equality professed than it was broken in favour of the five permanent Members. While sovereignty is being consecrated, certain sovereignties are more powerful than others.

13.4 A CONSENT BIASED IN BOTH THEORY AND PRACTICE

A critical reflection on consent to international law raises the question of whether the concurring will of States corresponds to an actual endorsement to this law on the part of the peoples comprising the global society. Various perils threaten the human community as a whole. To confront them, the human community needs solidarity, and, more than ever, international law has to be the link establishing the people of the world as a global political community. It is true that the consciousness of belonging to such a universal community is still embryonic. It becomes perceptible in the efforts to address common challenges such as environmental threats, or proven risks such as sanitary crises, wars and economic or commercial interdependences. The difficulty lies in the current absence of an institution representing what this 'world community' would be. The only existing institutions are international intergovernmental institutions that merely reflect the world's division into separate societies, when international law must respond to challenges that go beyond States or groups of States and must be addressed on a higher scale. The formal consent of States alone may not satisfy the critical need for endorsement of the norm on the part of those concerned by the application of the law that seeks to meet such challenges.

This legitimacy requirement sheds light on deficiencies that need to be addressed. As for the group of States considered as 'great democracies'(to be put in quotation marks), few of them subject their international commitments to the democratic process. The notion of 'national security secrecy' is used to conceal numerous decisions. In France, foreign policy and military commitments are the exclusive prerogatives of the Head of the State who incarnates sovereignty, without control by the people's representatives and with a mere duty to inform the Parliament. France's positions on international law are the reserved domain of its Head of State and its Minister of Foreign Affairs. Such positions are also subordinated to the French Constitution as applied by domestic courts. At times, these courts oppose international law's application in the domestic sphere on the pretence that some treaties are not self-executing. In such cases, the consent given to the norm's adoption does not amount to a guarantee of its application.

In many other States, power is not democratic or is only nominally democratic by virtue of the occurrence of 'elections' that do not reflect the people's actual consent to the norms enacted by those in power. In States with an official religion, elected assemblies only serve as a smoke screen for powers that are still considered to be of divine right. These assemblies ensure that secular norms coincide with the religion's imperatives, such as in States where Islam is the official religion.

Moreover, many groups have not reached Statehood or do not recognize themselves in the States in which they are included. This is the case, for example, for the millions of refugees and migrants who no longer reside in their own country and are not represented. Their accession to the status of subjects of international law requires an effort of institutional imagination that has not yet taken place. This is also the case for peoples without States, for some minorities, for so-called overseas territories, and, sometimes, for certain regions. These human groups have sometimes endowed themselves with political structures, and some Stateless peoples have acquired observer status in international institutions, but efforts to provide agency to these groups has not gone so far as to reconceptualizing how they could express consent or dissent under international law. Even when minorities, overseas territories or regions have purportedly representative institutions, those remain derivative of the sovereign States that oversee them. As a result, demands to take certain positions with regard to international law occasionally surface from the depth of these societies and spill over beyond their States. For example, some large cities have broken free from the views of their own State in matters relating to environmental protection or migrants.[18] But positive law is not able to take this into account; it is sovereignty that is at stake. Regions and cities, even in highly decentralized States, derive their powers, and even their existence, from an act of the State, the only subject endowed with sovereignty. For these entities to get access to the procedures of consent to international law on an equal footing as States, the paradigm upon which the international society is built would have to change. Yet, there is no indication that such a change is on its way.

Since international law is based on formalism, it adheres to the expressions of consent made by States. But the consent expressed by the majority of the States that participate in a vote cannot convey the international community's 'general will'. Such a contrivance is untenable. The vote in the UN General Assembly on the Resolution condemning the Russian aggression against Ukraine on 2 March 2022 offers a stark example.[19] This Resolution was apparently adopted by a large majority of States. But a look at the respective demography of the five States that voted against it, of the thirty-five that abstained, and of a few others that were absent at the time of the vote shows that almost half of the people who live on the planet did not support the measures taken by the Western States. Is it possible to consider that there has been 'consent' to that resolution?

The reflection on these issues must be renewed. But we are not left to begin from scratch: while contemporary international legal theory has not devoted much attention to the question of consent and its relationship to sovereignty, the topic had been addressed in a more comprehensive fashion in other periods. Léon Duguit's and Maurice Hauriou's public law theories on institutions, for example, can shed light on these questions. And, in particular, Hannah Arendt and the philosophers who have advanced her theories appear to be in a position to help with the elaboration of a theory of consent, one

[18] Samantha Besson and José Luis Martí, 'Cities as Democratic Representatives in International Law-Making', in Helmut Philipp Aust and Janne E. Nijman (eds.), *Research Handbook on International Law and Cities* (Cheltenham: Edward Elgar, 2021), pp. 341–353.

[19] UNGA Res. ES-11/1 (2 March 2022).

which would lead not to the wilting of democracy, but to its renewal on a global scale.

We must learn from Duguit and from the solidarist theories of the late nineteenth century that inspired him.[20] As the State has taken on additional functions in the economic and social realms, the doctrine of public service provided a backstop against the slide towards absolutism. This doctrine offered an alternative to the idea of public power and disputed the idea that public power could justify the use of force as a means of government. For Duguit, the State must end its position as a commanding power and become a group that works together. Social solidarity is the only possible legitimation of public action. This formula applies to the domestic level, but it could and should be transposed to the international level. Nowadays, social needs are of a plurinational scope. Satisfying such needs calls for solidarity. And yet, the compartmentalization of peoples in sovereign States places them in competition with one another, which exacerbates national self-interests and hinders the organization of interdependences.

The development of solidarities must be translated into institutions. Hauriou had noted this point, which further advances the path opened by Duguit. For Hauriou, institutions are social forms intended to be durable.[21] It is in that perspective that institutions can be alive and, at times, liberating. In the wake of these reflections, new institutions emerged such as social security in domestic societies or the International Labour Organization (hereafter ILO) at the international level. The ILO's tripartite structure is a source of inspiration for envisioning a consent to international law grounded in institutions more representative of social diversity than those only composed of States. Most specialized agencies of the UN system would gain from being administered by structures combining State representatives and representatives from the social fields relevant to their specialization. The legitimacy of norms adopted by these institutions would increase.

The demands for increased legitimacy must be pushed even further. If consent to law is key to its legitimacy – its fundamental, and not merely formal, legitimacy – and, as such, essential to its effectiveness, this consent must not be fictional. It must strive to express the endorsement of the social

[20] Claude Courvoisier, 'Propos introductifs', in Jean-Claude Beguin, Patrick Charlot and Yan Laidié (eds.), *La solidarité en droit public* (Paris: L'Harmatan, Logiques Juridiques, 2005), pp. 7–10, p. 10; Robert Lafore, 'Solidarité et doctrine publiciste: Le "solidarisme juridique hier et aujourd'hui"', in Maryvonne Hecquard-Théron (ed.), *Solidarité(s): Perspectives juridiques* (Toulouse: Presses Universitaires de Toulouse I Capitole, 2009), pp. 47–82.

[21] Maurice Hauriou, 'La théorie de l'institution et de la fondation: Essai de vitalisme social'(1925) 4 *Cahiers de la nouvelle journée* 1–147.

group in its plurality. Too often, the fiction of the general will is merely a mask for force imposing itself as law. Such a fiction is a negation of plurality. Walking in Hannah Arendt's footsteps, the philosopher Étienne Tassin has shown in a striking expression how 'the people do not want'.[22] It is so because the conception of democracy, that is the conception of liberty as developed by these philosophers in the wake of La Boétie, privileges the realities characterizing every society: otherness, multiplicity, dissensus, profuse contradictions. In such an effervescent environment, there is no pre-existing common will, as if it were expressing a spontaneous consent. A movement of the social body that could be identified as a consent to law must occur not as a supposed *general will*, but as the *will of all* expressed in a public deliberation and through a response elaborated on the basis of a clearly articulated solicitation (e.g. during a referendum), and provided that the right to interrogate the people be shared with the people itself, as is the case with the popular initiative referendum. It must be noted that when experiments in participatory democracy occur in domestic societies, these attempts are most often invested in by politically active groups to the detriment of groups that are not as active. This imbalance in participation means that some fundamental conflicts will remain latent: without groups to surface these core contradictions, they will never be overcome through the law. Such contradictions will remain unexpressed legally or politically.

At the international level, the development of social networks has in recent years allowed for the use of popular initiatives in the form of transnational petitions on global issues, particularly with regard to human rights or environmental challenges. But we are still far from a situation where it would be possible to consider some international norms as subject to popular consent. Some conditions must be met in order to conceive of the global society in its universality and in its incredible diversity, so that all may express themselves with the feeling of belonging to the human community, whose destiny is currently under dire threat.

The first and the most important of these conditions relates to the recognition of human rights-holders. In the current system based on the world's division into sovereign States, these rights depend on whether each individual holds a given nationality. As a result, a substantial number of human beings (migrants, refugees, stateless persons) are excluded from the protection of human rights, including political rights that safeguard participation to the

[22] Étienne Tassin, 'Le peuple ne veut pas' (2006) *Akadem*. Available at: https://akadem.org/sommaire/colloques/hannah-arendt-cent-ans-apres-sa-naissance/le-peuple-ne-veut-pas-27-11-2006-6793_4112.php, last accessed 13 December 2022.

procedures through which consent to the law is elaborated. Hannah Arendt forcefully denounced that situation. She stated that: '[t]he fundamental deprivation of human rights is manifested first and above all in the deprivation of a place in the world' and that 'the right to have rights, or the right of every individual to belong to humanity, should be guaranteed by humanity itself'.[23] Indeed, what foundation should we give to human rights other than belonging to the human community? What would be the meaning of the word 'universal' used in the 1948 Declaration if another conception prevailed? And yet, the foundation of human rights today remains a national foundation: the consent given by each State and in the terms according to which that consent was given through its accession to international conventions. The observation of the human rights situation in nearly every society reveals the dead end in which international law remains mired. Almost all States have, on the basis of their external sovereignty, consented to the recognition of the human rights defined in the various Covenants and Conventions. But a wide majority of States interpret their internal sovereignty as allowing them to repress their own population or the foreigners living within their territories, at times violently, in breach of those proclaimed rights. This raises the question of the authenticity of consent.

A new project by Tunisian lawyers for the creation of an International Constitutional Court would work to undergird that authenticity.[24] This effort stems from the observable lack of effective judicial review of the application by States in their domestic law of commitments made at the international level. The Human Rights Committee established to monitor the implementation of the Covenants has no binding force. A new jurisdiction seems required to verify the conformity of States' constitutions, legislation and administrative practices with their international commitments, and oblige States to change them if necessary. This would be nothing more than applying the well-known principle already recognized by many States of the primacy of international law over domestic law. The central justification for that proposal is the principle of good faith, by which a legal subject may not simultaneously pursue contradictory aims. The intervention of this new international judicial organ would compel States to adopt coherent policies, closing the gap between States' consent to written agreements and their consent as confirmed

[23] Hannah Arendt, *The Origins of Totalitarianism* (New York: HarperCollins Publishers, Mariner Books, 1976), pp. 296, 298.

[24] Constance Rémy, 'Le projet de création d'une Cour constitutionnelle internationale' (2019) 1(6) *Les Cahiers Portalis* 189–194; Monique Chemillier-Gendreau, 'Rendre possible le droit aux droits: à propos du projet de Cour Constitutionnelle Internationale', in *Mélanges en l'honneur de Dominique Rousseau* (Paris: LGDJ, 2020), pp. 621–627.

by practice. Yet, the requirement of a collective decision taken by States within the UN to create such a new judicial organ highlights the deadlock created by the domination of the notion of State sovereignty in the global political sphere.

The second condition for a truly universal approach to international law relates to the expression of consent in what could be an authentic conception of democracy on a global scale. Grounding such a conception in the expression of a general will is hazardous, because a general will may mask domination. Too many oppressive regimes manage to hide behind the name of democracy. Democracy can be revived for what it should never have ceased to be: a state of non-domination in the polity. But what are the ways to prevent the link between citizens from falling back under a hierarchy? This question is, of course, very pressing in domestic societies where so-called democratic models are increasingly strained. But it must be raised at the level of the global polity as well. How could we endow the human community with a common law that is not a tool for domination? The difficulty is daunting, because the individuals who compose that community are all similar due to their shared humanity, and all different due to their radical otherness. And the emergence of the human community is further hampered by the fact that humans are divided into sovereign States that have shared the administration of the planet's territories among themselves.

The prospects for addressing this issue remains amorphous. A slight opening was perceptible on 26 April 2022, when the United Nations General Assembly (UNGA) decided that in response to each instance of a permanent member of the Security Council employing a veto, it would automatically assemble to comment on that veto and demand justifications from that Member State.[25] Unprecedented avenues such as this one will have to be explored and invented for finding forms of consent to international law that are more reflective of the peoples concerned.[26]

As should be clear, the institutional question cannot be ignored. This question arises in each individual political community as well as in the global community. Peoples' consent to the law is channelled through their consent to the institutions charged with stating the law. Each people that has affirmed itself as a political community has developed its institutions, most often in a

[25] A/RES/76/262 26 April 2022.

[26] These points are further developed in Monique Chemillier-Gendreau, *De la guerre à la communauté universelle: Entre droit et politique* (Paris: Fayard, 2013); Monique Chemillier-Gendreau, *Pour un conseil mondial de la résistance* (Paris: Textuel, Petite Encyclopédie Critique, 2020).

State form. These differentiated communities were born out of (blood-stained) history but some bonds have formed that, over time, have proven to be lasting. These bonds deserve respect. But what must be taken into account are the particularities of each political community, and sovereignty is not needed for that. De facto interdependences require institutions enabling their realization. Yet, continental institutional levels must not absorb their constitutive communities. In that respect, the European Union (hereafter EU) has been remarkably innovative. Over time, and not without major difficulties, the EU successfully defined itself as a political community on a continental scale whose members are European citizens, but without eliminating the State communities of which it is composed. Most of all, it came into existence without asserting a new sovereignty.

Nothing would be more disastrous than to set the EU on the path of transformation into a new federal State. All the advantages of that double affiliation (of each citizen to his or her State and to the EU) would vanish. It seems preferable to advance this model further and accept the idea that cities, regions and ethnic minorities are political communities with a strong regime of autonomy that interlocks with national, continental and global communities. It is then necessary to define the allocation of competences among the different levels, but the subsidiarity principle appears to be the way to solve that repartition in accordance with principles of reason.

In any event, the political communities at these different levels need common norms and global institutions to adopt such norms in order to live and exchange with one another. Institutions created at the end of the Second World War do not seem suited to the current world. They are unable to tackle the many challenges that the peoples of the world have to face. In my view, it is the duty of lawyers to rethink the world's organization in a way that is responsive to the democratic imperative applied on a universal scale. It cannot be a new world government because that would inevitably result in a new form of domination. It is therefore necessary to take a new look at the reflection on cosmopolitanism and carve a new path that could serve as a matrix for fresh perspectives on the law and the institutions.

We must go beyond cosmopolitanism as theorized in Antiquity by the Stoics, who had imagined a world citizen abiding by a universal law common to all, and whose content was more ethical than political. Modern cosmopolitanism, which stemmed from the Renaissance's humanism and was revisited by Enlightenment thinkers, is another version. This conception of cosmopolitanism, which grew out of rival States waging war against each other, is animated by the yearning for peace, and the conviction that peace requires a political organization of the peoples articulated around the Kantian idea of a cosmopolitical law.[27] But Kant rejected the idea of a world State which would give rise to a new despotism. The only perspective left to this trend of cosmopolitanism was an alliance of the peoples that would be sealed in a Society of Nations.[28] The current international system is a bastardization of this idea: keeping State sovereignty as its central principle caused it to lose sight of the fact that citizens of States are also citizens of the world. We, humans, found ourselves confined in national identities, these locked cages depriving us from accessing the universal. To get cosmopolitanism out of this dead-end, it is necessary to follow the footsteps of Hannah Arendt and return to plurality, that is, to the welcoming of strangers despite conflict. In modern cosmospolitics, 'there are no strangers, as we all are citizens of the same world; and there are only strangers, as we all are strangers to each other'.[29] It is from there that we will be able to reinvent the relationships among States, peoples and citizens in the establishment of a common world. That common world transcends the existing communitarian worlds without disavowing them. It strives for a horizontal universal, for a community of communities. It disrupts the issue of consent, since it highlights the need to leave behind the formalist vision of consent to international law given by that law's subjects, States, and to move towards a more complex articulation of norms at various levels and resulting from diverse forms of consent.

On this point, as with others, the reflection on consent places us in a salutary situation of intellectual discomfort and I hope to have made you share that discomfort.

[27] Immanuel Kant, *On Perpetual Peace: A Philosophical Sketch*, translated by Ian Johnston (Arlington, VA: Richer Resources Publications, 2012).

[28] Norberto Bobbio, *L'état et la démocratie internationale: De l'histoire des idées à la science politique*, edited by Mario Telò and translated by Nicola Giovannini, Paul Magnette and Jean Vogel (Paris: Éditions Complexe, Études européennes, 2001).

[29] Étienne Tassin, *Un monde commun: Pour une cosmo-politique des conflits* (Paris: Seuil, La couleur des idées, 2003), p. 177: '*il n'y a pas d'étrangers puisque nous sommes tous citoyens d'un même monde; et il n'y a que des étrangers puisque nous le sommes tous les uns pour les autres.*'

14

From Equal State Consent to Equal Public Participation in International Organizations

Institutionalizing Multiple International Representation

SAMANTHA BESSON AND JOSÉ LUIS MARTÍ*

14.1 INTRODUCTION

International organizations[1] (hereafter IOs) have become pivotal to international law-making.[2] It is difficult, as a result, to imagine the international institutional order of, let us say, 2050 incorporating fewer or weaker IOs. One may not predict how IOs will evolve, of course, but it is easy to understand that they will, and probably should, become more pervasive and more powerful.

Admittedly, what IOs achieve today does not quite match the peoples of this world's expectations. It is a widely shared assessment that the law and institutions of existing IOs are not effective enough to address complex transnational challenges such as climate change, pandemics, war, hunger or extreme poverty. We need stronger IOs, able to adopt and implement

* Many thanks to Manon Fabre, Tamara Grigoras and Louis Hill for their editorial assistance, and to Paolo Palchetti, David Lefkowitz, Duncan B. Hollis, Catherine Brölmann and Pierre d'Argent for their comments and questions.

[1] '*International* organizations' are understood here as *inter-State* organizations (sometimes referred to, far too restrictively, as 'intergovernmental') or, more exactly, as *inter-public* ones. As we will argue, indeed, those IOs should be re-instituted as truly public international institutions, comprised of States and possibly of other public institutions (such as cities, regions) that may work as pivotal public institutional frameworks representing the 'peoples' or self-governing political communities: see Samantha Besson, 'Democratic Representation within International Organizations: From International Good Governance to International Good Government' (2022) 19 *International Organizations Law Review* 489–527; Samantha Besson, *The Public & Private Relation and International Law* (Leiden: Brill, in press, 2024), ch. 5. The chapter will draw no further distinctions between those IOs, including by reference to their scope, size or resources, and even when they present themselves as 'technical' and not 'political' as a result. Democratic legitimacy should be expected of all of them when they claim to adopt international law, albeit in different ways, of course.

[2] Because the answer to the analytical question of the 'legality' of international law cannot entirely be separated from that to the normative question of its 'legitimacy', we abstain from specifying the concept of international 'law-making' at this stage.

international law and exert institutional power to deliver effective solutions to those problems. True, some IOs already exert significant power over our lives, not the least through international law-making. Paradoxically, however, they are also often criticized for doing so, especially with respect to their lack of legitimacy. Most of the time, indeed, the powers they exercise in such cases are acquired by circumventing their Member States – or, at least, a majority of them to the advantage of a minority of powerful States – and the law they adopt outside their official intergovernmental procedures is usually referred to as 'informal' or 'soft' as a result. We certainly need our IOs to be more powerful. However, delegating some of our States' powers to them to make them more effective is often perceived as too dangerous, unless we are able to secure and strengthen their democratic legitimate authority in the first place.

It is against this background that this chapter develops its argument to enhance the democratic legitimacy of IOs.[3] It does so by focusing on one of its main articulating principles: the principle of equal State consent.[4] The equal acceptance of an IO's international law and decisions by its Member States *qua* main international representatives of their peoples is, indeed, often regarded as echoing the role of equal individual consent of those States' citizens in domestic democratic self-government. From a democratic self-government perspective, consent is one way to link the authorship of the law to the latter's legitimate authority.

Our main claim is that the principle of equal State consent should be approached as part of the problem, when addressing the effectivity and the democratic deficits of IOs, but also as part of the solution due to its democratic value.

At first sight, indeed, the principle of equal State consent seems to be strangling IOs from within. In many instances, States are not only the institutions that have prevented IOs from gaining more power and being more effective, but they have also not been very good at making them democratically accountable either. For instance, should we blame the World Health Organization (hereafter WHO) for not having been able to coordinate not only more effective, but also more legitimate responses to the COVID-19

3 For a first attempt at applying the proposed multiple international representation model to IOs, see Besson, 'Democratic Representation', fn. 1; Samantha Besson, 'L'égalité des États membres de l'Union européenne: Un nouveau départ en droit international de l'organisation des États?', in Edouard Dubout (ed.), *L'égalité des États membres de l'Union européenne* (Brussels: Bruylant, 2022), pp. 263–298.

4 See Samantha Besson, 'State Consent and Disagreement in International Law-Making: Dissolving the Paradox' (2016) 29(2) *Leiden Journal of International Law* 289–316, at 290, 295.

pandemic knowing that certain States (or, at least, their governments) had been delaying, sometimes for years, the delegation of more powers to the organization and more extensive compulsory public funding? Should we hold the United Nations (hereafter UN) system itself responsible for not having done more to prevent war or extreme poverty when it has been systematically paralyzed at all levels by the veto of certain members of the Security Council? And, finally, whom should we blame for the absence of an IO specifically designed to develop and coordinate effective global strategies to mitigate climate change but States?

By action or omission, then, States, invoking the principle of equal State consent, have hindered their IOs to develop not only a more effective, but also a more democratically legitimate government.[5] At the same time, however, States undoubtedly remain the institutions setting up, organizing and controlling most IOs and, accordingly, the main drivers of international law-making therein. As such, they are also the institutions that have contributed to the increasing empowerment of certain IOs, such as the European Union (hereafter EU), and the ones actually best organized to ensure democratic representation of their peoples in themselves, but also through the public and private institutions they have gradually associated to their IOs' law-making processes.

To escape what one may refer to as the 'double bind' of equal State consent from the perspective of enhancing both the effectivity and the legitimacy of IOs and its paralyzing *cum* enabling consequences, the time has come therefore to revise the principle of equal State consent in the international law of IOs and to reassess what it should require in democratic terms.

Our argument in this chapter is four-pronged and builds on our previous work on international democratic representation.[6] By opposition to a well-established technocratic trend in the literature that understands the legitimacy

[5] For the distinction between 'governance' and 'government' and why it is better to refer to the good 'government' of IOs, see Besson, 'Democratic Representation', fn. 1.

[6] Parts of Sections 14.1–14.3 are based on Besson, fn. 4; Samantha Besson and José Luis Martí, 'Legitimate Actors of International Law-Making: Towards a Theory of International Democratic Representation' (2018) 9(3) *Jurisprudence* 504–540; Samantha Besson and José Luis Martí, 'Cities as Democratic Representatives in International Law-Making', in Helmut Philipp Aust and Janne E. Nijman (eds.), *Research Handbook on International Law and Cities* (Cheltenham: Edward Elgar, 2021), pp. 341–353. Parts of Section 14.4 are based on Besson, 'Democratic Representation', fn. 1. A complete account of our proposal for the democratic legitimacy of international law is forthcoming in Samantha Besson and José Luis Martí, *Democratic International Law-Making* (Cambridge: Cambridge University Press, in press, 2024).

of IOs mostly as depoliticized and in terms of output legitimacy,[7] we characterize such legitimacy on classic input political legitimacy grounds, and especially democratic grounds. We regard democratic legitimacy as constituted by four basic democratic principles: the principle of ultimate, effective popular control; the principle of political equality; the principle of deliberative contestability; and the principle of human rights protection (Section 14.2). In a second part of the argument, we claim that States should remain central institutions in IOs' law-making and decision-making procedures, if the aim is to comply with these four democratic principles. Submitted to certain conditions, indeed, States are still the best institutions available to represent the peoples of the world and to institute them as the publics of international law. However, we also unpack and address the many deficits that afflict States and the principle of equal State consent from the perspective of the four democratic representation principles mentioned before (Section 14.3).

In the third prong of our argument, we turn to the growing role played in IOs by so-called 'non-State actors', both public (e.g. cities, regions) and private (e.g. non-governmental organizations (hereafter NGOs), transnational corporations (hereafter TNCs), religious organizations, unions). We claim that, despite their own respective democratic shortcomings and subject to certain conditions, those institutions and organizations may contribute to correcting or, at least, complementing the role of Member States *qua* main public representatives in IOs. In turn, this could improve the overall representation of the different 'peoples' of the world instituted as different 'publics' in the context of what we have referred to, in previous publications, as the 'multiple international representation system' (Section 14.4).

Finally, we argue for the re-institution of IOs as multi-public systems of representation capable of granting systemic democratic legitimacy to IO international law-making. After considering some of their institutional virtues in democratic terms such as publicity and generality, we also consider some of their institutional drawbacks in practice, including the paralyzing role of State consent and the circumvention of (most) Member States this has given rise to in IO decision-making processes. As a first and decisive step in the process of institutional reform of IOs, we argue that the principle of equal consent – whether it is applied to States or to other public representatives – is too narrow a principle of law-making: not only does it hinder the effective government of IOs, but, with the exception of a few cases which we specify, it is not required by their democratic legitimacy either, at least when taken in its strongest sense

7 See Marieke Louis and Lucile Maertens, *Why International Organizations Hate Politics: Depoliticizing the World* (Abingdon: Routledge, 2021).

of a veto or, at least, of a refusal power. It is best replaced, we argue, except in a few institutional circumstances that warrant for refusal rights, by the principle of equal 'participation' of States, but also, and in an articulated way, of other public representatives. While we claim that the multiple instituted publics of the world should have a right to participate in IOs' everyday decision-making processes, we also argue that State representatives should remain their main representatives and be vested with the primary responsibility of articulating further public and private representation in IOs (Section 14.5).

Methodologically, what this chapter proposes is an argument in normative international legal theory: it puts forward an interpretation of international law and institutions, especially IOs, that best fits and justifies their practice. More specifically, it defends a democratic interpretation of that practice. Although the proposed democratic approach to international law relies, at least in part, on some ideal theorization, the argument is primarily an exercise in non-ideal normative theory: it reacts to deficits in political legitimacy in the international legal and institutional order, and especially in democratic representation, by making proposals. It is to be expected therefore that some of its proposals may suffer from legitimacy shortcomings of their own.

A final remark pertaining to the scope of the chapter is in order. To the extent that our topic is democratic legitimacy and representation *in* IOs, we will not be discussing consent *by* IOs.[8] As of late, however, certain IOs have become members of other IOs and, more generally, active participants in international law-making processes that take place outside of the IO. When doing so, those IOs themselves should be regarded as representatives of their Member States' peoples, which adds another layer to the system of multiple international representation articulated in this chapter.[9] That additional layer of public representation cannot be addressed, however, before the role of

[8] On consent by IOs, see Brölmann, Chapter 4 in this volume; Bordin, Chapter 11 in this volume.

[9] This is a source of confusion in the literature where the term 'representation' is used to refer to different relations in IOs: (i) the participation of Member States and their representation in the IO *qua* members (through their accredited officials and hence 'representatives' *stricto sensu*) (see, e.g., Laurence Dubin and Marie-Clotilde Runavot, 'La représentativité et la légitimité des institutions internationales', in Evelyne Lagrange and Jean-Marc Sorel (eds.), *Traité de droit des organisations internationales* (Paris: LGDJ, 2013), pp. 77–103, pp. 82–88; Stephen Mathias and Stadler Trengove, 'Membership and Representation', in Jacob K. Cogan, Ian Hurd and Ian Johnstone (eds.), *The Oxford Handbook of International Organizations* (Oxford: Oxford University Press, 2016), pp. 962–984); (ii) the (political) representation of Member States' peoples through the participation of those States (and their representatives) and other public and private institutions within those IOs (see, e.g., Dubin and Runavot, fn. 9, pp. 88–93); and (iii) the representation of Member States and/or their peoples by the IO outside of the organization (see, e.g., Louis and Maertens, fn. 7, pp. 157–169).

those IOs as background public institutions in the multiple international representation system is fully unpacked. And the latter is this chapter's purpose.

14.2 THE DEMOCRATIC LEGITIMACY OF INTERNATIONAL ORGANIZATIONS

This chapter understands (input) political legitimacy, in quite a standard way, to refer to the normative questions of who has the right to rule (or the right to adopt legal norms or participate in the adoption of such norms) and how such a right to rule should be exerted in order to generate obligations for those subject to such rule.[10]

An opposite view, quite fashionable in normative international legal theory, grounds such obligations in what is called 'output legitimacy'. It refers to the substantive merits of international legal norms, be it their substantive justice or efficacy or both. We do not discuss that view here. It suffices to note that, regardless of the output and substantive merits of international law-making, the questions of who should rule and how still make normative sense and need to be addressed separately.

Turning to the values that may constitute the normative standard of political legitimacy, we assume here that any plausible standard of political legitimacy should be democratic.

In this respect, we distance ourselves from another fashionable view in normative international legal theory: the view that addresses the normative question of the legitimacy of international law-making by reference to the Razian account of authority.[11] Times precludes discussing that view here.[12] It suffices to stress that Razian accounts of the legitimacy of international law address an important, albeit different normative question: that of the circumstances under which international law may provide moral reasons for individuals and/or States to conform with its rules. Even if supporters of the Razian

[10] See Besson and Martí, 'Legitimate Actors', fn. 6, at 508–509.

[11] See, for example, John Tasioulas, 'The Legitimacy of International Law', in Samantha Besson and John Tasioulas (eds.), *The Philosophy of International Law* (Oxford: Oxford University Press, 2010), pp. 97–117; Samantha Besson, 'The Authority of International Law: Lifting the State Veil' (2009) 31(3) *Sydney Law Review* 343–380; Joseph Raz, 'The Democratic Deficit' (2018) *King's College London Dickson Poon School of Law, Legal Studies Research Paper Series, No.* 2018-07. Available at: https://papers.ssrn.com/sol3/papers.cfm?abstract_id=3101720#, last accessed 19 October 2022; Lefkowitz, Chapter 2 in this volume.

[12] For a view of political legitimacy that is very similar to ours, see Philip Pettit, *On the People's Terms: A Republican Theory and Model of Democracy* (Cambridge: Cambridge University Press, 2012).

view also claim to be interested in the questions of who has the right to rule and of how that right should be exerted, they usually assume that such a right to rule is correlated with a duty to obey the corresponding rules. We do not share that assumption. We consider them as two logically distinct questions and grant conceptual priority to the first one. It is only once we have clarified who – which institutions – possess the right to rule and how – through which procedures and which forms of participation – those institutions should exert it, that we may ask the further question of the conditions under which the decisions made with legitimate authority may provide the people(s) subject to them with moral reasons to comply. In turn, and as we will argue in detail, this difference explains why (State) consent may be relevant to the first set of questions relating to the political legitimacy of international law, and not to the second one.

More specifically, we propose that the democratic legitimacy of any law-making institution should be assessed by reference to four basic, scalar abstract principles.[13] This also applies at the international level given the identity of the ultimate individual subjects to both domestic and international law.[14]

First of all, the principle of *ultimate, effective popular control*. It derives directly from the ideal of popular sovereignty or self-government: all peoples[15] subjected to international law should have a say in the process of making that law. They may, of course, delegate that power to representatives. The peoples should, however, retain ultimate, effective control over their representatives (who may otherwise only claim to be such) and, through them, over international institutions and decision-making processes in order to make popular sovereignty or self-government possible. This may take place through periodic elections, but not only. Second, the principle of *political equality*. The peoples represented should have an equal say, directly or through their

[13] See José Luis Martí, 'Sources and the Legitimate Authority of International Law: Democratic Legitimacy and the Sources of International Law', in Samantha Besson and Jean d'Aspremont (eds.), *The Oxford Handbook of the Sources of International Law* (Oxford: Oxford University Press, 2017), pp. 724–745, pp. 733–735.

[14] See Besson, 'The Authority', fn. 11, at 349–350.

[15] In this chapter, we understand a 'people' as a political community or citizenry and, more specifically, as a 'public', that is an instituted people, by opposition to a 'nation' or 'society' or any community pre-existing its institution. This covers the peoples or publics of States, as much as those of subnational, international or supranational public institutions that re-institute the same peoples into different publics. There is, as of yet, no global people or public for lack of a global institution of global law. See also Besson, *The Public & Private Relation*, fn. 1.

representatives, in holding that ultimate power of control.[16] This means that no people should be able to impose its views unilaterally or have significantly greater political power to determine the law than others.

Third, the principle of *deliberative contestability*. The peoples – or their representatives – should be able to contest, through deliberation, the laws and decisions made internationally. They should also have the capacity to engage in deliberative interaction with each other, thus promoting public (formal and informal) debate.[17] Fourth, the principle of *human rights' protection*. Individuals' human rights that are constitutive of their basic moral equality and enable them to exercise ultimate control should also be protected in international law-making processes and institutions in order for the latter to be democratically legitimate.

What are those four principles' implications for the legitimate institutions of international law-making, including IOs? The first democratic principle is quite clear in this respect. Given that a system of direct popular decision-making is impossible at the international level, all peoples subjected to international law necessarily have to delegate their powers to representatives. This turns the question of the democratic legitimacy of international law into one of democratic representation. Accordingly, the assessment of the democratic legitimacy of current or potential institutions of international law-making crucially depends on whether those institutions, and IOs in particular, can be said to be representative of the peoples subjected to the decisions to be made, and, more importantly, on whether the peoples enjoy access to effective mechanisms of ultimate control over their representatives and over the decision-making system as a whole.

In our traditional (modern) understanding of representative democracy, at least when it applies to domestic law-making, these four principles have required the existence of a parliament with fundamental powers of legislation whose members are elected democratically, a directly or indirectly elected executive and an independent and self-standing judiciary, among other democratic institutions. Nothing like this, of course, exists (as of yet) at the international level, including in most IOs. To that extent, the proposed conception of the democratic legitimacy of IOs cannot, and probably should not, be that of a worldwide or global democratic State with a single global people or

16 See Thomas Christiano, 'Democracy', in Edward N. Zalta (ed.), *The Stanford Encyclopaedia of Philosophy* (2015). Available at: https://plato.stanford.edu/archives/spr2015/entries/democracy, last accessed 1 July 2021, s. 2.2.3.

17 See John Parkinson and Jane Mansbridge (eds.), *Deliberative Systems: Deliberative Democracy at the Large Scale* (Cambridge: Cambridge University Press, 2012); Samantha Besson and José Luis Martí (eds.), *Deliberative Democracy and Its Discontents* (Aldershot: Ashgate, 2006).

instituted public represented by various directly or indirectly elected officials organized in legislative, executive and judicial authorities.[18]

However, this does not imply that the principles of democratic legitimacy cannot be respected in other ways. If creating a world parliament and calling for a global election is not an available option in current, far from ideal, circumstances, we should explore other ways by which people can exert ultimate, effective control over international law-making and do so in conditions of political equality, deliberative contestability and human rights' protection. This is the larger project of which this chapter is just one part, with its specific focus on democratic representation in IOs.[19]

14.3 THE DEMOCRATIC AMBIVALENCE OF STATE CONSENT IN INTERNATIONAL ORGANIZATIONS

14.3.1 *The Democratic Value of States in the International Institutional Order*

The most obvious answer to the international democratic legitimacy challenge is that the legitimate institutions of international law-making *qua* representatives of the peoples of the world be their States. This also applies to those peoples' representation in IOs to the extent that most IOs are State-based: they are still largely dependent on their Member States for their institution, operation and control.

States-based representation in IOs usually means representation by a State's government (and a delegation or mission thereof) to the extent that the latter has the right, under the domestic constitutional order of most States and as confirmed by the international general rules on treaty-making powers (e.g. Articles 7(2), 8 and 46 of the Vienna Convention on the Law of Treaties (hereafter VCLT)), to conclude international agreements under the international law of treaties, to bind their States in the latter's external relations, and hence to speak for the people of those States on the international plane. This does not, however, exclude other forms of legislative or judicial representation of the same States in IOs. This is actually confirmed by the

[18] See, for example, Robert A. Dahl, 'Can International Organizations Be Democratic? A Skeptic's View', in Ian Shapiro and Casiano Hacker-Cordon (eds.), *Democracy's Edges* (Cambridge: Cambridge University Press, 1999), pp. 19–36; Mathias Koenig-Archibugi, 'International Organizations and Democracy: An Assessment', in Luis Cabrera (ed.), *Institutional Cosmopolitanism* (Oxford: Oxford University Press, 2018), pp. 154–185.

[19] See fn. 6.

modalities of State representation in certain IOs that, for instance, encompass parliamentary delegations in some of their law-making organs.

The fact that States continue to play a central part in international law-making, including in IOs, is uncontroversial from a descriptive point of view. But how should we evaluate this normatively?

There are, to quote Thomas Christiano, at least two reasons for considering States as the primary democratically legitimate institutions of international law-making at this relatively early stage in the development of IOs: 'one, States are still by far the most effective systems for making power accountable to persons',[20] and to do so in the greatest possible respect of political equality, deliberative contestability and human rights. Second, 'these States are in a position to represent their members to the larger community'.[21] They remain, accordingly, the most important institutional mechanism for making large-scale political institutions directly accountable to people.

Of course, States have been legally instituted in the course of time so as to best fit the requirements of democratic representation domestically. This is also true under the contemporary international law of statehood. That law guarantees the dimensions of statehood that best match some of the factual conditions for the justification of political equality and of the claim to democracy in the first place.[22] Those dimensions are, in particular, a territory, a stable population whose members (nationals) share an effective connection to one another and hence equal and interdependent stakes, and the capacity for effective government.[23]

Importantly, the inherent democratic qualities of statehood under contemporary international law also expand outside domestic borders to apply to international relations. This is, for instance, the case of the principle of 'sovereign equality', first guaranteed in writing in the 1945 UN Charter (Article 2(1)), and which expressly ties State sovereignty to State equality.[24] With the re-institution of States as equals in the 1945 international

[20] Thomas Christiano, 'Replies to David Alvarez, David Lefkowitz, and Michael Blake' (2016) 4 *Law, Ethics and Philosophy* 221–236, at 223.

[21] Ibid., at 223.

[22] Samantha Besson, 'Investment Citizenship and Democracy in a Global Age: Towards a Democratic Interpretation of International Nationality Law' (2019) 29(4) *Swiss Review of International and European Law* 525–547, at 534–536.

[23] Thomas Christiano, 'Democratic Legitimacy and International Institutions', in Besson and Tasioulas, fn. 11, pp. 119–138, pp. 121–122.

[24] Hans Kelsen, 'The Principle of Sovereign Equality of States as a Basis for International Organization' (1944) 53(2) *The Yale Law Journal* 207–220, at 208; Ulrich K. Preuss, 'Equality of States: Its Meaning in a Constitutionalized Global Order' (2008) 9(1) *Chicago Journal of International Law* 17–50, at 27; Marcelo G. Kohen, 'Article 2, paragraphe 1', in Jean-Pierre

institutional order, sovereign equality became closely related not only to peoples' equality in collective self-determination, but also to individual political equality within those States.[25] Of course, individual and State equality are not fully transitive and treating States equally may not lead to treating all individuals equally.[26] As we will see, democratic correctives (for instance, proportional voting, weighted majorities) are required to ensure the equality of domestic citizens even under conditions of perfect State equality in international law-making.[27] And the same may be argued about human rights to protect individual equality even in those circumstances. All the same, the guarantee of State equality under international law and State's equal rights in IOs in particular make the representation by equal States in IOs the best approximation of the equal representation of their peoples.

The main instrument, albeit not the only one, for the equal participation of States in international law-making, and hence for the representation of their people in that process, has been equal State consent. While State consent clearly has democratic value (Section 14.3.2), it also suffers from democratic deficits (Section 14.3.3), however.

14.3.2 *The Democratic Value of State Consent in International Organizations*

Even though it has changed in nature over time, and other chapters in this volume assess the depth and extent of that change, State consent still plays an important role in international law-making.[28] It is widely recognized as a principle of international law. To this day, indeed, international legal obligations are, but for a few exceptions, not imposed on a given State without its

Cot, Alain Pellet and Mathias Forteau (eds.), *La Charte des Nations Unies: Commentaires article par article*, 3rd ed. (Paris: Economica, 2005), pp. 402–404.

25 Samantha Besson, 'Sovereign States and Their International Institutional Order: Carrying Forward Dworkin's Work on the Political Legitimacy of International Law' (2020) 2(2) *Jus Cogens* 111–138, at 113, 127. See also Larry Siedentop, 'Political Theory and Ideology: The Case of the State', in David Miller and Larry Siedentop (eds.), *The Nature of Political Theory* (Oxford: Oxford University Press/Clarendon Press, 1983), pp. 53–73.

26 Lora Anne Viola, Duncan Snidal and Michael Zürn, 'Sovereign (In)equality in the Evolution of the International System', in Stephan Leibfried, Evelyne Huber, Matthew Lange, Jonah D. Levy, Frank Nullmeier and John D. Stephens (eds.), *The Oxford Handbook of Transformations of the State* (Oxford: Oxford University Press, 2015), pp. 221–236, pp. 231–232.

27 On the relationship between individual equality, the equality of peoples and State sovereign equality under international law, see Besson, 'L'égalité des États membres de l'Union européenne', fn. 3.

28 Besson, fn. 4, at 298–305; Besson, Introduction in this volume.

consent.[29] The requirement of State consent to international law is not only an observable reality, but also one that we argue is democratically justified.[30]

At this stage, it is worth emphasizing, however, that just as individuals' consent cannot be either a condition of the validity of domestic law or a moral reason to obey it,[31] State consent to international law, understood here as acceptance of that law, does not amount to a requirement of either the validity or the legitimate authority of international law understood in this limited, Razian way. Still, it is this chapter's argument that the role of State consent goes beyond merely enhancing general respect and compliance with international law, however.[32] Even if State consent does not give rise to an actual reason for that State to obey international law, its central role in contemporary international law has to do with its contribution to the latter's democratic legitimacy.[33] And even more so in the circumstances of widespread and persistent reasonable disagreement that characterizes international law-making today.[34]

At first, of course, such an argument for democratic State consent may sound paradoxical. Indeed, domestically, the role individual consent may play in furthering democratic legitimacy has long been disparaged precisely because of reasonable disagreement.[35] As a matter of fact, the equality-based justification of democracy accounts for majority rule instead of unanimity or even minority rule, thus making consent to law, at least when it is understood as a veto right, procedurally irrelevant to the latter's democratic legitimacy.

Importantly, however, democratic considerations in international law should not be conflated with domestic ones. Indeed, and contrary to what one often reads, States *qua* democratic representatives of their people cannot be treated as equal individual members of an international democratic polity in the same way as individuals are to be considered as equal members of a domestic democracy. Still, the importance of democratic legitimacy

29 See, for example, *Legality of the Threat or Use of Nuclear Weapons (Advisory Opinion)* [1996] ICJ Rep. 226, para. 21.

30 See, for a full argument, Besson, fn. 4, at 305–309; Samantha Besson, 'Law beyond the State: A Reply to Liam Murphy' (2017) 28(1) *European Journal of International Law* 233–240, at 238–240.

31 Joseph Raz, *The Morality of Freedom* (Oxford: Oxford University Press, 1986), pp. 88–94.

32 Liam Murphy, 'Law beyond the State: Some Philosophical Questions' (2017) 28(1) *European Journal of International Law* 203–232, at 229–232; Lefkowitz, Chapter 2 in this volume; Besson, 'The Authority', fn. 11, at 371–372.

33 Besson and Martí, 'Legitimate Actors', fn. 6, at 514–515.

34 Besson, fn. 4, at 305–312; Thomas Christiano, 'The Legitimacy of International Institutions', in Andrei Marmor (ed.), *The Routledge Companions to Philosophy of Law* (New York: Routledge, 2015), pp. 380–394.

35 Christiano, fn. 34.

domestically implies that we should try to respect the principles of democracy in the way we make international law, and especially the political equality of the peoples of democratic States.

In that context, State consent remains the most important means to protect the value of domestic self-government.[36] It amounts, after all, to the right to consent of a public and sovereign institution claiming to represent and bind a people and to institute it as a public domestically.[37] The way to link international law-making processes to domestic democratic legitimacy is precisely to respect the equality of each democratic State *qua* (States) people and *qua* equal (States)people. The requirement of equal consent of States enables small and weak States to resist the domination and the hegemony of large and powerful States or coalition of States. In turn, States' equal consent protects the individual citizens of those States' right to an equal voice in the broader international decision-making process they are participating in through their States as representatives.[38]

As a matter of fact, it is because democratic State consent should be considered an important dimension of the democratic legitimacy of international law that there also are inherent democratic limits to it.[39] Those limits, also sometimes referred to as *jus cogens* limits to State consent, amount to the protection of the basic conditions of democracy, that is political equality (including States' sovereign equality) and human rights. This explains why State consent may not be invoked as a democratic justification for the renouncement to equal participatory rights in an IO.[40]

14.3.3 *The Democratic Deficits of State Consent in International Organizations*

State consent also suffers from serious shortcomings from a democratic perspective. There are, we submit, at least six sources of concern with State consent by reference to two of the principles of democratic legitimacy

36 Christiano, fn. 23, pp. 123–124; Pettit, fn. 12, pp. 157–160; Philip Pettit, 'Legitimate International Institutions: A Neo-Republican Perspective', in Besson and Tasioulas, fn. 11, pp. 139–161, pp. 151, 155–160.

37 Besson, fn. 4, at 304–305; Timothy Endicott, 'The Logic of Freedom and Power', in Besson and Tasioulas, fn. 11, pp. 245–259, pp. 255–259.

38 Christiano, fn. 23, pp. 135–136.

39 Ibid., pp. 133–135; Besson, fn. 4, at 309–312.

40 Besson, 'L'égalité des États membres de l'Union européenne', fn. 3; Kohen, fn. 4, p. 402.

introduced in Section 14.2: ultimate, effective popular control and political equality.[41]

To start with, and in a nutshell, there are two main democratic deficits of State consent with respect to the democratic requirement of *representativeness* or effective, ultimate popular control.

First, the *existence of non-democratic States*. State consent only protects democratic self-government provided the State itself is democratic. Non-democratic States may claim to represent their people, but their claim is unwarranted for the latter cannot exercise ultimate, effective control over their State government's actions. The problem is that, currently, at least one half of the States in the world are non-democratic, according to very modest standards of democracy – for example, those of the Democracy Index.[42] Granting those non-democratic States a right to consent to international law leaves their citizens unrepresented.

Second, the *limited accountability of State governments*. State consent is blind to the actual domestic democratic accountability of State governments regarding international law-making, whether that control occurs indirectly through parliament (e.g. parliamentary approval of treaties) or directly through the people itself (e.g. popular referendum on treaties). To that extent, being a democratic State does not guarantee that its government is effectively representing its citizens. The problem then is that, since the international actions of State governments' officials are not necessarily submitted to ultimate, effective control of the people under domestic law, it is difficult to say that the consent of the government of a democratic State always ensures the international representation of that State's people.

Furthermore, even if the governments of all States in the world were democratic and internally accountable to their people, there are at least four further sources of democratic deficit of State consent that need to be addressed, this time with respect to the democratic principle of *political equality*.

First, *disproportions in demography*. Equal State consent does not pay sufficient attention to individual political equality by not being proportional to the demographic composition of States. To that extent, State consent treats the citizens of different States unequally. The problem is that, if all States have an equal right to State consent, then States with a very small population and

[41] On the democratic deficits relating to the other two democratic principles, see Besson and Martí, 'Legitimate Actors', fn. 6, at 519–520.

[42] The Economist Intelligence Unit Limited, 'Democracy Index 2021' (2022). Available at: www.eiu.com/n/campaigns/democracy-index-2021/, last accessed 20 October 2022.

their citizens hold, proportionally, much more power than those with larger ones, and this violates the principle of political equality. In effect, and without adequate correctives, the rule 'one State, one vote' in IOs tends to produce political inequalities between individuals across States. This is an implication of the lack of transitivity between individual and State equality mentioned in Section 14.3.2.

Second, the *imbalance of informal power among States*. Equal State consent does not pay sufficient attention to individual equality by not being sensitive to the power imbalance among States. To that extent, equal State consent treats the citizens of different States unequally. The problem is that, in IOs, more powerful States – in economic, military or cultural terms – are generally able to impose, formally or informally, their views and interests onto less powerful ones.[43]

Third, the existence of *permanent minorities*. Even in IOs in which State consent is not used as a veto power and to impose minority rule, there is a permanent risk of producing entrenched, persistent or permanent minorities. The problem is that even when State consent is put into practice through a mechanism of majority rule, the world can, and normally does, divide into regional or trans-regional coalitions or groups of interests. There is a risk, as a result, that some majorities and minorities of States freeze over time and over certain issues, preventing their taking turns on a broad range of issues that is required for democratic representation in law-making.[44] What this implies is that some people(s) will permanently be on the losing side in international decision-making processes because their State representatives are practically excluded from international law-making, thus violating the principle of political equality.

Fourth, the *unequal distribution of views*. State consent does not adequately reflect all views to the extent that those views are not necessarily distributed equally among States. Consequently, State consent may treat the citizens of different States unequally. For instance, the most vulnerable people according to global standards constitute a wide majority of citizens worldwide. However, they tend to be concentrated in a few, very populous countries that constitute a minority of States. As a result, and even if they share similar interests across countries, these most vulnerable people are represented very poorly by equal State consent and international law-making may be said to be unequally biased against them.

[43] Christiano, fn. 23, pp. 132–133.
[44] Ibid., pp. 133–134.

14.4 FROM STATES TO PUBLICS: MULTIPLE REPRESENTATION IN INTERNATIONAL ORGANIZATIONS

It should be clear by now that there are strong arguments of democratic legitimacy in favour of the representative role of States, especially democratic States, in IOs. Given the deficits of democratic State consent, however, the challenge is to improve the representation of the peoples who are currently under-represented by their States in IOs. This may be done by addressing two questions.

The first question pertains to the identity of the *subjects* who are to be represented in IOs' law-making processes. Contrary to a widespread understanding of IOs,[45] the subjects who should be represented by State officials in the institution and procedures of IOs are not States *per se*, but the 'peoples' that those States are particularly apt to represent internationally.

Accordingly, and to the extent that they should aim at ensuring ultimate, effective popular control, international democratic procedures cannot and should not be reduced to the kind of inter-State democracy propounded by (usually non-democratic) States that regard State equality and the principle of 'one State, one vote' in international law-making as the only requirement of international democratic legitimacy. On the contrary, from a democratic perspective, when States participate in international law-making, especially as members of IOs, it is as officials and representatives of their peoples, and not as such and in themselves.[46] Since the way those peoples are represented by their States in IOs is democratically deficient, we need to identify additional ways of representing the same peoples that may correct and complement State-based representation.

This raises a second question: could State-based representation co-exist with other *representatives* of the same peoples and, if so, which ones exactly? We argue that the same peoples may be instituted and re-instituted many times as *publics* by many different public institutions. Those public institutions may also serve as multiple representatives of those same publics in IOs, therefore. And the same may be argued about private organizations that

45 On representation at the United Nations see, for example, Catherine Amirfar, Romain Zamour and Duncan Pickard, 'Representation of Member States at the United Nations: Recent Challenges' (2022) 26(6) *ASIL Insights*. Available at: www.asil.org/insights/volume/26/issue/6, last accessed 20 October 2022.

46 Besson, 'The Authority', fn. 11, at 361–362; Jeremy Waldron, 'Are Sovereigns Entitled to the Benefit of the International Rule of Law?' (2011) 22(2) *European Journal of International Law* 315–343, at 329–330.

do not-reinstitute the same peoples as publics, but may contribute to their political representation all the same.[47]

As a matter of fact, many other public and private institutions or organizations already take part, in various capacities, in IOs procedures, including in the international law-making processes of IOs. Those other institutions are sometimes referred to as 'non-State actors' in international law. This denomination does not only reveal the latter's incomplete institutionalization under international law,[48] but also the need to differentiate them more adequately from States and then to articulate them to one another. Those non-State public institutions include, in particular, cities and regions, some elected and some not, but also other IOs. Private organizations include, for instance, NGOs, TNCs, religious organizations and trade unions.

Representation by those other public and private institutions may actually compensate for some of the democratic deficits of State-based representation in IOs by both correcting those deficits in certain cases and by complementing State-based representation of the same peoples in others. For instance, other non-State public institutions such as cities are often elected or, at least, more directly accountable to peoples than States, including with respect to international matters and even in non-democratic States. As to NGOs, they often protect the interests of domestic or international minorities and may correct some of the political inequalities of State-based representation.

Importantly, however, for this kind of complementary international representation to take place, those other public and private institutions should also be controlled effectively by the peoples they represent. More generally, they should comply with the four principles of democratic legitimacy presented in Section 14.2. This should be emphasized particularly for private organizations such as NGOs, which may only be considered as 'participants' in international law-making in a representative capacity, and not as such and in themselves. This approach certainly differs from what many authors seem to consider,[49] especially when they refer to 'civil society' or 'stakeholder' 'participation' in

[47] On the distinction between the 'public' and the 'political' and the distinction and articulation between public and private political representation, see Besson and Martí, 'Legitimate Actors', fn. 6, at 520–526, 529–533; Besson, *The Public & Private Relation*, fn. 1, ch. 1.

[48] Samantha Besson, *Reconstructing the International Institutional Order* (Paris: OpenEdition Books/Editions du Collège de France, 2021), paras. 81–82; Besson, *The Public & Private Relation*, fn. 1, ch. 5.

[49] See, for example, Dubin and Runavot, fn. 9, pp. 86–88.

IOs as a form of 'direct democracy' and independently from the question of democratic representation.[50]

Once we look at those non-State public and private institutions or organizations as representatives, however, it becomes clear that they actually not only suffer from democratic deficits akin to those of States, but also from some of their own. It is the case of non-State public institutions like cities that may not represent all peoples in the world equally, leaving rural population under-represented and over-representing urban interests and views. It is clearly also the case of private organizations such as NGOs, which are not equally distributed geographically and tend to over-represent certain groups of people. Nor are they usually controlled by those they claim to represent – provided they even claim to do so.

Due to their respective democratic deficits, therefore, neither public nor private institutions involved in international law-making should be considered as sufficient, taken on their own, to represent the peoples of the world in a way that may be considered democratically legitimate. This is what we have called elsewhere the 'insufficiency argument'.[51] In reaction to those deficits, we developed a second, systemic argument claiming that those public and private representatives should be approached not only as multiple in themselves with many publics, but also private institutions representing the same peoples at the same time, but also as constituting, together, the continuous and complementary parts of a Multiple International Representation System (hereafter MIRS).[52]

The MIRS reacts to the under-representation of peoples that characterizes the current international institutional order, including most IOs, where States

[50] See, for example, Anne Peters, 'Dual Democracy', in Jan Klabbers, Anne Peters and Geir Ulfstein (eds.), *The Constitutionalization of International Law* (Oxford: Oxford University Press, 2009), pp. 263–341, pp. 300–301, 332–333; Martin Krajewski, 'International Organizations or Institutions, Democratic Legitimacy' (last updated March 2019) in Rüdiger Wolfrum (ed.), *Max Planck Encyclopedia of International Law* (Oxford: Oxford University Press, 2008). Available at: https://opil.ouplaw.com/display/10.1093/law:epil/9780199231690/law-9780199231690-e495?rskey=okrplA&result=2&prd=OPIL, last accessed 13 December 2022, para. 19. Contra: Besson and Martí, 'Legitimate Actors', fn. 6, at 526–529 and 537–539; Martine Beijerman, 'Conceptual Confusions in Debating the Role of NGOs for the Democratic Legitimacy of International Law' (2018) 9(2) *Transnational Legal Theory* 147–173.

[51] Besson and Martí, 'Legitimate Actors', fn. 6, at 533.

[52] On the corresponding argument for multiple sovereignty, see Samantha Besson and José Luis Martí, 'Republican (Multiple) Sovereignty', in Mortimer N. Sellers and Franck Lovett (eds.), *The Oxford Handbook on Republicanism* (Oxford: Oxford University Press, in press, 2023).

often still have the monopoly of representation, albeit in a way that addresses and articulates the democratic strengths and weaknesses of the various non-State public and private institutions increasingly involved to compensate for that under-representation. It proposes to maximize the representation of peoples by enabling a variety of public and private institutions to play different, complementary representative roles by understanding those roles as part of a system of multiple or multi-public representation.

The multiplicity of representatives we endorse does not, however, equate with mere plurality. The proposed system[53] differs, therefore, from radical pluralist accounts of the international order which see that order, both descriptively and normatively, as the mere aggregation of several, separate institutional orders lacking any common set of rules. Multiple representation is not about aggregating representatives randomly in the hope of increasing the representativeness of the whole. Unless there is a clear articulation of those multiple representative institutions, allowing private institutions, such as TNCs or NGOs, to gain deliberative or even decision-making power in an IO in which other types of public representatives – for instance, States, regions and cities – are already representing the same peoples might end up undermining the overall representativeness of the particular IO.

As a matter of fact, and furthermore, multiplying international representative institutions without a systemic aspiration would also leave IOs exposed to a variety of conflicts among those multiple representatives. The only way to articulate competing claims to represent the same peoples is to approach IO representation primarily as a State-based system from the perspective of which Member States *qua* instituting powers of those IOs may decide on the complementary role of each further representative institution, public or private, so as to effectively enhance the democratic legitimacy of the IO. One of the implications of the systematicity of the MIRS, therefore, is that public representation should take priority over private representation, on the one hand, and that States should take priority over other non-State public representative institutions, on the other hand.

[53] Jane Mansbridge, James Bohman, Simone Chambers, Thomas Christiano, Archon Fung, John Parkinson, Dennis F. Thompson and Mark E. Warren, 'A Systematic Approach to Deliberative Democracy', in John Parkinson and Jane Mansbridge (eds.), *Deliberative Systems: Deliberative Democracy at the Large Scale* (Cambridge: Cambridge University Press, 2012), pp. 1–26; Felipe Rey, 'The Representative System' (2020) 25(1) *Critical Review of International Social and Political Philosophy* 1–24.

14.5 RE-INSTITUTING INTERNATIONAL ORGANIZATIONS: FROM EQUAL STATE CONSENT TO EQUAL PUBLIC PARTICIPATION

14.5.1 *International Organizations as Multi-Public Systems of Representation*

IOs possess many institutional virtues that make their re-institution as multi-public systems of international democratic representation possible.

This is true as much with respect to the institutional correctives, within a given IO's law, to the individual democratic shortcomings of each public or private institution representing the peoples of this world in the IO (e.g. regional quotas of NGOs), as to the mutual compensation of deficits between those multiple representative institutions through the articulation of complementary representation (e.g. additional, remedial representation by the cities or other territorial collectivities of non-democratic States).[54]

IOs present two institutional characteristics that should be emphasized in this respect. First of all, they are *public* organizations. Having States as main institutional members, IOs have the capacity to guarantee the central place and, as argued in Section 14.4, the priority of public representation in international law-making over the one exerted by private organizations. Their publicity makes them well suited, in turn, to require and to articulate the ultimate, effective popular control of the instituted publics over their multiple representatives, public or private. Second, IOs are *general*, whether they are universal or regional. They are not primarily organized as clubs, therefore, but are open to the membership of any State in the region or the world that is willing to join. This is one of the reasons why they are well suited to protect political equality,[55] not only by granting each State a seat and a vote, but also by reducing the existing political inequalities among (States)peoples through demographic correctives.[56]

Whatever the general virtues of IOs for the institution of a multiple international representation system, one should also warn against some of their in-built institutional defects that threaten that prospect by undermining

54 For a detailed analysis, see Besson, 'Democratic Representation', fn. 1.

55 Besson, 'L'égalité des États membres de l'Union européenne', fn. 3.

56 See, for example, Boutros Boutros-Ghali, 'Le principe d'égalité des États et les organisations internationales' (Volume 100) *Collected Courses of the Hague Academy of International Law*, 1960, pp. 9–71.

their publicity,[57] generality, and hence their own overall democratic representativeness.[58]

In turn, this actually explains why, in spite of their formally general and egalitarian legal framework, IOs have had a mixed record in terms of protecting political equality in practice. IOs' capacity to correct political inequalities between States and between the peoples they represent as publics is as high nowadays as their ability to multiply those inequalities and even entrench or institutionalize them. This may be exemplified by various types of 'hierarchical' and/or 'exclusive' multilateralism at work inside contemporary IOs.[59]

The reasons for this state of IOs lie primarily in the depoliticized and largely technocratic original institutional set-up of IOs, mentioned in the introduction of this chapter, and in its reliance on output legitimacy or on expertise-driven input legitimacy. As a result, State membership of IOs is mostly approached through a 'principal–agent' lens and not as a case of political institution and representation. The situation has worsened with the various 'good governance' and managerial measures adopted to contain the increase in IO powers since the 1990s and which have been criticized for their further depoliticizing effects.[60]

Ironically, what makes the situation even more difficult to criticize from a democratic perspective lies in the compensatory modes of association of non-State public and private institutions or organizations in IO processes adopted in the past few years in reaction to concerns for the political legitimacy of IOs. Those mechanisms are only political in name and not in content. They are usually justified by vague references to the need for greater 'inclusion' or

57 Thus, in light of their growing deformalization and public–private hybridization, IOs need to be re-instituted as public institutions so as to actually embody by law the public position they claim to hold and be vested by the instituted publics with the 'public authority' they claim to exercise in their 'public interest': see Samantha Besson, 'The International Public: A Farewell to Functions in International Law' (2021) 115 *American Journal of International Law Unbound* 307–311, at 311; Besson, *The Public & Private Relation*, fn. 1.

58 For a detailed analysis, see Besson, 'Democratic Representation', fn. 1.

59 Lora A. Viola, *The Closure of the International System: How Institutions Create Political Equalities and Hierarchies* (Cambridge: Cambridge University Press, 2020), pp. 187–188, 205–209; Viola *et al.*, fn. 26, pp. 230–231; Franck Petiteville, 'Bilan contrasté des organisations internationales', in Bertrand Badie and Dominique Vidal (eds.), *Un monde d'inégalités* (Paris: La Découverte, 2017), pp. 121–131; Besson, 'L'égalité des États membres de l'Union européenne', fn. 3.

60 Jochen von Bernstorff, 'Procedures of Decision-Making and the Role of Law in International Organizations', in Armin von Bogdandy, Rüdiger Wolfrum, Jochen von Bernstorff, Philipp Dann and Matthias Goldmann (eds.), *The Exercise of Public Authority by International Public Institutions: Advancing International Institutional Law* (Berlin: Springer, 2010), pp. 777–806, pp. 789–792.

'participation' of (more or all) 'stakeholders'[61] or of the 'most affected persons',[62] but without a truly political agenda. They do not articulate any representative claims, neither in themselves nor, and that is particularly striking, by reference to those of IOs' Member States.[63]

Multiple international representation cannot simply occur by chance, however. It calls for careful and systematic political reform of existing IOs and for a detailed institutional design of future ones. Those democratic reforms of the international institutional order need to be driven by the peoples represented by IO's Member States and by the other non-State public and private institutions or organizations at play, and hence by the corresponding sovereign publics themselves. This is the only hope to constrain the various public and private powers in place in the long run.

Given the centrality of States in IOs, we propose, to launch what amounts to a long series of necessary institutional reforms of IOs with a transformation of the role currently granted to equal State consent in the government of IOs. In order to launch such a democratic re-institution of IOs, equal State consent should not only be replaced, we argue, by a conception of equal State *participation* (Section 14.5.2), but the latter should also be expanded, more generally, to include the equal *public* participation of other non-State public representative institutions (Section 14.5.3).

Of course, the institutional design of international representation depends largely on the context, and there can be no 'one (institutional) design fits all'. The scope of this chapter precludes, however, addressing each IO in detail and our main albeit not exclusive example in this section will be the WHO. In several respects, indeed, the WHO exemplifies the democratic strengths and weaknesses of equal State consent in IOs,[64] not the least because of the

[61] See, for example, Joost Pauwelyn, Martino Magetti, Tim Büthe and Ayelet Berman (eds.), *Rethinking Participation in Global Governance: Voice and Influence after Stakeholder Reforms in Global Finance and Health* (Oxford: Oxford University Press, 2022).

[62] For a critical assessment, see Jochen von Bernstorff, 'New Responses to the Legitimacy Crisis of International Institutions: The Role of "Civil Society" and the Rise of the Principle of Participation of "The Most Affected" in International Institutional Law' (2021) 32(1) *European Journal of International Law* 125–157, at 152–155.

[63] Besson, 'Democratic Representation', fn. 1.

[64] See, for example, Samantha Besson, 'COVID-19 and the WHO's Political Moment' (2020) *EJIL Talk!*. Available at: www.ejiltalk.org/covid-19-and-the-whos-political-moment/, last accessed 13 December 2022; Oswald Jansen, 'Increasing the Legitimacy of the World Health Organization' (2020) *The Regulatory Review*. Available at: www.theregreview.org/2020/04/22/jansen-increasing-legitimacy-world-health-organization/, last accessed 13 December 2022; Hai Yang, 'Contesting Legitimacy of Global Governance Institutions: The Case of the World Health Organization during the Coronavirus Pandemic' (2021) 23(4) *International Studies Review* 1813–1834; Samantha Besson, 'Pour une représentation démocratique multiple au

unique international law-making powers of the World Health Assembly (hereafter WHA) (of States).[65]

14.5.2 *From Equal State Consent to Equal State Participation*

As explained in Section 14.3.2, States' representation role in IOs have been exercised primarily through State consent. Because the principle of equal State consent in IOs was originally understood in a strict sense as a right to veto, it quickly became incapacitating for the daily government of IOs. In turn, this explains why many IOs and their Member States have moved away from the strict enforcement of equal State consent in the internal organization and government of IOs. State consent has first turned unequal at the initiative of a few (more powerful) States. More generally, functionalism and its predominantly instrumental, expertise-oriented, and output-based approach to IO legitimacy[66] have contributed to make State consent itself largely dispensable in IOs' decision-making processes to the benefit of other original or emerging public and private powers.[67]

If loosening IOs from the grip of equal State consent has made them more effective in some respects, it has also left them out of control from their Member States' peoples. This has come at a very high cost in terms of political equality and of the other principles of international democratic legitimacy of IOs that equal State consent contributes, we have argued, to protecting. It may be time, therefore, to reinstate equal State consent in the institution, operation and control of IOs, albeit in a revised democratic understanding thereof that may correct its various democratic shortcomings.

So far, we have defined the principle of equal State consent in international law as 'acceptance', that is, as the equal right of States to accept the norms of international law to which they and their represented and instituted publics are subject to. The question, however, is what exactly should be understood by

sein de l'Organisation mondiale de la Santé', in Olivier de Frouville and Dominique Rousseau (eds.), *Démocratiser l'Espace-Monde* (Paris: Pedone, in press, 2023).

65 See, for example, José E. Alvarez, *The Impact of International Organizations on International Law* (Leiden: Brill, 2017), pp. 198–202; David P. Fidler, 'International Law and Global Public Health' (1999) 48 *Kansas Law Review* 1–58, at 20.

66 In the WHO context, see, for example, Jan Klabbers, 'The Normative Gap in International Organizations Law: The Case of the World Health Organization' (2019) 16 *International Organizations Law Review* 272–298, at 290–294. For a preliminary albeit very limited recent reckoning in this respect, see, for example, Lukasz Gruszczynski and Margherita Melillo, 'The Uneasy Coexistence of Expertise and Politics in the World Health Organization' (2022) *International Organizations Law Review* 1–31.

67 See, for example, von Bernstorff, fn. 60, pp. 776–800.

that right to accept international law, both in the practice of IOs and from a democratic perspective.

In its strongest, original version, the principle of State consent amounts to the capacity of States to exert a veto power over any legal norm or decision arising about or within an IO. It is famously exemplified by the five permanent members' veto right in the UN Security Council. Exercising such a veto in the Council means that a single State may block any decision or resolution. That right goes beyond enabling the States vested with that veto power to refuse to enter into an agreement or that a certain legal resolution agreed by others be binding for them. Indeed, their right also amounts to the capacity to prevent all others from reaching that agreement and hence from adopting any law. Interestingly, this strong version of the principle of State consent is not practised very much anymore in the internal organization of IOs. Member States' right to consent is mostly conceived of as a right of refusal or refusal power. It is also construed sometimes as a simple right to opt out at a later stage. Such refusal powers only pertain to that State's own obligations: they do not prevent other Member States in the IO from reaching an agreement and from adopting law.

This evolution of State consent in IOs from veto to refusal power is justified from a democratic perspective. The democratic value of State consent we argued for in Section 14.3.2 does not indeed require IOs' Member States to hold a veto power in that strong sense. It is enough for States to be granted a limited capacity to 'refuse' certain basic institutional decisions when they apply to them, and, for the rest, an equal capacity to participate in the making of other decisions.

The scope of this chapter precludes going into a full discussion of the egalitarian justification of majority rule in circumstances of reasonable disagreement,[68] especially when compared to minority rule or veto. Let us simply state that, first, minority rule endows minorities with more power proportionally to their number than majority rule. Second, minority rule protects organized minorities better than insular ones, although the latter need more protection against majorities than the former. Finally, although deliberation encourages the exchange of reasons, minority rule can induce minorities to use their veto to safeguard naked interests rather than reasonable opinions and convictions. By contrast to majorities, which have to be constituted in each case by deliberation, minorities know from the start that they can wave their veto and need not abide by the same deliberating rules as others.

[68] See, for example Jeremy Waldron, *Law and Disagreement* (New York: Oxford University Press, 1999), pp. 114–115; Hannah Arendt, *The Origins of Totalitarianism* (New York: Harcourt Brace Jovanovich, 1973), p. 164.

As explained in Section 14.3.2, however, one should not too quickly draw a parallel between deliberating citizens in a domestic democracy and States in IOs. The normative value of democratic State sovereignty and self-government explains the greater importance of (State) consent for the democratic legitimacy of international law than for that of domestic law. In turn, it gives us reasons to protect the refusal rights of States in a few residual areas of IO government. Outside those areas, the principles of political equality and deliberative contestability ground an interpretation of the principle of ultimate, effective popular control that may be reduced to granting (States)peoples an equal share in the control of international law-making in IOs.

Based on this qualified egalitarian defence of international majority rule, therefore, we propose moving from an understanding of the principle of State consent *qua* right to 'veto', to a principle of State 'participation' in IOs, on the one hand, qualified by a residual right to 'refuse' in a set of limited institutional circumstances, in which the cost for political equality is minimal, on the other hand.

Before clarifying our proposal and its egalitarian justification, it is useful to identify five key institutional moments or areas in the government of an IO in which States may be involved, ranging from the institution to the operation and the control of the IO: the *institution* of the IO – usually through a constitutive treaty such as the Constitution of the WHO; the *design and organization* of the IO, whether initially – through the constitutive treaty itself – or in the subsequent evolution and amendment of that design – either by amending the constitutive treaty or through the decision of the assembly of States or an equivalent body like the WHA in the case of the WHO; the *ordinary decision-making and law-making procedures* of the IO, which involves a great variety of decisions made by different bodies and at different levels – ranging from the WHA, Secretariat, General Direction or Executive Board, to lower committees, advisory boards or regional divisions, among others; the decision to *admit new members or exclude existing ones*; and the *control* of the IO, including responsibility mechanisms.

The distinction between those five institutional moments or areas is important to the extent that implementing a multi-public system of international representation in IOs calls for different solutions at each step of the institutional government of IOs. And the same applies to the role of State consent for purposes of democratic representation in those IOs.

First of all, Member States should be recognized a few, limited *refusal powers* in three sets of institutional circumstances: membership, exit and fundamental institutional decisions pertaining to the organization of the IO.

To start with, membership in IOs should not be mandatory. This means preserving the capacity of States to consent not only to institute an IO, but also to join an organization later on. Furthermore, this also implies preserving effective exit options for Member States. Finally, Member States should not have to leave an IO to refuse to take part in certain key normative developments. To that end, they should be guaranteed selective refusal rights pertaining to certain fundamental institutional obligations, for instance, through opt-out rights after a majority decision. This is, for instance, what Article 19 WHO Constitution foresees when it gives States the right not to approve the conventions or agreements adopted by a two-third majority in the WHA. What the WHO Constitution does not do, however, and we will get back to this later, is differentiate between opt-outs that pertain to fundamental institutional questions and others.

Granting refusal powers in those three instances does not amount to a serious infringement of the principle of political equality. On the contrary, not granting refusal powers to States in those circumstances would give every State a right to impose the conditions of membership to an IO on all others. This would be not only too important a departure from the current practice of international law, but would presumably benefit the most powerful States by allowing them to impose universal membership to IOs, which would result in greater political inequality. Granting equal refusal rights to every State, especially exit rights, might be the last, but crucial resort of weaker States seeking to escape the domination of more powerful ones in IOs.

Second, outside of that limited set of refusal powers, and for reasons pertaining to the democratic value of State representation, IO Member States should be guaranteed *rights to equal participation*.

This should not only apply to discussing the terms of the constitutive treaties, including the initial design of the IO, but also to the most important other decisions of the IO. Thus, those equal participation rights should include decisions to admit or to exclude a Member State and to hold the IO responsible. It is enough, in order to satisfy the requirements of democratic legitimacy, to guarantee all IOs' Member States an equal share in decision-making, that is, an equal seat, voice and vote in making those decisions.[69] Those decisions may, therefore, be adopted by majority rule, provided States have consented to that rule when instituting the IO in the first place.[70] As a

69 *Article 3, Paragraph 2, of the Treaty of Lausanne (Frontier Between Turkey and Iraq)* (Advisory Opinion) [1925] PCIJ Ser. B No. 12, p. 29.

70 Francis Cheneval, *The Government of the Peoples: On the Idea and Principles of Multilateral Democracy* (New York: Palgrave Macmillan, 2011), pp. 133–140.

matter of fact, two thirds of existing IOs today apply some kind of majority-based voting procedures. Scope precludes going into the detail of how best to design them in practice here.[71]

To illustrate our argument, it may be interesting to turn to the WHO again. States have the right to participate on an equal basis in deliberations and an equal right to vote in the decisions of the WHA, decisions that are adopted by majority rule (either a simple majority or a two-third one). As argued before in this section, it should, however, be considered democratically legitimate that those various applications of the right to equal participation do not also imply an additional veto or even a refusal power of each Member State.

Let us take the example of the United States (hereafter US) at the WHO. The US were free to join the WHO when it was instituted in 1946. And by virtue of its sovereignty, the US federal government may still decide to withdraw from the organization at any time, under the conditions established in the Constitution of the organization. For the rest, the US government has a claim to exercise its right to participate on equal terms in a number of important decisions about and in the WHO, such as decisions pertaining to how to amend its structure and organizations, how to finance it, which programmes should be most strategic, which further powers States should confer to the organization, whether a new member should be admitted or whether a current member should be excluded or, finally, whether to hold the organization responsible.

Imagine now that the WHA adopts a new treaty on pandemic prevention and preparedness that the US government considers contrary to its interests. Given that the US has the option to withdraw from the organization, the principle of equal State consent does not require, on the proposed account, giving the US, besides an equal right to vote, an additional right either to veto the convention or to opt out from that convention after the vote. Unfortunately, this is not what currently applies in the WHO. As mentioned previously in this section, the WHO Constitution grants every Member State a right to opt out from any convention or agreement adopted by a majority of the WHA (Article 20 WHO Constitution), including within the scope of the regulatory powers of the WHA (Articles 22 WHO Constitution). What this means therefore is that all Member States may exercise their consent as a refusal power. Thus, if the US considers that the proposed convention is contrary in any way to its interests, it may simply refuse it and it will not be bound by it.

[71] For a detailed discussion see, for example, Boutros-Ghali, fn. 56; Besson, 'L'égalité des États membres de l'Union européenne', fn. 3.

We consider this too strong an interpretation of what the principle of State consent requires from a democratic perspective. Certain exceptional topics that might impose a serious burden on States interests could and should be identified as such in the WHO Constitution and justify opt-out rights. In other cases, however, the WHA should be able to adopt new conventions by majority rule, as it currently does, but States in the minority should accept the result of the voting process without being granted a refusal power. They could indeed always withdraw from the organization. Admittedly, the distinction between fundamental issues that impose significant burdens on certain States' interests and those that do not, is not always clear and has to be identified specifically in each IO.

This example illustrates how the principle of State consent is often interpreted *qua* refusal power in the contemporary international law of IOs. This is also the case in universal, public and general IOs such as the WHO that have innovated by turning a veto right into a mere right to refuse and opt out at a later stage. To go back to our earlier analysis of the double bind of State consent in IOs, such a restrictive interpretation of State consent *qua* refusal power actually explains why such IOs and their Member States have found ways of disempowering or, at least, circumventing Member States' assemblies or other representative organs in practice, transferring some of their decision-making powers to less accountable technical bodies or secretariats or even to private organizations.

Against this background, the conception of the principle of State consent that we have defended here is, on the one hand, more restrictive, to the extent that it replaces, with a few exceptions, a refusal power with a right to equal participation. In so doing, the conception is, on the other hand, also more protective of State consent than the current practice of international decision-making within IOs that has mostly dispensed with equal State consent in regular decision-making processes. Our proposal's objective is to re-empower, within egalitarian limits, democratic States in their representative role in IO decision-making processes.

Note that even if State consent is understood along the proposed participatory lines and its role reformed in IOs on grounds of the political equality of States, additional reforms will be required to correct the other democratic deficits of State-only representation identified earlier in Section 14.3.3. This includes issues of demographic disproportions or permanent minorities and the further breaches of the political equality of peoples and individuals they give rise to despite the formal political equality of States.

14.5.3 *From Equal State Consent to Equal Public Participation*

Once the participation rights of States as representatives are revisited in the form of participation rights in IOs, it is important to explore not only how that public participation may be articulated with representation by other non-State public institutions, but also what those other public institutions' (distinct) participation rights should be and what they should apply to. Note that we are not considering the modalities and contexts of equal participation of other non-State private representative organizations in this chapter.[72]

Interestingly, as mentioned in Section 14.4.4, certain IOs have started reforming and defining mechanisms for their so-called 'interaction' with what they usually refer to, in a bulk, as 'non-State actors'.[73] Most of those interactions, however, are not constructed as political, as explained in Section 14.5.1, and are certainly not approached from a representative perspective. As a matter of fact, those allegedly 'participatory'[74] mechanisms, including so-called partnerships with 'stakeholders', have not even been organized so as to be very effective in participatory terms: they are mostly advisory (e.g. they give them a 'voice', but no 'vote').

Among those new mechanisms' political deficits, one should mention, first of all, that they do not clearly distinguish the participation of non-State public institutions from that of non-State private organizations. Furthermore, most of those mechanisms do not propose a clear articulation of those other institutions' and organizations' 'participation' in IOs with Member States' own participatory rights in those IOs, and this despite the fact that they represent the same peoples. As a consequence, the other public or private institutions' distant involvement in IO processes somehow dispenses those IOs and their Member States from drawing the full institutional consequences of those newly included institutions' representative role.[75] Worse, the increasing involvement of those non-State public and private institutions in IOs has actually also often come at the price of the latter's Member States' own participatory rights.[76]

The relevance of some of those critiques are best exemplified by reverting to the WHO example. Indeed, the WHO belongs to one of the most active IOs

[72] On those non-State private actors' 'consent', see Duncan B. Hollis, 'Why Consent Still Matters – Non-State Actors, Treaties and the Changing Sources of International Law' (2005) 23(1) *Berkeley Journal of International Law* 137–174. See also Besson, 'Pour une représentation démocratique multiple au sein de l'Organisation mondiale de la Santé', fn. 64.

[73] Pauwelyn *et al.*, fn. 61.

[74] See, for example, Peters, fn. 50, pp. 269, 320–322; Krajewski, fn. 50, paras. 19–20.

[75] Peter J. Spiro, 'Accounting for NGOs' (2002) 3(1) *Chicago Journal of International Law* 161–169, at 166–167.

[76] Andrew Hurrell and Nicholas Lees, 'International Organizations and the Idea of Equality', in Bob Reinalda (ed.), *Routledge Handbook of International Organization* (Abingdon: Routledge, 2013), pp. 106–118, pp. 115–116.

in extending participatory rights to non-State institutions or organizations, both public and private.[77]

To start with, WHO law has been receptive to the need to organize various interactions with other IOs. This explains how the WHO has been able to reach significant agreements of collaboration, reciprocal representation and mutual control with other IOs. However, nothing comparable has yet been articulated regarding the WHO's interactions with other non-State public institutions such as regions and cities. This is surprising given the increasing *ad hoc* implication of cities in some other IOs' standard-setting processes.[78] Of course, under Article 8 of the WHO Constitution, the latter could become Associate Members of the organization. That provision refers, indeed, to the granting of rights and obligations to 'territories or groups of territories which are not responsible for the conduct of their international relations'. However, this would require a proposition by their respective Member State that is still regarded therefore as the sole representative of the people.

True, in 2016, the WHO was the first IO to adopt the so-called Framework of Engagement with Non-State Actors.[79] Sadly, and despite its name, the Framework focuses on private organizations only.[80] It does not address the participation of non-State public institutions such as cities or regions, and the complex but sophisticated ways in which various non-State public institutions may combine to correct and complement State representation at the WHO. Moreover, even with respect to private organizations, the Framework adopts a depoliticized cost–benefit approach and, within that context, mostly emphasizes the 'risks of engagement' rather than its benefits. Finally, the Framework focuses mostly on the risks of capture by the 'private sector' involved in public–private partnerships or privatization and does not consider the representative benefits of the inclusion of other non-profit private organizations such as NGOs.

Clearly, therefore, more work is needed in specifying the participatory rights of non-State public institutions in IOs and their exact scope. It is actually an ancient question to the extent that the first IOs were open to the membership

77 See, for example, Pauwelyn *et al.*, fn. 61, s. III, and especially chs. 13, 18, pp. 245–269, 381–393.

78 Katz Cogan, 'International Organizations and Cities', in Aust and Nijman, fn. 6.

79 WHO, 'Framework of Engagement with Non-State Actors', Adopted by the World Health Assembly, WHA69.10 (28 May 2016). See also Besson, 'Pour une représentation démocratique multiple au sein de l'Organisation mondiale de la Santé', fn. 64.

80 Ayelet Berman, 'Between Participation and Capture in International Rule-Making: The WHO Framework of Engagement with Non-State Actors' (2021) 32(1) *European Journal of International Law* 227–254.

of other public institutions than States such as regions in particular.[81] Moreover, certain IOs have actually remained open to non-State institutions' membership or, at least, been revised in their constituting treaty so as to enable the inclusion of other IOs, such as the EU, as members.

Importantly, as argued in Section 14.5.2, the multi-public system of international representation does not commit us to the idea that all public representatives should enjoy the same status and rights in IOs as those of Member States.[82] Quite the opposite, actually. Two arguments may be made here with respect to political equality.

First of all, the principle of political equality should be instantiated *differently for different kinds of public institutions.*

For the reasons examined in Section 14.3.2, there are democratic reasons to grant distinct participatory rights to States only, such as the right to vote in an IO Member States' assembly. States are, after all, the primary international representatives of their peoples. Political equality therefore applies, first and foremost, to the reciprocal relations among those States. It requires that whatever rights are given to some of them, particularly in universal IOs, such as the WHO, are also granted to all other States on an equal basis.

Other types of public institutions may therefore be recognized rights different from States' without a violation of the principle of political equality. When applied to other non-State public institutions, the principle of political equality only requires that they be treated equally among themselves. For instance, if a universal IO like the WHO recognizes a city as an Associate Member with certain rights and obligations, it should grant similar rights and obligations to other cities around the world. There may be exceptions, of course, related to the remedial (and arguably temporary) role played by non-State public representatives in the current non-ideal circumstances of international law-making. It suffices here to mention the special remedial role US cities could play at the WHO in the context of a hypothetical US withdrawal from the organization. The representative role those cities would play would indeed be substantially different from that of other cities in other WHO Member States.

Second, the principle of political equality should be instantiated *differently for different processes and situations.* When we apply the principle of equal

[81] See, for example Jean-Marc Sorel, 'La prise en compte des collectivités territoriales non-étatiques par les organisations internationales à vocation universelle', in Société française pour le droit international (ed.), *Les collectivités territoriales non-étatiques dans le système juridique international* (Paris: Pedone, 2002), pp. 125–153.

[82] Besson and Martí, fn. 52.

participation to non-State public institutions, it is important to clarify what their participation consists in and what it applies to.

Thus, voting in a decision-making process, especially if it is in the WHA, cannot be identified with merely participating in a deliberative process. And the same may be said about the difference between voting on a treaty and voting on a recommendation, or voting for a lower level decision of the Board. Note, however, that the common distinction between 'having a voice' and 'having a vote' is not always very easy to make in practice. And there may be certain decisions that, even if they are crucial to the ordinary government of a particular IO, are not the kind of decisions made by its assembly of Member States. In such an instance, extending voting rights on those decisions to other public institutions, like regions, cities or even other IOs, might be the best way to enhance the democratic representativeness of the IO.

14.6 CONCLUSION

Even if, strictly speaking, consent can neither be a condition of international law's validity nor amount to a moral reason to comply with it, most obligations of international law are still regarded as 'based' on State consent and State consent contributes to the legitimacy of international law. In spite of its many drawbacks, including the slowing down of international law-making, there are, this chapter argued, good reasons for the principle of equal State consent to international law, especially from a democratic legitimacy perspective. If our concern is the democratic legitimacy of international law-making in IOs and their representativeness in particular, then equal State consent should not be dispensed with. If it is in many cases part of the problem for the effectivity of IOs, it is also part of a democratic solution thereto and should be revised accordingly.

Even in its qualified version of 'democratic State' consent, the principle of equal State consent in IOs suffers from important deficits from the point of view of democratic legitimacy. The chapter envisaged several institutional proposals to correct or, at least, complement the role of equal State consent in the institution, operation and control of IOs. While being aware of the high complexity and diversity of IOs, it developed a non-ideal normative argument for the latter's re-institution to enhance their democratic legitimacy. That process should start, it argued, with the replacement of the principle of equal State consent by that of equal public participation in IOs: doing so does not only avoid reducing State consent in IOs to State veto or even refusal powers, but it also extends the personal scope of those participatory rights to other non-State public institutions.

The chapter's proposal should be read as the first of many steps in the institutionalization of a system of multiple representation of the world's peoples *qua* multiple instituted publics. A lot remains to be clarified, however. More research is needed in particular on the increasing international representative role of IOs themselves, including in other IOs.

15

Autonomy in International Law

About the Legal and Societal Limits to the Exercise of Consent

YANNICK RADI

15.1 INTRODUCTION

'[W]hat in our usual discourse do we more familiarly and knowingly make mention of than time? ... What is time then? If nobody asks me, I know; but if I were desirous to explain it to one that should ask me, plainly I know not.'[1] Saint Augustine's well-known remark about time suits consent in international law very well; it aptly reflects the bewilderment that it causes to international lawyers. Like Saint Augustine, they seem to know what consent is at first glance. It is a matter of 'free will' and 'acceptance';[2] acceptance of a rule, of a regime, of international law as a whole. Some even argue that consent constitutes the foundation of the international legal order.[3] But, when they look at it more closely, from a practical and a theoretical standpoint, their certainties vanish and the concept remains largely indeterminate.[4]

This uncomfortable feeling has been shared by international lawyers for a long time and has led to the publication of numerous writings.[5] And yet,

[1] Saint Augustine, *Confessions*, Vol. 2 (Cambridge, MA: Harvard University Press, 2014), pp. 238–239.

[2] Samantha Besson, 'State Consent and Disagreement in International Law-Making: Dissolving the Paradox' (2016) 29(2) *Leiden Journal of International Law* 289–316, at 295.

[3] See, for example, Catherine E. Sweetser, 'Humanity as the A and Ω of Sovereignty: Four Replies to Anne Peters' (2009) 20(3) *European Journal of International Law* 549–555, at 550: 'Consent, rather than simply non-intervention, can be seen as constitutive of the international legal order; treaties and even customary international law are based on norms of state consent, whether explicit or tacit.'

[4] In this respect, Laurence Boisson de Chazournes asks whether the international community really knows what consent means beyond the general presumption within that community that consent is understood: see Boisson de Chazournes, Chapter 10 in this volume.

[5] In addition to the material referred to in this chapter, see, for example, Matthew Craven, 'The Ends of Consent', in Michael J. Boon and Dino Kritsiotis (eds.), *Conceptual and Contextual Perspectives on the Modern Law of Treaties* (Cambridge: Cambridge University Press, 2018),

consent remains an 'old chestnut' that still puzzles many theorists, as noted by Samantha Besson.[6] The present volume, which is based on presentations made by theorists and practitioners at the Collège de France, sheds interesting and complementary lights on this 'old chestnut'. This chapter, which is itself based on the concluding remarks delivered at the end of the conference, pursues a twofold objective. First, it stresses the salient ideas and remarks formulated by those speakers as also reflected in their written contributions. Second, it aims at contributing to the epistemic endeavour to better understand the 'ins and outs' of consent in international law or, to use the terms rightly chosen for the conference's and volume's title, the 'ins and outs' of consenting to international law.

As a starting point, it is worth noting that State consent has long been demythologized since *The S.S. "Lotus"*[7] in both international legal theory and international legal practice. As a matter of international relations, it is obvious that States do not hesitate to challenge consent in concrete situations when their interests so require, even though they adhere to it in general as a key principle.[8] Also, the exercise of consent – or rather the refusal to exercise it – has led to situations which have been criticized for making international law ineffective or immoral, criticisms which are more generally formulated by some about the consensual structure of international law.[9]

pp. 103–135; Duncan B. Hollis, 'Why Consent Still Matters – Non-State Actors, Treaties and the Changing Sources of International Law' (2005) 23(1) *Berkeley Journal of International Law* 137–174; Alain Pellet, 'The Normative Dilemma: Will and Consent in International Law-Making' (1992) 12(1) *Australian Yearbook of International Law* 22–53.

6 Besson, Introduction in this volume.

7 *The Case of the S.S. "Lotus" (France* v. *Turkey)* (Judgment) [1927] PCIJ Ser. A No. 10, p. 18: 'International law governs relations between independent states. The rules of law binding upon States therefore emanate from their own free will as expressed in conventions or by usages generally accepted as expressing principles of law and established in order to regulate the relations between these co-existing independent communities or with the view to the achievement of common aims. Restrictions upon the independence of States cannot therefore be presumed.' This dictum has been read as grounding international law in State consent, or in any case as acknowledging this: see, for example, Wouter G. Werner, 'State Consent as Foundational Myth', in Catherine Brölmann and Yannick Radi (eds.), *Research Handbook on the Theory and Practice of International Lawmaking* (Cheltenham: Edward Elgar, 2016), pp. 13–31, p. 13.

8 Guy Ladreit de Lacharrière, 'Tendances contradictoires en matière de consentement des États', in Société française pour le droit international, *L'élaboration du droit international public. Colloque de Toulouse* (Paris: Pedone,1975), pp. 183–203, pp. 199–201.

9 See, for example, Laurence R. Helfer, 'Nonconsensual International Lawmaking' (2008) 1 *University of Illinois Law Review* 71–125; Andrew T. Guzman, 'Against Consent' (2012) 52(4) *Virginia Journal of International Law* 747–790; Fernando R. Teson, A *Philosophy of International Law* (Abingdon: Routledge, 1998); Christian Tomuschat, 'Obligations Arising

And yet. The adherence of States to consent is obviously *à géométrie variable*; the hegemony of State consent leads obviously to situations where, for instance, the lack of effectiveness of international law is without doubt. But, is not State consent, both empirically and normatively speaking, the 'worst modality of government except for all the others', to borrow Winston Churchill's words about democracy?[10] It is probably so. In a horizontal society like the international one as it has existed since the seventeenth/eighteenth century, where there is no de jure power – neither immanent nor transcendent – there can only be relations between formal equals, each constituting, so to speak, its own 'power' in a 'constitutional' sense. In a society like the international one, the legal system is, as a matter of principle, based on autonomy: law is made of the rules each of these equals consents to be bound by or, to put it differently, it is made of the rules each of these equals gives to itself.

As it appears, consent is linked to autonomy, and more precisely, consent is the manifestation of autonomy, its vector, its vehicle. Shedding light on this link between consent and autonomy allows us, not only to better understand the concept of consent, which is not a static concept but a dynamic one,[11] but also to better understand how consent operates in practice, its importance and its limits. The exercise of autonomy, and what it teaches us about consent and consenting in international law, constitutes the focus and the common thread of this chapter.

For that purpose, it is worth specifying at the outset what autonomy means and entails in international law. As above-mentioned, being autonomous for States means that each gives itself – through its consent – the rules that apply to it. This holds true for the rules that each State gives to itself to regulate its conduct, that is for primary rules; this holds true as well for the rules that it gives to itself to ensure the enforcement of those primary rules, meaning for secondary rules. As discussed in Section 15.2.1, the autonomy of States with regard to primary rules is at the core of the theory of the sources of international law. As for enforcement, beyond the obligation for States to settle

for States Without or Against Their Will' (Volume 241) *Collected Courses of the Hague Academy of International Law*, 1993, pp. 195–374.

10 Winston Churchill, Speech delivered on 11 November 1947. Available at: https://winstonchurchill.org/resources/quotes/the-worst-form-of-government/, last accessed 10 November 2022.

11 In that sense, it is worth emphasizing the title of this volume which refers to '*consenting*' to international law and not to '*consent*' as most of the literature does. This choice also reflects the dynamic nature of the concept.

their disputes pacifically under international law,[12] their autonomy is enshrined in the principle of the free choice of means.[13] States are autonomous in that regard as they can decide the method to be used to settle the disputes to which they are a party. Compared to domestic legal orders, this autonomy is particularly remarkable in relation to adjudication, on which this chapter focuses. Indeed, courts' jurisdiction therein is characterized by its automatic and compulsory nature.[14]

That being said, it would be wrong to overestimate the prerogatives that autonomy confers to States. There are contextual limits to the exercise of autonomy – and thereby to consent – which are actually inherent in the two components of the term 'autonomy': '*auto*' (the self) and '*nomos*' (the law). Giving oneself its own rules does not take place in a societal *vacuum*. Societal constraints, linked to the relations with others and events, exist and leave no other choice to the self than taking into account circumstances and otherness in the exercise of its autonomy, and even sometimes to capitulate to others. Besides, rules, systems of rules, and the law more generally display inner-features which all come as a limit to the hegemony of the self while it gives itself its own rules. Among these features, the indeterminacy of law as a language and the argumentative nature of interpretation are key. Because of them, the rules that States give to themselves are to a large extent normative by-products of processes which are marked by the conflicting societal

[12] Art. 2(3), Charter of the United Nations and Statute of the International Court of Justice (hereafter UN Charter and ICJ Statute), 1 UNTS XVI (adopted 26 June 1945, entered into force 24 October 1945).

[13] See, for example, the Manila Declaration on the Peaceful Settlement of International Disputes, UNGA Res 37/10 (15 November 1982), para. 3: 'International disputes shall be settled on the basis of the sovereign equality of States and in accordance with the principle of free choice of means in conformity with the obligations under the Charter of the United Nations and with the principles of justice and international law.'

[14] In that sense, Brigitte Stern noted: 'On the national level, when there exists a substantive right, there is always automatically a means to protect such a right through the jurisdictional system … In contrast, on the international level, most rights cannot be enforced through a jurisdictional process, it is only when, exceptionally, the State has given its consent … that such a "jurisdictional treatment" complements the substantive treatment granted by the international rules': *Impregilo S.P.A.* v. *Argentine Republic*, ICSID, Award (21 June 2011) Case No. ARB/07/17, Concurring and Dissenting Opinion of Professor Brigitte Stern (21 June 2011), para. 45; see also *Abaclat and Others (Case formerly known as Giovanna a Beccara and Others)* v. *The Argentine Republic*, ICSID, Decision on Jurisdiction and Admissibility (4 August 2011) Case No. ARB/07/5, Dissenting Opinion of Georges Abi-Saab (28 October 2011), para 7.

dynamics and by the conflicting epistemic forces which are at play within the international society and within the international legal community.[15]

Overall, and as explained across the chapter, all these constraints pertaining to the 'self' (*auto*) and to the 'law' (*nomos*) explain why the exercise of autonomy, and thereby why consenting to international law, is to be regarded as a dialectic collective practice. To shed light on all this, Sections 15.2 and 15.3 analyse autonomy and consent respectively in relation to international law-making and dispute settlement. Based on these analyses, the concluding section addresses prospectively the future of autonomy and consent in international legal theory and practice (Section 15.4).

15.2 CONSENT IN INTERNATIONAL LAW-MAKING

If one takes for granted the dictum of the Permanent Court of International Justice (hereafter PCIJ) in *The S.S. "Lotus"*, notably the views according to which '[i]nternational law governs relations between independent States' and '[t]he rules binding upon them . . . emanate from their own free will',[16] there seems to be little to say about consent in international law-making. And yet, a lot has been said about this issue, an issue which, what is more, has always acutely puzzled international lawyers, be they academics or practitioners. This puzzlement has become even more acute throughout the years because of the diversification of the law-making paths and of the role played therein by new entities, typically international organizations (hereafter IOs). To understand and make sense of the old and new problems raised by consent in international law-making, this section looks at them successively from the perspective of the theory of the sources of international law and from that of institutional law-making.[17]

[15] On those matters, see, for example, Jean d'Aspremont, *Epistemic Forces in International Law: Foundational Doctrines and Techniques of International Legal Interpretation* (Cheltenham: Edward Elgar, 2015); Andrea Bianchi, Daniel Peat and Matthew Windsor (eds.), *Interpretation in International Law* (Oxford: Oxford University Press, 2015); Anne Lise Kjaer and Joanna Lam (eds.), *Language and Legal Interpretation in International Law* (Oxford: Oxford University Press, 2022); Ingo Venzke, *How Interpretation Makes International Law: On Semantic Change and Normative Twists* (Oxford: Oxford University Press, 2012).

[16] See fn. 7.

[17] This distinction aims at ensuring the clarity of the analyses provided. It goes without saying that there exist overlaps between the theory of the sources of international law and institutional law-making, notably in relation to treaties.

15.2.1 *The Theory of Sources*

The theory of sources which underpins Article 38 of the Statute of the International Court of Justice (hereafter ICJ),[18] in particular as it is construed by voluntarists like Prosper Weil,[19] is built on the hegemony of State autonomy and that of State consent. As such, this approach appears largely disconnected from the societal context in which States actually exercise their autonomy. Indeed, it fails to take into account the interplay, the dialectic between 'the individual State' and 'the group of States' within which autonomy is exercised.[20] This is true in relation to both the role of State consent and the nature of State consent, which are discussed in turn.

15.2.1.1 The Role of Consent in the Theory of Sources

As noted by Alain Pellet,[21] the 'consent load' of the formal sources of international law varies from one source to the other. This variation can be represented by a sliding scale. On one side of it, there are general principles of law recognized by civilized nations for which consent plays no role. Indeed, those general principles are to be deduced, typically by courts and tribunals, from rules in force in a large number of representative domestic legal orders. States express no specific consent in that deductive process; their consent is

[18] UN Charter and ICJ Statute, fn. 12.

[19] See in particular Prosper Weil, 'Vers une normativité relative en droit international?' (1982) 86(1) *Revue générale de droit international public* 5–47; Prosper Weil, 'Towards Relative Normativity in International Law' (1983) 77(3) *American Journal of International Law* 413–442.

[20] In relation to the debate between voluntarists and objectivists concerning the foundation of international law, the issue of the relations between international law subjects appears to be key for the understanding of international law-making: see Pierre-Marie Dupuy, *Droit international public*, 8th ed. (Paris: Dalloz, 2008), p. 353: 'Loin de garder l'idée simpliste de la nécessité de choisir son camp en privilégiant dans la formation de la coutume soit la volonté soit la société, on doit au contraire comprendre que la contrainte sociale naît elle-même de l'affrontement des volontés initialement contradictoires, mais amenées à composer les unes avec les autres. Autant dire qu'il peut y avoir des situations dans lesquelles un ou plusieurs États se verront pratiquement contraints d'accepter l'opposabilité à leur égard de la règle générale, ce qui, ainsi que l'affirment les objectivistes, manifeste la puissance normative de contraintes sociales.' For a voluntarist approach and an objectivist approach to customary international law, see, for example, Dioniso Anzilotti, *Cours de droit international*, edited by Pierre-Marie Dupuy and Charles Leben, translated by Gilbert Gidel (Paris: Édition Panthéon-Assas, 1999); Georges Scelle, 'Essai sur les sources formelles du droit international', in *Recueil d'études sur les sources du droit en l'honneur de François Gény*, Vol. 3 (Paris: Recueil Sirey, 1934), pp. 400–429.

[21] Pellet, Chapter 1 in this volume.

not required to turn legal rules under domestic laws into general principles under international law. At best, they can acknowledge (or not) this transmutation as a matter of fact. On the other side of that 'consent load' sliding scale, we find treaties for which consent is paramount; the expression by each State of its consent to be bound is required under the law of treaties. The importance of State autonomy as for treaties is also reflected in reservations which, as coined by Samantha Besson, constitute 'pockets of disagreements'.[22] Each State can give itself its own rules in those pockets or, to put it differently, each State can decide therein not to give itself the rules agreed on by States parties.

That being said, in relation to the dialectic between the 'individual State' and 'the group of States', it is worth insisting that no parallel can be drawn between the process of entering into a treaty and that of terminating it. The former is based on the consent of each State; the latter on the consent of all States parties. When a State has consented to be bound by a treaty, to use the words of Alain Pellet, 'the trap closes . . . and its will is captive and will be freed only through processes in which the will of an individual State will have little or nothing to do'.[23]

The domination of 'the group of States' over 'the individual State' also holds true as regards customary international law. Indeed, Article 38 of the ICJ Statute requires the existence of a *general* practice accepted as law;[24] likewise, the doctrine of the two elements is based on the general acceptance of the practice as law, and not on the acceptance by individual States.[25] As a result, a State can be bound by a customary rule without having consented to it. Of course, the persistent objector doctrine can be seen as contradicting this line of reasoning. Indeed, this doctrine allows, so to speak, each State to – pre-emptively – decide not to give itself the upcoming customary rule, which will derive from the corresponding general practice accepted as law. That being said, it is fair to say that this doctrine has little relevance in real – international – life.[26]

15.2.1.2 The Nature of Consent in the Theory of Sources

In the international society, setting aside unilateral acts, States' autonomy can only materialize in bilateralism or multilateralism.[27] This societal necessity

[22] Besson, fn. 2, at 313.
[23] Pellet, Chapter 1 in this volume.
[24] See fn. 12.
[25] See notably ILC, 'Draft Conclusions on Identification of Customary International Law, with Commentaries', in ILC, 'Report on the Work of the Seventieth Session' (2018), UN Doc. A/73/10, pp. 122–156, pp. 124–126.
[26] Pellet, Chapter 1 in this volume.
[27] Dupuy, fn. 20, p. 285.

means that States are faced with one another to give themselves their own rules. This also means that their 'footprint' in that process depends on the bargaining power of each. As a result, the consent given by States when they exercise their autonomy does not always reflect an 'affirmative attitude'; it actually sometimes/oftentimes reflects something more passive.[28]

Even though the coercion of a State representative and of the State itself are prohibited under the law of treaties,[29] the consent given by States to be bound by treaties displays obviously such diverse attitudes.

This holds true as well with regard to customary international law. The attitude adopted by States depends here as well on their respective bargaining power. Brigitte Stern noted in that sense:

> [c]ertains États auront le sentiment d'être liés parce qu'ils auront voulu, parce qu'ils y auront librement consenti, certains États au contraire auront le sentiment d'être liés parce qu'ils ne peuvent pas ne pas le vouloir, parce que la règle leur est imposée . . . Est règle coutumière internationale celle qui est considérée comme telle par la volonté d'États pouvant imposer leur point de vue.[30]

As it appears, the dialectic between 'the individual State' and 'the group of States' is key to understand the diversity that characterizes both the nature of consent and its the role. Consent and autonomy are limited by the societal context in which the self (*auto*) gives its own rules to itself. These considerations apply *mutatis mutandis* to institutional law-making.

15.2.2 *Institutional Law-Making*

Institutional law-making nowadays takes place in two types of settings, which, for the sake of the discussion, can be said to stand 'within' and 'outside' international law. The former includes law-making in IOs and in treaty regimes. The latter refers to all those processes, often labelled informal law-making, whose output is non-binding.[31] At play in those settings, there is not only the dialectic between

28 Pellet, Chapter 1 in this volume.

29 Arts. 51, 52 of the Vienna Convention on the Law of Treaties (hereafter VCLT), 1155 UNTS 331 (adopted 23 May 1969, entered into force 27 January 1980).

30 Brigitte Stern, 'La coutume au cœur du droit international: Quelques réflexions', in *Mélanges offerts à Paul Reuter: Le droit international: unité et diversité* (Paris: Pedone, 1981), pp. 479–499, p. 498.

31 See in particular Joost Pauwelyn, Ramses Wessel and Jan Wouters (eds.), *Informal International Lawmaking* (Oxford: Oxford University Press, 2012). In this volume, see notably Joost Pauwelyn, 'Is It International Law or Not, and Does It Even Matter?', in Pauwelyn *et al.*, ibid., pp. 125–161; Weil, 'Vers une normativité relative en droit international?', fn. 19; Weil, 'Towards Relative Normativity in International Law', fn. 19.

'the individual State' and 'the group of States', but also the dialectic between States and other entities. Both settings are discussed in turn.

15.2.2.1 Institutional Law-Making 'Within' International Law

The law-making processes which are at play in IOs and in treaty regimes display paradoxical trends as for State consent: consent as a limitation and limitation of consent. This phenomenon results from the features and the functioning of the international society. In this respect, Guy Ladreit de Lacharrière made this interesting diagnosis, which sheds light on this paradox:

> Le resserrement des liens entre nations et le développement de la solidarité mondiale font prendre conscience de l'opportunité de réglementations universelles si l'on veut éviter que la non-participation de quelques-uns ne ruine le dessein commun. Par-là, se trouve alimentée une tendance à l'extrapolation des institutions étatiques et donc aux procédures de contrainte des contestataires au nom de la volonté générale. Mais à l'inverse, l'hétérogéneité de la communauté internationale en termes de systèmes politiques ou de niveaux de développement conduit les États à insister sur leurs différences qualitatives irréductibles et à rejeter une règle majoritaire qui ne peut jouer qu'entre entités se reconnaissant pour fondamentalement semblables.[32]

Constitutive of one trend, mechanisms like majority-based decision-making processes come as a limit to the hegemony of State consent. Through these processes and mechanisms, law is made of the rules that 'the group of States' decides to give itself. Despite the existence of 'opt-out' mechanisms, which confer to each State the possibility not to give itself the rules agreed on by the group, this trend leads, as put by Catherine Brölmann, to the disaggregation of State consent.[33]

On the other hand, another trend is at play in those settings where, to use the terms of Samantha Besson and José Luis Martí, State consent strangles IOs from within.[34] The archetypal example of this trend is obviously the veto power of the permanent members of the Security Council and the way they use it. In such cases, the refusal of one State to consent prevents, or at least makes it more difficult for the others to give themselves – collectively – their own rules. As noted by Jutta Brunnée in relation to the climate regime, the interplay between the individual and collective aspects of the consent process

[32] Ladreit de Lacharrière, fn. 8, p. 200.

[33] Brölmann, Chapter 4 in this volume.

[34] Besson and Martí, Chapter 14 in this volume.

can have a dark side indeed, by slowing down the progress in a regime towards more ambitious requirements, or even by resulting in a standstill.[35]

Due to the necessity to react – swiftly – to phenomena like global warming and climate change, new mechanisms are yet created to endeavour to cope with the inextricable situations in which the dialectic between 'the individual State' and 'the group of State' places the international society. Hector was right in *La guerre de Troie n'aura pas lieu*; 'le droit est (à coup sûr) la plus puissante des écoles de l'imagination'.[36] This is well illustrated by the non-binding 'nationally determined contributions',[37] under the Paris Agreement.[38] As said by Jutta Brunnée, the bottom-up approach that characterizes this mechanism is remarkable: to unlock the situation, it disentangles the individual and collective dimensions of consent under the auspices of an international agreement.[39] Such a mechanism, and more generally the international climate change regime, are also of great interest as they tie closely the international legal order to domestic legal orders. In particular, they confer a key role to domestic courts, which can be seized – and have actually been seized – on those matters. The *Urgenda* v. *Netherlands* case exemplifies this possibility and trend.[40] This involvement of domestic courts is another manifestation of their contribution to the functioning of the international legal order and of their growing role in the international society.[41]

35 Brunnée, Chapter 8 in this volume.

36 Jean Giraudoux, *La guerre de Troie n'aura pas lieu* (Paris: Flammarion, 2015), p. 24.

37 On the 'nationally determined contributions', see United Nations for Climate Change, 'Nationally Determined Contributions (NDCs)'. Available at: https://unfccc.int/process-and-meetings/the-paris-agreement/nationally-determined-contributions-ndcs/nationally-determined-contributions-ndcs#eq-1, last accessed 10 November 2022. In the literature, see, for example, Sandrine Maljean-Dubois, 'The Paris Agreement: A New Step in the Gradual Evolution of Differential Treatment in the Climate Regime?' (2016) 25(2) *Review of European, Comparative and International Environmental Law* 151–160.

38 Paris Agreement, 3156 UNTS (adopted 12 December 2015 and entered into force 4 November 2016).

39 Brunnée, Chapter 8 in this volume.

40 Supreme Court of the Netherlands (Hoge Raad), *The State of the Netherlands (Ministry of Economic Affairs and Climate Policy)* v. *Stichting Urgenda*, Judgment of 20 December 2019, No. 19/00135.

41 See, for example, Filiz Kahraman, Nikhil Kalyanpur and Abraham L. Newman, 'Domestic Courts, Transnational Law, and International Order' (2020) 26(1) *European Journal of International Relations* 184–208; Yuval Shany, 'National Courts as International Actors: Jurisdictional Implications' (2009) 15 *Rivista di diritto pubblico italiano, comparato, europeo*. Available at: www.federalismi.it/ApplOpenFilePDF.cfm?artid=13810&dpath=document&dfile=29072009111203.pdf&content=National%2Bcourts%2Bas%2Binternational%2Bactors%3A%2Bjurisdictional%2Bimplications%2B%2D%2Bdottrina%2B%2D%2Bdottrina%2B%2D%2B, last accessed 10 November 2022; Antonios Tzanakopoulos, 'Domestic Courts in

Whatever the creativity that the 'nationality determined contributions' displays, it remains that this mechanism will likely fail to sufficiently limit global warming and its consequences within the very short period of time that is left ahead. Such instances of ineffectiveness of the institutional law-making processes 'within' international law are often said to have triggered institutional law-making 'outside' international law to which this section now turns.[42]

15.2.2.2 Institutional Law-Making 'Outside' International Law

The regulation of the contemporary international society is not only confronted with the long-observed difficulties raised by State autonomy, but it is also faced with unprecedented societal and natural phenomena. Global warming, which is mentioned in Section 15.2.2.1, illustrates this. Another such phenomenon is globalization.

In this respect, it is argued by some that the acceleration of globalization exacerbates the deficiencies inherent in the traditional structure of the international society and leads to the emergence of functionality as a leading principle alongside territoriality. The latter has traditionally grounded and served as a key justification for the prevalence of States' consent and their claim to be the highest authority.[43] On the other hand, the rise of functionalism brings experts to the forefront[44] of society and of normativity, be it considered as a legal normativity or not. This is reflected in the increasing importance of private and hybrid groups whose normative activities affect individuals and peoples directly or indirectly. This is well illustrated by the International Organization for Standardization.[45] Also characterized by informalism and linked to the complexities brought by globalization, groups

International Law: The International Judicial Function of National Courts' (2011) 34(1) *Loyola of Los Angeles International and Comparative Law Review* 133–168.

42 See fn. 9.

43 Werner, fn. 7, p. 26.

44 This results also from the growing complexity of societies and from the phenomenon that has been conceptualized as the autonomization of social subsystems, in particular by Niklas Luhmann: see notably Niklas Luhmann, *Law as a Social System* (Oxford: Oxford University Press, 2004). For an application of this conceptualization to the international society, see Gunther Teubner, 'Global Bukowina: Legal Pluralism in the World Society', in Gunther Teubner (ed.), *Global Law without a State* (Brookfield: Dartmouth, 1997), pp. 3–28.

45 For a discussion of the role played by the International Organization for Standardization, see, for example, Janelle M. Miller, 'Private Standardization in Public International Lawmaking' (2012) 33(3) *Michigan Journal of International Law* 481–536.

gathering a limited number of States or State agencies like, for instance, the G7 or the Financial Action Task Force, also flourish.[46]

Informalism is not a new phenomenon in law and in international law in particular.[47] Yet, its recent quantitative growth has qualitative implications. The normative activities of those groups raise mainly two series of issues.

With regard to those groups in particular wherein States are not involved, expertise appears obviously as challenging State consent. More fundamentally, the growing empowerment of expertise and technocracy raises a democratic issue and calls for a democratic control, as highlighted by Samantha Besson.[48] Although those groups may well be effective and may thereby well be seen as enjoying an output legitimacy, they do nonetheless lack an input and a throughput legitimacy.[49] A way forward would be to better tie expertise to democratic State consent,[50] and more generally to reinforce public participation. Thereby, autonomy would be fostered inasmuch as those individuals and peoples who are actually impacted by the normative activities of those groups would – at least partially – be giving rules to themselves.

As for the groups of States, they run the risk of fostering hierarchy and control. Not only are those groups tools which empower their members *vis-à-vis* less powerful third States, but – within – they also empower the most powerful of their members. Of course, and as discussed above in Section 15.2.1.2, power politics and bargaining power also come into play in the formal sources of international law. But the informalism that characterizes the processes 'outside' international law can only exacerbate this reality of

46 For a discussion of this entity and other similar ones, see Nico Krisch, 'The Decay of Consent: International Law in an Age of Global Public Goods' (2014) 108(1) *American Journal of International Law* 1–40.

47 See, for example, Christine B. Harrington, 'Informalism as a Form of Legal Ordering', in Gregory A. Caldeira, R. Daniel Kelemen and Keith E. Whittington (eds.), *The Oxford Handbook of Law and Politics* (Oxford: Oxford University Press, 2008), pp. 378–396; Charles Lipson, 'Why Are Some International Agreements Informal?' (1991) 45(4) *International Organization* 495–538; Michael W. Reisman, 'The Concept and Functions of Soft Law in International Politics', in Emmanuel G. Bello and Prince Bola A. Ajibola (eds.), *Essays in Honour of Judge Taslim Olawale Elias*, Vol. 1 (Leiden: Martinus Nijhoff, 1992), pp. 135–145.

48 Besson, fn. 2, p. 311.

49 On these notions, see, for example, David Lefkowitz, 'The Legitimacy of International Law', in David Held and Pietro Maffetone (eds.), *Global Political Theory* (Cambridge: Polity Press, 2016), pp. 98–116; Vivien A. Schmidt, *Europe's Crisis of Legitimacy: Governing by Rules and Ruling by Numbers in the Eurozone* (Oxford: Oxford University Press, 2020), ch. 2, pp. 24–84; Rüdiger Wolfrum and Volker Röben (eds.), *Legitimacy in International Law* (Berlin: Springer, 2008); see in particular Daniel Bodansky, 'The Concept of Legitimacy in International Law', in Wolfrum and Röben, ibid., pp. 309–317.

50 Besson, fn. 2, at 311.

international relations.[51] Quite ironically, it appears that the attempts made to clear the hurdles created by State consent 'within' international law tend in fact to make them higher 'outside' it.

For that reason in particular, instead of looking for a panacea in informal law-making, it is likely preferable to focus on the reform of law-making processes 'within' international law. As part of this endeavour, it is crucial to think of the proper role to be played by State consent, an issue which is discussed in the conclusion after the analysis of consent in international dispute settlement.

15.3 CONSENT IN INTERNATIONAL DISPUTE SETTLEMENT

In international law, autonomy is also central to dispute settlement. As touched upon in the introduction, States can decide the method to be used to settle the disputes to which they are a party. They can notably opt for adjudication, on which this section focuses. The exercise of this autonomy materializes into the consent to be given by the disputing parties for international courts and tribunals to have jurisdiction to settle their disputes; it also designs the scope of that consent. Also, with regard to applicable law, the rules to be applied by those courts and tribunals are the ones that the disputing parties consented to in their capacity as law-makers, the ones that they gave themselves, as discussed above in Section 15.2.[52]

It is worth emphasizing at the outset that consent is nowhere as pivotal and sensitive as it is in the adjudicatory setting. This is due to the fact that States are therein 'in the hands' of a third entity, be it a permanent court or an arbitral tribunal. Because adjudication entails to confer to that third entity a legal power, that is notably the power to resolve disputes and to apply/interpret the law, the existence of State consent is crucial. But, once empowered, that

[51] *Mutadis mutandis*, the same risk results from the rise of unilateralism, which is partly due to the hurdles created by State consent in the multilateral context. This is well illustrated by extraterritorial policies. On unilateralism in international law, see, for example, Pierre-Marie Dupuy, 'The Place and Role of Unilateralism in Contemporary International Law' (2000) 11 (1) *European Journal of International Law* 19–29; Krisch, fn. 46; Leonard J. Theberge, 'Unilateralism: The Direct Challenge to International Law' (1979) 9(2) *California Western International Law Journal* 553–562.

[52] The freedom of choice is even more important in arbitration as the disputing parties can choose the law applicable to the settlement of their disputes, procedural matters and the identity of the arbitrators.

third entity takes to a large extent control over the determination of the meaning and ambit of that consent. This is true with regard to both consent to jurisdiction and 'substantive consensualism'.[53] According to Christian Tams, this 'takeover' is the necessary implication of two prerogatives: the *Kompetenz-Kompetenz* principle and the power of courts and tribunals to resolve disputes authoritatively.[54] As mentioned in the introduction and as explained further below in this section, this is also the necessary implication of the inner-features of *nomos*, that is, of the inner-features of international law. This is discussed in turn as regards jurisdiction and applicable law.

15.3.1 *Consent to Jurisdiction*

Investor-State arbitration, which is analysed by Laurence Boisson de Chazournes in her contribution to this volume,[55] is certainly the international adjudicatory setting where consent to jurisdiction and its scope are most discussed by tribunals, parties and academics. More precisely, this is the consent of States – and not that of foreign investors – which attracts the attention in the investment law community. Therefore and although consent to jurisdiction is of course regime specific,[56] this setting appears to constitute an incomparable 'laboratory', on which this section relies to shed light on the limits faced by State consent in jurisdictional matters.

In reference to her dissenting opinion in *Garanti Koza* v. *Turkmenistan*,[57] Laurence Boisson de Chazournes reminds us that the interpretation of consent is fundamental as 'the principle of compétence de la compétence

[53] Fuad Zarbiyev distinguishes 'substantive consensualism' from 'threshold consensualism'. The latter 'refers to the fundamental notion that a State is not bound by a treaty without its consent to be bound by it'. 'Substantive consensualism' boils down to their consent to the content of the treaty. He notes in this respect that the treaty interpretation regime that currently prevails is inhospitable to 'substantive consensualism': Zarbiyev, Chapter 7 in this volume.

[54] Tams, Chapter 3 in this volume.

[55] Boisson de Chazournes, Chapter 10 in this volume.

[56] Tams, Chapter 3 in this volume. Consent to jurisdiction also displays nuances and differences *within* some international law regimes, in particular because consent can be expressed therein in instruments of a different nature. This is well illustrated by investor-State arbitration, as discussed by Laurence Boisson de Chazournes in her contribution to this volume: see Boisson de Chazournes, Chapter 10 in this volume.

[57] *Garanti Koza LLP* v. *Turkmenistan*, ICSID, Decision on the Objection to Jurisdiction for Lack of Consent (3 July 2013) Case No. ARB/11/20, Dissenting opinion by Laurence Boisson de Chazournes, para. 5.

requires an international court or a tribunal to establish the extent and limits of its jurisdiction *objectively*, that is on the basis of the title of jurisdiction'.[58]

'Objectively' is the key term in that statement and 'objectivity' is a key guide in the process of establishing jurisdiction in order to ensure that State consent to jurisdiction is respected. To reach that objective, international courts and tribunals shall notably interpret compromissory clauses neither liberally, nor restrictively. This is often recalled by investor-State arbitral tribunals,[59] as it was by Rosalyn Higgins in relation to the ICJ case law.[60] Despite the consensus on this matter, a problem remains. Indeed, the reasoning to determine the scope of a compromissory clause can be seen, by some, as being restrictive and, by others, as not being restrictive. This is well illustrated by *Daimler* v. *Argentina*. In that case, the majority of the Tribunal considered that the requirement to have affirmative evidence of consent does not amount to a restrictive approach,[61] while the Dissenting Arbitrator considered that it does.[62] What is objectivity then and where does it lead arbitrators?

This directs our attention towards interpretation and the limits that the inner-features of international law place on State consent, an issue that is discussed further in relation to applicable law in Section 15.3.2. With regard to the interpretation of compromissory clauses, among other types of clauses, the issue is not only – and likely not mainly – their lack of clarity, but also the clash between the various epistemic forces which are at play within the investor-State arbitral community. Indeed, these clauses are interpreted by arbitrators who have different views about the legal principles, values and interests which underpin investor-State arbitration and international investment law more generally.[63]

This is also well illustrated by the conflicting views expressed in the arbitral practice about the status of pre-conditions to arbitration, like the local remedy

58 Boisson de Chazournes, Chapter 10 in this volume (emphasis added).

59 See, for example, *Michael Anthony Lee-Chin* v. *The Dominican Republic*, ICSID, Partial Award on Jurisdiction (15 July 2020) Case No. UNCT/18/3, para. 120.

60 *Case concerning Oil Platforms (Islamic Republic of Iran* v. *United States of America)* (Judgment) [1996] ICJ Rep. 803, Separate Opinion of Judge Higgins, pp. 847–861, p. 857, para. 35: 'The Court has no judicial policy of being either liberal or strict in deciding the scope of compromissory clauses: they are judicial like any other.'

61 *Daimler Financial Services AG* v. *Argentine Republic*, ICSID, Award (22 August 2012) Case No. ARB/05/1, para. 175.

62 Ibid., Dissenting Opinion of Judge Charles N. Brower (15 August 2012), para. 3.

63 In that sense with regard to international law more generally, see Martti Koskenniemi, *From Apology to Utopia: The Structure of International Legal Argument* (Cambridge: Cambridge University Press, 2005), p. 341.

requirement,[64] or the applicability of the most-favoured-nation clause to the dispute settlement mechanism of international investment agreements.[65] Typically, conflicting interpretations of the same treaty provisions by tribunals' majorities and dissenting arbitrators have spread in the arbitral practice on all these issues.[66] The diverging reasonings that they adopted were largely based on the various legal principles, values and interests they relied on, elements rooted in diverse *corpus* of law and disciplines, notably public international law, commercial arbitration and private law.[67]

Irrespective of the theoretical and sociological foundations of this diversity, interpretations reached by some tribunals or arbitrators have had real-life consequences; notably, they have given a picture of State consent to jurisdiction that States have failed to recognize. This raises the issue of the relation between the intention of treaty parties and the interpretations reached by tribunals; this issue is specifically discussed below in Section 15.3.2 with

64 Referring to the case law of the ICJ, the majority of the Tribunal in the case *Daimler* v. *Argentina* concluded that the local remedy requirement contained in the Argentina-Germany bilateral investment treaty (hereafter BIT) pertains to jurisdiction and constitutes a pre-condition to the host State's consent to arbitrate. On the contrary, the Tribunal in the case *Hochtief* v. *Argentina* considered that the very same requirement (in the very same treaty) does not pertain to jurisdiction but to admissibility instead: see *Daimler* v. *Argentina*, fn. 61, paras. 193–194; *Hochtief AG* v. *The Argentine Republic*, ICSID, Decision on Jurisdiction (24 October 2011) Case No ARB/07/31, para. 96.

65 See, for example, *RosInvestCo UK Ltd.* v. *The Russian Federation*, SCC, Award on Jurisdiction (1 October 2007) Case No. V 079/2005, para. 131: 'While indeed the application of the MFN [most-favoured-nation] clause of Article 3 [of the United Kingdom-Union of Soviet Socialist Republics BIT] widens the scope of Article 8 [Dispute Settlement Provision] and thus is in conflict to its limitation, this is a normal result of the application of MFN clauses, the very character and intention of which is that protection not accepted in one treaty is widened by transferring the protection accorded in another treaty.' On the other hand, the Tribunal in the case *Telenor Mobile* v. *Hungary* argued that 'an MFN clause in a BIT providing for most favoured nation treatment of investment should not be construed as extending the jurisdiction of the arbitral tribunal to categories of dispute beyond those set out in the BIT itself in the absence of clear language that this is the intention of the parties'; *Telenor Mobile Communications A.S.* v. *The Republic of Hungary*, ICSID, Award (13 September 2006) Case No. ARB/04/15, para. 91.

66 The issue of the applicability of the MFN clause to the dispute settlement mechanism of international investment agreements (hereafter IIA) has actually attracted the greatest number of dissenting opinions in investor-State arbitration, see Yannick Radi, *Rules and Practices of International Investment Law and Arbitration* (Cambridge: Cambridge University Press, 2020), pp. 130–135.

67 On those divergences that characterize the international investment law epistemic community more generally, see, for example, Anthea Roberts, 'Clash of Paradigms: Actors and Analogies Shaping the Investment Treaty System' (2017) 107(1) *American Journal of International Law* 45–94; Stephan W. Schill, 'W(h)ither Fragmentation? On the Literature and Sociology of International Investment Law' (2011) 22(3) *European Journal of International Law* 875–908.

regard to applicable law. As for consent to jurisdiction, it matters to emphasize here the practical consequences of those decisions establishing jurisdiction and its scope, which are not seen by States as being objective. In investor-State arbitration, this has undermined their trust in the regime and has contributed to its legitimacy crisis. It is worth noting in this respect that Laurence Boisson de Chazournes warned the arbitral community of such a risk in her dissenting opinion in *Garanti Koza* v. *Turkmenistan*. She explained indeed that 'the trust and confidence in third-party adjudication is dependent on the respect by international courts and tribunals of the limits of the jurisdiction conferred upon them'.[68]

Similar considerations apply *mutatis mutandis* to State consent in relation to applicable law.

15.3.2 *Applicable Law*

'[A] treaty is not the end of a process, but the beginning of another process',[69] a process in which, as noted by Samantha Besson, interpretation is marked by disagreements.[70] These disagreements are of two types, which can yet overlap depending on the views and strategies adopted by States and adjudicators. Both types of disagreements are very telling about the role of State consent – in relation to State intent – and about the limits it faces as for applicable law.

The first type of disagreements consists in disagreements between the States parties themselves. In the context of a dispute, States adopt typically different views about the meaning of the rules to be applied; they have a different idea about what they consented to. Such views may be based on bad faith, a party or the parties refusing – in contravention with Article 31 of the VCLT[71] – to do justice to their *ab initio* common intention. In other situations, the matter does not boil down to bad faith, but simply to the lack of an *ab initio* common intention. This is so in particular when the rules to be applied were – on purpose – left ambiguous. States use this strategy in treaty drafting in particular to continue promoting their interests at the stage of treaty interpretation.[72]

[68] *Garanti Koza* v. *Turkmenistan*, fn. 57, Dissenting Opinion by Laurence Boisson de Chazournes (3 July 2013), para. 6. More generally, Christian Tams also stresses that the reasonable exercise of inherent power is necessary to ensure the continued State consent to binding dispute settlement: see Tams, Chapter 3 in this volume.

[69] Philip Allott, 'The Concept of International Law' (1999) 10(1) *European Journal of International Law* 31–50, at 43.

[70] Besson, fn. 2, at 314.

[71] VCLT, fn. 29.

[72] On purposive ambiguity in treaty drafting, see, for example, Guy Ladreit de Lacharrière, *La politique juridique extérieure* (Paris: Economica, 1983), pp. 90–101; Ladreit de Lacharrière, fn. 8, pp. 188–193.

To borrow Clausewitz's words about war and politics,[73] treaty interpretation appears in such situations as the prolongation of disagreement by means other than treaty negotiation. In the adjudicatory setting, this is then *in fine* to the adjudicator to deal with the matter and to provide an authoritative interpretation of the rules.

The second type of disagreements consists in disagreements between States and adjudicators as to the meaning and the normative substance of the rules to be applied. This situation relates to the very old debate among international lawyers concerning the object of treaty interpretation. In particular, the question that has been fiercely debated is whether it aims at determining the meaning of the text, which is deemed to reflect the intent of the parties, or whether it consists in an enquiry into their actual intent.[74] As stressed by Fuad Zarbiyev, there is a strong trend against the intentionalist paradigm in the official regime of treaty interpretation based on the VCLT.[75] As a result of this trend and thereby of the focus on the text as the primary object of interpretation, State consent has become less compelling in this process.[76] Two remarks are warranted in this respect.

First of all, and as noted by Martti Koskenniemi, it can be suggested that the reliance on the text, that is the declared intent, instead of the actual intent, is in fact non-consensual.[77] This is due to the fact that its point can be seen, not as being to give effect to the real will, but as being to meet the expectations of other States, in particular in relation to legal certainty. This holds true, for instance, of the expectations of acceding States parties which often have little insight into the actual intent of the negotiating States, the text constituting for them the only evidence of their intent. Because of those considerations, Martti

[73] Carl von Clausewitz, *On War*, edited and translated by Michael Howard and Peter Paret (Princeton: Princeton University Press, 1989), p. 280: 'war is the continuation of politics by other means'.

[74] Those debates were well reflected during the work of the International Law Commission (hereafter ILC) on the law of treaties as well as during the Vienna Conference on the law of treaties. For an account of those debates, see in particular Francis G. Jacobs, 'Varieties of Approach to Treaty Interpretation: With Special Reference to the Draft Convention on the Law of Treaties before the Vienna Diplomatic Conference' (1969) 18(2) *International & Comparative Law Quarterly* 318–346; John G. Merrils, 'Two Approaches to Treaty Interpretation' (1971) 4(1) *Australian Year Book of International Law* 55–82. For recent contributions to this old debate, see, for example, Eirik Bjorge, *The Evolutionary Interpretation of Treaties* (Oxford: Oxford University Press, 2014); Andrea K. Bjorklund, 'The Enduring but Unwelcome Role of Party Intent in Treaty Interpretation' (2018) 112 *American Journal of International Law* 44–48.

[75] Arts. 31, 32 VCLT, footnote 29.

[76] Zarbiyev, Chapter 7 in this volume.

[77] Koskenniemi, fn. 63, p. 343.

Koskenniemi considers such an approach as a standard of justice.[78] This would be another illustration of the role of legal principles and values in treaty interpretation that is emphasized in Section 15.3.1.

Second, the focus on the text in the interpretative process can be seen, as argued by Fuad Zarbiyev in reference to Stephen Neff,[79] as causing a shift from 'rule consent' to 'regime consent'.[80] Such a 'regime consent' is seen as leading international courts and tribunals to inferentially interpret treaty provisions. Most notably, this shift leads to situations where States can be said to be bound by the inferential consequences of their treaty obligations, to which they would not be said to have consented to under a 'rule consent' approach.[81]

No doubt, such a conception and practice of treaty interpretation leads to an empowerment of international courts and tribunals; indeed, in such an inferential practice, the legal principles, values and interests they rely on are key. It is all the more true as there is only one step between, on the one hand, grounding an interpretation on the conviction by implication that States *must* have given their consent and, on the other hand, grounding an interpretation on the conviction that States *should* have given their consent. This latter approach does exist in the practice of international courts and tribunals, as stressed by Duncan B. Hollis in relation to the case law of the ICJ and of the International Tribunal for the Law of the Sea.[82]

As with regard to consent to jurisdiction, such interpretations based on inferences can provide a picture of State consent that States fail to recognize. Here again, international courts and tribunals can be expected to act cautiously in order to ensure that States continue to trust them, a trust which, as explained by David Lefkowitz, is paramount to ground the consent of States to international authorities.[83]

15.4 CONCLUSION

As a matter of reality and as a matter of legitimacy, State consent is central to international law. This reality, the way States exercise their autonomy is

78 Ibid., p. 344.
79 Stephen C. Neff, 'Consent', in Jean d'Aspremont and Sahib Singh (eds.), *Concepts for International Law: Contributions to Disciplinary Thought* (Cheltenham: Edward Elgar, 2019), pp. 127–140, p. 128.
80 Zarbiyev, Chapter 7 in this volume.
81 Ibid.
82 Hollis, Chapter 6 in this volume.
83 Lefkowitz, Chapter 2 in this volume.

sometimes/oftentimes problematic. Even though State consent has provided a modicum of order and stability, as noted by Fernando Bordin and Duncan B. Hollis,[84] it has prevented or slowed down action which should yet have been taken quickly to tackle societal emergencies. It is also problematic inasmuch as, as explained by Samantha Besson and José Luis Martí, State consent displays a democratic deficit.[85] That being said, State consent also displays a democratic value. Indeed, to use the words of Thomas Christiano, States 'remain ... the most basic mechanisms for the accountability of political power to persons'.[86] This is why State consent can also be said to be central to international law from a legitimacy point of view.

Taking into account these two sides of State consent – positive and negative – Samantha Besson and José Luis Martí make a powerful call for the establishment of a multi-public system of representation and sovereignty, based on participation, in which non-State actors would complement or correct the role played by States.[87]

This approach is *mutatis mutandis* shared by other contributors to this volume, for instance, by David Lefkowitz, who argues that justice is most likely to be realized through the development of a multilevel institutional structure. For him, such a structure would generate the best possible integration of information and understanding that human beings can achieve.[88] Likewise, Monique Chemillier-Gendreau calls for the reshuffling of political communities at several territorial levels. She urges us to think of the international society in its universality and its plurality, to make it possible for all to express themselves having the feeling to belong to the human community.[89]

To inform the reflection on participation as a substitute/complement to consent, a few remarks are warranted about these last words of Monique Chemillier-Gendreau: 'the feeling to belong to the human community'. From a descriptive point of view, it suffices to look at the wave of populism all over the world to realize that this feeling to belong to the human community does not exist, or at best, that it hardly exists. But is there any possibility that it may flourish in the future? Two factors may make this possible.

The first factor is connected to the dramatic consequences of global phenomena, in particular climate change, that populations are enduring

84 Bordin, Chapter 11 in this volume; Hollis, Chapter 6 in this volume.
85 Besson and Martí, Chapter 14 in this volume.
86 Thomas Christiano, 'Climate Change and State Consent', in Jeremy Moss (ed.), *Climate Change and Justice* (Cambridge: Cambridge University Press, 2015), pp. 17–38, p. 17.
87 Besson and Martí, Chapter 14 in this volume.
88 Lefkowitz, Chapter 2 in this volume.
89 Chemillier-Gendreau, Chapter 13 in this volume.

worldwide. Fear and pain are spreading everywhere as a result of these phenomena and this may precisely foster the feeling that we belong to the human community. The work of Ernest Renan, one of the most influential thinker of nationhood, helps to realize this. In a famous conference he delivered at La Sorbonne in 1882 about what a nation is, he claimed in that sense: '"avoir souffert ensemble"; oui, la souffrance en commun unit plus que la joie!'.[90]

The second factor which may contribute to fostering the feeling that we belong to the human community boils down to participation. Indeed, the virtue of participation is not only to foster democracy in international law,[91] but it may well also be to foster the feeling of the individuals, the peoples, that they belong to one – human – community. To understand this, the work of Hannah Arendt about the relation between 'will' and 'freedom' is paramount,[92] in particular in the way it has been relied on by Étienne Tassin. He analysed in his work 'the belief in the will' (la croyance en la volonté) and conceptualized 'the people who does not want' (le peuple qui ne veut pas).[93] Interestingly, he made a distinction between two types of peoples: the people who comes to exist 'because it wants to' (le peuple naissant de son vouloir) and the people who comes to exist 'because it acts' (le peuple naissant de son action).[94] On the basis of this distinction, Étienne Tassin formulated an interesting proposition which is worth reflecting on to pursue the epistemic endeavour to conceptualize and design participation in international law: 'Il nous revient de penser le peuple, non pas sous couvert d'une entité subjective, mais d'une pluralité active, non pas sous couvert d'une domination souveraine, mais d'une liberté entendue comme pouvoir de commencer, non pas sous couvert d'une volonté autonome, mais d'une interaction conflictuelle de la pluralité.'[95]

90 Ernest Renan, *Qu'est-ce qu'une nation?* (Paris: Fayard, Mille et une nuits, 2014), p. 22.

91 Besson and Martí, Chapter 14 in this volume.

92 Hannah Arendt, *Qu'est-ce que la politique?*, edited by Jerome Kohn, translated by Carole Widmaier, Muriel Frantz-Widmaier, Sylvie Taussig and Cécile Nail (Paris: Seuil, 2014); Hannah Arendt, *De la révolution*, translated by Marie Berrane (Paris: Gallimard, 1985); Hannah Arendt, *La vie de l'esprit*, translated by Lucienne Lotringer (Paris: Presses Universitaires de France, Quadrige, 2013).

93 Étienne Tassin, 'Le peuple ne veut pas', in Anne Kupiec, Martine Leibovici, Géraldine Muhlmann and Étienne Tassin (eds.), *Hannah Arendt, Crises de l'État-Nation: Pensées alternatives* (Paris: Sens & Tonka, 2007), pp. 305–315 (my translation).

94 Ibid., p. 303 (my translation).

95 Ibid., p. 304.

Index